Refashioning Iran

Orientalism, Occidentalism and Historiography

Mohamad Tavakoli-Targhi
Associate Professor of Historiography and Middle Eastern History
Illinois State University
Normal, Illinois

First published 2001 by
PALGRAVE
Houndmills, Basingstoke, Hampshire RG21 6XS and
175 Fifth Avenue, New York, N. Y. 10010
Companies and representatives throughout the world

PALGRAVE is the new global academic imprint of
St. Martin's Press LLC Scholarly and Reference Division and
Palgrave Publishers Ltd (formerly Macmillan Press Ltd).

ISBN 0–333–94922–6

This book is printed on paper suitable for recycling and made from fully managed and sustained forest sources.

A catalogue record for this book is available from the British Library.

Library of Congress Cataloging-in-Publication Data
Tavakoli-Targhi, Mohamad, 1957–
    Refashioning Iran : Orientalism, Occidentalism, and
    historiography / Mohamad Tavakoli-Targhi.
        p. cm. — (St. Antony's series)
    Includes bibliographical references and index.
    ISBN 0–333–94922–6 (cloth)
    1. Iran—Historiography. 2. Orientalism—Iran. 3. Nationalism–
    –Iran. 4. Historiography—Iran. 5. Historiography—India. I. Title.
    II. St. Antony's series (Palgrave (Firm))
    DS271.5 .T38 2001
    955'.007'2—dc21
                                                        2001035430

10 9   8   7   6   5   4   3   2   1
10 09 08 07 06 05 04 03 02 01

Printed and bound in Great Britain by
Antony Rowe Ltd, Chippenham, Wiltshire

For Jennifer, Azadeh, and Afsaneh

.

Contents

Preface and Acknowledgments

Refashioning Iran is the product of an intellectual journey that began with the Iranian Revolution of 1979 but which then detoured into an exploration of modernity, Orientalism, nationalism, and the writing of history. Dissatisfied with the conventional accounts of the Revolution and my own dissertation on the subject, I began to explore the making of modern Iranian identity. An initial inquiry into the narrative identity of the nineteenth century led me back to a set of Iran-centered *dasatiri* texts (named after *Dasatir*, a collection of writings attributed to ancient Iranian sages) that were produced by an exile community of Zoroastrian scholars who had settled in India in the late sixteenth century. These *dasatiri* texts, which were popularized by the late eighteenth- and early nineteenth-century Orientalists, intensified my curiosity about the formation of Orientalism and "Oriental studies" in India. The inquiry into the works of early Orientalists, conversely, interested me in Persianate scholars who had informed and educated these "pioneers." Exploring the works of Persian scholars who collaborated with Orientalists, in turn, prompted my study of Persian travelogues on Europe. Exploring Persian travelogues, once again, I came full circle and found myself encountering the themes that informed the constitutionalist and revolutionary discourses in Iran.

As a byproduct of these intellectual detours and zigzags, *Refashioning Iran* is not a traditional historical monograph. Like episodes in the *Thousand and One Nights*, each chapter may stand on its own but it also shares the overarching concerns of the others. The issues explored in this book were once intended as two separate monographs; but the ticking of the academic clock and my self-deconstruction made such a project inexpedient. This was conveyed to me most forcefully by my colleagues, Ahmad Karimi-Hakkak, Fatema Keshavarz, Ahmet Karamustafa, and Jennifer Jenkins, who are to be credited for the completion of this book.

Refashioning Iran is an historiographical project that challenges the conventional national histories of Iran, which often depict modernity as an historical epoch inaugurated by "Westernizing" and state-centralizing reforms. By viewing modernity as a global process that engendered various strategies of self-refashioning, this study seeks to break away from the dehistoricizing implications of "Westernization" theories that are predicated upon the temporal assumption of the non-contemporaneity of European and non-European societies. This assumption informs the hegemonic Iranian understanding of modern history since the early nineteenth century. In a recent expression of this dehistoricizing and detemporalizing presumption, Dariush Shayegan, a leading Iranian critic, inviting his readers to "to be rational for once" and claiming to "stay with the facts" argued, "For more than three centuries we, the heirs of the civilizations of Asia and Africa, have been 'on holiday' from history. We succeeded so well in crystallizing time in space that we were able to live outside time, arms folded, safe from interrogation."[1] Informed by the same temporal assumption of non-simultaneity with Europe, Riza Davari, an Iranian philosopher who has set himself the task of transcending "Western" humanism, asserted that "the past of the West is our future."[2]

The temporal comprehension of these *engagé* critics is genealogically related to the ironic and self-Orientalizing rhetorical argument of an early twentieth-century Constitutionalist who contended that if Adam, the forefather of humanity, could return today, he would be pleased with his Iranian descendants who have preserved his mode of life for many millenniums, whereas his unfaithful European children have totally altered Adam's tradition and mode of life. With the exception of a short-lived ancient cultural efflorescence, this rhetorical argument was similar to the Hegelian postulate of the fundamental similarity of the ancient and contemporary Persian mode of life, a postulate which Hegel shared with his contemporary Orientalists. Such Hegelian and Orientalist temporal assumptions have been reinforced by Iranian historiographical traditions that equate modernity with Westernization.

Departing from these dehistoricizing traditions, I articulate an alternative understanding of modernity and nationalism. Here my focus is less on rationality and individualism and more on the simultaneity of a global process that contributed to the hybridization of cultures and the invention of national selves. Instead of confining Persianate modernity to the nation-state of Iran, this book explores the wider Persianate (Persian-writing) world, which is divided by area studies conventions into two autonomous cultural zones of South Asian India and Middle Eastern Iran. This allows for the discussion of the forgotten and what I have called *homeless texts* that have fallen between the cracks of area studies and nation-states of Iran and India, where Persian, despite its abrogation as the official language in 1830s, continued to serve as a *lingua franca* until the end of the nineteenth century. In this dialogic account, the revival of pre-Islamic history, stylistic and narratological developments in the Persian language, and the productive encounters with the *heterotopic* communities of European settlers and travelers are explored in a pre-bordered historical setting when geographical lines separating Iran from India were not constituted as the "natural" divide of two divergent national characters, traditions, and cultures.

The first four chapters explore the interrelations of modernity, Orientalism, and Eur(ope)ology – a body of knowledge about Europe that has been hailed as "invisible Occidentalism" by the historian Juan Cole and as "Orientalism in reverse" by political scientist Mehrzad Boroujerdi.[3] The remaining three chapters explicate the emergence of an Iran-centered historiography and a constitutionalist discourse that was facilitated through a "secondary identification" with the Iranian *homeland* (*vatan*).[4] Identification with Iran, as a maternal homeland (*madar-i vatan*), provided the foundation for the making of modern nationalist subjects and subjectivities in Iran.

Informed by recent scholarship, Chapter 1 evaluates the conventional accounts of modernity as a byproduct of "Occidental rationalism" and offers an alternative approach for the exploration of Persianate modernity. This chapter was originally prepared for a St Antony's conference on "The Coming of Modernity in Qajar Iran," the proceedings of which were published in *Comparative Studies of South Asia, Africa, and the Middle East* (1998). A later version of it also appeared in *Cultural Dynamics* (2001). The completion of this chapter was made possible by a 1998 Iranian Fellowship at St Antony's College, Oxford. I am grateful for the support provided by the Middle East Centre and its faculty and staff, including Derek Hopwood, Eugene Rogan, Mustafa Badawi, Ahmed al-Shahi, Avi Shlaim, Elizabeth Anderson, and Mastaneh Ebtehaj who made my work at the Centre productive and pleasant. I am also grateful to John Gurney, Shahrzad and Reza Sheikholeslami, Julie Meisami, Farhan Nizami, John Piscatori, Colin Wakefield, Neguin Yavari, Wadad al-Kazi, Parviz Nieman, Mastaneh Ebtihaj, and Homa Katouzian who provided a supportive social and intellectual environment.

"Orientalism's Genesis Amnesia" (Chapter 2) explores the institutional erasure of the labor of Persianate scholars who contributed to the making of Orientalism as an area of academic inquiry. Reexamining the intellectual career of Anquetil-Duperron (1731–1805) and Sir William Jones (1749–94), I interrogate an intellectual exchange that authorized European scholars but marginalized their Persianate associates. Exploring the intertextuality of European printed texts with forgotten Persian manuscripts, this chapter seeks to correct a current critical tendency that focuses solely on European scholarly productions without inquiring into the contribution of native scholars in the making of Oriental studies. An earlier version of this chapter appeared in *Comparative Studies of South Asia, Africa, and the Middle East* (1996). I am particularly thankful to Sucheta Mazumdar and Vasant Kaiwar, the editors of CSSAAME, for their support for my scholarship. The research for this chapter was made possible by a fellowship from the American Institute of Indian Studies (1992–3) and institutional affiliation with the Centre for Historical Studies of Jawaharlal Nehru University, New Delhi. I particularly benefited from intellectual interaction with my gurus Harbans Mukhia and Muzaffar Alam. Khuda Bakhsh Oriental Public Library (Patna, India) provided me with valuable sources. I am grateful for the generosity of Dr Abid Reza Bedar, the library's exceptionally efficient director. Earlier versions of this chapter were presented at a symposium on "Questions of Modernity," organized by the Department of Middle Eastern Studies and Anthropology, New York University, April 19–20, and the Rockefeller Humanities Institute on "South Asian Islam and the Greater Muslim World," sponsored by the Triangle South Asia Consortium Workshop, Chapel Hill, NC, May 23–26, 1996. This chapter benefited from the comments and critiques of conference participants including Lila Abu-Lughud, Talal Asad, Partha Chatterjee, Dipish Chakrabarty, Gyan Prakash, Michael Gilsanon, Khalid Fahmey, Stefania Pandolfo, Zachary Lockman, Timothy Michell, Faisal Devji, Gregory Kozlowski, Vali Nasr, David Lelyveld, Sandria Freitag, Barbra Metcalf, David Gilmartin, Tony Stewart, Vasant Kaiwar, Sucheta Mazumzdar, Mariam Cook, Bruce Lawrence, and Carl Ernst. I am also appreciative of Alison Bailey's and Charlotte Brown's editorial suggestions for this and other chapters.

"Persianate Europology," Chapter 3, analyzes late eighteenth- and early nineteenth-century Persian accounts of Europe. Familiarity with Europe and European modes of life, I argue, facilitated the development of a "double consciousness" whereby Persianate ethical standards were used to evaluate European cultural practices and European perspectives were deployed for the censuring of Indian and Iranian societies. Earlier drafts of this chapter were presented in April and May 1997 respectively at the South Asia Seminar, the University of Chicago, and the Triangle South Asia Consortium Workshop at North Carolina State University. Participants at these two gatherings provided invaluable feedback and criticism. I am particularly indebted to Richard Eaton, Mushirul Hasan, Frank Korom, Claude Markovits, Omar Qureshi, Mohammed Kalam, Aisha Khan, Dipish Chakrabarty, and C. M. Naim who initially encouraged me to look beyond a nationalist frame of historical analysis. Tony Stewart, John Richards, Katherine Ewing, David Gilmartin, Bruce

Lawrence, and Carl Ernst, the organizers of the Triangle South Asia Consortium, provided an invaluable environment for intellectual dialogue in three consecutive years.

"Imagining European Women," Chapter 4, explores late eighteenth- and early nineteenth-century Persian travelers' impressions of European women. These travelers' reports of "self-experience" provided the narrative basis for instituting Europe as a new significant cultural Other. Positive accounts of European women informed the nationalist call for unveiling and educating women in Iran. Negative accounts, on the other hand, prompted the formation of a Europhobic discourse that warned against the Europeanization of Iranian women. The earliest version of this chapter was prepared for the 1990 "Round-Table on Identity Politics and Women," which was organized by Valentine Moghadam and sponsored by the World Institute for Development Economics Research at the United Nations University in Helsinki. Later versions were presented at a 1994 conference on Nineteenth-Century Persian Travel Memoirs at the Center for Middle Eastern Studies, University of Texas, Austin, and at a 1995 University of Virginia symposium on "Shifting Boundaries of Gender Categories in South Asia and the Middle East," which was sponsored by Middle East Studies Program, Women's Studies Program, and the Center for South Asian Studies. Having gone through many revisions and rethinking, this chapter has benefited from the critical readings of the organizers and participants in these conferences, including Valentine Moghadam, Farzaneh Milani, Richard Barnnet, Elton L. Daniel, Abbas Amanat, Juan Cole, Amin Banani, M. R. Qanoonparvar, and Hafez Farmayan. This chapter, which came to shape much of my later scholarship, received invaluable support from Afsaneh Najmabadi and Lynne Withey of University of California Press, who offered me a book contract on the "Women of the West Imagined." Concerned with the use-value of this project in scapegoating Muslims and Iranians in the United States, I hesitantly abandoned it in mid-course. But the intellectual questions that this hesitation and change of heart posed for me contributed to the maturing of my historiographical perspective.

Chapter 5, "Contested Memories," explores the allegorical meanings of Iran's pre-Islamic history, a point of contention between Islamist and secular–nationalist visions of Iran. It explains that the meanings of pre-Islamic Iran are embedded in narratives that terminate in the Muslim conquest and death of the last Sasanian king in 651. In early Islamic historical writings, the termination of Sasanian rule signified the moral superiority of Islam. This was altered by a neo-Zoroastrian narrative that was formulated by Azar Kayvan and his cohorts, who had migrated to India in the late sixteenth century. Popularized in the nineteenth century, this *dasatiri* account sought to displace the Qur'anic sacred history with an Iran-centered proto-nationalist history. The work on this chapter, like that of Chapter 2, was made possible with an American Institute of Indian Studies travel grant that enabled me to roam around Indian libraries and familiarize myself with Persian language texts written and printed in India. This chapter owes a great deal to Hossein Ziai, who offered a long and detailed criticism of an earlier draft. He made me aware of the political underpinnings of the temporal coding "pre-Islamic" and the scholarship on ancient Iran and Illuminationist (*Ishraq*) philosophy. I am also indebted to Sholeh Quinn, Alison Bailey, Charlotte Brown, Houchang Chehabi, and Afsaneh Najmabadi, who offered invaluable suggestions for revision. Earlier drafts of this chapter have appeared in *Iranian Studies* (Winter 1996) and *Medieval History Journal* (Winter 2000). I am thankful to Abbas Amanat and Harbans Mukhia, the editors of these journals, for their mentoring and intellectual support.

"Crafting National Identity," the sixth chapter, explores the emergence of a secular national identity in the nineteenth century. Informed by *dasatiri* texts, many nineteenth-century historians represented the pre-Islamic past as a "golden age," which come to a "tragic end" with the Muslim conquest. Linking the end of the "enlightened" pre-Islamic times to origins of human history, this representation made possible the crafting of a new memory, identity, and political reality. This invented past was used to project Iran's "decadence" onto Arabs and Islam and to introject desirable attributes of Europeans to the pre-Islamic Iranian Self. This chapter is a product of extensive dialogue with many friends and colleagues, including Afsaneh Najmabadi, Palmira Brummett, C. M. Naim, Catherine Hobbs, Khosrou Shakeri, Ahmad Karimi-Kakkak, as well as Houchang Chehabi and Abbas Amanat. An earlier draft of this chapter appeared in *Iranian Studies* (1990).

Chapter 7, "Patriotic and Matriotic Nationalism," explores two competing styles of national imagination. The official nationalism identified Iran as a "familial home" headed by the "crowned father" (*pidar-i tajdar*). This patriotic style was contested by a counter-official discourse that identified the "homeland" (*vatan*) as a dying mother in need of immediate care. In this matriotic style of nationalist imagination all Iranians were called upon to care for and to protect the motherland. In a close reading of Persian newspapers from the 1870s to the 1900s, I explain how the engendering of the national body as a mother symbolically eliminated the father-Shah as the guardian of the nation. I also explore how this contributed to the emergence of popular sovereignty – the participation of "the nation's children" (both male and female) in determining the future of the "mother-land" (*madar-i/mam-i vatan*). In developing this chapter, I have benefited from correspondences with Afsaneh Najmabadi and discussions with Jennifer Jenkins, Valentine Moghadam, Juan Cole, and Rebecca Saunders with whom I developed and taught a course on "Nations and Narration." Earlier drafts of this chapter were presented at the South/West Asian Seminar Series at Illinois State University and at the Center for Middle Eastern Studies Lecture Series at the University of Chicago in 1997. It was also presented at a Social Science Research Council Project on "Nationalism After Colonialism," Berkeley, November 1997. An earlier draft of this chapter has appeared in *Strategies* (November 2000) and can be viewed at http://www.tandf.co.uk/journals.

The postscript explores the rhetoricality and theatricality of Iran's modern constitutionalist discourse. It explains that maneuvers among alternative forms of Iranian-ness foregrounded Iranian identity, setting up the twentieth-century vacillations between secular and Islamic identities and cultural politics. The diverse range of issues addressed in this book inevitably raise more questions than I have been able to answer. Thus, this book should not be seen as a conclusive account of Iranian modernity and nationalism but as a preliminary reexamination of their fundamental assumptions.

The final production of this book was aided by the diligent and punctual editorial work of Valery Rose, to whom I am deeply grateful.

Notes on Romanization and Dates

This book utilizes a simplified version of the Library of Congress (LC) romanization system for Persian names and titles. Conventionally used by most on-line library catalogues, this system drops all defamiliarizing diacritical marks. Thus readers can conveniently locate the cited titles in on-line library catalogues. In a few self-evident cases, such as Tehran instead of Tihran, I have deviated from the LC convention.

For the period covered in this book, the lunar Hijri calendar was conventionally used in Persian sources. When necessary, I have supplied both Hijri and Gregorian dates.

1
Modernity, Heterotopia, and Homeless Texts

Modernity and heterotopia

A shift toward "historical epistemology" has altered the nature of scholarship on modernity and nationality.[1] Departing from objectivist and Eurocentric historiographies, postmodern and postcolonial scholars have began to *reactivate* the *sedimented* practices that naturalized "the nation" and instituted Europe as the original home of modernity.[2] As the foundation of modern historical narratives, "the nation" is being revisited by scholars who view it not as a concrete and observable reality but as a modernist style of collective imagination, societal organization, and self-disciplining of citizens.[3] By the contingent deployment of territory, history, language, ethnicity, and culture, the architects of modern *cosmopolitical* order naturalized the nation as a serially continuous and homogeneous entity endowed with a distinct identity and characteristic. By structuring thought-ways, patterns of identity, nations and nation-states regulated the modern time's expanding gap between the "space of experience" and the "horizon of expectation."[4] In the *new age* of "fateful simultaneity of spring and autumn"[5] when everything seemed "pregnant with its contrary,"[6] the apocalyptic expectation of the radical rupture of the time to come was transformed into an anticipated and planned "progress" toward the future. Displacing divine decree with human agency, the modernist notion of *progress* combined experience and expectation and thus "served the purpose of theoretically anticipating future historical movement and practically influencing it."[7] Revolution, development, progress, and liberation – these and other *temporalized* concepts – were employed to awaken a nation to "self-consciousness" and to normalize the experience of everyday life in rapidly changing modern times. The binary opposites of these concepts – reaction, tradition, stagnation, and despotism – were often deployed against a nation's internal "foes" who were marginalized and excluded from the national-political scene.

The reexamination of the Eurocentric definition of modernity has been at the center of recent historical *reactivations* of "modern times."[8] The conventional Enlightenment story treats modernity as a peculiarly European development and as a byproduct of "Occidental rationalism."[9] Viewed from within this hegemonic paradigm, non-European societies were "modernized" as a result of Western impact and influence.[10] Thus Westernization, modernization, and acculturation were conceived as interchangeable concepts accounting for the transition of "traditional" and "non-Western" societies.[11] These assertions have been reevaluated by scholars examining the cultural genealogies and etiologies of modernity.[12] Locating "the West" in a larger global context beginning with the "Age of Exploration," Stuart Hall suggests that "The so-called uniqueness of the West was, in part, produced by Europe's contact and self-comparison with other, non-western, societies (the Rest), very different in their histories, ecologies, patterns of development, and cultures from the European model."[13] Demonstrating the critical importance of "the Rest" in the formation of "Western" modernity, Hall submits that "[w]ithout the Rest, (or its own internal 'others'), the West would not have been able to recognize and represent itself as the summit of human history."[14] Hall's revised conception of modernity allows for an expanded framework of analysis encompassing what I call the formative role of *heterotopic* experiences in the formation of the *ethos* of modernity.

In contrast to *utopias*, the imaginary places in which human societies are depicted in perfect forms, Michel Foucault explored *heterotopias* as alternative real spaces. As existing loci beyond the everyday space of experience, heterotopias "are something like counter-sites, a kind of effectively enacted utopia in which the real sites, all other real sites that can be found within the culture, are simultaneously represented, contested, and inverted." These loci of alterity served the function of creating "a space of illusion that exposes every real space . . . a space that is other, another real space, as perfect, as meticulous, as well arranged as ours is messy, ill-constructed, and jumbled." Calling the latter type a "compensatory" heterotopia, Foucault speculated that "on the level of the general organization of terrestrial space" colonies might have "func-tioned somewhat in this manner."[15] He offered as historical examples the regulated colonies established by Jesuits and Puritans. Similarly, sixteenth-century reports of European exploration of exotic hetero-topias deepened the Renaissance "humanists' understanding of human motives and action" and enlarged their framework of understanding.[16] "As late as the 18th century," according to Stephen Toulmin, "Montesquieu and Samuel Johnson still found it helpful to present unusual ideas by attributing them to people in a far-off land like Abyssinia or Persia."[17] The attribution of "unusual ideas to people in a far-off land" was not merely a "literary device."[18] For instance, the physical presence of the Persian Ambassador Muhammad Riza Bayk (d. 1717) in France in 1715–16 provided the pertinent context for the imaginary scenarios informing the "unsual ideas" and the central question of *Persian Letters*: "How can one be Persian?"[19] As spectacles and as native informants of exotic heterotopias, travelers like Muhammad Riza Bayk inspired native European spectators who in turn provided them with a space of self-recognition and self-refashioning. Considering the material significance of the "Rest" in the formation of "Western modernity," such attributions can be considered as residues of a genesis amnesia in European historiography. Such a historiographical amnesia has made possible the fabrication of a coherent and continuous medieval and modern "Western Civilization." As Maria R. Menocal has demonstrated, the "European Awakening" was "an Oriental period of Western history, a period in which Western culture grew in the shadow of Arabic and Arabic-manipulated learning."[20]

By recovering the significance of heterotopic experiences in the formation of the ethos of modernity, the lands beyond Europe, instead of being the reverse image of enlightenment and modernity, served as "laboratories of modernity," as sites of the earliest sightings of "the hallmarks of European cultural production."[21] This has been explored in the historiographical works of Paul Rabinow, Sidney Mintz, Timothy Mitchell, Uday Mehta, Benedict Anderson, Gwendolyn Wright, and Nicholas Dirks, among others.[22] Summarizing the contribution of these scholars, Ann Stoler observed that, "These reconfigured histories have pushed us to rethink European cultural genealogies across the board and to question whether the key symbols of modern western societies – liberalism, nationalism, state welfare, citizenship, culture, and 'European-ness' itself – were not clarified among Europe's colonial exiles and by those colonized classes caught in their pedagogic net in Asia, Africa, and Latin America, and only then brought 'home'."[23] For instance, in his study of French colonialism in Morocco Paul Rabinow observed that "[t]he colonies constituted a laboratory of experimentation for new arts of government capable of bringing a modern and healthy society into being."[24] In *Imagined Communities* Anderson demonstrated that Creole communities developed "early conceptions of their nation-ness – *well before most of Europe*."[25] Locating Foucault's *History of Sexuality* in a larger trans-European context, Stoler contends, "One could argue that the history of Western sexuality must be located in the production of historical Others, in the broader force field of empire where technologies of sex, self, and power were defined as 'European' and 'western,' as they refracted and remade."[26] In the following chapter, I explain how the "founding" of Orientalism was informed by the works of *Persianate* scholars and scholarship in India.

In light of these recent studies it can be argued that modernity was not a homemade product of "Occidental rationality," as asserted by Max Weber and universalized by "modernization" theorists. Alternatively, modernity can be viewed a product of a globalizing network of power and knowledge that informed the heterotopic experiences of crisscrossing peoples and cultures and thus provided multiple scenarios of self-refashioning. Whereas Europeans reconstituted the modern self in relation to their non-Western Others, Asians and Africans began to redefine the self in relation to Europe, their new significant Other. But what Toulmin calls the "counter-Renaissance" search for certainty,[27] constituted European modes of self-refashioning as archetypically universal, rational, and modern. This dehistoricizing universalist claim enabled European rationalists to obliterate the heterotopic context of their self-making and thus constitute themselves as the originators of modernity and rationality. This *amnesiac* or *forgetful* assertion gained hegemonic currency and thus constituted "non-Western" modernity as "Westernization."

The universalist claims of European enlightenment has blackmailed non-European modernity and debilitated its historiography by engendering a tradition of historical writing that used a dehistorized and decontextualized "European rationality" as its scale and referent. Iranian historians and ideologues, like their Indian and Ottoman counterparts,[28] developed a fractured conception of historical time that viewed their contemporary European societies ahead of their own time. This conception of historical time parallels the time-distancing devices of European anthropologists who denied *coevalness* to their contemporary non-Western societies.[29] Such a *schizochronic* conception of history informs the nationalist historiography of Iranian modernity, a historiography that assumes the non-contemporaneity of the contemporaneous Iranian and European societies.

Discursive affinities of nationalism and Orientalism

Recognized as the heterotopia of modernity and scientific rationality, Europe has been constituted as the horizon of expectation for the Iranian passage to modernity. Thus European history, as the *future past* of the desired present, has functioned as a normative scenario for the prognosis or forecasting of the future Iran. This anticipatory modernity introduced a form of historical thinking that narrated Iranian history in terms of the European past. By universalizing that past, historical deviations from the European norm have been misrecognized as abnormalities. Thus, the development of feudalism, capitalism, the bourgeoisie, the proletariat, democracy, freedom, scientific rationality, and industry in the "well-ordered" Europe have informed the diagnoses of their lack, absence, retardation, and underdevelopment in Iran.[30] In other words, alternative non-European historical processes have been characterized as the absence of change and as unhistorical history. For instance, John Malcolm, the author of an influential Orientalist *History of Persia* (1815), which was translated into Persian in 1876, observed:

> Though no country has undergone, during the last twenty centuries, more revolutions than the kingdom of Persia, there is, perhaps, none that is less altered in its condition. The power of the sovereigns, and of the satraps of ancient times; the gorgeous magnificence of the court; the habits of the people; their division into citizens, martial tribes, and savage mountaineers; the internal administration; and the mode of warfare; have continued essentially the same: and the Persians, as far as we have the means of judging, are at the present period, not a very different people from what they were in the time of Darius, and the Nousheerwan.[31]

In a more concise statement, Hegel (1770–1831) similarly asserted that, "The Persians . . . retained on the whole the fundamental characteristics of their ancient mode of life."[32] This dehistoricizing assumption – that is, the contemporaneity of an early nineteenth-century "mode of life" with that of ancient times – informs both Orientalist and nationalist historiographies that constitute the heightened period of European colonialism and imperialism as the true beginning of rationality and historical progress in Iran. Whereas a progressive conception of time informs the modern European historiography from the late eighteenth century to the present, the accounts of modern Iran, like that of other non-Western societies, are unanimously based in a regressive conception of history. Thus the passage to modernity has been constituted a radical break with the "stagnant" and eternally recurring Iranian mode of life.

Malcolm viewed Islam and "the example of the prophet of Arabia and the character of some of the fundamental tenets of his faith" as the most prominent factors "in retarding the progress of civilization among those who have adopted his faith." These "retarding" factors explained why "every country inhabited by Mahomedans" never "attained a state of improvement which can be compared with that enjoyed by almost all those nations who form the present commonwealth of Europe." He concluded his recounting of the Iranian past with a reflection on its future. "The History of Persia, from the Arabian conquest to the present day," he claimed, "may be adduced as a proof of the truth of these observations: and while the causes, by which the effects have been produced, continue to operate, no material change in the condition of that empire can be expected." Malcolm wondered whether "the future destiny of this kingdom" could be altered with "the recent approximation of a great European power." The experience of the Ottomans who "wrapt up in the habits of their ancestors and . . . have for ages resisted the progress of that civilization with which they were surrounded" did not seem promising to him. Thus the proximity with European powers and the "consequent collision of opposite habits and faith, was more likely to increase than to diminish those obstacles which hitherto prevented any very intimate or social intercourse between Mahomedan and Christian nations."[33] This prognosis, a forerunner of the "Clash of Civilizations," was grounded in the epistemological differentiation of the progressive Christian "commonwealth of Europe" and the stagnant "Mahomedan nations" of Asia.

  With the global hegemony of "the West," this binary opposition became an ever more significant component of an Iranian national historiography venerating progress, development, and growth. With these concerns, a celebratory history of Europe provided the normative manual for deciphering the abnormalities of Iran's past and for promoting its modernization, that is, Westernization. For instance, Ervand Abrahamian, the author of one of the most sophisticated accounts of modern Iran, offers a paradigmatic view of the nineteenth century, a view that is embedded in Persian historical writings. "Traditional Iran," in his estimation, "in sharp contrast to feudal Europe, thus had no baronial rebellions, no magna carta, no legal estates, and consequently no representative institutions." These and other *lacks* constitute the foundation for explaining a series of reformist failures of the nineteenth-century Qajars: "The attempt to construct a statewide bureaucracy failed. . . . The Qajars were equally unsuccessful . . . in building a viable standing army . . . [and] even failed to recapture the full grandeur of the ancient shah-in-shahs." By narrating a failed version of European history, this progressive historian of Iran assumes a typically Orientalist vantage: "For the nineteenth-century Europeans, the Qajar dynasty was an epitome of ancient oriental despotism; in fact, it was a failed imitation of such absolutism."[34] Such a characterization is a common feature of Orientalist, nationalist, and also Marxist historiography of nineteenth-century Iran.[35] The opening paragraph of Guity Nashat's *The Origin of Modern Reforms in Iran* is, likewise, a testimony to the centrality of Europe in the horizon of expectation for "traditional" Iran:

> In 1870 a young Iranian of modest background, Mirza Huseyn Khan, was presented with an opportunity to regenerate Iran. During the next ten years he introduced regulations that were designed to transform the country's traditional political, military, and judicial institutions to resemble Western models. He also attempted to introduce Western cultural innovations and Westernized modes of thought.[36]

Viewed as a "Western model" used to transform "traditional" societies, "the modern," as in the above case, is commonly understood "as a *known history*, something which has *already happened elsewhere*, and which is to be reproduced, mechanically or otherwise, with a local content." As a mimetic plan, Iranian modernity, like its non-Western counterparts, can at best be hailed as a "project of positive unoriginality."[37] An eternally recurring Iranian premodernity was thus superseded by an already enacted "Western" modernity.

Viewing modernity as belated reduplication of "Western models," historians of Iran often invent periodizations that are analogous to standard European historical accounts. Recognizing Descartes's *Discours sur la Méthode* and Newton's *Principia* as two founding texts of modern thought in Europe, Iranian historians have the same expectations for the Persian rendering of these texts. In a modularized periodization of the Iranian "discovery of the West" and the "dissemination of European 'new learning'", Mangol Bayat, a historian of Qajar Iran, writes that a Persian translation of René Descartes's *Discourse* was commissioned by Arthur Gobineau and published in 1862.[38] Referring to I'tizad al-Saltanah's *Falak al-Sa'adah* (1861),[39] she adds that only one year earlier Isaac Newton and the idea of heliocentricity had been "introduced to the Iranian public."[40] This periodization concerning the introduction of modern European philosophical texts is similarly advanced by Faraydun Adamiyat, Elie Kedourie, Nikki Keddie, Jamshid Bihnam, and Alireza Manafzadeh.[41] Adamiyat, a pioneering historian of Iranian modernity, contended that *Falak al-Sa'adah* and the Persian translation of *Discourse* provided the "context for rational transformation" (*zaminah-'i tahavvul-i 'aqlani*) of nineteenth-century Iran. To dramatize the historical significance of

Descartes's translation, he speculated that all copies of an earlier 1853 edition of the text might have been burned.[42]

In these accounts, the Comte de Gobineau, a French diplomat in Tehran as well as an infamous anti-Semite,[43] is credited as the initiator of the rationalizing tasks of translating Descartes's generative text of European modernity into Persian. Although Gobineau commissioned this translation, he doubted whether Iranians and other Asians were capable of absorbing modern civilization.[44] Like Gobineau, Iranian historians of scientific modernity often assume that "the defense of geocentricism was of greatest importance for Muslim traditional scholars, just as it was for the medieval church."[45] In such accounts the endeavor for modernity is often depicted as a contention between the rational European astronomy and the irrational Muslim astrology.[46] For example, Bayat writes that I'tizad al-Saltanah "rose in defence of Newton and other European scientists' theories, and he declared obsolete the 'knowledge of the ancients.'"[47] Likewise, Arjomand argues that I'tizad al-Saltanah's work "is the first book of its kind, aimed at combating the belief in traditional astronomy and astrology and bringing what might be termed scientific enlightenment to 19th-century Iran."[48]

Recounting the contentions for scientific rationality, historians of modern Iran often select scholars who endorsed astrology and opposed heliocentrism as Muslim representatives, ignoring those who did not fit into this schema. By claiming that the Persian publication of Descartes in the 1860s is the beginning of a new age of rationality and modernity, these historians provide a narrative account that accommodates and reinforces the foundational myth of modern Orientalism, a myth that constitutes "the West" as ontologically and epistemologically different from "the Orient."[49] This Orientalist problematic has been validated by a nationalist historiography that constitutes the period prior to its own arrival as a time of decay, backwardness, and despotism.[50] By deploying the basic dogmas of Orientalism for the enhancement of its own political project, in this sense Iranian nationalist historiography has participated "in its own Orientalizing."[51] As self-designated vanguards of modernity and national homogenization, both official and counter-official Iranian nationalists have naturalized and authenticated the working assumptions of Orientalism.

Homeless texts

In the mid-seventeenth century a purely self-congratulatory view of European civilization as the paragon of universal reason and the concurring "blackmail of the Enlightenment" had not yet been formed. Similarly, Europe's Oriental-Other had not yet been dehistoricized as only "traditional," "static," and "unchanging," and Muslims were not viewed as "anti-scientific." More significantly, historical thinking had not yet been confined to the boundaries of modern nation-states. It is during this period that an alternative account of a Persianate modernity can be retrieved. Predating the consolidation of modern nation-states and the co-optation of modernity as a state-legitimating ideology, following Foucault, modernity may be envisaged as an ethos rather than a well-demarcated historical period.[52] By envisaging modernity as an ethos rather than as a decisive epoch of the nation, historians of Iran and India may imagine a joint fact-finding mission that would allow for reactivating what the poet Mahdi Akhavan Salis has aptly recognized as "stories vanished from memory" (*qissah-ha-yi raftah az yad*).[53] These vanished stories may be retrieved from a large corpus of texts made homeless with the emergence of *history with borders*, a convention that confined historical writing to the borders of modern nation-states.

The convention of history with borders has created many *homeless texts* that have fallen victim to the fissure of Indian and Iranian nationalism. Although abolished as the official language of India in the 1830s, the intellectual use of Persian continued and Persian publications in nineteenth-century India outnumbered those produced in other languages. Publishers in Calcutta, Bombay, Lucknow, Kanpur, Delhi, Lahore, Hyderabad, and other cities in the Indian subcontinent also published more Persian books than their counterparts in Iran. Many of the literary and historical texts edited and published in India achieved canonical status in the neighboring Iran. Rammahan Roy, the acclaimed "father of modern India," was in fact the editor of one of the first Persian newspapers, *Mir'at al-Akhbar* (1822). This Indo-Iranian intellectual symmetry continued until the end of the nineteenth century, when a Persian newspaper, *Miftah al-Zafar* (1897), campaigned for the formation of Anjuman-i Ma'arif, an academy devoted to the strengthening of Persian as a scientific language.[54] Whereas the notion of "Western civilization" provided a safety net supplementing European national histories, no common historiographical practice captures the residues of the colonial and national conventions of historical writing that separates the joint Persianate literary culture of Iran and India – a literary culture that is irreducible to Islam and the Islamic civilization. A postcolonial historiography of Indian and Iranian modernity must begin to reactivate the concurring history that has been erased from memory by colonial conventions and territorial divisions.

The conventional account of Persianate acquaintance with the Cartesian notion of "I think, therefore I am", differs radically from an account retrievable from the *Travels* of François Bernier (b. 1620), a French scholar who resided in India for a few years. Approximately 200 years prior to Arthur de Gobineau, Danishmand Khan Shafi'a Yazdi (d. 1670?), a Mughal courtier and Iranian émigré who was aware of current intellectual developments in Europe, dared to be wise (in Kant's sense of *sapere aude*) and commissioned Bernier to translate into Persian the works of René Descartes (1560–1650), William Harvey (1578–1657), and Jean Pecquet (1622–1674).[55] Bernier (a student of the philosopher Gassendi and a recipient of a "Doctor of Medicine" in 1652), who is considered as a founding figure of modern Orientalism,[56] was an employee of Mirza Shafi'a, who was granted the title "Danishmand" (scholar/scientist) for his intellectual endeavors. Bernier reported of "explaining to my Agah [master] the recent discoveries of Harveus and Pecquet in anatomy... [and] discoursing on the philosophy of Gassendi and Descartes, which I translated to him in Persian (for this was my principal employment for five or six years)." Illustrating the intellectual courage and curiosity of Danishmand Khan, Bernier wrote:

> [M]y Navaab, or Agah, Danech-mend-khan, expects my arrival with much impatience. He can no more dispense with his philosophical studies in the afternoon than avoid devoting the morning to his weighty duties as Secretary of State for Foreign Affairs and Grand Master of the Horse. Astronomy, geography, and anatomy are his favourite pursuits, and he reads with avidity the works of Gassendi and Descartes.[57]

Danishmand Khan, who is known to have espoused and "disseminated many of the innovating principles of that [European] community" (*aksari az ahkam-i tahrifat-i an jama'at tikrar minimud*) desired to know "European sciences" (*'ilm-i ahl-i farang*) at a time when Europe was still plagued with religious wars.[58] His sustained interest in European intellectual developments is evident from his securing of a promise from Bernier "to send him the books from *ferngistan* [Europe]."[59] It was within the dynamic intellectual community around Danishmand Khan that Bernier became familiar with Persian translations of classical Sanskrit texts, including the *Upanishads*, which he brought back to Paris.[60] But the writings of Danishmand Khan and his cohorts who trained Bernier – this pedagogue of the "educated society in the seventeenth century" Europe – have remained virtually unknown. This is in part because of the stereotypical perception of the period of the Indian Mughal Emperor Aurangzayb's rule (1658–1707) as the age of Muslim bigotry and medieval decline. Confined within the grand narratives of "historical stages" and counter-colonial Hindu nationalism, historians of "medieval" India have mostly found facts of decline, all too often the only facts that they have searched for. During the same period François Martin, a friend of Bernier who visited Iran in 1669, observed that Persians "love the sciences, particularly mathematics." Contrary to received ideas, Martin reported: "It is believed that they [the Persians] are not very religious."[61] Likewise Pietro della Valle (1586–1652) could still confide that the Persianate scholar Mulla Zayn al-Din Lari, who has remained unknown to historians of Iran, "was comparable to the best in Europe."[62]

The scholarly efforts of Raja Jai Singh (1688–1743) provide another precolonial example of Persianate scholars' engagement with the modern sciences. Jai Singh built the observatories of Delhi, Banaris, and Jaipur, and based on new observations prepared the famous Persian astronomical table *Zij-i Muhammad Shahi* of 1728.[63] After the initial draft of his astronomical calculations, he sent a mission to Portugal in 1730 to acquire new observational equipment and to inquire about recent astronomical findings. The mission, which included Father Emmanuel de Figueredo (1690?–1753?) and Muhammad Sharif, returned with an edition of Phillipe de La Hire's *Tabulae Astronomicae* from 1702.[64] Mubashshir Khan provides a brief account of Jai Singh's scientific mission in his *Manahij al-Istikhraj*, an eighteenth-century guide for astronomical observation and calculations. Mubashshir Khan reported that Mirza Muhammad 'Abid and Mirza Khayr Allah were two "Muslim engineers" who assisted Raja Jai Singh in the building of observatories. He had met Mirza Khayr Allah, who explained to him how Jai Singh, with the assistance of "Padre Manuel", acquired European observational equipment and a copy of de La Hire's *Tabulae*. La Hire's calculations were used by Jai Singh in a revised edition of his *Zij-i Muhammad Shahi*.[65] This astronomical table, which was well known to eighteenth-century Iranian scholars, has remained virtually unknown to historians of Iran.[66] It is significant to note that almost a century earlier Shah 'Abbas II (1642–66) also had sent a mission to Rome to learn European painting techniques. The delegation included Muhammad Zaman "Paulo", who joined the ranks of the artists of the royal court and left a long-lasting imprint on representational art in both India and Iran.[67]

Works of Tafazzul Husayn Khan (d. 1800), well known to his Iranian friends and associates, are among other homeless texts that are elided from both Indian and Iranian annals of modernity. Hailed as an *'Allamah* (arch-scholar), he was an exemplary figure of the late eighteenth century who interacted closely with the first generation of British Orientalists in India and actively promoted local inquiry into modern science. In the 1780s he translated Isaac Newton's *Principia*, Emerson's *Mechanics*, and Thomas Simpson's *Algebra*.[68] In his obituary in 1803 *The Asiatic Annual Register* remembered Tafazzul Husayn Khan as "both in qualities and disposition of his mind, a very remarkable exception to the general character of Asiatic genius." Taking an exception to William Jones's assessment that "judgment and taste [were] the prerogative of Europeans," the obituary stated, "But with one, at least, of these proud prerogatives, the character of Tofuzzel Hussein [Tafazzul Husayn] unquestionably interferes; for, a judgment at once sound, clear, quick, and correct, was its indistinguishable feature."[69] To document the accomplishments of this "Asiatic" who had "cultivated ancient as well as modern European literatures with ardour and success...very uncommon in any foreigner," *The Asiatic Annual Register* published letters received from Ruben Burrows (1747–92),[70] David Anderson,[71] and Lord Teignmouth (or John Shore, 1751–1834). Lord Teignmouth remarked that for Tafazzul Husayn Khan, "mathematics was his favorite pursuit, and perceiving that the science had been cultivated to an extent in Europe far beyond what had been done in Asia, he determined to acquire a knowledge of European discoveries and improvements; and with this view, began the study of the English language." He further noted that in two years, Tafazzul Husayn Khan

was not only able to understand any English mathematical work, but to peruse with pleasure the volumes of our best historians and moralists. From the same motives he afterwards studied and acquired the Latin language, though in a less perfect degree; and before his death had made some progress in the acquisition of the Greek dialect.

Tafazzul Husayn Khan's knowledge of classical Indo-Islamic sciences were utilized by the British Orientalists William Jones, Richard Johnson, and Ruben Burrows, with whom he was acquainted.[72]

Mir 'Abd al-Latif Shushtari (1172–1220/1758–1806), a close associate of Tafazzul Husayn Khan who traveled to India in 1788, provided a synopsis of European modernity, modern astronomy, and new scientific innovations in his *Tuhfat al-'Alam* (1216/1801).[73] Shushtari constituted the year 900 of Hijrah (1494/95 CE) as the beginning of a new era associated with the decline of the caliphate (*khilafat*) of the Pope (*Papa*), the weakening of the Christian clergy, the ascent of philosophy, and the strengthening of philosophers and scientists. Referring to the

English Civil War, he explained the historical conditions for the decline of religion. While both philosophers and rulers affirmed the unity of God, they viewed "as entirely myths" (*hamah ra afsanah*) prophecy, resurrection, and prayers. He also explained the views of Copernicus and Newton on heliocentricity and universal gravitation. Shushtari rejected the astrological explanations of "earlier philosophers" (*hukama-yi ma taqaddam*) and found affinities between the contemporary British scientific views and the "unbounded rejection of astrologers in the splendid *Shari'ah*" (*kah hamah ja dar Shari'at-i gharra' takzib-i munajimin varid shudah ast*). Critical of the classical explanation of tides, as recounted by 'Abd Allah Jazayiri (d. 1173/1760) in *Tilism-i Sultani*, he offered a Newtonian account, relating the tides to gravitational actions of the sun and moon on oceanic waters.[74] Accordingly, he explained why the magnitude of the high tides in Calcutta differed from that of the coastal cities of the Persian Gulf. Shushtari viewed Newton as a "great sage an a distinguished philosopher" (*hakim-i a'zam va filsuf-i mu'azzam*) and ventured that in view of Newton's accomplishments all the "the golden books of the ancients" (*gawharin namah'ha-yi bastaniyan*) are now "similar to images on water" (*nimunah-'i naqsh bar ab ast*).[75] Shushtari's critical reflections on European history and modern sciences was appreciated by Fath 'Ali Shah who assigned the historian Vaqayi' Nigar (d. 1250/1834) the task of editing an abridged edition of *Tuhfat al-'Alam*, which is known as *Qava'id al-Muluk* (Axioms of Rulers).[76] Given Shushtari's competence in both classical and modern astronomy, a periodization of Iranian "scientific modernity" that lionizes I'tizad al-Saltanah's *Falak al-Sa'adah* (1861) as the harbinger of scientific modernity needs serious reconsideration. This is particularly important since I'tizad al-Saltanah was familiar with *Qava'id al-Muluk*.[77]

Aqa Ahmad Bihbahani Kirmanshahi (1777–1819), an Iranian Shi'i scholar and a friend of Shushtari who visited India between 1805 and 1810, devoted a chapter of his travelogue, *Mir'at al-Ahval-i Jahan Nama* (1810), to "the classification of the universe according to the school of the philosopher Copernicus." In the introduction he explained that "eminent philosophers are so numerous in Europe that their common masses [*avvam al-nas*] are inclined philosophically and seek mathematical and natural sciences." Like many other Muslim scholars, Bihbahani linked the "new views" (*ara'-i jadidah*) of Copernicus to those of ancient Greek philosophers, but emphasized that "most of his beliefs are original" (*mu'taqidat-i u aksari tazigi darand*).[78] He explained favorably the heliostatic system, the sidereal periods for the rotation of planets around the sun, the daily axial and annual orbital revolutions of the earth, and the trinary rotations of the moon. This Muslim theologian found no necessary conflict between Islam and modern astronomy.[79]

The corpus of homeless texts of modernity includes Mawlavi Abu al-Khayr's concise account of the Copernican solar system, *Majmu'ah-'i Shamsi* (1807), which appears to have been known in Iran.[80] Like the works of Tafazzul Husayn Khan, *Majmu'ah* is a product of dialogic inter- action between Persianate scholars and the British colonial officers. Among topics discussed in the *Majmu'ah* are the movements of the earth, the law of inertia, the planetary motions, and universal gravitation. In the introduction Mawlavi Abu al-Khayr noted that his book was based on English language sources and was translated "with the assistance" (*bi-i'anat*) of Dr William Hunter.[81] It is significant to note that Hunter had introduced Raja Jai Singh's *Zij-i Muhammad Shahi* to the English reading public in an article appearing in *Asiatic Researches* (1799).[82] It is likely that Mawlavi Abu al-Khayr had assisted Hunter in understanding and translating this highly technical Persian text.

During the first three decades of the nineteenth century numerous other texts on modern sciences were written in Persian that do not appear in accounts of Iranian and Indian modernity.[83] Muhammad Rafi' al-Din Khan's treatise on modern geometry and optics, *Rafi' al-Basar* (1250/1834),[84] was one such text. The author was informed by English sources brought to his attention by Rev. Henry Martyn (1781–1812),[85] a renowned Christian missionary and a translator of the Bible into Persian.[86] With an increased mastery of modern science, Persianate scholars can be seen as becoming active themselves in the production of scientific knowledge. In *A'zam al-Hisab*, a treatise on mathematics completed in 1814, Hafiz Ahmad Khan A'zam al-Mulk Bahadur (d. 1827) took issue with the Scottish astronomer James Ferguson on reckoning the differ- ence between the Christian and the Muslim calendar.[87] Aware of the self-congratulatory views of Europeans, "particularly among the people of England," A'zam al-Mulk Bahadur wrote a treatise on astronomy, *Mir'at al-'Alam* (1819) in order to "disprove" the assertion that Muslims were "uninformed of mathematics and astronomy."[88] Based on Coper- nican astronomy and informed by the most recent observations and discoveries at the Madras Observatory, this treatise likewise remains homeless and among those not yet included in the Indian and Iranian nationalist accounts of modernity.

This familiarity of the Persianate world with the modern sciences was commonly reported by European travelers. Referring to Abu al-Khayr's *Majmu'ah-'i Shamsi*, John Malcolm reported, "An abstract of the Coper- nican system, and the proofs which the labors of Newton have afforded of its truth, have been translated into Persian; and several individuals of that nation have laboured to acquire this noble but abstruse subject... "[89] The British Orientalist James Fraser reported meeting in December 1821 Fath Ali Khan Saba (d. 1822), the Qajar poet laureate, whom he viewed as "singularly well informed in, and has a great taste for, mechanics; having constructed several complicated pieces of machinery of his own invention, in a very ingenious manner, and even succeeded in making a printing press, from the plates of the *Encyclopaedia Britannica.*" In February 1822 in Mashhad, Fraser met Amirzadah Nasir al-Din Mirza, whose "observations upon astronomy were pertinent and good; and the solutions he had devised for various difficulties that met him in his way, were ingenious and often perfectly just." Mirza Abd al-Javad, son of Mirza Mahdi the Mujtahid of Mashhad, was also acquaintanted with modern sciences. Reporting on his conversation with Mirza Abd al-Javad, Fraser wrote:

> He asked me many very pertinent questions relating to geography and astronomy; and he pushed me so hard on subjects connected with the theory of optics, and the nature of the telescope, that I found I had neither language nor science sufficient to satisfy him. He was particularly well skilled in mechanics, and produced several very ingenious articles of his own construction, with others of European fabric, as dials, dividers, and other mathematical instruments, such as I never expected to find in Khorasan; and the uses of which he so well understood, that he had contrived to repair some of them which had accidentally been broken.[90]

Mirza Abd al-Javad's interest in modern astronomy is evident from a Persian manuscript, *Tufah-'i Muhammadiyah* (1610)[91] which was copied for him. The manuscript included an appendix (written at a later time) on Europe, modern scientific instruments, the solar system, and notes on Newton. Mulla Aqa Abu-Muhammad, another acquaintance of Fraser in Mashhad, was so keenly interested in astronomy and Fraser's telescope that he invited the non-Muslim Fraser to dine with him. Fraser believed that "I owed this invitation entirely to his wish to see my large telescope, and to view the stars through it, rather than to any desire for its master's company."[92]

Decolonizing historical imagination

The preceding synopsis of Persianate familiarity with the modern sciences and its dialogic relations with Europe calls for the decolonization of historical imagination and the rethinking of what is commonly meant by South Asian and Middle Eastern modernity. By anticipating a period of decline that paved the way for the British colonization, historians of Mughal India have searched predominantly for facts that illustrate the backwardness and the disintegration of this empire. Mughal historiography in this respect has a plot structure similar to the late Ottoman history. In both cases, the dominant themes of "decline" and "disintegration" are based on a projection about the rise and progress of Europe. In a similar manner, historians of modern Iran inherited historiographical traditions that militate against the construction of historical narratives about the pre-Constitutional and/or pre-Pahlavi times as anything but an age of ignorance (*bikhabari*), stagnation, and despotism. Anticipating the coming of the Constitutional Revolution of 1905–9, historians have crafted narratives of intolerable conditions that instigated the coming of the revolution.[93] Written by a participant of the revolution between 1910 and 1912, the title of Nazim al-Islam Kirmani's paradigmatic account of the revolution, *Tarikh-i Bidari-i Iraniyan* (The History of the Awakening of Iranians), reveals this prevalent assumption of pre-revolutionary dormancy. To legitimate the Pahlavi dynasty (1926–79) as the architect of Iranian modernity and progress, Pahlavi historians likewise depicted the Qajar period (1794–1925) as the dark age of Iranian history. These two Iranian historiographical traditions have been informed by, and in turn have informed, Orientalist accounts of Qajar Shahs as absolute Oriental despots and Islam as only a fetter to rationalization and secularizaion. Inscribing the history of Europe on that of India and Iran, both Indian and Iranian historians have deployed a regressive conception of time that constitutes their respective histories in terms of lacks and failures.

These bordered histories have rendered homeless texts that yield a different account and periodization of Persianate modernity. Historians of modern India often view Persian as a language only of the "medieval" Muslim Mughal court and thus find it unnecessary to explore the Persian texts of modernity.[94] Viewed as solely Iranian language, historians of Iran also consider unworthy Persian texts produced outside of the country. The conventional Persian literary histories, moreover, regard poetry as a characteristically Iranian mode of self-expression. With the privileged position of poetry in the invented national *mentalité*, the prose texts of the humanities are devalued and scholarly efforts are infrequently spent on editing and publishing non-poetic texts. Thus a large body of historically significant prose texts of modernity have remained unpublished. This willful marginalization of prose is often masked as a sign of the prominence of poetry as an intrinsically Iranian mode of expression. These factors account for the elision of texts produced in India, which are stereotypically considered as either linguistically faulty or as belonging to the corpus of the degenerate "Indian style" (*sabk-i Hindi*) texts. Consequently, Persian language texts documenting precolonial engagement with the modern sciences and responding to European colonial domination have remained nationally "homeless" and virtually unknown to historians working within the confines of modern Indian and Iranian nationalist paradigms. This has led to several historiographical problems. Exclusion of these "homeless texts" from national historical canons, on the one hand, has contributed to the hegemony of Eurocentric and Orientalist conceptions of modernity as something uniquely European. On the other hand, by ignoring the homeless texts, both Indian and Iranian historians tend to consider modernity only under the rubric of a belated "Westernization." Such a conception of modernity reinforces the exceptionality of "Occidental rationality" and corroborates the programmatic view of Islamic and "Oriental" societies and cultures as static, traditional, and unhistorical. This historical imagination is simultaneously grounded on two problematic conceptions of historical time. On the one hand it is grounded in the presupposition of the non-contemporaneity of the contemporaneous Western and "Oriental" societies, and on the other hand it is based on the dehistoricizing supposition of the contemporaneity of the non-contemporaneous early nineteenth-century and ancient modes of life. With the onset of Westernization, consequently, the premodern repetition of ancient modes of life is replaced with the repetition of Western modernity.

2
Orientalism's Genesis Amnesia

A genealogy of Orientalism

The formation of Orientalism as an area of European academic inquiry was grounded on a "genesis amnesia"[1] that systematically obliterated the dialogic conditions of its emergence and the production of its linguistic and textual tools. By turning "the Orient" into an object of analysis and gaze, Orientalism as a European institution of learning anathematized the Asian pedagogues of its practitioners. Embedded in an active process of forgetting, histories of Orientalism have attributed to the "pioneers" of the field the heroic tasks of entering "this virgin territory," breaking into "the walled languages of Asia," unlocking "innumerable unsuspected scriptures," and making "many linguistic discoveries."[2] This modulated account of the history of Orientalism appropriates as its own the agency, authorality, and creativity of its Other. As a hegemonic and totalizing discourse, Orientalism celebrates its own perspectival account as scientific and objective while forgetting the histories and perspectives informing its origins.

The sedimentation and institutionalization of Orientalism authorized the history of its other. In recent years the growth of Orientalism as a field of critical inquiry has further contributed to the underdevelopment of that history. A few exemplary statements by Bernard Lewis, a renowned Orientalist scholar, and Edward Said, a leading critic of Orientalism, display the unequal development of Orientalism and its nemesis, Europology (Europe + logy). In direct contrast to "the Oriental renaissance" and "Europe's rediscovery of India and the East," Bernard Lewis asserts that "there was a complete lack of interest and curiosity among Muslim scholars about what went on beyond the Muslim frontiers in Europe." Lewis observes that, by the end of the eighteenth century, there was a "total lack of any such literature in Persian or – with the exception of Moroccan embassy reports – in Arabic." The more advanced Ottoman writings on Europe "had not yet amounted to anything very substantial." Evaluating the "Muslim scholarship about the West," he postulates that "the awakening of Muslim interest in the West came much later, and was the result of an overwhelming Western presence."[3] Lewis suggests that Asians lacked the curiosity of Europeans in the study of languages and religions:

> Europeans at one time or another have studied virtually all the languages and all the histories of Asia. Asia did not study Europe. They did not even study each other, unless the way for such study was prepared by either conquest or conversion or both. The kind of intellectual curiosity that leads to the study of a language, the decipherment of ancient texts, without any such preparation or motivation is still peculiar to western Europe, and to the inheritors and emulators of the European scholarly tradition in countries such as the United States and Japan.[4]

Discussing how the "fear of the West has proven itself a spur to humanistic studies" and "scientific knowledge of the West," G. E. Von Grunebaum similarly observed, "The urge to acquaint oneself with cultural phenomena outside one's own civilization is, broadly speaking, a peculiarity of the post-Renaissance West." Having assumed that interest in other cultures represents a peculiarly European style of thinking, Von Grunebaum takes a 1948 Iranian call to establish a field of Europology (*Farangshinasi*) as a symptom of acculturation:

> Somewhat surprisingly to our [Western] point of view, the Muslim East has never developed anything comparable to Western "Oriental-ism"; thus it seems an important innovation and, if you wish, a sig-nificant symptom of acculturation when an Iranian scholar-politician like Dr. Fakhr al-Din Shadman (who in 1948 published a book with the characteristic title *The Subjection of Western Civilization* [*Taskhir-i tamaddun-i firangi*]) calls for *firang-shinasi*, that is, for a study of Western civilization in all its aspects.[5]

While critical of such historically inaccurate accounts, Edward Said grounded his pioneering work on the assumption that Orientalism "had no corresponding equivalent in the Orient." Viewing Orientalism as a "one way exchange," Said argues that it would be unlikely "to imagine a field symmetrical to it called Occidentalism." Likewise, he observes that "the number of travelers from the Islamic East to Europe between 1800 and 1900 is minuscule when compared with the number in the other direction."[6] Oddly enough, both Said and Lewis agreed on the absence of Occidentalism or Europology. Criticizing Said's Foucaultian analysis of power/knowledge, Bernard Lewis wrote,

> The "knowledge is power" argument is no doubt emotionally satisfying, to some extent even intellectually satisfying, and it serves a double purpose: on the one hand, to condemn the Orientalism of the West; on the other, to make a virtue of the absence of any corresponding Occidentalism in the East.[7]

These exemplary observations were based on the binary assumption of "Oriental silence" and "Western writing" and were products of Orientalism's genesis amnesia. The assumed silence and lack of scientific curiosity among the Orientals were strategic choices for authorizing the "disciplinization" of Orientalism and legitimating its claim to objective knowledge. Without these assumptions the perspectival nature of Orientalist knowledge, which has been skillfully elucidated by Edward Said, would have been obvious from the outset. By retrieving the dialogic conditions of the emergence of modern Orientalism, this chapter retraces the contributions of Persianate scholars to the education of "pioneering" Orientalists and the production of their texts. In retracing the dialogic relations between European and Persianate scholars I hope to retrieve an unexplored history of Indian and Iranian *vernacular modernity*, a common history elided by the nationalist historiography.

The Columbus of Oriental studies

The modular histories of Orientalism grounded exclusively in a European context the intellectual contributions of Anquetil-Duperron (1731–1805), Sir William Jones (1746–94), and other "pioneering" Orientalists. This historiographical selection played a strategic role in constituting "the West" as the site of innovation and "the Orient" as the locus of tradition. The fully differentiated East and West were the historical products of these paradigmatic selections and deletions.

But in its formative phase Orientalism was a product of cultural and intellectual hybridization. Its development into "a style of thought based upon an ontological and epistemological distinction between 'the Orient' and (most of the time) 'the Occident'"[8] was a later development.

Orientalism's transformation into a discourse on Western domination was ultimately connected to colonization and obliteration of all traces of "Oriental" agency, subjectivity, voice, writing, and creativity. This chapter offers an account of the conjoined process of the silencing of "the Orientals" and the authorizing of Western writers. More particularly, I will elucidate the Persianate scholarly and textual culture that authorized Anquetil-Duperron and William Jones as "pioneers" of Orientalism. Viewed by Max Müller (d. 1900) as "the discoverer of Zend-Avesta,"[9] Anquetil-Duperron was in essence "a disciple of Indian Sages."[10] During his residence in India between 1755 and 1761,[11] Anquetil-Duperron was trained to read and decipher Pahlavi texts by Zoroastrian scholars Dastur Darab bin Suhrab, also known as Ustad Kumana Dada-Daru of Surat (1698–1772), Dastur Kavus bin Faraydun (d. 1778), and Manuchihrji Seth.[12] The study of Avestan and Pahlavi texts had been an important component of Parsi intellectual life in India well before Anquetil-Duperron translated and published his *Zend-Avesta* (1771). Yet, according to Raymond Schwab, Anquetil-Duperron for "the first time...succeeded in breaking into one of the walled languages of Asia."[13] But the breakthroughs in comparative religion and linguistics, which were the high marks of "the Oriental Renaissance"[14] in Europe, were in reality built upon the intellectual achievements of Mughal India.

Aspiring to create a harmonious multi-confessional society, Emperor Akbar (r. 1556–1605) sponsored debates among scholars of different religions and encouraged the translation of Sanskrit, Turkish, and Arabic texts into Persian.[15] Persian translations of Sanskrit texts included *Ramayana*, *Mahabharata*, *Bhagavad-gita*, *Bhagavat-purana*, *Nalopakhyana*, *Harvamsa*, *Atharva-veda*, and *Jug-bashasht*, among many others.[16] In the introduction to the Persian translation of *Mahabharata*, Abu al-Fazl 'Allami (1551–1602) described Akbar's motivation for sponsoring these translations:

> Having observed the fanatical hatred between the Hindus and the Muslims and being convinced that it arose only from mutual ignorance, that enlightened monarch wished to dispel the same by rendering the books of the former accessible to the latter. He selected, in the first instance the *Mahabharata* as the most comprehensive and that which enjoyed the highest authority, and ordered it to be translated by competent and impartial men of both nations.[17]

These efforts helped to make Persian the *lingua franca* of India. Furthermore, Akbar encouraged the expansion of the lexical repository of the

Persian language by commissioning the compilation of a dictionary "containing all of the old Persian words and phrases" that had become obsolete "since the time that Arabs gained domination over the Persian land [*bilad-i 'Ajam*]."[18] To facilitate the learning of Persian by Sanskrit pundits who were increasingly employed in translation projects, Vihârî-Srî-Krishna-dâsa-Misra wrote a book on Persian grammar in Sanskrit, *Parasi-prakasa* (1717), dedicated to Emperor Akbar.[19] In addition Mirza Jan Ibn Fakhr al-Din Muhammad wrote his *Tuhfat al-Hind*, an original study of Sanskrit and Indian prosody, poetics, and music.[20] Upon the request of the lexicographer Mir Jamal al-Din Inju (d. *c.*1626), who was commissioned to compile a comprehensive Persian dictionary, Akbar invited Dastur Ardshir Nawshirvan of Kirman to the court in 1597 to assist Inju with the compilation of the "Zand and Pazand" component of *Farhang-i Jahangiri*.[21] This dictionary functioned as an essential tool for Siraj al-Din Khan Arzu, who ascertained the affinity of Persian and Sanskrit, a significant event in historical linguistics, a few decades before Sir William Jones. It also provided the semantic resources for the nineteenth-century nationalist attempts to purify Persian of Arabic terms and concepts.

The cultural and intellectual environment in India provided a pertinent context for the Oriental Renaissance in Europe. Contrary to Eurocentric historical accounts, the compiling and collating of Avestan and Pahlavi manuscripts were not methods invented by Orientalists. The late sixteenth-century neo-Zoroastrian *dasatiri* movement, which is discussed in Chapter 5, prompted an interest in pre-Islamic textual traditions. A religious controversy among the Zoroastrians of India in the early eighteenth century likewise motivated the development of textual criticism.[22] In response to this controversy the Zoroastrian scholar Dastur Jamasb Vilayati was invited from Kirman for advice. He visited Surat in 1720, bringing a collection of manuscripts, and offered Avestan and Pahlavi lessons to young *dasturs* Darab Kumana of Surat, Jamasp Asa of Navsari (d. 1751), and Dastur Kamdin of Broach.[23] Among the rank of Dastur Jamasb's students were the "Indian sages" who later educated Anquetil-Duperron during his residence in India from 1755 to 1761. The translation and the publication of *Zend-Avesta* (1771) by Anquetil was made possible by Dastur Darab, Dastur Kavus, and other Parsi scholars who taught him Pahlavi language and manuscript collation.[24]

Neither was the comparative studies of religions a uniquely European phenomenon. Prince Dara Shikuh's (1615–59) interest in comparative understanding of Hinduism and Islam prompted him to seek assistance from the pundits of Banaris with a Persian translation of the *Upanishads*.

Completed in 1657 as *Sirr-i Akbar* (The Great Secret) or *Sirr-i Asrar*,[25] this text was retranslated into English by Nathaniel Halhed (1751–1830)[26] and into French and Latin by Anquetil-Duperron and published in 1801–2.[27] As Schwab remarked, "the pandet of Dara Shikoh … was the famous translator who provided the Persian version of the *Upanishads* which Bernier was to bring back to Paris and which Anquetil was to translate." Francois Bernier, who rendered "India familiar and desirable to educated society in the seventeenth century" Europe,[28] had served as a physician and translator for Danishmand Khan Shafi'a Yazdi (d. 1081 H/1670), a Persian–Indian courtier and scholar. This enabled Bernier to interact with Hindu pundits:

> My Aqah [master], Danechmend-khan, partly from my solicitation and partly to gratify his own curiosity, took into his service one of the most celebrated Pendets in all the Indies, who had formerly belonged to the household of Dara, the eldest son of the King Chah-Jehan [r. 1628–58]; and not only was this man my constant companion during a period of three years, but also introduced me to the society of other learned Pendets, whom he attracted to the house.[29]

In its formative phase, Orientalism was not a discourse of domination but a reciprocal relation between European and Indian scholars. However, with European hegemony and the rise of a heroic model of science in the eighteenth century, Orientalists increasingly marginalized and deemed non-objective the contribution of non-Europeans. This marginalization and denial of agency of the Other provided the foundation for the Orientalists' claim of creativity and authorality. Most histories of Orientalism, from Raymond Schwab to Edward Said, fail to take into account the intellectual contribution of native scholars to the formation of Oriental studies. In a typical example, Anquetil-Duperron was portrayed as the Columbus of Oriental studies by the suppression of the contributions of indigenous scholars in "his discovery" of *Zend-Avesta*.

Jones and the affinity of languages

Sir William Jones (1746–94), who is viewed as the founder of British Orientalism as well as "one of the leading figures in the history of modern linguistics,"[30] also relied heavily on the intellectual labor of numerous Persianate scholars. He was supported by an extensive network of scholars whom he labeled as "my private establishment of readers and writers."[31] This network of "readers and writers" included Tafazzul Husayn Khan

(d. 1801),[32] Mir Muhammad Husayn Isfahani,[33] Bahman Yazdi,[34] Mir 'Abd al-Latif Shushtari,[35] 'Ali Ibrahim Khan Bahadur,[36] Muhammad Ghaus,[37] Ghulam Husayn Khan Tabataba'i (1727–1814?),[38] Yusuf Amin (1726–1809), Mulla Firuz, Mahtab Rai, Haji Abdullah, Sabur Tiwari, Siraj al-Haqq, and Muhammad Kazim.[39] In addition, Jones was assisted by many pundits, including Radhacant Sarman.[40] In one letter he specified that, "My pendits must be *nik-khu, zaban-dan, bid-khwan, Farsi-gu* [well-tempered, linguist, Vedantist/Sanskrit-reader, and Persophone]."[41] As the manager of an extensive scholarly enterprise, William Jones appropriated as his own the finished works that were the products of the intellectual capital and labor of Indian scholars.

Jones's connection to Persianate scholars predated his 1783 arrival in India. Mirza I'tisam al-Din, an Indian who traveled to England between 1766 and 1769, reported that during his journey to Europe he helped to translate the introductory section of the Persian dictionary *Farhang-i Jahangiri,* which was made available to Jones when he composed his academic bestseller *A Grammar of the Persian Language* (1771). As Munshi I'tisam al-Din recounted:

> Formerly, on ship-board, Captain S[winton] read with me the whole of the Kuleelaah and Dumnah [*Kalilah va Dimnah*], and had translated the twelve rules of the Furhung Jehangeree [*Farhang-i Jahangiri*], which comprise the grammar of the Persian language. Mr. Jones having seen that translation, with the approbation of Captain S[winton], compiled his Grammar, and having printed it, sold it and made a good deal of money by it. This Grammar is a very celebrated one.[42]

While at Oxford, Munshi I'tisam al-Din met William Jones and "went to the libraries" with him.[43] In the preface to the *Grammar of the Persian Language,* Jones acknowledged the assistance of an unidentified "foreign nobleman," who was later identified as Baron Charles Reviczky by the editor of his collected works.[44] As Jones acknowledged:

> I take a singular pleasure in confessing that I am indebted to a foreign nobleman for the little knowledge which I have happened to acquire of the Persian language; and that my zeal for the poetry and philology of the Asiaticks [*sic*] was owing to his conversation, and to the agreeable correspondence with which he still honours me."[45]

In light of Munshi I'tisam al-Din's remark in his travelogue, one may doubt the editor's assertion that Jones had intended to thank Reviczky,

whom he had met in 1768.[46] By leaving the "foreign nobleman" unidentified, Jones may have intended to use this ambiguity to simultaneously
account for different individuals who assisted him with his Persian,
including Mirza, his "Syrian teacher."[47] It is significant that in the preface
to *A Grammar of the Persian Language*, Jones distinguished his work from
that of others:

> I have carefully compared my work with every composition of the same
> nature that has fallen into my hands; and though on so general a
> subject I must have made several observations which are common to
> all, yet I flatter that my own remarks, the disposition of the whole
> book, and the passages quoted in it, will sufficiently distinguish it as
> an original production.[48]

Demonstrating the extent of Jones's originality in *A Grammar of the Persian
Language* is beyond the scope of this study.[49] But it should be noted that
the text bore a Persian title, *Kitab-i Shikaristan dar Nahv-y Zaban-i Parsi
tasnif-i Yunis-i Oxfordi*, where Jones or "*Yunis-i Oxfordi*" (Yunis of Oxford
or Oxonian Jones) is identified as the compiler of the work.

Publication of Jones's *A Grammar of the Persian Language* (1771) coincided with that of Anquetil-Duperron's *Zend-Avesta*. Jones, who had
claimed in the "Preface" to be working on "a history of the Persian language from the time of Xenophon to our days,"[50] seemed unaware of
the Avestan and Pahlavi languages from which Anquetil had translated
his work. To protect his own reputation, Jones attacked the authenticity
of the texts that Anquetil had translated.[51] Relying upon the authority
of John Chardin (1643–1713), Jones argued that the "old Persian is a
language entirely lost; in which no books are extant . . . ".[52] Jones argued
that the translation of "the rosy-cheeked Frenchman," ascribed to Zoroaster, was in fact "the gibberish of those swarthy vagabonds, whom we
often see brooding over a miserable fire under the hedges."[53] John Richardson (1741–1811), a leading Persian lexicographer and the compiler
of *A Dictionary: Persian, Arabic, and English* (1777–80), joined Jones in his
attack against Anquetil, arguing that the two languages of Zend and
Pahlavi were mere fabrications. Having evaluated the work of Anquetil,
Richardson, like Jones, concluded: "Upon the whole, M. Anquetil has
made no discovery which can stamp his publication with the least
authority. He brings evidence of no antiquity; and we are only disgusted with the frivolous superstition and never-ending ceremonies of
the modern Worshippers of Fire."[54] Richardson, offering a philological
reason, maintained that inauthenticity of Zend and Pahlavi was evident

from numerous Arabic words found in both.[55] This conjecture fueled the imagination of Jones who later entertained the thesis that Pahlavi was related to Arabic and Hebrew.[56]

Jones, who had grown more erudite and informed by 1789, revisited the controversy with Anquetil-Duperron in his "The Sixth Discourse: On the Persians." His observation that "Zend was at least a dialect of the Sanscrit"[57] earned him recognition as "the creator of comparative grammar."[58] In Max Müller's estimation, however, "[t]his conclusion that Zend is a Sansckrit dialect, was incorrect, the connection assumed being too close; but it was a great thing that the near relationship of the two languages should have been brought to light."[59] While Jones continues to be lionized for his remarks concerning the affinity of languages,[60] the Persian–Indian scholars and texts that informed Jones's work have remained unknown.

A few decades prior to Jones, the Persian lexicographer and linguist Siraj al-Din Khan Arzu (*c.*1689–1756) wrote a comprehensive study of the Persian language, *Muthmir* (Fruition), discerning its affinity with Sanskrit.[61] Textual evidence indicates that Jones might have been familiar with this work and so might have used it in writing the lecture that gained him recognition as "the creator of the comparative grammar of Sanskrit and Zend."[62] In his study of phonetic and semantic similarities and differences of Persian, Arabic, and Sanskrit, and the interconnected processes of Arabization (*ta'rib*), Sanskritization/Hindization (*tahnid*), and Persianization (*tafris*) in Iran and India, Arzu was fully aware of the originality of his own discernment on the affinity of Sanskrit and Persian. He wrote, "Amongst so many Persian and Hindi [Sanskrit] lexicographers and researchers of this science [*fann*], no one except *faqir* Arzu has discerned the affinity [*tavafuq*][63] of Hindi and Persian languages." Arzu was amazed that lexicographers such as 'Abd al-Rashid Tattavi (d. *c.*1658), the compiler of *Farhang-i Rashidi* (1064/1653) who had lived in India, had failed to observe "so much affinity between these two languages."[64] The exact date of the completion of Arzu's *Muthmir* has not been ascertained. But it is clear that Arzu had used the technical term "*tavafuq al-lisanayn*" (the affinity/concordance of languages) in his *Chiragh-i Hidayat* (1160/1747), a dictionary of rare Persian and Persianized concepts and phrases.[65] In this dictionary he offered examples of words common to both Persian and Hindi (Sanskrit).[66] Since Arzu died in 1756, *Muthmir* must have been written prior to that date. Arzu's works on the affinity of Sanskrit and Persian certainly predated the 1767 paper by Father Coeurdoux, who had inquired about the affinity of Sanskrit and Latin.[67]

Based on a set of Zand and Pazand terms, *Lughat-i Zand va Pazand* (technically known as *Huzvarish*[68] and appearing in an appendix to *Farhang-i Jahangiri*), Arzu also conjectured the "affinity of Pahlavi and Arabic languages"*(tavafuq-i lisanayn-i Pahlavi va 'Arabi)*. What Arzu failed to recognize was that in Pahlavi Aramaic words were occasionally used as ideograms for conveying their Persian equivalents. These words were written in Aramaic but were read as Persian equivalents. Arzu's mistake was similarly repeated by Jones who a few decades later asserted that "the Zend bore a strong resemblance to Sanscrit, and Pahlavi to Arabick [*sic*]."[69] More consistently historical in his thinking than Jones, Arzu argued that the change from Pahlavi to Dari and contemporary Persian was due to diachronic linguistic changes.[70] He likewise attributed the differences between the Zoroastrian texts *Avesta*, *Zand*, and *Pazand* to a historical transformation of the Persian language.[71]

Arzu's study of the transformation of Persian language was motivated by the intensified linguistic conflict among the Persian poets of Indian and Iranian descent. His essays, *Dad-i Sukhan*, *Siraj-i Munir*, and *Tanbih al-Ghafilin*, all focused on these tensions. In search of courtly patronage in India, poets from Iran sought to advance their lot by questioning the linguistic competence of the poets of Indian descent. For example, Shayda Fatihpuri (d. 1042/1632), whose poem was analyzed in Arzu's *Dad-i Sukhan*, complained that Iranians dismissed him because of his Indian lineage.[72] Unlike his Iranian nemesis, Shayda argued that "being Indian or Iranian can not become an evidence of excellence" (*Irani va Hindi budan fakhr ra sanad nagardad*).[73] Abu al-Barakat Munir Lahuri (d. 1054/1644), another poet whose work was evaluated in Arzu's *Siraj-i Munir* and *Dad-i Sukhan* had also responded to the same ethnic–professional tension that inspired Shayda to criticize the work of the Iranian Malik al-Shu'ara [King of Poets] Muhammad Jan Qudsi (d. 1056/1646). Like Shayda, Munir Lahuri complained that Iranian lineage (*nasab-i Iran*) – in addition to old age (*piri*), wealth (*tavangari*), and fame (*buland avazigi*) – was unfairly viewed as a criterion for the recognition of one's mastery of language. He observed, "if a Persian makes one-hundred mistakes in Persian, his language will not be questioned. But if an Indian, like an Indian blade [*tiq-i Hindi*], reveals the original essence [of Persian], no one will applaud him."[74] He complaind that despite his achivements in the Persian language, "if the infidel I [Munir Lahuri] tell the truth and reveal that the land of India is my place of descendence [*nizhadgah-i man-i kafir*], these villains of the earth will equate me with the black soil."[75] Munir Lahuri elaborated his views in his *Karnamah*, an outstanding text challenging the Iranian poets' self-congratulatory definition of linguistic competence.

These productive tensions inspired Arzu to undertake a pioneering historical study of the Persian language and the processes of lexical Arabization (*ta'rib*), Persianization (*tafris*), and Sanskritization (*tahnid*). His discernment of the affinity of Persian and Sanskrit bolstered his argument that Indians were authorized to resignify Persian words and phrases and use Hindi concepts in their writings. Pursuing such a historically informed path, students of Arzu initiated a process of vernacularization and cultivation of literary Urdu, *Urdu-yi mu'alla*.[76] It was for this reason that Muhammad Husayn Azad (*c*.1834–1910) argued that Arzu "has done for Urdu what Aristotle did for logic. As long as all logicians are called the descendants of Aristotle, all Urdu scholars will also be called the descendents of Khan-e Arzu."[77] In other words, vernacularization was a result of poetic and literary contestation among Indian and Iranian poets and was well under way prior to the British colonization of India.

Like Arzu, Jones's speculation concerning the historical relation of Sanskrit, Persian, and Arabic was informed by the historical imagination of *Dabistan-i Mazahib*, which had been introduced to him by Mir Muhammad Husayn Isfahani.[78] *Dabistan* and other "dasatiri texts" provided a mythistorical narrative inaugurated by the pre-Adamite Mahabad, who was supposed to have initiated the great cycle of human existence well before Adam. Compiled, composed, or "translated" by Azar Kayvan (1529–1614) and his disciples, these texts fashioned a new historical framework that challenged the hegemonic biblical/Islamic imagination in which human history begins with the creation of Adam.[79] This proto-nationalist historical imagination provided Jones with necessary "evidence" for establishing the origins of languages and nations. Writing about his "discovery" of *Dabistan*, Jones explained: "A fortunate discovery, for which I was first indebted to Mir Muhammed Husain, one of the most intelligent Muslims in India, has at once dissipated the cloud and cast a gleam of light on the primeval history of Iran and the human race, of which I had long despaired, and which could hardly have dawned from any other quarter."[80] The historical narrative of *Dabistan*, by extending the history of Iran to pre-Adamite eras of Abadiyan, Jayan, Sha'iyan, and Yasa'yan, offered a new origin for languages and races:

> If we can rely on this evidence, which to me appears unexceptionable, the Iranian monarchy must have been the oldest in the world; but it remains dubious, to which of the three stocks, Hindu, Arabian, or Tartar, the first King of Iran belonged, or whether they sprang

from a fourth race distinct from any of the others; and these are questions, which we shall be able, I imagine, to answer precisely, when we have carefully inquired into the languages and letters, religion and philosophy, and incidentally into the arts and sciences, of the ancient Persians.[81]

The theoretical possibility of "a fourth race distinct from any of the others" inspired Max Müller (1823–1900) to map the Aryan race and family of languages.[82] Based on the historical imagination of *Dabistan* and *Dasatir*, Jones argued that Kayumars, a progenitor of humankind in Zoroastrian cosmology, "was most probably of a different race from Mahabadians, who preceded him."[83] By assuming a racial difference between Kayumars and Mahabad, responding to the dispute with Anquetil-Duperron, Jones was "firmly convinced, that the doctrines of the *Zend* were distinct from those of the *Véda*, as I [Jones] am that the religion of the Brahmans, with whom we converse every day, prevailed in Persia before the accession of Cayumers [Kayumars], whom the *Parsis*, from respect to his memory, consider as the first of men, although they believe in a universal deluge before his reign."[84] Speculating further on the basis of *Dabistan*, Jones conjectured "that the language of the first Persian empire was the mother of the Sanscrit, and consequently of the Zend, and Parsi, as well as of Greek, Latin, and Gothick; that the language of Assyrians was the parent of Chaldaick and Pahlavi, and that the primary Tartarian language also had been current in the same empire; although, as Tartars had no books or even letters, we cannot with certainty trace their unpolished and variable idioms."[85] The historical narrative of *Dabistan*, in other words, enabled Jones, as it had inspired Khan Arzu, to imagine both linguistic and racial diversification of human societies.

In his significant lecture "On the Persians," which earned him a permanent place in the history of comparative linguistics, Jones solicited recognition for his originality: "In the new and important remarks, which I am going to offer, on the ancient *languages* and *characters* of *Iran*, I am sensible that you must give me credit for many assertions, which on this occasion it is important to prove; for I should ill deserve your indulgent attention, if I were to abuse it by repeating a dry list of detached words, and presenting you with a vocabulary instead of a dissertation[.]"[86] Describing his reliance on evidence, Jones noted:

since I have habituated myself to form opinions of men and things from *evidence*, which is the only solid basis of *civil*, as *experiment* is of *natural*, knowledge; and since I have maturely considered the question which I mean to discuss, you will not, I am persuaded suspect my testimony, or think that I go too far, when I assure you, that I will assert nothing positively, which I am not able to satisfactorily demonstrate.

Yet after these introductory remarks Jones went on to explain the affinity of Persian and Sanskrit without offering any examples: "I can assure you with confidence, that hundreds of Parsi [Persian] nouns are pure Sanscrit, with no other change than such as may be observed in numerous *bhasha*'s, or vernacular dialects, of India; that very many Persian imperatives are the roots of Sanscrit verbs." As Richardson had noted earlier in his criticism of Anquetil-Duperron's translation of *Zend-Avesta*, Jones asserted that "in pure Persian I find no trace of any Arabian tongue, except what proceeded from the known intercourse between Persians and Arabs, especially in the time of Bahram."[87] With the assistance of Bahman Yazdi, a Zoroastrian scholar who had fled Iran,[88] Jones was able to articulate the theses that established him as "the creator of comparative grammar of Sanskrit and Zend:"[89]

> I often conversed on them with my friend Bahman, and both of us were convinced after full consideration, that the *Zend* bore a strong resemblance to *Sanscrit*, and the *Pahlavi* to *Arabick*. He had at my request translated into *Pahlavi* the fine inscription, exhibited in the *Gulistan*, on the diadem of Cyrus; and I had the patience to read the list of words from *Pazand* in the appendix to the *Farhangi Jehangiri*: this examination gave me perfect conviction that the Pahlavi was a dialect of the Chaldiack; and of this curious fact I will exhibit short proof.

In support of the thesis that Pahlavi was a Chaldiack dialect, Jones offered the following evidence: "By the nature of the Chaldean tongue most words ended in the first long vowel like *shemia*, heaven; and that very word, unaltered in a single letter, we find in the Pazand, together with *lailia*, night, *meya*, water, *nira*, fire, *matra*, rain, and a multitude of others, all Arabick or Hebrew with Chaldean termination . . . " This list of common terms in Chaldiack and Pahlavi offered by Jones–*shemia* (heaven), *lailia* (night), *meya* (water), *nira* (fire), *matra* (rain)[90] – were among the first few words that appeared in a list of over 40 terms analyzed by Arzu under the heading "On Lexical Affinity" (*dar tavafuq-i alfaz*).[91]

Given the evidences cited, it is apparent that Persianate scholars such as Arzu and Bahman Yazdi and texts such as *Muthmir, Dabistan,* and *Farhang-i Jahangiri* figured prominently in the shaping of William Jones and his contributions to comparative linguistics and Oriental studies. Clearly Orientalists such as Anquetil-Duperron and Jones had entered into the fields of "Oriental" languages, religions, and history as novices. Their intellectual developments and contributions would not have been possible without the expertise and the cultural capital of the native scholars whom they had employed. The European nativist accounts of Orientalism have erased these pertinent non-Western contexts informing the intellectual development of the field.

Intertextuality and postcolonial historiography

Similar to the capitalist process of commodification and reification,[92] histories of Orientalism have concealed the traces of creativity and agency of the intellectual laborers who produced the works that bear the signature of "pioneering" Orientalists. The archives of unpublished Persian texts commissioned by eighteenth- and nineteenth-century British Orientalists reveal this underside of Orientalism. Having examined the works of the British who commissioned these unpublished works, it appears to me that they had "authored" books that closely resemble their commissioned Persian works. For instance, Charles Hamilton's *Historical Relation of the Origin, Progress, and Final dissolution of the Rohilla Afghans* (1787) corresponds closely to Shiv Parshad's *Tarikh-i Fayz Bakhsh* (1776).[93] Similarly W. Francklin's *History of the Reign of Shah-Aulum, the Present Emperor of Hindustan* (1798) is comparable in content and form to Ghulam 'Ali Khan's *Ayi'in 'Alamshahi.*[94] Likewise, a large set of Persian language reports on Tibet provided the textual and factual foundations for Captain Samuel Turner's *An Account of an Embassy to the Court of the Teshoo Lama in Tibet Containing a Narrative of a Journey Through Bootan, and Part of Tibet* (1800).[95] The most fascinating of these textual concordances is William Moorcroft's *Travels in the Himalayan Provinces of Hindustan and Panjab.*[96] Moorcroft is recognized as "one of the most important pioneers of modern scientific veterinary medicine" and is also viewed as "a pioneering innovator in almost everything he touched." In 1812 Moorcroft commissioned Mir 'Izzat Allah to journey from Calcutta to the Central Asian city of Bukhara. Along the way, Mir 'Izzat Allah collected invaluable historical and anthropological information which he recorded in his "Ahval-i Safar-i Bukhara."[97] Mir 'Izzat Allah's findings, similarly, provided the factual foundations for the "pioneering" *Travels* of Moorcroft. A preliminary inquiry indicates that Moorcroft may not have personally made the recounted journey that is praised for its "accuracy of historiographical and political observations."

Based on these and other collated texts, it seems that in its formative phase European students of the Orient, rather than initiating "original" and "scientific" studies, had relied heavily on research findings of native scholars. By rendering these works into English, the colonial officers in India fabricated scholarly credentials for themselves, and by publishing these works under their own names gained prominence as Oriental scholars back home.[98] The process of translation and publication enabled the Europeans to obliterate the traces of the native producers of these works and thus divest them of authorality and originality, attributes which came to be recognized as the distinguishing marks of European "scholars" of the Orient. In many of these cases, European scholars differentiated their works by adding the scholarly apparatuses of footnotes and references, citations that were already available in the body of the commissioned texts.

In some other cases, scholarly competition helped to preserve the name of the original authors. For instance, Mirza Salih Shirazi served as a guide for the delegation led by Sir Gore Ouseley (1770–1844), the British Ambassador Extraordinary and Plenipotentiary, who visited Iran between 1811 and 1812.[99] Mirza Salih accompanied and kept records of the journey of this delegation, which included leading Orientalists William Ouseley (1767–1842), William Price, and James Morier (1780–1849).[100]

Mirza Salih composed a set of dialogues in Persian which were published in William Price's *A Grammar of the Three Principal Oriental Languages*.[101] According to Price, "While we were at Shiraz, I became acquainted with Mirza Saulih, well known for his literary acquirements: he entered our train and remained with the Embassy a considerable time, during which, I prevailed upon him to compose a set of dialogues in his native tongue, the pure dialect of Shiraz."[102] In his *Travels* of thirteen years earlier William Ouseley had cited an "extract from some familiar Dialogues, written at my request by a man of letters at Shiraz . . . "[103] The extract offered by Ouseley was the opening of the "Persian Dialogues" written by Mirza Salih.[104] Both Ouseley and Price claimed that the "Dialogue" was written at their request.[105] These competing claims may account for the preservation of the name of Mirza Salih as its author. In the introduction to the "Dialogue," Price humbly noted, "having myself no motive but that of contributing to the funds of Oriental literature, and of rendering the attainment of the Persian language to students; I have given the Dialogues verbatim, with an English [*sic*] translation as literal as possible."[106] Mirza Salih also assisted Price in the research for his *Dissertation*.[107] William Ouseley likewise credited Mirza Salih for providing him with a "concise description and highly economiastick [*sic*]" narrative on historical and archaeological sites used in his *Travels in Various Countries of the East, More Particularly Persia*.[108] Having relied on Mirza Salih's contribution, Ouseley viewed part of the work as "the result of our joint research. . . . "[109] Oddly enough, Mirza Salih is only remembered as a member of the first group of Iranian students sent to England in 1815 who were supposedly in need of "instruction in reading and writing their own language."[110]

The obliteration of the intellectual contributions of Persianate scholars to the formation of Orientalism coincided with the late eighteenth-century emergence of authorship as a principle of textual attribution and creditation in Europe. The increased significance of authorship is attributed to the Romantic revolution and its articulation of the author "as the productive origin of the text, as the subjective source that, in bringing its unique position to expression, constitutes a 'work' ineluctably its own."[111] With the increased cultural significance of innovation (*inventio*), European interlocutors constituted themselves as the repositories of originality and authorship. It was precisely at this historical conjuncture that contemporary works of non-European scholars began to be devalued and depicted as *traditio*. This rhetorical strategy authorized the marginalization of Persianate scholarship at a time when the existing systems of scholarly patronage in Iran and India were dislocated. Without stable institutional and material resources that authorized the Persianate scholars, Orientalists were able to appropriate their intellectual works. The institutionalization of Orientalism as a field of academic inquiry, and its authorization of "original sources," enabled European scholars to effectively appropriate the works of their non-Western contemporaries, who were denied agency and creativity.

The challenge of postcolonial historiography is to re-historicize the processes that have been concealed and ossified by the Eurocentric accounts of modernity. This challenge also involves uncovering the underside of "Occidental rationality." Such a project must go beyond a Saidian critique of Orientalism as "a systematic discourse by which Europe was able to manage – even produce – the Orient politically, sociologically, militarily, ideologically, scientifically, and imaginatively." Said's *Orientalism* provided the foundation for immensely productive scholarly works on European colonial agency but these works rarely explore the agency and imagination of Europe's Other, who are depicted as passive and traditional. This denial of agency and *coevality* to the "Rest" provided the ground for the exceptionality of the "West." By reconstituting the intertextual relations between Western texts and their repressed "Oriental" master-texts, the postcolonial historiography can reenact the dialogical relations between the West and the Rest, a relationship that was essential to the formation of the ethos of modernity. The reinscription of the "homeless texts" into historical accounts of modernity is essential to this historiographical project.

3
Persianate Europology

Perspectival knowledge

Recounting a situation experienced by most eighteenth- and nineteenth-century "Occidental" and "Oriental" travelers,[1] Mirza I'tisam al-Din, who journeyed to England in 1766–9 recounted: "The young and old gazed at my countenance and shape and I stared at their beauty and face. I journeyed for a spectacle and became a spectacle myself."[2] Some 70 years later another Persian traveler, Prince Riza Quli Mirza, is reported to have turned abruptly to his translator and urged, "let us just sit down here on this bench, and look at these people passing before us." Acutely aware that he was himself a spectacle, the Prince added, "[w]herever I sit they will be sure to come fast enough. I am as great a *tamasha* (rare show) myself, as anything here."[3] Commenting on this incident, his translator, the renowned Orientalist James Ballie Fraser, recalled, "And, sure enough, he was right. No sooner had we seated ourselves than the crowd began to gather round, passing and re-passing us in a manner that enabled us to see much more than we should have done had we been walking about; and my friend, now in a state of greater comfort, made free and amusing remarks."[4] Like Persian voyagers, Europeans also experienced the interlocking of gazes during their journeys to the "exotic Orient." On a tour to the outskirts of Julfa in Isfahan on November 29, 1824, R. C. Money remarked:

> In fact, in these busy and hurried scenes of life is much the same all over the world, whether in London or Paris, Pekin or Ispahan. Only here a Feringee [*Farangi*, European] creates a great stir. All run to look and stare; and I am induced sometimes to think that some malicious spirit had turned me into a curiosity, and that I am not what I am.[5]

Seeing oneself being seen, that is, the consciousness of oneself as at once spectator and spectacle, grounded all eighteenth- and nineteenth-century Oriental and Occidental *voy(ag)eurs'* narrative emplotment of alterity. The traveling spectators appeared to the natives as traveling spectacles; *voy(ag)eurs* seeking to discover exotic lands were looked upon by the locals as exotic aliens.

The anxiety and the desire to represent and narrate alterity were reciprocal amongst Asians and Europeans. The formation of modern European discourses on the Orient were contemporaneous with Persianate explorations of Europe (*Farang/Farangistan*).[6] Asians gazed and returned the gaze and, in the process of "cultural looking," they, like their European counterparts, exoticized and eroticized the Other.[7] In the interplay of looks between Asians and Europeans, there was no steady position of spectatorship and no objective observer. As understood by Asad Khayyat, the Lebanese companion of three Iranian princes who traveled to England in 1836, visitors and natives did not see things "with the same eyes." In Asad Khayyat's estimation, all narratives of alterity were perspectival and validated the cultural perspective of the reporter:

> Some who are acquainted with the scenes through which their Royal Highnesses passed, and were in company with them at the time, will perhaps be astonished that they themselves saw not the same things which they described. To this it is but candid to reply, that their Royal Highnesses could not see with the same eyes as Englishmen, and being in a strange land, their language must seem to be quite *de traverse*, while yet it expresses the impressions which were made upon their own minds.[8]

There were recurrent European attempts to label as "uncivilized" those who did not see things "with the same eyes." Yet Persianate travelers narrated the spectacle of Europe and European onlookers reported the spectacle of the "exotic" Persians in their midst. The field of vision and the making of meaning were perspectival, contestatory, and theatrical.

Thus Oriental and Occidental travelers each saw themselves being seen and narrated the locals who narrated them. This conjunction of knowing subjects from different cultures, who gazed simultaneously at the Other and exhibited the Self, foregrounded the *trans*formation of modern national identities. In these ambivalent encounters, the narrator-spectacles often fetishized the spectators and reduced them to visible signs of otherness.[9] Through a process of projection and introjection, the visible features of the Other became loci for self-reflection and self-fashioning for both Asian and European narrators.[10] In this conjoined process the other served as a vantage for cultural mimicry and mockery.

As divergent strategies of identification and disidentification, mimicry and mockery were anchored in contesting local, regional, and global networks of power and knowledge. In the nineteenth-century Iranian political discourse, for example, identification with *heterotopic* Europe served as an oppositional strategy for the disarticulation of the dominant Islamicate discourse and for the construction of a new pattern of self-identity grounded on pre-Islamic history and culture. Mimesis (*taqlid*) did not signify only mindless imitation but was rather a strategy for the creative reconstruction of Iranian history and identity.[11] Correspondingly, Iranian counter-modernists represented Europe as a *dystopia* and thus sought to preserve dominant power relations and to subvert this oppositional strategy of secularization and de-Islamization. Thus mockery was not a "reactionary" and "traditionalist" rejection of Europe. By mocking Europe, counter-modernists were able to remake the Perso-Islamic tradition and culture in contradistinction to Europe. Both the secularist Europhilia and the Islamist Europhobia constituted Europe as a point of reference and created competing scenarios of vernacular modernity.

Persianate accounts of Europe, like Orientalist narratives, based their authority on self-experience and eyewitness accounts of alterity. Exotic others were observed and witnessed either at home or abroad. Montesquieu's *Persian Letters*, for instance, was partly motivated by the visit of an Iranian envoy to France in 1715. Similarly, traveling Europeans ignited the imagination of the multitudes who viewed the exotic *Farangis* passing through their homeland. Among the multitude who surveyed the *Farangis* were the Indian and Iranian state-appointed *mehmandars* (guestkeepers), who were assigned to the distinguished foreign visitors.[12] James Morier (1780–1849), who traveled through India and Iran in 1810–12, described the *mehmandar* as "an officer of indispensable necessity in a country where there are no public inns, and little safety on the roads, for strangers" According to Morier, the *mehmandar* "acts at once as commissary, guard, and guide; and also very much in the same capacity as Tissaphernes, who in conducting the ten thousand Greeks through Persia, besides providing markets for them, was also a watch upon them, and a reporter to the king of all their actions."[13] J. P. Ferrier, who served as the Adjutant-General of the Iranian army, explained the notion of *mehmandar* as follow:

Foreign ambassadors, and European travellers of distinction, are generally favoured by the government with the attendance of a *mehmendar*, whose task varies according to that of the person he is appointed to travel with. The English and Russians have in their treaties determined the rank of the *mehmendars* who are to accompany their ambassadors. The officer is responsible for all losses, accidents, and vexations that may happen to the person confided to his care; he rides forward to prepare all things necessary for his comfort and accommodation, which, by the terms of the *firman*, every village at which the party halts is obliged to provide gratis.[14]

Traveling in Iran between 1627 and 1629, Sir Thomas Herbert (1606–82) was assigned to Khwajah 'Abd al-Riza, whom he identified as a harbinger.[15] Sir John Malcolm, traveling in 1809, identified one of his *mehmandars* as Mahomed Sheriff Khan Burgashattee, who had shown him "a journal he had written for the information of the court by whom he was deputed, in order to enable them to judge, by the aid of his observations, what kind of a person and nation they had to deal with."[16] Sheriff Khan, whom Sir Malcolm described as "a keen observer,"[17] reported:

> What I chiefly remark is, that neither he [Sir Malcolm] nor any of the gentlemen sleep during the day, nor do they ever, when the weather is warm, recline upon carpets as we do. They are certainly very restless persons; but when it is considered that these habits cause their employing so much more time every day in business, and in acquiring knowledge, than his majesty's subjects; it is evident that at the end of a year they must have some advantage. I can understand, from what I see, better than I could before, how this extraordinary people conquered India. My office is very fatiguing, for the Elchee [Ambassador], though a good-natured man, has no love of quiet, and it is my duty to be delighted with all he does, and to attend him on all occasions.[18]

The *mehmandars*, who as early as the sixteenth century closely observed the visiting Europeans, can be viewed as important authorities for the dissemination of knowledge about Europe and Europeans.[19]

Persianate *voy(ag)eurs*

Persianate travelers played a generative role in the development of Eurpology and the dissemination of "eyewitness" accounts of Europe. Persian speakers traveled to Europe as early as 1599 and kept records of their encounters with the *Farangi*-other.[20] Husayn 'Ali Bayg, accompanied by Antony Sherley, four secretaries, and 15 servants was dispatched to eight European courts in 1599. The four secretaries were 'Ali Quli Bayg, Uruj Bayg Bayat (also known as Don Juan of Persia), Bunyad Bayg, and Hasan 'Ali Bayg. The first three of these secretaries defected by converting to Christianity and respectively adopting the names Don Philip, Don Juan, and Don Diego of Persia. Don Juan wrote a memoir (1604), which was first published in Castilian, but no trace of the original Persian manuscript has been found.[21]

In the first decades of the seventeenth century, an Iranian woman journeyed to Europe. Teresia, daughter of Isma'il Khan, a member of the court of Shah 'Abbas, married Robert Sherley (1581?–1628) and accompanied him on two diplomatic missions on the Shah's behalf to Europe.[22] It is reported that in February 1610 she landed "at Lisbon from Hamburgh" and "her lodging was appointed by order of the King of Spain in the Monastery of English Nuns..."[23] In the autumn of 1611 she visited England, where she gave birth to a son, Henry, who was named after the Prince of Wales.[24] She remained in England "about a year and half" and then returned to Iran via India. She departed for Europe for the second time in 1616, a journey that lasted until 1627. Teresia's return to Iran was prompted by the arrival of another Persian envoy, Muhammad Zaman Naqd 'Ali Bayg (d. November 1627), who challenged the credentials of her husband as the ambassador of Persia. Naqd 'Ali Bayg arrived in England in February 1626 with his son, Khwajah Shahsavar, and Khwajah's son Muhammad Shahsavar. Naqd 'Ali was granted an audience with Charles I on March 6, 1626.[25] To resolve the diplomatic confusion over the true ambassador of Persia, the King sent Robert Sherley, Teresia Sherley, and Naqd 'Ali Bayg back to Iran accompanied by his own envoy, Sir Dodmore Cotton. On the way back Naqd 'Ali Bayg and Muhammad Shahsavar suspiciously died before reaching India. Likewise Robert Sherley and Dodmore Cotton passed away after reaching Qazvin, the Safavid capital. "Teresia Comitissa ex Persia,"[26] described as "thrice-worthy and heroic lady," survived her husband and left for Europe after his death in 1628; she died in Rome in 1668.[27] The details of Lady Teresia's European voyages are not well known; but she must have provided invaluable information about Europe to the Safavids, who appointed her husband as a Persian ambassador to the "princess of Christendom."[28] In addition to these delagates, it is also reported that during 1642–3 Shah 'Abbas II, who appreciated European arts, dispatched a group of students to Rome to acquire Western painting techniques. It is believed that the delegation included Muhammad Zaman, also known as Paulo Zaman.[29] He joined the rank of royal artists during the reign of Shah Sulayman and left an impact on Persian representational art.[30] The seventeenth-century delegations, like the later diplomatic missions, usually included secretaries, translators, and attendants.[31] Both the high- and low-ranking members of these delegations became disseminators of knowledge about Europe. Likewise the defectors, who converted to Christianity, contributed to the formation of religious-based stereotypes and heightened the anxiety of establishing contacts with European Christians. Such anxieties became a defining element of the counter-modernist discourse.

Persianate knowledge of Europe increased in sophistication in the eighteenth century. Muhammad Riza Bayg (d. 1716) was one of that century's first travelers to Europe. As an envoy of the Safavid Shah, he reached Paris in February 1715, but skeptics like Montesquieu viewed him as an impostor. As a locus of public attention, Muhammad Riza Bayg was indeed a source of inspiration for Montesquieu's *The Persian Letters*. He had fallen in love with La Marquise Depinay Roussy, whom he married prior to his departure for Iran.[32] Having outlived her husband who died when they reached the Iranian territories, Mrs Roussy-Bayg continued her journey to Isfahan, the Safavid capital, where she later remarried to her brother-in-law.[33] Not much is known about Mrs Roussy-Bayg but it is likely that she served as a native informant offering invaluable information about France and the rest of Europe to Iranian courtiers. Joseph Émïn (1726–1809), a native of Hamadan, was another traveler who visited England in 1751 and wrote an account of his life and adventures in English, which was edited by Sir William Jones in 1788 and printed in London in 1792.[34] In 1765, Munshi I'tisam al-Din, accompanied by Muhammad Muqim, journeyed to England, and his *Shigirf Namah* is one of the earliest available eyewitness reports of Europe written in Persian. Textual evidence indicates that Mirza Abu al-Hasan Shirazi had access to it when he wrote his *Hayrat Namah*.[35] Munshi Isma'il also visited England between 1772 and 1773 and wrote a travelogue, *Tarikh-i Jadid* (New History).[36] Many other eighteenth-century Persianates traveled to Europe but their reports and travelogues have joined the rank of other homeless texts. During his journey to Iran in 1821–2, for instance, James Morier reported that he had seen a book by Mulla Muhammad Isfahani, "who visited Europe, and England in particular, some sixty years ago, and who appears to have written a fairly succinct account of what he saw, with a short history of Europe and its political situation and divisions at the time."[37] Mulla Muhammad Isfahani, whose work remains unaccounted for, also wrote "a short notice regarding America, its discovery by Columbus, and its subsequent revolutions."[38] An account of Europe and modern astronomy was also written in 1774 by Mir Muhammad Husayn (d. 1205/1790) who had visited France and England.[39] Like other eighteenth-century homeless texts of Persianate modernity, Mir Muhammad Husayn's *Risalah-'i Ahval-i Mulk-i Farang va Hindustan* remains in manuscript form.[40] Mirza Abu Talib (1752–1806) also reported that while in Ireland he visited Din Muhammad Murshidabadi, who had written an autobiography and description of the customs of India in English.[41]

Among the Persianates who traveled to Europe during the first decade of the nineteenth century were Mirza Abu-Talib Khan (1752–1806) and Mirza Abu al-Hasan Ilchi (1780–1860), the Persian Envoy to the court of King George in 1809–10. Viewed as a "Persian Prince," Mirza Abu Talib traveled in Europe from 1799 to 1802 and was a locus of public gaze. Prior to his travel to Europe, he wrote *Lubb al-Siyar va Jahan Nama* (1208/1793), a general description of Europe and America, along with a brief outline of the works of Copernicus and Newton.[42] Returning from his European tour, Mirza Abu Talib wrote a travelogue which was translated and published in English (1810), Dutch (1813), French (1819), and German.[43] According to Richard Herber (1773–1833), who reviewed the English translation of Mirza Abu Talib's travelogue in *The Quarterly Review* (1810), the book "appeared at a time, when the world, or at least all the idle part of it [England], was still on the stretch of curiosity, respecting His Excellency Mirza Abdul Hassan [Ilchi]." Herber began his review by noting that "[i]t is difficult to imagine any character whose first impressions would excite more natural curiosity, than an Asiatic traveller in Europe." Explaining the significance of the appearance of a report on Europe by a "boná fide Mahommedan," he wrote:

> Now, when the ladies had once ascertained, by actual experiment, the length of a Persian's beard, and the texture of his skin and clothing; when their minds were pretty well made up what to think of their formidable guest, it was surely no unnatural desire to know that guest's opinion of them.

Herber viewed Mirza Abu Talib's travelogue as "a very agreeable present to the Western World," and hoped that in the East it would also "excite a spirit of imitation among those, who before considered the Europeans as a race of warlike savages."[44]

Mirza Abu al-Hasan Ilchi, who traveled to England on a diplomatic mission in 1809–10, became "a gazing-stock for multitudes." His letter of May 19, 1810, to the *Times of London*, expressing "my thought of what

I see good and bad [in] this country," nurtured the public curiosity.[45] Convinced by the stereotypical views of Muslim men, a reporter noted that "His excellency has not availed himself of the Mussulman privilege which allows a plurality of wives. Although no man is more sensible of the beauty's power (as his admiration of our English ladies sufficiently evinces) he has (we understand from good authority) but one wife, and by her but one child."[46] The report added, "The progress which he had made both in speaking and writing English, within a few months, surprises all those who have the honour of his acquaintance; and we are assured, that he also converses freely in the Turkish and Hindoostanee languages."[47] On December 24, 1809, *The Examiner* reported that "Wednesday being the day appointed for presenting the Persian Ambassador to his Majesty, crowds not only assembled in the Park, but also in the streets leading to his Excellency's house, in Mansfield-Street, before twelve o'clock." In response to a countess's request "to obtain from me every information in my power concerning my friend the Persian," Lord Radstock wrote *A Slight Sketch of the Character, Person, ...* of Aboul Hassen.[48] The extravagant "style of elegance" and expenditure for a "Dinner in Honour of the Persian Ambassador" at London Tavern, where the dignitaries toasted the "natural union between Persia and Great Britain," provided an occasion for political criticism in *The Examiner* (1810).[49]

Mirza Abu al-Hasan Khan returned to Europe in 1819 and was again met with much public enthusiasm. Augustus de Nerciat reported, "During the residence of the above distinguished personage in Paris, he was so great an object of public curiosity, that he could not leave his hotel without being surrounded by a multitude of gazers."[50] Citing extracts from the French journals, de Nerciat quoted:

> The Persian Ambassador, on returning the other day from a ride, found his apartments crowded by ladies, all elegantly dressed, though not all equally beautiful. Astonished at this unexpected assemblage, he inquired what these European Odalisques could possibly want with him. The Ambassador was surprised to find himself an object of curiosity among a people who boast of having attained the apogeon of civilization; and was not a little offended at conduct which in Asia would have been considered an unwarrantable breach of good breeding.[51]

Interestingly enough, Mirza Abu al-Hasan had found Europeans wondrous enough to title the report of his 1809–10 travel "The Book of Wonders" (*Hayrat Namah*),[52] a title connotatively similar to Munshi I'tisam al-Din's *Shigirf Namah*. Whereas in Europe Mirza Abu al-Hasan was taken as evidence of exotic Persia, back in Iran his eyewitness report became evidence of self-experience in Europe. The exotic Persian of London became the narrator of the tales of the exotic *Farang*. James Fraser, traveling in Iran in 1821–2, reported that Mirza Abu al-Hasan "talks openly by name of the ladies of rank, duchesses and others, with whom he has had affairs of gallantry, and a whole host of minor females, some of whose letters he produces in Persian." Disgusted by Mirza Abu al-Hasan's representation of English women, Fraser added, "He produces, too, a miniature picture, which has been shown to the King as that of his mistress, without concealing the name; which, I regret to say, is that of a lady highly connected, and, I believe, considered respectable."[53] Such accounts were also reported by James Alexander, who visited Mirza Abu al-Hasan in 1826.[54] Having visited Mirza Abu al-Hasan's modern house, Fraser noted, "it was sufficiently apparent that he had picked up some idea of convenience, as well as other good things in England; he did not however approve completely of the plan of our English houses; he thought them deficient in ground space, and that the rooms were much too small."[55]

Impressed by Mirza Abu al-Hasan's reports on Europe, in 1811 Crown Prince 'Abbas Mirza sent two students to England.[56] Mirza Haji Baba Afshar, who studied medicine, returned in 1819 and was appointed physician to both the Crown Prince and the Shah.[57] In 1815, 'Abbas Mirza sent an additional five students to England.[58] With the exception of Mirza Ja'far Tabib, these students returned to Iran in 1819. Among them, Mirza Salih had served as a guide to Sir Gore Ouseley's delegation that reached Iran in 1811 and provided valuable information for the works of William Ouseley, William Price, and James Morier.[59] He also served as secretary for Sir Henry Lindsay-Bethune (1787–1851).[60] Like Mirza Salih, who was familiar with Europe and Europeans prior to his departure for England, Mirza Riza Muhandisbashi, also known as Muhammad Riza Tabrizi, was familiar with Napoleonic Europe and had translated an Ottoman book on this subject in 1807.[61] Contrary to an established view, these students were well educated and familiar with Europe and Europeans prior to their departure for England.[62] Muhammad 'Ali Chakhmaqsaz, another student, returned with his English wife Mary Dudley, whom he had married prior to his departure. Mirza Ja'far returned in the following year after the completion of his studies in medicine. Among these students, Mirza Ja'far and Mirza Abu Talib returned to Europe at later times.

Upon their return, the students made significant contributions to the building of new institutions and the dissemination of modern sciences.

Mirza Ja'far Mushir al-Dawlah Husayni authored a number of scientific treatises and taught mathematics and engineering.[63] Among his contributions is a comparative study of European and Iranian forms of governance.[64] He was appointed as the Ambassador to Constantinople from 1834 to 1844 and returned to England on a diplomatic mission in 1860. Likewise, Mirza Salih Shirazi returned to Europe in 1822–3 on a diplomatic mission. He founded *Kaghaz-i Akhbar* (1837),[65] the first Persian newspaper published in Iran, and wrote an influential account of the students' journey to Europe. Mirza Salih's travelogue offered a detailed political history of England and modern Europe, which included accounts of the English, American, and French revolutions. He published a version of his travelogue in the 1820s; and a selection from it was translated into English and published in 1824 in *Oriental Magazine*, a Calcutta publication, and reprinted in the *Asiatic Journal*.[66] Like his cohorts, Mirza Riza Muhandisbashi Tabrizi became an engineer helping the Iranian war efforts agiant Russia. Among his other accomplishments were translations of texts on Napoleon and the Napoleonic Wars.[67] In 1831, he also translated Gibbon's *Rise and Fall of the Roman Empire*.[68] The organized efforts of Mirza Riza and his cohorts were the manifestation of an emerging field of *Europloy* in Persian.

These and other Persian travelers, by constituting Europe as a differentiated site of analysis and gaze, produced a significant body of knowledge about European history, politics, culture, science, and economy. The knowledge about Europe, instead of constituting an isolated branch like Orientalism, was integrated into a general repository. The dialogic interaction of European and Persianate knowledge set in motion the dynamic process of modern cultural (trans)formations. Whereas European modernity actively suppressed the heterotopic context of its emergence, Persianate modernity celebrated its transformative conversance with Europeans. This active remembrance of the creative process of cultural hybridization and diversification is often misunderstood by the historians of modern Iran as an undifferentiated process of Westernization. Thus the rich textual sources of Persianate modernity, instead of being viewed as hybrid texts containing a double consciousness, are often dubbed as bad copies of originally European views and ideas.

The anthropology of modern Europe

Modern Europe was a topic of intense interest to Persianate travelers. They were all conscious that European ascendancy was a recent historical development and sought to uncover the mechanisms of societal change in Europe. Writing in the late 1810s, Mirza Salih Shirazi argued that until 400 years ago the people of England were "wicked reprobates and blood-shedders" (*sharirah-'i mufsid va khunriz*). Riza Quli Mirza believed that "in earlier times Europeans, particularly the English, were like wild beasts and animals and lacked industry." Due to disorder and the extremity of oppression, the Europeans who were deprived of tranquillity left for the New World and other islands. Writing in the 1830s, he argued that the new order in England emerged only about 250 years ago and viewed their newly-acquired wealth as based solely on commerce and industrial inventions.[69] The Persianate travelers' understanding of mechanisms of change in Europe provided the imaginary scenarios for the transformation of their own society.

To elucidate the anthropological and sociological insights embedded in Persian travelogues, the following section focuses on Mirza Abu Talib's evaluation of modern-age characteristics of the English in a section of his travel report devoted to "Virtues and Vices of the English" (*zikr-i fazayil va razayil-i Inglish*), which was written after the 1802 conclusion of his European journey. Using the taxonomy of philosophical ethics, Mirza Abu Talib divided his observations into broad categories of virtues (*fazayil*) and vices (*razayil*). He viewed these as "new age" (*jadid al-'ahd*) characteristics with differential impacts on "the elite" (*akabir*), "the intermediates" (*mutavvasitin*), "the subalterns" (*kaminah-ha*), and peasants "whose diet consists solely of potatoes" (*khurak-i ishan munhasir bah putatus ast*). Conscious of the increased class "revenge and animosity" (*bughz va 'idavat*) due to the "extravagence" (*ta'ayyush*) of some and "hardship" (*ta'ab*) of others, he forewarned of a great uprising like the French Revolution.[70]

Mirza Abu Talib viewed "self-respect" (*'izzat-i nafs*) as the first virtue of the English, particularly the elite. He argued that this quality was inculcated in individuals through "childhood education" (*parvarish saba*) and was maintained by the public censuring of those who lacked it. Consequently, the English were intolerant of "disrespect" (*bihurmati*) and were willing to sacrifice their lives and possessions in defense of their honor. "Acknowledgment" (*qadr-shinasi*) of individual achievements and "excellence" (*kamal*) was viewed as a second virtue. This elevated individuals' opinion of each other and promoted their "national honor and credence" (*abru va ihtiram-i qawm*). But in other countries (*mulkha*) individual accomplishments, "even when a person's excellence is proven" (*ba isbat-i vujud-i kamal*), remain unacknowledged because of the "false assumption" (*khiyal-i batil*) of individuals' unexceptionality. He discerned an affinity between individual and national self-respect and excellence. Whereas the recognition of individuals' excellence resulted in the "the production of honor and respect for [the English] nation" (*mawjib-i tawlid-i abiru va i'tibar-i qawm...gashtah ast*), the failure to acknowledge individuals' excellence in places like India had the adverse effect of contributing to the lack of regard for greatness (*'izam*), disrespect by foreigners (*biganigan ham ta'zim nakunand*), "the disappointment of artists" (*dilshikastigi-i ahl-i hunar*), and the nation's declining reputation and feeling of self-inferiority (*qillat-i abiru va hiqarat-i nafs dar qawm*).[71] This linkage of individual and collective accomplishments was a novel contribution to Persianate modernity and modern subjectivity.

Mirza Abu Talib identified "the fear of law-breaking and the abiding of self-limits" (*hadd-i khish*) as the third virtue. The primary "civil benefits" (*favayid madani*) of this virtue was the promotion of "social cohesion" (*ittifaq-i jama'at*) and "the stability of collective and state power" (*paydari-yi quvvat-i millat va dawlat*). He argued that a "nation" (*qawm*) that possesses such a characteristic "will never regress" (*hargiz nazil nashavad*). The hesitation to "transgress the law" (*shikastan-i qanun*) contributed to "individual tranquillity" (*aram-i nafs*). This was achieved because of the "satisfaction with the imminently fulfillable desires and enjoyments" instead of "harboring distant wishes" that could not benefit the majority of the people.[72] Linking the status of a "nation" (*qawm*) to "social cohesion," "civil benefits," and "individual tranquillity," Mirza Abu Talib's conceptualization transcended the conventional paradigm of Persianate political theory and its overwhelming concern with the stability of state and religion. His articulation of *millat, nafs,* and *favayid-i madani* (civil benefits) altered the conventional signification of these concepts. Applied to modern England, his notion of *millat* no longer signified a religious community. More significantly, his usage of *nafs* connoted "the individual" or "the subject" and not "the soul" as understood in classical Islamic philosophy.[73] In his evaluation of the English character, Mirza Abu Talib discerned a close linkage between the civil and communal welfare and the tranquillity of the individual.

The linkage of collective and individual welfare was embedded in a fourth virture: "their rationalists' inclination for public welfare and aversion to public harm" (*righbat-i 'uqala-yi ishan bar favayid-i 'amm va tanaffur az muzzirat-i 'amm*). This inclination to public welfare was "essentially beneficial to everyone" (*mawjb-i fayidah-'i zati-yi harkas*). Conversely, the lack of concern for public good was viewed as an "erroneous opinion and shortsightedness" (*zann-i ghalat va kutah-andishi*).[74]

Offering an insightful understanding of modernity and consumption, Mirza Abu Talib explained the English's "enthusiastic endorsement of new mode" (*iqbal-i ishan tarz-i jadid ra*). He conceptualized modernity as *tarz-i jadid*, a phrase used to refer to poetic innovations introduced by seventeenth- and eighteenth-century Indian–Persian poets. Applying *tarz-i jadid* to social innovations, Mirza Abu Talib argued that the desire for a "new mode" induced "the replacement of the older articles" (*tajdid-i asbab-i qadim*): "The renovation of forms of dress, furniture and other necessities have reached such an extent in London that the used articles of the previous year and season are abandoned and their possession and use is degraded." Cognizant of the aggregate effect of the desire to consume new commodities, Mirza Abu Talib observed that such expenditures were beneficial to "the manufacturing class" (*ahl-i hirfah*) and induced the rationalist "to ponder and innovate permanently" (*hamishah dar fikr va ikhtira'and*). The new innovations, in turn, resulted in cost and labor reduction. To illustrate how innovations led to labor reduction, he explained that "while fifteen male and female servants might be insufficient in an Indian household, due to the simplification of tasks a man and a woman is adequate here." The English desire for the "new mode" was explained by their inclination toward "task-facilitating instruments and appliances."[75]

Concluding his observations on the "virtues of the English" (*faza'il-i Inglish*), he explained their peculiar conception of "perfection" (*kamal*).[76] Having in mind the Islamicate notion of *kamal* as absolute perfection, he ascertained that the English "notion of *kamal* and human endeavor for its attainment is in essence based on a prior state and not the absolute." Elaborating this peculiarity, he reported that, according to the English, "if a human moves himself/herself from the state of an Ethiopian savage and cannibal and eventually reaches the state of the Philosopher Newton, there will be a time in the future that he/she will improve to the extent that in comparison, Newton will appear like the above mentioned Ethiopian." He explained this evolutionary and undisruptive progression as "a sequential and normal movement from a lower to a higher state." Disregarding his racist view of Ethiopians, Mirza Abu Talib keenly observed a European redefinition of *kamal* that displaced "spiritual *profectus*" with "worldly *progressus*." Writing on the modern notion of "progress," Reinhart Koselleck explains that, "The concept of progress was first minted toward the end of the eighteenth century at the time when a wide variety of experiences from the previous three centuries were being drawn together.... As part of a group, a country, or finally, a class, one was conscious of being advanced in comparison with the others; or one sought to catch up with or overtake the others."[77] As an outsider, Mirza Abu Talib fully understood the significance of this conceptual innovation. Later Persianate observers of Europe internalized this concept and sought to explain the widening gap between the progress of Europe and the decline of their own society. This led to a *schizochronia*, or a fractured view of time of the self and time of the Other.

Mirza Abu Talib's list of English virtues was followed by a longer and more detailed outline of vices. "Prominent among their vices is the disbelief in religion and resurrection, and their inclination toward philosophy." He viewed "dishonesty" (*'adam-i diyanat*) as an outcome of irreligiosity, particularly among the "subalterns of the land" (*kaminah-ha-yi mulk*). "Despite the fear of transgression against the law," he observed that "they never pass the opportunity of purloining and plotting to appropriate the property of the rich." For this reason, "the houses of nobility are always shut and they deal and speak only with their acquaintances." Observing that as yet "the ill effects of this [vice] are not apparent," he asserted that its prevalence could "affect the foundation of the government and have undesirable consequences."[78]

"The arrogance induced by the past fifty years of power and good fortune" was listed as another modern vice. Due to price inflation and high taxes, he found England on the "verge of a protestation and an uprising" (*nalishi va qarib-i balva mibashand*) because of the high price of provisions and the imposition of new taxes." But due to arrogance, "they view as improbable imminent incidents and fail to prepare to avert them." Despite the vigilance of the police and arrangements to crush popular protestation, Mirza Abu Talib felt that the English government "fails to address the foundational problem" (*tadaruk-i asl nimi-namayand*). He asserted that such an arrogant neglect at the time of peace precipitates "high costs with the occurrence of the incident, as demonstrated with the [execution of the] late King of France, but then, it will be too late."[79] Like his contemporary Immanuel Kant (1724–1804), Mirza Abu Talib was deeply impressed by the experience of the French Revolution. Whereas Kant saw the French Revolution as the "historical sign" of evolutionary improvement of humankind,[80] Mirza Abu Talib viewed it the exemplar of what is called the "age of revolution."[81]

A third vice was "passion for money and worldly affairs." He ascertained that "this characteristic is not harmful amongst them since they appreciate wealth and make utmost efforts to save." Protected by "security and legal arrangements" wealth and possessions were beneficial to their owners. But Mirza Abu Talib believed that passion for material possessions "produced negative effects by fostering vile qualities such as jealousy, illiberality, and arrogance at times of weakness." He expressed his own preference for generosity in a poem written for the enlightening of a person who preferred accumulating over spending money. In this poem Mirza illustrated that, unlike his rival, he preferred the treasure of Ms Grand's love to the love for worldly treasures.[82]

"Enormous desire for comfort and ease" was another modern vice. This only prevailed amongst the elite and the powerful and not among "the *bangis* as in India and the Ottoman Anatolia." To illustrate the English desire for ease, he explained that his friends were often hesitant to help him with translations or mediate on his behalf. He reported that, whenever helped, aversion was so conspicuous in the continence of his British friends that he desisted asking for help. "If you carefully reflect, you will discern that the English have left absolutely no time for assisting friends and acquaintances."[83] In comparison, he found the French quite courteous and willing to spend time with and assist others.

"Irritability and ill-temper" (*zud ranji va nizakat-i nafs*) was identified as a vice related to the desire for comfort and ease. Due to ill temper, the English were viewed as intolerant of "practical or verbal disagreements" (*harkat ya sukhan-i mukhalif mazaj az digari*). Mirza Abu Talib found this understandable in relation to "aliens" (*biganigan*) but inappropriate with regard to friends. For in his view "the tolerance of harsh and shrill words of friends" was a necessity of "civilization" (*tamaddun*). Mirza speculated that waspish temperament "would lead to the rupture of unifying links" (*mawjib-i qat'-i silsilah-'i ittihad*) amongst the people and could bring about "the disintegration of the state" (*zival-i dawlat*).[84]

Objectifying the English, Mirza Abu Talib observed that they "spend excessive time sleeping, dressing themselves, fixing their hair, and shaving." To promote beauty, "they wear no less than twenty-five different articles of dress." Taking into account the time spent on dressing, undressing, shaving, fixing hair, eating, entertaining, and sleeping, he calculated that they usually have no more than six hours left for work. The nobility, he observed, usually have only four hours for business. Critical of multiple layers of clothing, he viewed the coldness of weather as an unacceptable excuse for overdressing. If the English paid less attention to "beauty" (*zibayi*), they could easily reduce the layers from 20 to ten. He recognized as "unnecessary necessities [*luzum-i malayalzam*] the changing of day-wears to night-wears, daily shaving, and the norm of hair pressing."[85]

Another modern vice was "the multiplicity of needs and desires for pleasurable household appliances." A major defect of this characteristic was the wasting of invaluable time on shopping, changing, and install-ing despicable items in one's [living] quarters. Attention to such matters required "attentiveness to the essence of the self [*zat-i khud*] and natural inclination [*'alaqah-'i tab*] toward details." In Mirza's view such pre-occupations "cause the unfreedom of mind" (*mawjib-i 'adam-i azadi-yi khatir migardad*). While appreciating the comfort of tables and chairs, he suggested that the English could build their living quarters in a manner that would render the purchasing of chairs and tables unnecessary. Critical of English eating habits, he remarked that "more urgently they should give up excessive consumption of meats, drinks, and etc., un-necessary necessities that are contrary to reason and religion, and cause illness." Contrasting the luxurious life of the English with earlier empires, he wrote, "if one reflects on the history of Arab and Turkish conquests, two significant contributory factors could be identified for their victor-ies: First, their minimal need for unnecessary equipment accounted for the rapidity of their movement, their freed nature (*azadi-i tab'*), and their devotion of plenty of time to the acquisition of arts and sciences." The second factor contributing to these successful imperial expansions was their "minimal expenditures." These two factors reduced the costs of maintaining the empire and enabled the imperial rulers to cut taxes in half. By lowering taxes, "the people preferred them to their *ancien* rulers and befriended them." Mirza Abu Talib observed that "bravery and national unity (*ittifaq-i qawm*), cavalry, and weapons such as spears and arrows contributed to [Arab and Turkish] victories, but these alone could not account for rapidity of their conquests."[86]

"Error in the recognition of the boundaries of sciences and languages" was identified as an eighth defect. Elaborating on this vice, he observed that "by learning a few words they consider themselves linguists and by learning a few scientific principles claim to be scientists and compose books on these subjects and print and circulate their nonsense." He noted that Greeks and the French had also confirmed his observation. Rejecting the assertion that "imperfect knowledge is better than absolute ignorance," Mirza Abu Talib argued that "their books do not contain [even] a fraction of accurate knowledge. It is indeed a misrepresentation and deforming of knowledge." He believed that "once these deformed views are imprinted on one's mind, [the person] will be incapable of accepting accurate knowledge." As an example, Mirza Abu Talib explained the negative impact of Sir William Jones's *Grammar* on students who sought his assistance: "My efforts to educate anyone who had studied that book prior to coming to me was rendered futile." He concluded that books like Jones's *Grammar* "are so abundant in London that soon it will be impossible to distinguish exact books from the rest."[87]

"Selfishness and profiteering" (*khud gharazi va qabugari*) was identified as another vice. He observed that "in the hope of personal benefit, they do not hesitate to cause extensive losses to others." Mirza Abu Talib explained that his personal experience in London was limited to inter-actions with owners of inns. "But the conduct in India of Colonel Hannay, Mr. Middleton, Mr. Johnson, and Dr. Blane gave me convincing proofs of it; for whenever they had any point to carry they would accept of no excuse from me; and having, by fine promises, prevailed upon me to undertake their business, as soon as they obtained their wishes they forgot their promises, and abandoned me to the malice of the enemy. Besides my own experiences in India, this [defect] is so evident that no one could doubt it."[88]

Another modern vice was "the escaping of girls with their partners, the pre-nuptial copulation of wives and husbands, and the scarcity of chastity among women and men." These were caused by "the excess of women's freedom and the multiplicity of taverns and courtesans in London" (*kisrat azadi-yi zanan va vufur-i kharabat-khanah ha va favahish-i Landan ast*). To support this claim, he reported that there were 60,000 prostitutes in the parish of Mary-la-bonne in London. It was ironic that courtesans resided predominantly in districts with religious names like "'Paradise Street,' 'Modest Court,' 'St. James Street,' 'St. Martin's Lane,' and 'St. Paul's Churchyard'." Mirza observed that prostitutes usually resided near opera houses and theaters and that in such localities rooms were not rented to men.[89]

Viewing their own culture as "flawless and proper," the English "rarely inquired into the advantages of customs and religions of others." Such self-congratulatory assertions were, in Mirza Abu Talib's estimation, "contrary to reality" (*haqiqat bar khalaf-i an budah*). As an example, he recounted being ridiculed for sleeping with his pants on instead of going to bed naked like the English. Having found the English natives unwilling to listen to his reasoned justification concerning his own cultural habits, Mirza abandoned the effort "to respond to their inquiries with logical explanation of the advantages of our own customs." Based on personal experience, he was convinced that "their mind [*dil*, literally "heart"] cannot be cleared of foolish imaginations and regrounded on a new truthful foundation." Having given up on reasoned com-parative cultural discourse, he instead chose "to respond to them in their own fashion, which silenced them immediately." For instance, he responded to the ridiculing of Islamic ceremonies of pilgrimage (*hajj*) and circumambulation of Ka'ba, by asserting that "it is similar to the Christianization of children via baptism in a church by clergymen." He proudly announced that during his European journey, "I offered thousands of such silencing responses."[90]

Mirza Abu Talib viewed these defects as "new age" (*jadid al-'ahd*) vices. He attributed their appearance to "the abundance of affluence and the continuity of the government" (*kisrat-i ni'mat va tavatur-i dawlat*). He observed that as of yet no negative consequences ensued from these vices, in part because of English power and the prevalence of similar vices in neighboring lands. But he was convinced that the hesitancy of the English to acknowledge their vices paved the way to a detrimental future. Unwilling "to concede to these vices," the English were similar to "the contemptuous of India and the ignorant and arrogant Ottoman rulers." Compounding the ill effect of these vices was the English intolerance of praise for other nations: "If someone praises the ancient Arabs, Turks, and Iranians, they will deny the accuracy of these reports." He believed that "to a sharp intellect the weakness of their opinion is obvious."

Mirza Abu Talib attributed modern vices to "fashion" (*fashin*) and the frequent urge "to renovate the order of things." This habit was notable amongst Londoners who spent excessively on "unnecessary necessities most of which are lavish and intended for self-gratification" (*hazz-i nafs*). Observing the daily price inflation for carriages, horses, servants, theaters, balls, and masquerades, he argued that this promoted dishonesty (*bidiyanati*) and thievery since legitimate professions could not produce sufficient profits to support such expenses. He warned, "if they read incisively the books of history, they will learn that governments were overturned after the appearance of excessive expenses." Drawing a lesson from the colonization of India, he argued that in such an intolerable situation the English "could hand their land to rivals out of necessity like the people of Italy and India." Identifying the widening gap between the nobility and the lower classes as a cause of the French Revolution, he warned that extravagance, excessive taxation, and price inflation could similarly lead to "a great revolution" (*fitnah-yi 'azim*) in England. Such a revolution could bring about "the fragmentation of English power and the receding of their progress."[91] In this sociological prognosis, Mirza Abu Talib did not take into account the function of colonial wealth in the lessening of social tensions in England.

As this detailed review of Mirza Abu Talib's understanding of contemporary Britain indicates, Persianate travelers were not gaping at an advanced culture. As keen observers of Europe, they were endowed with a critical "double-consciousness." They critiqued European social settings with their own ethical standards and censured their own society from a European perspective. As anthropologists of modern Europe, they provide critical outsiders' perspectives on the emerging modern social ethos. These unexplored perspectives on Europe offer alternative sources for the study of modern European social norms. As critiques of their own societies, travelers like Mirza Abu Talib provided new perspectives on the dominant sociopolitical ethos. Fully aware of Europe as a significant new Other, travelers' oral and written reports of self-experience served as self-refashioning scenarios for Indians and Iranians.

4
Imagining European Women

Farangi women

The European woman (*zan-i Farangi*) was the locus of gaze and erotic fantasy for many eighteenth- and nineteenth-century Persianate *voy(ag)eurs* of Europe. The travelers' recounting of their self-experience provided the material for the formation of competing discourses on women of Europe. With the political hegemony of Europe, a woman's body served as an important marker of identity and difference and as a terrain of cultural and political contestations. The eroticized depiction of European women by male travelers engendered a desire for that "heaven on earth" and its uninhibited and fairy-like residents who displayed their beauty and mingled with men. The attraction of Europe and European women figured into political contestations and conditioned the formation of new political discourses and identities. These contestations resulted in the valorization of the veil (*hijab*) as a visible marker of the self and the other. For Iranian modernists, viewing European women as educated and cultured, the veil became a symbol of backwardness. Its removal, in their view, was essential to the advancement of Iran and its dissociation from Arab–Islamic culture. For the counter-modernists who wanted to uphold the Islamic social and gender orders, the European woman became a scapegoat and a symbol of corruption, immorality, Westernization, and feminization of power. In the Iranian body politic the imagined European woman provided the subtext for political maneuvers over women's rights and appearance in the public space.

The early Persian travelers described Europe as "heaven on Earth" (*bihisht-i ru-yi zamin*), "the birth-place of beauty" (*zad bum-i husn*), and the "beauty cultivating land" (*mulk-i husn khiz*).[1] The attraction of Europe masqueraded the attraction to "houri-like" (*hurvash*), "fairy-countenanced" (*hur paykar*), and "fairy-mannered" (*firishtah khuy*) women of Europe.[2] Appearance of unveiled women in public parks, playhouses, operas, dances, and masquerades impressed the Persian *voy(ag)eurs* who were unaccustomed to the public display of female beauty. For them, the only cultural equivalent to the public display of male–female intimacy was the imaginary Muslim heaven. Unlike the Shari'ah-bound earthly society, the pious residents of heaven were to be rewarded with "the fair ones . . . whom neither man nor jinni will have touched before them."[3] Like many other Persianate travelers, Mirza I'tisam al-Din, who traveled to England in 1765, was attracted to the spectacle of male–female intimacy in public parks. Recalling the observed scenes of a public park near the Queen's Palace in London, for example, he wrote:

> On Sunday, men, women, and youths, poor and rich, travelers and natives, resort here. This park enlivens the heart, and people overcome with sorrow, repairing thither, are entertained in a heavenly manner; and grieved hearts, from seeing that place of amusement, are gladdened against their will. On every side females with silver forms, resembling peacocks, walk about, and at every corner fairy-faced ravishers of hearts move with a thousand blandishments and coquetries; the plain of the earth become a paradise from the resplendent foreheads, and heaven (itself) hangs down its head for shame at seeing the beauty of the lovers. There lovers meet their fairy-resembling sweethearts: they attain their end without fear of the police or of rivals, and gallants obtain a sight of rosy cheeks without restraint. When I viewed this heavenly place, I involuntarily exclaimed:
>> If there is a paradise on earth,
>> It is this, oh! It is this.
>> (*Agar firdawsi bar ru-yi zamin ast*
>> *hamin ast u hamin ast u hamin ast*).[4]

Like I'tisam al-Din, Mirza Abu al-Hasan Khan Ilchi, who had traveled to Europe in 1809–10, described Hyde Park and St James's Park in a remarkably similar fashion.

> If a sorrowing soul traverses these heavenly fields, his head is crowned with flowers of joy, and looking on these saffron beds – luxurious as Kashmir's – he smiles despite himself. In the gardens and on the paths, beauteous women shine like the sun and rouse the envy of the stars, and the houris of paradise blush with shame to look

upon the rose-cheeked beauties of the earth below. In absolute
amazement, I said to Sir Gore Ouseley:[5]
   If there be paradise on earth
   It is this, oh! it is this![6]

The practice of male–female physical intimacy in public places differentiated Europe, "the land of heavenly ordinances" (*sarzamin-i bihisht ayin*),[7]
from an actual Muslim society where such a behavior was thought to be
indecent, a sign of moral and social disorder. By employing the familiar
images of the Muslim heaven in their description of modern European
norms of gender relations, the Persianate Riza Quli Mirza in *Safar Namah*
made these norms respectable to their readers and audiences. What was
only imaginable in the promised heaven was reported to exist on earth
by travelers returning from Europe.

   Conscious of the religious implication of reporting the mixing of
men and women in Europe, Prince Riza Quli Mirza Qajar, who visited
England in 1836 along with his brothers Taymur Quli and Najaf Quli,
recalled a *Hadith* (saying of Muhammad, the Messenger of Islam) that
"The world is a prison for a believer and a paradise for an unbeliever."
Elaborating on this saying, he assured himself that: "All conveniences
that the Lord of the universe has promised to His special servants in the
hereafter is available for their [European] view in this world. But the
difference is that these intoxicates and pleasures are temporary and
those [heavenly] conveniences are eternal."[8] As perfect and desirable
places beyond home, European lands displaced the heaven as sites of
sexual fantasies and ideal sociopolitical imagination.

   Persianate travelers often used the conventional symbols and meta-
phors of women from classical Persian poetry in describing Europeans.
In these strategies of familiarization, European women were compared
to literary and historical personalities such as Zubaydah, Asiyah, Zubba',
Gharah, 'Azra, Vis, Sarah, Balqis, Salma, Zulaykha, Layli, and Shirin. Mirza
Abu Talib, for instance, favourably compared Lady Palm with such
fictional women characters and observed: "I am an impostor, if I had
ever seen a woman like Lady Palm in Europe and Asia. While these great
women [*mahbanuvan*] have been mentioned in ancient myths, I have
never seen one [in real life]." In another poem dedicated to Miss Garden,
he said he found in London the promised Muslim heaven: "while I
have heard the description of the garden of paradise enough times,
in London I have seen better than it many times." He considered the
women of London much more attractive than the imaginary fairies of
paradise. In the same poem, while addressing the Muslim ascetics, he

stated, "In every street a hundred fairies appear in blandishment; for how long would you babble about the houris, it's enough!"

> To you, the ascetic, merry be the houris!
> I am content with the face of Miss Garden
> With honey and apple, you deceive me like a child
> But I am content with the gem and apple of the chin.[9]

Mirza Abu Talib judged European women according to Persian aesthetic values. He viewed beauty and nature as synonymous and so compared female beauty to the moon, sun, flowers, trees, and animals. He appreciated natural beauty but considered cosmetic changes as deceptive. For example, narrating the differences between French and English women, he remarked:

> Although the French women are tall, corpulent and rounder than the English, they are not comparable to the beauty and excellence of the English women. Because of their lack of simplicity, girlish shyness, grace and good behavior, [the French women] appear rather ugly.

He found the French women's hairstyles contrary to his standards of female beauty and equated them with those of "the base and whorish women of India." Unlike the idealized Muslim women, French women were viewed as "fast walkers, big talkers, fast chatters, loud-voiced, and quick responders." Mirza Abu Talib disapproved of the behavior of French women, and while in Paris, he "abandoned" voyeurism:

> Although I am by nature amorous and easily affected at the sight of beauty, I have lost the desire for the profession of voyeurism that I had in London. Now, my heart desires a different profession. In the Palace Royal I encountered thousands of women day and night, but I was not at all impressed and none were attractive to me.[10]

Some Persian travelers were infatuated with the women that they met and their poems expressed their genuine sensual desire. For instance, Mirza Abu al-Hasan, in a party at the residence of Lady Buckinghamshire[11] (held on January 15, 1810), "noticed groups of sunny-faced girls and *houri*-like ladies chatting together, their beauty illuminated by the candlelight." On that night he talked to many women whose beauty dazzled him. He was talking to a "rare beauty" when "another fairy creature" attracted him. That night he met a young lady, Miss Pole, who "inflamed" his heart. Inspired by this "girl of noble birth," who bashfully distanced herself from him after a short conversation, Mirza Abul Hasan recited this quatrain:

> Like a cypress you proudly stand, but when did a cypress walk?
> Like a rosebud your ruby lips, but when did a rosebud talk?
> Like a hyacinth's blooms are the ringlets of your sweet hair;
> but when were men's hearts enslaved by a hyacinth's stalk?[12]

Mirza was so infatuated with "Miss Pole" that he did not notice the presence of the Princess of Wales at that gathering.[13] The story of his love even circulated around the high circles of London. For example, the Queen is reported to have asked Sir Gore Ouseley, Ilchi's official *mehmandar*: "I have heard that the Iranian Ambassador is so enamoured of a certain young lady that the affairs of Iran are far from his thoughts!"[14]

One day's *houris*, however, on other occasions were denigrated as witches. For example, writing about his observations at a party at the house of the Marquis of Douglas and his wife Susan Euphemia, Abu al-Hasan wrote that the Marquis "has recently married a lady whose flawless beauty makes other women look like witches. She has a matchless singing voice: the nightingale's song is like a crow's compared to hers!" Having met her for the first time, he wrote, "I lamented that – just on the eve of my departure – I should be ensnared by the curve of a straying lock":

> It is not only I whom your ringlets ensnare,
> There's a captive tied up by each lock of your hair.

Abu al-Hasan reported that one night he was so absorbed by "the beauty of that *houri*-faced girl" that he had no interest in eating and drinking.[15] In a Sufi-style poem, where Susan Euphemia was the beloved, he declared, "This 'I' is not 'I', if there is an 'I' it's you" (*in man nah manam, agar mani hast tu'i*).[16]

Infatuated with the unveiled feminine beauties witnessed in Europe, a few Persian travelers like Mirza Abu al-Hasan and Mirza Abu Talib uttered poems and statements similar to unorthodox utterances, *shathiyat*, of intoxicated Sufis. The classical Sufi poems were basically ambiguous, leaving unspecified the beloved and the nature of the love. Yet in the poetic utterances of *voyeugers*, occasionally heaven was compared with parks, European women with *houris*, and Islam was abandoned in favor of physical love. It was no wonder that Riza Quli Mirza referred to some European women as "plunderers of heart and religion" and noted that thousands would abandon their religion like the Shaykh of San'an, a Muslim mystic who converted from Islam in order to unite with his Christian beloved.[17]

The pioneering Persian *voyageurs* were often invited to ballrooms, theaters, concerts, and masquerade parties during their European travels. They found the level of male–female intimacy at these gatherings to be radically different from public gatherings in India and Iran. The public dancing of unveiled women with men was shocking to travelers who were accustomed to seeing women veiled in public gatherings in the Islamic world. Within their own public space, the physical proximity of women and men was viewed as a sign of the disintegration of political and moral orders. The observed/imagined irregularities and differences of public women provided the loci for imagining the life and power of *Farangi* women.

As heterotopic spaces, radically different from actual spaces of everyday life, playhouses, operas, dances, and masquerades provided sites for alternative experiences in Europe. Mirza Abu Talib viewed the visit to playhouses as "sensual employment" (*mashghalah-'i nafs*) and wrote a detailed description of a playhouse in Dublin, explaining the arrangement of the stage, seats, spectacles, and spectators. He even drew a detailed blueprint of the playhouse. He was often accompanied to playhouses by Miss Garden, whom he described as a "fanatic in religion and used to the habits of old London."[18] During his stay in England, Mirza Abu al-Hasan was also invited to many plays and operas. After attending the opera of *Sidagero* at the King's Theatre in December 1809, he remarked: "Dancers and sweet-voiced singers appeared one after the other to entertain us, acting and dancing like Greeks and Russians and Turks." He found pleasing the well-disciplined crowed at the theater: "It is amazing that although 5000 people may gather in the theater, they do not make a loud noise . . . ".[19] On that night a historical ballet entitled *Pietro Il Grande*, by Signor Rossi, was performed. He commented that "the dancers imitated the Emperor and the Empress of Russia and the Pasha of Turkey and his wife and other Turks." Lord Radstock, in a letter, described Mirza Abu al-Hasan's reaction to the historical ballet:

He laughed heartily at the folly of bringing forward Peter the Great and his Empress as dancing to divert the throng. "What!" exclaimed he, "is it possible that a mighty monarch and his queen should expose themselves thus? how absurd! how out of nature! how perfectly ridiculous." Were I to translate the look that followed these words it would be thus: "Surely a nation that can suffer so childish and preposterous an exhibition, and be pleased with it, can have little pretensions either to taste or judgement."

Radstock further reported that Mirza Abu al-Hasan had jokingly said, "When I get back to my own country, the King shall ask me, 'What did the English do to divert you?' I will answer, 'Sir, they brought before me your Majesty's great enemies, the Emperor and Empress of Russia, and made them dance for my amusement.'" Radstock added, "This he repeated with the highest glee, as if conscious of saying a witty thing."[20]

Mirza Abu al-Hasan also attended a few plays, including an improved version of *King Lear* at the Royal Opera House. "Walking around the theater," he noted that "my companions and I saw beautiful ladies, beautifully dressed, casting flirtatious glances from their boxes." He attended the performances of Angelica Catalan (1789–1849), the famous Italian soprano, saying that "her performance was superb and her talent was highly praised by those who attended the Opera regularly." Mirza was astonished by her salary: "a high ranking general is said to receive a salary of 1000 tomans a year, yet a female entertainer is paid 5000 tomans for three nights' work!" After seeing Mlle Angiolini's performance of the "Persian Wedding Dance," he wrote: "The Italian woman called Angiolini, who is a good dancer, performed a 'Persian Wedding Dance,' which bore no resemblance at all to the real thing. Such novelties are mounted to attract the money of the idle rich who are forever seeking new diversions."[21]

Most Persian travelers thought of theaters as respectable and entertaining places. But Mirza Fattah Garmrudi, who visited England in 1839, viewed them as "the gathering places of whores and adulteresses and rendezvous of well-experienced pimps." He took the intermission between performances to be an occasion for sex between the performers and their customers.[22] Such intentional misunderstanding played an important role in shaping the popular opinion about Europe and European-style theaters.

Masquerade parties were another site of attraction for Persian travelers. Mirza Abu Talib viewed masquerading as a way of "testing the limits of each other's cleverness." He identified "maximum freedom for a short period of time," as a benefit of masquerading. "Since the identities of individuals are not apparent," according to Mirza Abu Talib, "they can behave in any manner." He found the diversity of nations represented in the masquerades appealing and noted, "since the English have traveled all over the world and are more familiar with the conditions of most other nations, London masquerades are perfect. In their masquerades Iranian, Indian, Arab, Turkuman, Hindu, Yogi,...and a hundred other types can be found. Some mimic to the extent that it affects their language and bodily movement."[23] The most attractive aspect of the masquerade for Mirza Abu Talib, who was called the "Persian Prince,"[24] was the masking of class distinctions so that "the nobility wear the clothing of the artisans and appear like barbers, flower-sellers, and bakers, imitating them so well that it is not possible to distinguish the original from the imitated/fake."[25] Among the memorable masquerades described by Mirza Abu al-Hasan was "a lady [Lady William Gordon] unknown to me, who was disguised as a priest, introduced herself to me: the English call such behaviour 'forward.'"[26] The accumulated reports of male–female interactions in ballrooms, theaters, and masquerades constituted "the woman of Europe" (*zan-i Farangi*) as the site of cultural gaze and as a fetishized marker deployed in the crafting of an extensive network of ethnic, religious, and political differences with Europe.

Comparing women

Misogyny and ethnocentrism were the shared characteristics of both European and Persian narration of the Other. European fascination with the imagined women of harems, seraglios, and gynoecium paralleled the Persianate view of Europe as an eroticized "heaven on earth" and European women as lascivious and licentious.[27] Both Persians and Europeans constituted the body of the "other" women as a site for sexual and political imagination. Traveling in Iran in 1812, James Morier explained that the residents of the Iranian city of Bushir showed a "feeling of great wonder" about women who accompanied the British delegation to Iran: "Above all things, that which excited their curiosity, was the circumstance of our ambassador having brought his *harem* with him; for although the Easterners look upon it as indecorous to make inquiries about each other's women, yet still we could observe how anxious they were to know something about ours." Morier, who had traveled to Iran a few years earlier, explained that this inquisitiveness was reciprocal:

Perhaps their curiosity about the women of Europe is quite as great as that of Europeans about those of Asia. I can state, in confirmation of the last assertion, that one of the first questions put to me by my acquaintances in Europe, has ever been on that subject; and from the conversations I have had with Asiatics upon the same topic, both parties have universally appeared to entertain in their imaginations the highest ideas of beauty of each other's women.[28]

The idealized women of the other became objects of male desire. Seeking the fulfilment of their fantasies, journeymen pursued exotic sex unobtainable at home. For many Europeans, as Said has observed, "the Orient was a place where one could look for sexual experience unobtainable in Europe."[29] Likewise Ibrahim Sahhafbashi, a late nineteenth-century Iranian traveler, ascertained that, "Anyone who wrote a travelogue, exalted [Europe] and anyone who heard these reports desired [to visit] it." These desires for Europe were displaced desires for European women. Such "preprogrammed expectations" overdetermined what travelers sought, saw, and cited.[30]

Thus women figured prominently in the travelers' understanding of the rising political dominance of Europe. They often established a causal relation between the education of women and the progress of Europe. For them the public appearance and behavior of European women symbolized a different order of politics and gender relations. I'tisam al-Din, for example, recognized the significance of schooling in the shaping of social and gender relations:

In England it is usual for the people of rank to send both their sons and daughters to a distant place for education.... The people of wealth in England, commencing at the age of four years, keep their sons and daughters constantly employed in writing, reading, and acquiring knowledge; they never permit them to be idle. If a man or woman not be acquainted with the musical art, be unable to dance or ride, he or she is accounted by people of substance as descended from a mean parentage, and taunts and reproaches are not spared.... The ladies, particularly, who can neither dance nor sing, are considered in a very inferior light; they will never get well married.

I'tisam al-Din found the institutionalized disciplining in England more beneficial to the children of the elite than the Indian practice of hiring private teachers at home. Like nineteenth-century reformers, he praised the European devotion to education and scientific inquiry, contrasting it to the worthless Persian–Indian quest for the beloved:

They are not like the people of this country, who repeat Hindi and Persian poems in praise of a mistress's face, or descriptive of the qualities of the wine, of the goblet, and of the cup-bearer, and who pretend to be in love.[31]

Mirza Abu-Talib, like I'tisam al-Din, was interested in the European educational system, especially that of women. Commenting on the "apparent freedom" (*azadi-i zahiri*) and education of English women, Mirza Abu-Talib noted that through education the English "have cleverly restrained" women from deviant deeds. He viewed education and the veiling as two diverse patterns of disciplining women. He observed that "the institution of the veil as a form of restraining is [also] an instigator of sedition and corruption."[32] Similarly Mirza Salih, who resided in England from 1815 to 1819, explained that the English women, while unveiled as a result of education, "do not have the propensity of committing wicked acts."[33] Disciplining women through education was more appealing to Persian travelers who viewed the veil as an instigator of moral depravation. Mirza Abu al-Hasan, for instance, in a conversation with Mrs Perceval in January 1810, comparing European and Persian women, remarked: "Your custom is better indeed. A veiled woman, with downcast eyes [*zan-i masturah-'i chashm bastah*], is like a caged bird: when she is released she lacks even the strength to fly around the rose garden."[34] Likewise, in a Persianized English letter published in the London *Morning Post* (May 29, 1810) and reprinted in many other newspapers and journals, Mirza Abu al-Hasan observed:

> English ladies [are] very handsome, very beautiful ... I [have] see[n] best Georgian, Circassian, Turkish, Greek ladies – but nothing so beautiful as English ladies – all very clever – speak French, speak English, speak Italian, play music very well, sing very good – very glad for me if Persian Ladies [were] like them.[35]

On many other occasions Mirza Abul Hasan wished that Iranian women could become like British women. The patriarchal example of the English woman who was devoted to her husband provided a modular form of familial organization that was free from the extensive network of female relatives who made the Persian wife autonomous of her husband.

> As God is my witness, I wish the women of Iran could be more like the women of England. Iranian women are chaste because they are forced to be – they are shut away from men; but the English women are chaste by choice. They are free and independent and responsible only to their husband, whom they look upon as the only man in the

world. They do not hide themselves away, but appear veil-less in society.[36]

Such arguments became fashionable among modernist men who linked the unveiling of women to the progress of the nation. Likewise women utilized the same rhetoric in their struggle for suffrage and participation in public life. For instance Bibi Khanum Astarabadi, in her *Vices of Men*, argued that European men serve their wives and live with them "in perfect harmony and concord" whereas Iranian men "all endeavor to humiliate women."[37] Such rhetorical comparisons became an essential component of the discourse on women's rights in Iran.

Persian travelers were also conscious of the legal order that made women's participation in the public sphere less restrictive. I'tisam al-Din explained the sexual liberty of Europeans in contrast to Muslim women in terms of the different legal systems:

> The courts have nothing to do with cases of simple fornication, unless a woman complains that she was forcibly violated. . . . If a man and woman commit fornication in a retired house, or even in any place whatever, they may do so with impunity, and neither the *cutwal* [police] nor the censor (*muhtasib*) can take any notice of it; for it is a common saying, "what business has the superintendent inside a house?" (*Muhtasib ra dar durun-i khanah chah kar?*) In England it is completely the reverse of what it is in this country, for there the *cutwal* and the censor have little or nothing to do, and don't have the power of seizing either a fornicator or a fornicatress, whatever the people may say.

He further observed that "the King of England is not independent in matters of government . . . and can do nothing without first consulting and advising with his ministers and nobles and a few selected men." By focusing on the relative freedom of women and the restriction on the power of sovereign, he shifted the meaning of freedom (*azadi*): "It is the English but also the European norm of freedom (*rasm-i azadi*) . . . that neither the elite nor the poor ever subjugate themselves to others." Contrasting this to the conventional historical practices, he observed that their norm is different from those of other countries where people "are proud of the title of the servant of the king" (*binam-i ghulami-i padishah fakhr kunand*).[38]

Such observations on gender and political "space of experience" in Europe expanded the "horizon of expectation" for the travelers and their circles of audience. *Azadi* (freedom) was among the first temporalized concepts deployed by travelers to project the observed experiences in Europe into the expected future for their own homeland. It also became a key concept for "diagnosing" norms of life at "home" and for legitimating interventions for their future progress (*tarraqi*). This is evident in Sahhafbashi's observation that "We raise our girls in a cage and would not teach them anything besides eating and sleeping . . . Unfortunately we comprehend the enjoyment of eating and intercourse more than progress and education (*tarraqi va tarbiyat*)."[39] The futurist concept of *azadi* produced its own counter-concept of *istidbad* (tyranny/despotism), which was used to characterize the mode of governance in Qajar Iran. To strengthen their nation, many nineteenth-century Persian travelers, either directly or indirectly, called for the establishment of a constitutional government and the participation of women in the public sphere.

Libertine women

Unlike many nineteenth-century travelers, Mirza Fattah Garmrudi, who traveled to Europe in 1838, developed a distaste for European manners and characteristics and warned against closer contacts with them. He called upon the *'ulama* and the political elite to distance themselves from this "wicked group" (*guruh-i nabikar*). Aware of the colonization of India, he warned that Europeans should not be trusted. For if opportune, they would "damage the religion and the state and destroy the Shari'ah traditions." He referred to Europe (*Farangistan*) as the land of the infidels (*Kufristan*) and concluded his 1842 *Shab Namah* (Nocturnal Letter) by noting that "due to the emotional depression and immensity of regret and sorrow that resulted from my observation of the state of affairs in *Kufristan*, I have been able to narrate no more than a seed from a donkey's burden and a drop in a sea about the obscene acts and indecent behaviors of this malevolent people [*in qaum-i bad sigal*]."[40] Mirza Fattah's pornographic view of Europe was the precurser of a Europhobic political imagination that sought to protect Iran from the "feminization of power" and European domination by guarding Iranian women from the malady of Europeanization. Like the earlier genre of *Lizzat al-Nisa'* (Joy of Woman), which was widely disseminated in homosocial male gatherings, *Shab Namah* was the prototype of a new erotic literature that constituted the uninhibited women of Europe as the locus of male sexual fantasies and arousal.

Mirza Fattah Garmrudi was a member of an Iranian delegation which was dispatched to Europe in 1838 and traveled to Vienna, Paris, and

London. The main objective of the mission, led by Mirza Husayn Khan Ajudanbashi, was to offer condolences to Queen Victoria (r. 1837–1901) on the death of William IV (1765–1837), to congratulate her on her accession to power, and to ask the British government to recall John McNeil, its Minister Plenipotentiary, for being unsympathetic to Iran's political claim to the city of Herat.[41]

This delegation, arriving in London in April 1839, faced a most discourteous reception. Queen Victoria declined to see them. The British government refused to receive them as governmental guests. Lord Palmerston pointed out that "[t]he Persian Ambassador must be Europeanized" by making him pay for all of his expenses.[42] This was a reversal of the earlier protocol according to which the British government, like its Iranian counterpart, paid all the expenses of diplomatic guests for the duration of their stay. Adding to the insult, the Iranian delegate was asked to revise Muhammad Shah's (r. 1834–48) letter to Queen Victoria, changing her title from *Malikah* to *Padshah*, for, according to Palmerston, "we have no sexual distinction for our sovereign," a distinction which was implied in the concept *malikah* but not in *padshah*.[43] This hostility, instead of the expected hospitality, shaped the Iranian delegates' image of *Farangistan* and perception of *Farangis*.[44] This is clearly illustrated in Mirza Fattah's *Shab Namah* (1842). He recounted about 20 anecdotes and incidents witnessed by him or Iqbal al-Dawlah, his newly found Persian–Indian friend who was in England at that time.[45] Mirza Fattah constructed a pornographic view of Europe that focused particularly on the sexual debauchery of British women.

After discussing the source of his anecdotes, Mirza Fattah noted that he would "briefly explain some of the conditions and characteristics of the women and their husbands."

> In this land of diverse persuasions, women and girls are generally pantless and without a veil [*chadur*] and have a constant desire for able pummelers. Covered women are rare and unacceptable. Women are masterful in the realization of the wishes of men. They are addicted to pleasure and play, and are free from suffering and toil [*az ranj va ta'ib azad*]. In actualizing the demands of their partners, they are always daring and exquisite. But they are incompetent and frail in preserving their own honor.

According to Mirza Fattah, "A common characteristic of women is their extreme desire for sexual intercourse." In his view,

They have escaped from the trap of chastity into freedom and have masterly leapt from the snare of purity. They have extreme desire for union with men and are endlessly coquettish and flirtatious. They glorify freedom and appreciate self-reliance [*bah azadi tafakhur darand va bah khud sari tashakkur*].

He equated English women's freedom with a lack of honor and chastity. This constituted the nodal point of the emerging Europhobic and misogynist discourse. Women and men, according to Garmrudi, were united night and day in ballrooms, theaters, coffeehouses, and whorehouses. To highlight the sexual debuchery of the English, he offered a pornographic description of how some women satisfied their sexual desires by keeping dogs at home. He explained that this practice was accepted and appreciated by the husbands:

In this land, due to the enormity of a woman's lust, a man does not have the strength to satisfy and realize her wishes promptly. Consequently, if a woman has an affair with another man and receives from him a payment, or due to her nobility and magnanimity, doesn't receive anything, according to the law of the nation [*qanun-i millat*] the poor husband has no right to punish her. Under such a condition the zealous husband is thankful that the dog has done the job for her instead of a neighbor or an ignorant rogue in the street. To be just and fair, the poor husband cannot be blamed.[46]

Men's sexual impotence and their inability to punish their wives was viewed as a cause of women's bestiality. To further illustrate the legal restrictions on men and the resultant sexual appetite of women, Garmrudi recounted the story of a wife who was "ugly and bad looking, and singularly ill-created and ill-humored." Her husband had become repulsed and preferred "living in a cave with a snake" to her companionship:

But since in their nation [*millat*] it is established that a man cannot have more than one wife, he was compelled to give in to his destiny and persevere, always praying to God for mercy and his liberation from her yoke of damnation.

One day the husband came home to find his wife with another man. He asked the adulterer why he was not looking for a better woman. The adulterer replied, "I do not have such bad taste. I am laboring and getting paid for it." Because of the incompetence of European men and

the voracious sexual appetite of European women, Garmrudi reported
that women had to rely on extramarital relations or on dildoes to satisfy
their desires. But he also described in graphic detail the pleasures of oral–
genital sex between men and women.

Why did Mirza Fattah write such a disparaging account of European
women, when earlier travelers had offered exalting reports? One is
the obvious fact that the special mission was ill-treated by the British
government. But there are a number of other factors which may illu-
minate his motivation for the writing of *Shab Namah*. For example, he
wrote:

> With all these destructive conditions and deplorable actions, if a person
> in the nations of *Farangistan*, especially in England, unintentionally
> (which is the necessary nature, meaning that it is the second nature
> of human beings) names chest and breast, or vagina and phallus, or
> the like among women, they will immediately print and register
> them in the newspapers and will disseminate it around the world
> that so and so in such and such gathering, had no shame and talked
> about such and such in front of women.

So Mirza Fattah and his colleagues might well have been victims of
journalistic admonishment and intrigue, which capitalized on the Persian travelers' unfamiliarity with European norms, mocked them, and
portrayed them as indecent and uncivilized. Might this also explain
Mirza Fattah's rather negative view of newspapers, which earlier Persian
travelers greatly admired? He wrote,

> Since the majority of newspapers print pure lies and they lie thor-
> oughly, then it is clever of them to clean their posteriors with these
> papers. There is no better use for them. They believe that with these
> papers the feces is cleaned from their rears, but this is neither clear
> nor obvious. It is not clear whether in reality their rears are cleaned
> by the papers, or whether the newsprint is actually purified by the
> excrement.

The members of the special mission had become extremely sensitive to
and angry with journalists who seemed to have reported on all that
seemed irregular and unfamiliar to their readers. There are other possible
explanations for Mirza Fattah's negative representation of Europeans.
As this same text suggests, Mirza Fattah was responding to a denigrating
European view of Iran.

With all these desolate affairs and deplorable conditions, they [Europeans] have written some books to reproach and reprimand Iran. Especially the Englishman [James Baillie] Fraser has vulgarly denigrated Iran and has gone to extremes in this regard. Among his charges is that the men of Iran have excessive desire for beardless teenagers and some men commit obscene acts with them. Yes, in the midst of all nations of the world, some fools, due to the predominance of lascivious spirit and satanic temptations, commit some inappropriate acts. It is far from just that the people of *Farangistan*, with all of their imperfect attributes and obscene behaviors for which they are characterized and are particularly famous, i. e. the establishment of homo-houses [*amrad-khanah*] and whore-houses, where they go at all times and pay money and commit obscene acts, that they characterize the people of Iran with such qualities and write about them in their books.[47]

After expressing his disapproval of Fraser's generalizations about and condemnation of Iranians,[48] Mirza Fattah narrated the story of an Italian lord who copulated with the son of an English gentleman after gaining the consent of the boy's father. He concluded that:

The above incident, besides indicating unfairness and engagement [of Europeans] in demeaning behaviors, is also an indication of the stupidity and foolishness of this people; but they ignore all these incidents and occurrences amongst themselves and attached their own characteristics to others.

As Mirza Fattah Garmrudi observed, Europeans were reading their own behavior and ways into Iranian character. Reflecting on the European perception of Iran, Garmrudi recognized the importance of power in determining the type of relations Europeans establish with other countries:

Apparently, they always interact on an appropriate and humane basis with strong states and never initiate opposition. With a state which appears weaker, however, they constantly search for excuses, make downright illogical statements and resist listening to logical views.

Mirza Fattah did, however, praise some European political institutions. Concerning the parliamentary arrangements, he remarked, "Individually, the people of *Farangistan* are not very wise or mature nor are they endowed with much eloquence or intelligence; but the parliament and the house of consultation [*mashvirat khanah*] that they have established apparently conceal these shortcomings." Despite their parliamentary form of government, he observed that on most occasions Europeans "deploy shenanigan and deception." He concluded that, "in fairness, any government whose elite are addicted to this habit are not considered amongst the wise and the mature but should be regarded as swindlers and ignoramuses."[49] The *Shab Namah* ends with a warning that the governmental elite should distance itself from the "wicked" Europeans, for they would damage the foundation of the state and religion.

During the nineteenth century, pornographic views of Europe, similar to Mira Fattah's *Shab Namah* provided the ammunition for an intensified struggle against the reformists who were idealizing Europe. Such pornographic denunciation of Europe entered into the Islamist discourses on the danger of unveiling and women's suffrage. The threat of feminization of power played a pivital role in the articulation of a counter-modernist Islamist political discourse. In the counter-modernist discourse the "fairy-faced" women of Europe appeared now as demonic. Mirza Fattah was amongst the originators of such a Europhobic discourse, a discourse in which the political threat of Europe was connected to the sexual debauchery of European women. By its erotic condemnation of sexualized European women the discourse interfaced the erotic and political genres. The success of this politico-erotic literature created a serious cultural opposition to the traveling of Iranian women to Europe.

Narrative plots and the scapegoating of women

Fascination with non-Muslim women has a long history in the Perso-Islamic literary culture. The mystical "Story of Shaykh San'an" by Farid al-Din 'Attar (d. *c.*1230) is one of the most famous and often narrated tales expressing the Persian imagination on the erotic and the exotic.[50] Shaykh San'an, the keeper of Mecca's holy place and an accomplished mystic with 400 disciples, had fallen in love with a Rumi (Roman/Greek) Christian girl whose beauty "was like the sun in splendor." Her eyes "were a lure for lovers," her face "sparkled like a living flame," and "the silver dimple of her chin was as vivifying as the discourses of Jesus." To unite with the Muslim mystic, the Christian woman set forth four difficult conditions: "prostrate yourself before the idols, burn the Qur'an, drink wine, and shut your eyes to your religion." After accepting these apostatizing conditions and converting to Christianity, instead of the usual dowry, the woman requested, "Now, for my dowry, O imperfect man, go and look after my herd of pigs for the space of a year, and then we shall pass our lives in joy or sadness." Deeply in love, Shaykh accepted this "unkosher" task: "Without a protest the shaykh of the Ka'aba, this saint, resigned himself to becoming a hog-ward."[51] At the end of the tale, Shaykh reconverted and his Christian beloved also accepted Islam. This and other similar stories provide a glimpse of how the exotic and erotic Christian women figured in the mystical and religious formation of identities in premodern South and South-west Asia.

In the course of the nineteenth century, pornographic views of European women became as prevalent as the views that they were educated, decent, and self-restrained. Sahhafbashi, who praised the education of women, also observed that in Europe "virgin women are rare and womanizing [*dukhtar bazi*] is like eating bread and yogurt in Iran and is not offensive."[52] Reports of the sexual laxity of European women provided the Iranian clerisy (*'ulama*) with effective moral ammunition to attack the modernists who were questioning their moral and intellectual leadership. An early example of clerical scapegoating of European women is evident in the writings of Hajj Muhammad Karim Khan Kirmani (1810–71), a leading Shaykhi theologian.[53] Writing in 1856, Kirmani believed that Iran was becoming infected with a "new malady" which was the result of "pleasure-seeking individuals, who refuse to associate with the ulama, and would no longer abide by religious principles."[54] Relying on the eyewitness account of Europe narrated to him by "a leading Iranian notable" who had taken refuge in England,[55] he warned of the ensuing feminization of power in Iran.

Can any Muslim allow incompetent women to have affairs in their hands so that they could go wherever they choose, sit with whomever they desire, leave the house whenever they wish? They [Europeans] have not yet gained firm control of Iran but they are already ordering our women not to cover themselves from men. Would any Muslim consent to women wearing makeup, sitting in the squares and at shops, going to theaters? Can any Muslim consent to the independence and beautification of his wife and allow her to go to the bazaar and buy wine and drink it and get intoxicated . . . and sit with rogues and ruffians [*alvat va awbash*] and do whatever she chooses? God forbid! Would anyone consent to allowing freedom and losing charge of one's daughter, wife, slave, and housekeeper? And allow them to go wherever they please and do whatever they like and sit with whomever they choose and have available in their gatherings any kind of wine they desire and mingle with rogues, and not be able to protest because an unbeliever has ordered the establishment of a land of freedom [*vilayat-i azadi*]?[56]

Kirmani described his antagonist as an "ignorant, conceited youth who, upon hearing the call of freedom, immediately make themselves look like Europeans, adopting European customs and betraying Islam and Islamic values."[57] He warned:

When they hear the call to freedom [*nida-yi azadi*] they would shape themselves like the *Farangis*, organize their assemblies and associations patterned after Europeans, model their behaviors on the bases of European customs, and turn away from Islam and Islamic traditions.[58]

Fearing that the imitation of Europe would lead to the de-differentiation of gender and religious identities, Muhammad Karim Kirmani cautioned Muslim men:

Then if your wife abstains from you, if she chose to convert to Armenianism, she would go to a church and after she is baptized in public, she would enter the Christian religion ... If the deviant women wish to become apostates no one can protest. Due to freedom a large number of people would become apostates and the clerisy and others would have no power to speak out. In conclusion, they would establish schools, and classes would be taught by European teachers ... and then the simple minded people would send their children to European schools and they would become totally Christianized.[59]

He further warned the male believers that if Iranian women mingled with European women, they would be tempted to dress like Europeans, dance in public celebrations and gatherings, drink wine, and sit with men on benches and chairs and joke with strangers. By becoming a "land of freedom" (*vilayat-i azadi*), women of Iran would copulate with Europeans and no one would dare to protest. Muhammad Karim Khan concluded his counter-modernist essay by declaring that "anyone who befriends a European would be considered an European himself ... and thus has apostatized and adopted the religion of the Europeans."[60] This line of argument became a significant component of an Iranian counter-modernity that equated undesirable sociopolitical reforms with the Europeanization and Christianization of Iran. Iranian modernity was always constrained by the terms established by its powerful counterpart.

Persian travelers' accounts of their journeys to Europe frequently followed the narrative plot of the "Story of Shaykh San'an." While enthusiastically reporting on the liberty of European women – their mixing with men in masquerades and dancing parties and their sexual laxity – at the same time they often sought forgiveness for deviating from the straight path during their journey to "infideldom" (*kufristan*). For example, Mirza Abu Talib confessed to having abandoned his cherished goal of learning "English sciences" (*'ilm-i Ingilish*) in favor of "love and gaiety" in London. On his return journey to Calcutta he visited the shrines of the Shiite imams 'Ali, Husayn, and Zayn al-'Abidin and sought their forgiveness for his sins in Europe.[61] He also composed two elegies in praise of 'Ali and Husayn,

> Whilst at Baghdad, I had them beautifully transcribed, on gold paper, and suspended them near the tombs of those illustrious saints at Karbela and Najaf. These elegies were much approved by both the superintendents; and they promised me to take care they were not removed, but they should be preserved, a testimony of my zeal.[62]

Not all travelers visited Muslim shrines, repenting for their experiences in Europe like Mirza Abu Talib; instead many assumed the posture of objective and disengaged observers in the recounting of their self-experience. This objectivist posture, like repentance, enabled the travelers to reintegrate themselves into their own society by eroticizing and exoticizing Europe.

Through the narrative recounting of their *observations* in Europe, the Persianate travelers induced the production of two competing Europhiliac and Europhobic discourses. In the Europhiliac discourse Europe was represented as an orderly and law-bound *heterotopia* with educated and disciplined women who were perfect companions to their husbands. In the Europhobic discourse Europe was depicted as an *ectopia*, an abnormal place with lewd and libertine women who could not be sexually satisfied by their husbands. These competing representations of Europe were deployed by Iranian modernists and counter-modernists in their divergent strategies of refashioning Iran. Identification with Europe served as a strategy for the subversion of the dominant Islamicate discourse and the construction of a new pattern of identity rooted in pre-Islamic history and culture. By mocking Europe, counter-modernists sought to preserve the existing order and to subvert the political strategy of de-Islamizing Iran. Both the modernist Europhilia and the counter-modernist Europhobia deployed Europe as a point of reference; both, however, were actively involved in creative construction of alternative bodypolitics and vernacular modernities.

Seeing oneself being seen

The Persian travelers narrated the spectacle of Europe and the European onlookers reported the spectacle of the exotic Persians in their midst. The surveyors of Europe and its cultural differences found themselves surveyed by Europeans. Reflecting on his own experience as a spectacle, I'tisam al-Din wrote:

> Whenever I went outdoors, crowds accompanied me, and the people in the houses and bazaars thrust their heads out of the windows and gazed at me with wonder. The children and boys took me for a black devil, and being afraid kept at a distance from me.[63]

Mirza Abu Talib recalled happier experiences. Remembering his visit to Dublin, he wrote:

> As I would walk out of the house they would surround me and every one would say nice things about me. Some said that I must be the Russian General, who had been for some time expected; others guessed that I am a German ruler, and still others would view me as a Spanish noble. But the greater part perceived me as a Persian Prince.[64]

Observing the details of English social and political life, Mirza Abu al-Hasan was likewise constituted as an object of popular gaze and amazement. According to *The London Literary Gazette*, he was so great an object of public curiosity, that

> he could not leave his hotel without being surrounded by a multitude of gazers. When he attended fashionable parties, the eagerness evinced by the ladies to gain a sight of him, subjected him to a degree of embarrassment the more insupportable, as the people of the East entertain notions very unfavourable to that kind of female curiosity.[65]

Abu al-Hasan's appearance provided a signifying surface for the rearticulation of cultural differences and the replaying of European sexual fantasies. Drawing on the culturally available resources, *The Morning Herald* (March 29, 1810) offered a spectacularized description of his appearance:

> The Persian Ambassador attracts the particular attention of the Hyde Park belles as an equestrian of a singular order, for he rides in silken pantaloons of such a wide dimension, that, being inflated by the wind makes his Excellency appear [more] like flying to a Turkish Harem, than riding for the pure air in Rotten Row.[66]

The *harem*, a misrecognized space, had already become an exotic site for the projection of European sexual fantasies. As a symbolic condensation of the Muslim Orient, the *harem* became a point of reference for culturally placing the Persian travelers who were often asked about polygamous practices.

The Persian visitors were the objects of intense public voyeurism. To ward off the public eye, they went "native" and cross-dressed. By replacing their Persian dress with European costumes, the visitors hoped to de-exoticize themselves and remove the most obvious sign of their otherness. Such transvestite protection from public voyeurism sought by Muhammad Riza Bayk (d. 1714), a Persian envoy to France, provided Montesquieu with material for the *The Persian Letters*. A central episode of *The Persian Letters* terminated with the question "How can one be Persian" (*Comment peut-on etre Persan?*). The Persian Rica found the excessive public curiosity to be burdensome and so decided "to give up Persian costume and dress like an European."[67]

The protective shield of cultural transvestism was occasionally sought by Mirza Salih Shirazi. On the occasion of King George's birthday, Mirza Salih was asked by his friends to participate in the public celebration. Worried about the public gaze and harassment, Mirza Salih intended to wear a European costume instead of Persian attire. But his friends advised him against it, arguing that he should not be worried since he was to be accompanied by Englishwomen and men. Upon their insistance, Mirza Salih wore his Persian garments and, holding hands with a certain Miss Sara Abraham, accompanied his friends to the public celebration. But the sight of an "exotic Persian" walking hand-in-hand with an Englishwoman intensified public curiosity: "All of a sudden, the masses, who had not seen a person dressed like me, appeared from all sides and in a short time five hundred people gathered around me." Mirza Salih escaped from the scene, went to his apartment, and after changing into European dress, rejoined his friends. According to his own report, no one harassed him after he cross-dressed.[68] Such harassing public curiosity was also reported by European travelers who visited the Middle East in the eighteenth and nineteenth centuries.

With the global hegemony of European perspectives, the Persian mode of dress became associated with premodernity. The Persian travelers who were conscious of the use of dress as a *time-distancing* device in European imagination, *contemporized* themselves by shedding their Persian dress in favor of European mode. The European dress, as it will be explained in Chapter 6, was initially adopted as a military uniform in 1839 by the modernizing Muhammad Shah. Having likewise internalized the time-distancing European perspectives, almost a century later Riza Shah sought to visually *contemporize* Iran with Europe by imposing European dress on men and by unveiling women. These policies of self-refashioning were driven by two interlocking inferiority complexes: a sense of inferiority to *contemporary* Europeans and a feeling of inferiority to the imperial ancient Persians, an imperial tradition that was created in the sixteenth century and popularized in the nineteenth century.

5
Contested Memories

Narrative emplotment[1]

The historical accounts of pre-Islamic Iran have contested allegorical meanings that are essential to the configuration of Iranian identity. These meanings are embedded in narrative structures that terminate in the Muslim conquest of Iran and the death of Yazdigird III (d. 31/651 or 652), the last Sasanian king. In early "Islamicate" historiography the accounts of ancient Iran served as an allegory of the Persian (differentially identified as *Furs*, *'Ajam*, and *Majus*)[2] submission to Islam. The narrative termination of Persian sovereignty (*saltanat*) coincided with the commencement of Islam and with the closure of the cycle of prophecy inaugurated by Adam. The co-termination of the Sasanian dynastic rule and the cycle of prophecy mark the transition to a new and "superior" moral and political order – divinely sanctioned to last until "the end of time" (*akhar-i zaman*).

The allegorical meaning of pre-Islamic Iran was altered radically by the pioneers of a late sixteenth- and early seventeenth-century exilic movement. Known as Azari, Kayvani, or Dasatiri, this movement was led by Azar Kayvan (939 or 940–1027/1533–1618) and his disciples, who migrated to India in response to the repressive religious policies of the Safavids (1501–1722). Responding to the threat of physical elimination, the architects of this neo-Mazdean intellectual movement wrote themselves back into history by projecting an Iran-centered universal historical narrative that subordinated the Biblico-Qur'anic "mythistory" to its own all-encompassing framework.[3] In the generative texts of *Dasatir*, *Sharistan-i Danish va Gulistan-i Binish*, and *Dabistan-i Mazahib* human history begins not with Adam, but with the pre-Adamite Mahabad. Linking the history of Iran to pre-Adamite times, the Azaris reframed the inaugural, medial, and terminal events of Islamicate historiography imposed by early Muslim historians on the accounts of pre-Islamic Iran. This enabled the Azaris to reconfigure the textual terraces of Iran's ancient past that had been subordinated to the narrative motifs of Islam-icate prophetography (*tarikh-i anbiya'*). By extending and ethnicizing history, the non-biblical framework of these texts inspired the proto-scientific endeavors of early Orientalists,[4] Zoroastian Khushnumists,[5] and Iranian Baba'is and nationalists.[6] This framework enabled Sir William Jones (1746–94) and other Orientalists to construct new theories on the origins of languages and races.[7] It incited the nineteenth-century Iranian nationalists to reconfigure the pre-Islamic past as a "golden age" coming to a "tragic end" with the Muslim conquest.

The first part of this chapter offers an outline of the Islamicate patterns of encoding the ancient history of Iran. It explains how the claims of Kayumars and Adam as progenitors of humankind were resolved by the imposition of a Qur'anic framework, which supplied the inaugural, medial, and terminal events of the ancient history. It then explores how Azar Kayvan and his disciples recentered Iran and altered the allegorical meaning of its pre-Islamic history.

Islamicating history

Historical accounts of the pre-Islamic past often appear in chronicles, which encompass the emergence and proliferation of Islam and end with the chroniclers' own time. In their overarching structures as "chronicles," these narratives abruptly terminate in *medias res*, without a conclusion that endows the chain of events with a meaningful closure. Unlike the accounts of the Islamic period that lack the formal cohesion of a "well-made story," the narratives of pre-Islamic history come to full closure and are endowed with a "moral meaning."[8] As accounts of a putatively vanished world displaced by Islamdom, the pre-Islamic Persian histories have an autonomous narrative structure that clearly demar-cates them from Islamic history. Islamic authority and its containment of counter-narratives often prefigures into the plot structures of pre-Islamic histories.[9]

In their narration of Biblico-Qur'anic and Persian mythistories, Early Muslim historians were concerned with coordinating the claims of origin of the two traditions. The Islamic encodement of the historical field was most apparent in the attempts to subordinate Persian histor-ical narratives to the inaugural, medial, and terminal events of Muslim prophetography: Adam's creation, Noah's Flood, and Muhammad's prophecy. Reconciling the originary claim of Adam and Kayumars proved the most challenging aspect of historical synchronization.[10] Its solution determined the chronological ordering of subsequent events. The resolution of these two irreconcilable claims necessitated the altera- tion of Kayumars's genealogy. The reconfiguration of Kayumars, as the ancestor of Iranians, was also coordinated with the claim that Noah's flood covered the entire earth. As inaugural and medial motifs of Islamic prophetography, the stories of Adam and Noah overdetermined the chronological reordering of Persian historical narratives.

Kayumars (Avestan *Gayö maretan*; Pahlavi *Gayümart*, meaning "mortal life") was a problematic alternative figure for Muslim historians writing on the beginning of human history. According to Mazdean sources, Kayumars, an androgyne, appeared in *Iran-vij* (Iran-land) and upon death a seed from her/his back impregnated the earth with rhubarb plants (*ribas*), which grew into the first human couple, Mahryag and Mahryanag (also known as Mashya and Mashyani or Mashi and Mashy- nah).[11] The androgynous identity of Kayumars and the perception of her/him as the progenitor of humankind was irreconcilable with the Biblico-Qur'anic view of Adam as the primal man.[12] Early Arab historians such as Dinawari (d. 281/897), Mas'udi (d. 345/956), Baladhuri (d. 279/ 892), and Tabari (d. 310/923) recounted diverse and often conflicting reports about Kayumars. Views on Kayumars were so diversified that Tabari claimed "[i]t would make this book of ours too long to mention them all."[13] The multiplication of reports on the lineage of Kayumars offered Muslim historians a wide range of options in their attempts to reconcile the Persian and Biblico-Qur'anic mythistories. The Mazdean perception of Kayumars as the androgynous progenitor was irreconcil- able with the Qur'anic creation story and was consequently viewed as unreliable, absurd, and irrational.[14]

For Muslim historians the synchronization of biblical and pre-Islamic Persian historical narratives had to correspond with the beginning and ending motifs provided by Islamic prophetography: a chain of divine appointments beginning with Adam and terminating with Muham- mad. This framework fashioned the historical field and determined the credibility of non-Qur'anic historical accounts. Events irreconcilable with the Qur'anic historical imagination were considered suspect and even offensive. For instance, Ya'qubi argued that "Persians make many claims for their kings which cannot be accepted."[15] Finding them to be "jesting and make-believe," he decided to "set [them] aside because our principle is to excise offensive reports."[16]

In his attempt to reconcile different narrative traditions and con- struct a sequential account of pre-Islamic history, Tabari recognized the significance of relying on each people's account of their own history: "Every people is more familiar than others with their own forefathers, pedigrees, and accomplishments. With respect to every complex matter, one must have reference to those who were [directly] involved." After recounting the views of "Persian scholars" on Kayumars, Tabari apologetically remarked:

> I mention this information about Jayumart [Kayumars] in this place only because none of the scholars of the [various] nations disputes that Jayumart is the father of the non-Arab Persians. They differ with respect to him only as to whether he is Adam, the father of mankind, as stated by those mentioned by us, or somebody else.

For Tabari and other early Muslim historians who were interested in constructing a narrative account of ancient peoples culminating in the victory of Islam, Persian historical accounts were of paramount importance. Explaining the significance of these narratives, Tabari notes:

> [I refer to Jaumars] because his rule and that of his children continued in the East and the mountains there uninterrupted in an orderly fashion, until Yazdjard b. Shahriyar [d. 31/651 or 652], one of his descendants – May God curse him! – was killed in Marw in the days of 'Uthman b. 'Affan. The history (or chronology) of the world's bygone years is more easily explained and more clearly seen based upon the lives of the Persian kings than upon those of the kings of any other nation. For no nation but theirs among those leading their pedigree back to Adam is known whose realm lasted and whose rule was continuous. . . . Thus, a history based upon the lives of the Persian kings has the soundest sources and the best and clearest data.[17]

The continuous annals of Persian kings enabled Muslim historians to construct a richly textured account of the pre-Islamic world. In such narratives, the Qur'anic historical imagination or prophetography provided the principle of selection and "colligation."[18] The Creation of Adam constituted the inaugural motif, the universal deluge during Noah's time the transitional motif, and Muhammad's prophecy the terminal motif toward which the pre-Islamic history unfolded. As fully enclosed narratives terminating in the commencement of Islam, the stories of pre-Islamic Persian kings were allegories of the moral and political eminence of Islam. The moral superiority of Islam was signaled not only by the outcome of that history but also by the evidentiary use of the Qur'an in altering the sequence of historical events and the establishment of its truth.

Encoded with the inaugural and the terminal frame of Islamic mythistory, Persian kings and historical events were endowed with a new genealogy and chronological order of occurrence. Kayumars was transformed from an androgyne to a man, and quite a virile one for that matter, since, as Tabari reported, he "married thirty women who gave him many children. His son Mari and daughter Mariyanah were among those born at the end of his life."[19]

The "son" and "daughter" of Kayumars were the first human couple of the Mazdean tradition. In that tradition they were believed to have emerged from the contemporaneous metamorphoses of "a one-stemmed rivas-plant" after the death of Kayumars.[20] Concerning the first human couples, Abu Rayhan Biruni (362–440/973–after 442/1048) recounted that as Kayumars neared death,

> two drops of sperma fell down on the earth. And out of these drops grew two Rîbâs bushes (Rheum ribes), from among which Mêshâ and Mêshâna sprang up, i.e. the Persian Adam and Eve. They are also called Malhâ and Malhayâna, and the Zoroastrians of Khwârizm call them Mard and Mardâna.[21]

Recounting another tradition, Biruni reported that Kayumars, after living in Paradise 3,000 years and on the earth for another three millennia, at last desired to die, "whereupon God killed him."

> At the same moment two drops of sperma fell down out of his loins on the mountain Dâmdâdh in Istakhr, and out of them grew two Rîbâs-bushes, on which at the beginning of the ninth month the limbs (of two human bodies) began to appear, which by the end of that month had become complete and assumed human shape. These two are Mêshâ and Mêshyâna.[22]

Once the identity of Kayumars, Mashi, and Mashyana were transformed, Tabari had a basis for reconciling the differences between the Biblico-Qur'anic and Persian accounts of the two claimants of primordiality. In his discussion of the ancestry of Hushang, Tabari entertained the possibility that Adam and Kayumars might be identical.[23] But when no reconciliation seemed possible, as in the case of the universal deluge, the Qur'an established the basis for "telling the truth about history."

In providing a new beginning for human history, the story of Noah constituted another essential component of the Qur`anic account of the ancient world. This new beginning reintegrated all histories into a single homogenized universal narrative. But the convergence of different narratives into a universally experienced flood required a radical rearrangement of the chronological order of Persian accounts. This rearrangement was necessary since the Persians, along with Indians and Chinese, had not recounted the occurrence of a universal flood. Tabari, like Abu Rayhan Biruni, reported that,

> The Magians have no knowledge of the flood. They say: Our rule continued uninterrupted since the age of Jayumart – who they say is identical with Adam. It was inherited by consecutive rulers to the time of Feroz b. Shahriyar. They [also] say: If [the story of the Flood] were sound, the pedigrees of the people would have been disrupted and their rule dissolved. Some of them acknowledge the Flood and assume that it took place in the clime of Babil and nearby regions, whereas the descendants of Jayumart had their dwellings in the East, and the Flood did not reach them.[24]

Tabari, responding to the discrepancies between the "Magians" and the Qur`anic accounts, boldly expressed his own position: "Abu Ja`far [al-Tabari] says: The information given by God concerning the Flood contradicts their statement, and what He says is the Truth: 'Noah called upon Us – and surely, good are those who respond! We delivered him and his family from the great distress and made his offspring the survivors.'[25] God thus indicated that Noah's offsprings are the survivors, and nobody else."[26] In response to this exclusivist view of the historical truth many Muslim historians found it more pragmatic to represent Kayumars as a descendant of Noah rather than as identical with Adam. Ibn Athir (d. 630/1232), recounting Tabari's version, argued that Kayumars was really Ham, son of Japhet, son of Noah.[27] Tabari reported that some scholars regarded Kayumars as Gomer b. Japhet b. Noah.[28] After recounting the Persian explanation of the deluge, Biruni remarked,

> These discrepancies in their reports inspire doubts in the student, and make him inclined to believe what is related in some books, viz. that Gayômarth was not the first man, but that he was Gomer ben Yaphet ben Noah, that he was a prince to whom a long life was given, that he settled on the Mount Dunbâwand, where he founded

an empire, and that finally his power became very great, whilst mankind was still living in [elementary] conditions, similar to those at the time of the creation, and of the first stage of the development of the world.[29]

Biruni also recounted another opinion that "Gayômarth was Emîm ben Lûd ben Arám ben Sem ben Noah." While early Muslim historians subordinated the Persian mythistorical tradition to the Islamicate historical discourse, the Arab–Persian rivalries of the Shu'ubiyah movement contributed to diversifying the ancient Persians' genealogical connection to biblical personages.[30] The reconfiguration of the identity of Kayumars also necessitated the linguistic designation of his name as Syriac rather than Persian.[31] This misidentification was not accidental, for such a designation served as further evidence of "his" biblical pedigree.

Instead of concocting a postdiluvian genesis for the Persian historical development, Abu Hamid Muhammad Ghazzali (450–505/1058 or 1059–1111), a leading medieval religious thinker, found a pragmatic solution to the political problem of synchronization. Conveying the "disintegration of the caliphal empire" and the rise of autonomous sultanates in eleventh- and twelfth-century Islamdom,[32] Ghazzali fashioned a divinely sanctioned bifurcated history with similar beginnings and conclusions. According to Ghazzali, human history began with Adam and was divinely ordained into two separate ecclesiastic and royal histories, each with its own distinct function:

> You should understand that God on High selected two classes of the Sons of Adam and endowed these two classes with superiority over the rest: one being prophets, blessing and peace be upon them, and the other kings. To guide His slaves to Him, He sent prophets; and to preserve them from one another, He sent kings, to whom He conferred his rank.

After establishing that "kingship and divine effulgence [*farr-i izadi*] have been granted to them [kings] by God," Ghazzali offered a truncated account of the genealogies and characters of the pre-Islamic Persian kings. To endow the Persian kings with "divine effulgence" and the Qur'anic inaugural motif, he reported:

> It is related in the (Persian) traditions that Adam, on whom be peace, had many sons. From their number he chose two, Seth and

Kayumarth, to whom he gave forty of the Great Books, by which they were to work. Then he charged Seth with the preservation of religion and (affairs of) the next world, and Kayumarth with the affairs of this world and the kingship. (Kayumarth) was the first of the kings of the world, and his reign lasted 30 years.[33]

Thus Ghazzali invented physical embodiments for the metaphorical view of the state (*dawlat*) and religion (*din*) as twin brothers.[34] In his enumeration of the kings of Pishdadian, Kayanian, Ashkanian, and Sasanian dynasties, Ghazzali identified Yazdigird b. Shahriyar as "the last of the kings of the Persians." In conclusion, he remarked: "After him there was no other king of their community; the Muslims were victorious and took the kingship out of their hands. The power and dominion passed to the Muslims, through the benediction of the Prophet [Muhammad], God bless him." As a fully enclosed narrative, Ghazzali's version of the pre-Islamic Persian kings began with Adam and terminated with the victory of Islam.

While configured within an Islamic framework, the history of ancient Persians had its own autonomous logic of continuity and rupture: "the development or desolation of this universe depends upon kings; if the king is just, the universe is prosperous and the subjects are secure, as was the case in the times of Ardishir, Firidun, Bahram Gur, Kisra, and other kings like them; whereas when the king is tyrannical, the universe becomes desolate, as was in the times of Øahhak, Afrasiyab, and others like them."[35] Outlining the political wisdom that guided the historically recounted actions of kings, Ghazzali explained:

They would not tolerate any [infraction] small or great, because they knew beyond all doubt that where injustice and oppression are present, the people have no foothold; the cities and localities go to ruin, the inhabitants flee and move to other territories, the cultivated lands are abandoned, the kingdom falls into decay, the revenues diminish, the treasury becomes empty, and happiness fades among the people. The subjects do not love the unjust king, but always pray that evil may befall him.

Expounding the significance of justice (*'adl*) in the maintenance and preservation of state power, Ghazzali outlined the syllogism that prefigured into the narrative accounts of the cycles of rise and fall of dynasties: "The religion depends on the monarchy, the monarchy on the army, the army on supplies, supplies on prosperity, and prosperity on justice [*'adl*]."[36] This "circle of justice" (*dayirah-'i 'adalat*),[37] as a universal law of causal relations, provided the metahistorical presuppositions that operated in most mediaeval Persian historical writings.

Unlike the ethnographic histories that were regulated by "the circle of justice," the ecclesiastical narratives were grounded in "the Qur'anic paradigm of repeated prophetic challenge, followed either by rejection and punishment or (more rarely) by acceptance and prosperity."[38] Whereas the repeated cycle of dynasties served as warnings to tyrannical kings, the cycle of prophets served as warnings to transgressing nations. As moralizing narratives, the ecclesiastic history invited the people to submit to God and the ethnographic history invited kings to the practice of justice.

The pedagogical value of the pre-Islamic history gave rise to a bifurcated narrative structure best exemplified in medieval Persianate historical writings. Instead of reconciling the pre-Islamic with the Biblico-Qur'anic and Persian mythistorical accounts, most Persianate historians and chroniclers framed their work into two autonomous ecclesiastic and ethnographic narratives with similar points of inauguration and termination. One chapter would recount the history of prophets from the Creation of Adam to the messengership of Muhammad. The succeeding chapter would narrate the annals of pre-Islamic Persian kings from Kayumars – often viewed as a descendent of Noah – to the conquest of Persia by the Muslim armies. The termination of both narratives signaled Islam's moral and political superiority. This bifurcated narrative structure was embedded in Nasir al-Din 'Abd Allah Bayzavi's *Nizam al-Tawarikh*, Hamd Allah Qazvini's *Tarikh-i Guzidah*, Mir Khwand's *Rawzat al-Safa*, and Khwand Mir's *Habib al-Siyar* (930/1523).

Nizam al-Tawarikh (completed in 674/1275) begins with a chapter on "prophets, testators, and philosophers," followed by a chapter on Persian kings (*muluk-i furs*), which included the non-Persian rulers Zahhak, Afrasiyab, and Istihan. Although he knew of the Mazdean [Mughan] view of Kayumars, Bayzavi found it more plausible to construe Kayumars as a descendant of Shem ben Noah.[39] He concluded the narrative on Persian kings with the death of Yazdigird, with whom "the sovereignty of Persian kings was discontinued completely and became a trustee of Muslims (*Musalmanan ra musallam gasht*)."[40] Hamd Allah Qazvini's *Tarikh-i Guzidah* (730/1329), also adhered to the same narrative structure. The first chapter recounts the story of biblical and Qur'anic messengers and prophets. The chapter on pre-Islamic kings begins with Kayumars and ends with Yazdigird. The latter is identified as "the last of the Persian kings" (*akhar-i muluk-i 'Ajam*).[41]

Following the same narrative convention, Mir Khwand (838–902/ 1433–98) devoted more than half of the first part of his *Rawzat al-Safa* (completed in 899/1493) to prophetography and follows this with annals of the Persian kings (*muluk-i 'Ajam*) from Kayumars to Yazdigird, whose assassination led to the "lowering of the flags of infidelity [*kufr*] and the rising of the banners of Islam."[42] Mir Khwand, like other historians, recounted different stories of Kayumars. He explained, "The Magi assert that Kaiomars [Kayumars] is synonymous with Adam, the progenitor of the human race: they also style him Gilshah, or Earth-king, because in his time scarcely anything had been called into existence, over which his authority could extend, except water and clay."[43] Narrating diverse Muslim traditions, including Ghazzali's, Mir Khwand asserted: "Amidst such a diversity of traditions, the chief historians however agree, that Kaiomars [Kayumars] was the first sovereign who placed the yoke of obedience and submission on the necks of refractory, and spread the carpet of justice [*basat-i ma'dilat*] over the habitable world."[44] In this, as in other Persian historical texts, kings were entrusted with the responsibility of maintaining justice and preserving the moral and political order of the world.[45] This divinely sanctioned responsibility of kings, mediated through the principle of "divine effulgence" (*farr-i izadi*), was often projected as the realization of the following Qur'anic verse: "Say: 'Lord, Sovereignty of all sovereignty, You bestow sovereignty on whom You will and take it away from whom you please'."[46] Appearing in the preamble of Ghazzali's account of pre-Islamic Persian kings, this and another Qur'anic verse were utilized to infuse history with the moral and political principles of Islam.[47] Because of their pedagogical value, the anecdotes of various Persian kings figured into the manuals of statecraft and mirrors for princes which were authored for the education of Muslim rulers and administrators.[48] By bringing the theories and practices of ancient Persian kings into the service of Islamicate political culture, the notions of *farr-i izadi* (divine effulgence) and *Zill Allah fil arz* (the shadow of God on Earth) became atemporal expressions of divine authority.

Recentering Iran

Three-quarters of a century after the Safavids' establishment of Shi'ism as the state religion of Iran, a neo-Mazdean renaissance, led by Azar Kayvan (939 or 940–1027/1533–1618) and his disciples, set out to recover the memories of the pre-Islamic past and to alter the allegorical meaning of Iran's ancient history and culture.[49] The disciples of Azar Kayvan included Zoroastrians, Jews, Muslims, and Hindus. Fath Allah Shirazi (d. 997/1588), a close advisor of Emperor Akbar, was among his most influential students.[50] Abu al-Fazl 'Allami was also considered a "total believer" in Azar Kayvan.[51] Well grounded in Islamic philosophical traditions, Azar Kayvan and his cohorts, collectively known as Azaryan (Azaris) or Kayvanyan (Kayvanis), attempted to highlight the circular relationship and reciprocal influences between Mazdaism and Islam. Combining erudition and imagination, they tried to recover the suppressed memories and marginalized views of ancient Persians. They constructed a narrative framework that extended back to pre-Adamite times, and subsumed Islamic prophetography by reassembling and re-encoding scattered fragments of Islamic and Mazdean textual traces. *Dasatir*,[52] *Dabistan-i Mazahib*,[53] *Sharistan-i Danish va Gulistan-i Binish* (popularly known as *Sharistan-i Chahar Chaman*),[54] and *A'in-i Hushang*,[55] all known as *dasatiri* texts, were the exemplary products of their creative intellectual efforts. The publication and dissemination of these Iran-centered neo-Mazdean texts provided a master-narrative well suited to the needs of nineteenth-century nationalists. Compiled, composed, or "translated" by Azar Kayvan and his disciples, these texts provided a mythistorical narrative inaugurated by the pre-Adamite Mahabad, who claimed to have initiated the great cycle of human existence well before Adam.

Azar Kayvan, a Zoroastrian philosopher, emigrated from the religiously intolerant Safavid Iran in the 1570s and settled in Patna, India, where he died at the age of 85.[56] The religious policies of the Mughal Emperor Akbar (963–1014/1556–1605) provided a suitable intellectual environment in India for an active reconstruction of Mazdaism,[57] which had suffered from centuries of Islamic political hegemony in Iran. By incorporating Illuminationist philosophy (*Hikmat-i Ishraq*) into a Mazdean cosmology,[58] Azar Kayvan and his cohorts constructed a world-view characterized as "Zoroastrian Ishraqi."[59] Whereas Mazdaism provided the latent content of a manifestly Islamic Illuminationist philosophy, Azar Kayvan and his followers incorporated the terminology of Islamic Illuminationism into a manifestly Mazdean perspective, identified with 16 pre-Islamic Persian sages (*vakhshuran/vakhshwaran*): Mahabad, Ji-Afram, Shay-Kaliv, Yasan, Gil-Shah (Kayumars), Siyamak, Hushang, Tahmuris, Jamshid, Faraydun, Manuchihr, Kay-Khusraw, Zartusht (Zoroaster), Sikandar (Alexander), Sasan-i Nukhust (Sasan I), and Sasan-i Panjum (Sasan V).[60] The presumed epistles of these sages,[61] collected in the *Dasatir*, constituted the foundational canon of the neo-Mazdean renaissance. These epistles, according to Azaris, were originally written in a "celestial language" (*zaban-i asmani*) but were translated into Persian with added commentary by the Fifth Sasan, who was considered a contemporary of Muhammad (d. 632 CE) and the Sasanian ruler Khusraw Parviz (r. 590–628 CE). Dating the commentary to a period immediately preceding the Musim conquest of Iran was intended to serve as evidence for the unique and exemplary prose of the *Dasatir*, which was devoid of Arabic terms and concepts and included many "obsolete" Persian terminologies.[62] The *dasatiri* terminologies were incorporated in *Burhan-i Qati'*, an influential Persian dictionary compiled by Muhammad Husayn Khalaf Tabrizi in 1062/1651, and widely circulated and used by poets and writers in India and Iran. On account of its lack of Arabic words, *Dasatir* became an inspiring text for generations of Persian purists from Abu al-Fazl ʿAllami (958–1011/1055–1602) to Ahmd Kasravi (1890 or 1891–1946) who sought to purge from Persian any "alien" Arabic lexicons.

A historiographically significant aspect of *Dasatir* was the attribution of the first four epistles to sages who were anterior to Kayumars, the progenitor of humankind in the Mazdean tradition. This newly fashioned framework was designed to challenge the hegemonic Islamic historical imagination that marginalized and distorted the Persian mythistory. In this scenario, Kayumars is preceded by four sages who were respectively the founders of the eras of Abadiyan, Jayan, Shaʾiyan, and Yasaʾiyan.[63] According to the system of reckoning introduced in *Dabistan-i Mazahib*, a text arguably written by Azar Kayvan's son Kaykhusraw Isfandyar,[64] these astronomical eras were measured in Saturnian years – with a sidereal revolution equal to 29.46 years – as follows: Abadiyan for 100 *zad* or 60^{12} years; Jayan for 1 *aspar* or one billion years; Shaʾiyan for 1 *shumar* or 10 million years, and Yasaʾiyan for 99 *salam* or 9,900,000 years.[65] This involved a revolutionary expansion of time, a temporal expansion that was seriously considered in Europe only with the 1830 publication of Charles Lyell's *Principles of Geology*.[66]

These *dasatiri* cosmic ages were followed by the eras of Gilshaʾyan, founded by Gilshah (the Earth-King) or Kayumars. As recounted in most Arabic and Persian classical and medieval historical texts, the Gilshaʾyan era was divided into the periods of Pishdadiyan, Kayaniyan, Ashkaniyan, and Sasaniyan. The sovereignty of Gilshaʾyan that began with Kayumars was brought to an end with the death of Yazdigird (d. 31/651 or 652). According to *dabistan*, this period was equal to 6024 years and five months.[67] It is significant to note that this number was calculated by adding the "Greek Christian" (Antiochian era) reckoning of 5,992 years from the "Creation of Adam" to the Hijrah of Muhammad, as cited by Tabari, to the 31 years from the Hijrah of Muhammad to the

Muslim conquest of Iran, with an additional 17 months to account for the fraction of years. This calculation was based the *dasatiri* assumption that Adam was the alias for Kayumars.

In a dialogic relation with Islamicate texts, Bahram ibn Farhad, the author of *Sharistan*, sought to "remove the mistakes and quibbling" (*rafʿ-i ishtibahat va iʿtirazat*)[68] that hindered the appreciation of ancient Iranian accomplishments: "People do not view favorably the history and the deeds of Persians (*Parsiyan*); and the annals of their accomplishments are buried under the obscurity of words; and men of affairs, utilizing the authority of pen, have fastened them with locks."[69] To unlock that past, he questioned the validity of hegemonic views concerning the genesis of humankind and the universality of the flood of Noah. He also challenged the excellence of Arabs over Persians and the eloquence of Arabic language in comparison with Persian.

Bahram ibn Farhad, like the author of *Dabistan*, contended that "on philosophical ground human existence has no temporal genesis."[70] His view of time corresponds with the Mazdean notion of "shore-less time" (*zurvan akanarak*)[71] and the writings of Ibn Sina (370–428/980–1037) and Suhrawardi (549–87/1153–91).[72] Bahram connected the emergence of human beings to a double process of "reproduction" (*tavallud*) and "generation" (*tavalud*). He argued that unlike *tavallud*, which is reproduction of the same species, *tavalud* leads to the generation or the birthing of a new species. According to Bahram ibn Farhad's proto-evolutionary scheme, "a series of ruptures" – beginning with the mixture of earth, water, and fire – caused the birth and growth of vegetation, animals, and humankind. This non-creationist explanation assumed that "Adam the father of humanity" (*Abu al-Bashar Adam*) had a "father" of his own and could have raised the religiously inspired question of "why was the father of Adam not named in the Qurʾan." Anticipating such a question, Bahram asserted that, like the case of Christ, this implied not the absence of a biological father but a father from whom Adam could have inherited and received an education. After establishing that "the world is eternal" (*giti qadim ast*) and that there is no "temporal genesis for mankind," he introduced Mahabad as the First Sage (*avval-i vakhshuran*).[73] The author of *Dabistan*, elaborating on Bahram's postulation, reported that Mahabad initiated human settlements, farming, industry, and the division of people into four distinct classes, a view at odds with orthodox Zoroastrianism.[74]

The imaginary view of Mahabad as the originator of urbanity and civility enabled Bahman ibn Farhad to resolve "the dispute of Arabs and Persians in regard to the precedency of Adam and Kayumars." He took as indisputable the claim that "none other than Kayumars was the father of Persians" (*pidar-i 'Ajam Kayumars ast la ghayr*). According to *Sharistan*, "a difficulty was posed by the Arabs' insistence that Noah's flood was universal and the claim that after the settling of the wind none of his contemporaries survived." He argued that "Persians [*ahl-i Furs*] repudiate this claim and assert that the flood did not occur in Persia [*zamin-i Furs*]." The historical continuity of Iran was cited as evidence for this claim. Anticipating a historically fashionable objection, he argued: "But if they say that this was anterior to Kayumars and their history began after him, we say their history dates from the time of his Majesty Abad the Great [Mahabad] hundreds of thousands of years earlier."[75] Bahram ibn Farhad established that no mention of a flood was made in that known period of history by citing the authority of Tabari who had reported that "Noah lived in the time of Bewarasb . . . who is called Zahhak"[76] and the general agreement that Zahhak had revolted at the time of Jamshid. He argued that the flood was limited to Babylon. Citing the Qur'anic verse, "We had sent forth Noah to his people,"[77] he averred that the flood was a punishment inflicted upon the people who had revolted against Noah. Having argued that the flood was a local rather than a universal phenomenon, he offered a metaphorical reading of the flood associated with the identity of King Jamshid and Solomon.

To appreciate the significance of this shift, it is important to recall the earlier traditions concerning the similarity of these two powerful kings of Persian and Judeo-Christian traditions. The attempts to subordinate ancient Persian historical traditions to the Qur'anic prophetography created a reciprocal movement for the identification of Judeo-Christian patriarchs as Persian kings. This mutual transferential effect also led to the intertextualization of the two narrative traditions and consequent similar biographical information concerning certain Persian kings and Qur'anic prophets. Citing a report by Ibn Muqaffa', Dinawari reports the Persian claim that King Solomon was the same person as King Jamshid: "Ignorant Persians, and such as have no science, suppose that King Jam[shid] was Solomon the son of David, but this is an error, for between Solomon and Jam was an interval of more than 3,000 years."[78] Writing about the reign of Jamshid, Mir Khwand also reported that, "Many of the Persians reckon him as a prophet; and also state, that he was the thirtieth in the order of mission." Recounting the report attributed to Ibn Muqaffa', Mir Khwand additionally notes: "Some ignorant Persians [*juhhal-i Furs*] suppose him to be the same as Sulimán; but this opinion is absurd in every respect, as between the age of Jemsheed and that of Sulimán (on whom be salvation!) more than two thousand years intervenes."[79] Mir Khwand discredits this claim by citing the authority of the Qur'an: "Jemsheed apostatized in the end of his reign; whereas the Almighty himself expressly declares, 'Truly Sulimán committed no infidelity'."[80] Comparing the portrayals of Jamshid and Solomon, he concluded, "all writers agree that the All-powerful Creator never permitted an enemy to prevail over Sulimán; whereas Zahák completely subdued Jemsheed."[81] This point is in accord with the portrayal of Jamshid in the *Avesta* and the *Shahnamah* of Firdawsi.[82] According to the *Avesta*, the illustrious reign of Jamshid came to an abrupt end with his claim of divinity.[83] Jamshid's "untruthful" utterances led to the Divine withdrawal of "Kiyani effulgence" (*farr-i kiyani*) and his consequent defeat by Zahhak.[84]

Bahram ibn Farhad challenged the validity of such reports, contending that Jamshid remained pious to the end of his life and that Zahhak had been sent by God as a punishment to the "rebellious people" who had broken the covenant with Jamshid.[85] In asserting the piety of Jamshid, he also established a Persian origin for the Arabs by arguing that Zahhak was a descendent of Siyamak, a son of Kayumars.[86] He rejected the oneness of Firaydun and Namrud – "that famous infidel king of the lands of the East and the West"[87] – as reported in *Rawzat al-Safa*,[88] and maintained that Noah was in fact the Persian king Faraydun who brought to an end the tyrannical rule of Zahhak.

By reconciling the accounts of Jamshid and Faraydun with Solomon and Noah, Bahram ibn Farhad provided the basis for a metaphorical interpretation of the flood: "It is apparent that Noah was sent to Zahhak. The flood of Noah, then, is a metaphor for the extremity of Zahhak's oppression including the punishment for the people who broke the covenant ['*ahd*] with Jamshid. The ship is the approval of Faraydun." He argued, by expanding the parallelism between Noah and Faraydun, that the three sons of Noah were no other than the three sons of Faraydun (Salm, Tur, and Iraj) who inherited the inhabited parts of the earth. In similar fashion Bahram ibn Farhad asserted that Seth was an alias for Siyamak, Idrish for Hushang, Lughman for Tahmuris, Soloman for Jamshid, and Noah for Faraydun, Abraham for Zoroaster, and Khizr and Alyas for Kaykhusraw.[89] These supposed similarities were based on earlier reports often dismissed as unreliable by Muslim historians.[90] By recontextualizing these reports and integrating them into a well-connected narrative on the excellence of Persian sage-kings, Bahram ibn Farhad successfully sought to reverse the Islamication of pre-Islamic Persian historical memory and to fashion a glorified Iran-centered past. This reversal was, however, as conjectural as the attempt of Muslim historians who refashioned the Persian historical accounts by placing them in the all-encompassing frame of Biblico-Qur'anic historical imagination. One sought to Islamicate ancient history and the other to Persicate Islamic prophetography. At different levels of intensity, this reciprocal relationship has been a permanent factor in (trans)forming Perso-Islamic culture.

Arab–Persian ethnic and linguistic rivalries were significant components of tensions embedded in the narrative structure of *Sharistan*. This latent tension surfaced in a discussion of the nobility of the Arabs and the eloquence of Arabic in comparison with Persians and their language. The Islamicate privileging of Arabs and Arabic was grounded in their rhetorical association with the Prophet and the Qur'an, the embodiments of the Islamic *Sunnah* and the *Shari'ah*. The subversion of such discursive associations was significant to the followers of Azar Kayvan. It was the subject of the following debate, which was reported in detail in *Sharistan*.

An Indian scholar inquired about Azar Kayvan's opinion of a statement on "the people of Persia" (*mardum-i Pars*) appearing in *Farhang-i Jahangiri* (1017/1608), an authoritative Persian dictionary compiled by Mir Jamal al-Din Husayn Inju Shirazi (d. *c*.1626), which states, "Beside Arabs, no people is as excellent as the people of Persia; and after Arabic no language is as eloquent and better than Persian."[91] This description was not satisfactory to the Pers-centric cohorts of Azar Kayvan who claimed that "According to the Persians and those residents of Iran [*sikanah-'i Iran*] who have remained on the same ancient path [*tariq-i qadim*], descendants of Persia [*abna-yi Pars*] are the noblest of created beings [*afzal-i makhluqat'and*]." As approvingly reported in *Sharistan*, Mubad Hush – a close companion of Azar Kayvan – argued that the divine appointment of Muhammad could not account for the nobility of Arabs over Persians. He contended that the Prophet Muhammad was "an intermediary between God and people and he had nothing to do with the Arabs." Contrasting Persians who were credited with the worldwide "dissemination of philosophy" (*intishar-i hikmat*) with the Arabs to whom the Prophet Muhammad was sent, Mubad Hush argued that prophets were sent to "the wretched" (*ashqiya*) and "the sinning nations" (*firqah-'i 'usat*) so that they could be led to the right path. Accusing the Arabs of extremism, including insatiable sexual desire, he concluded that Iranians "are more eloquent and intelligent than Arabs" (*az A'rab afsah va a'qal'and*).[92]

Mubad Hush, comparing the Arabic and Persian languages, further argued that the eloquence of the Qur'an, as a revealed text, was not attributable to the Arabic language. In an Arabophobic argument he asserted that the Qur'an was revealed in Arabic because, unlike other peoples, Arabs could not get accustomed to the use of foreign languages. To demonstrate the eloquence of Persian over Arabic he contended that "Arabic is excessive" (*'Arabi tavil ast*) whereas "Persian is minimal in letters and maximal in meanings" *(Parsi qalil al-lafz va kasir al-ma'ni'ast)*. He argued that there are many Arabic verses and reports concerning "the people of Persian descent and the excellence of their language." To support this claim he cited the Qur'anic verse 4: 59, "Obey God and obey the Apostle and those in authority among you,"[93] a verse frequently used by Muslim political theorists to assert the believers' obligation to support the ruling sovereigns.[94] Recoding this verse as a sign of Persian excellence, he proudly asserted that, "by consensus, the prevalence and the credibility of royalty [*saltanat*] and the persistence of government [*hukumat*] is accredited to Persian kings [*muluk-i 'Ajam*]." Bahram ibn Farhad concluded his report of the debate between the entourage of Azar Kayvan and Indian scholars by declaring, "it was proved by reason and tradition that with the exception of sages/philosophers [*navamis*], Persians [*Parsiyan*] are the most righteous of all people [*a'dal-i anva'*] and excel over all other nations [*jamahir-i aqvam*]."[95] Such assertions of ethnic and linguistic superiority in the early seventeenth century anticipated a nationalist discourse that became hegemonic three centuries later.

Dabistan-i Mazahib, supplementing the historical claims of *Sharistan*, elaborated the religious views of the followers of Azar Kayvan. Among the historiographically significant assertions in this text was the view that the Muslim shrines of Mecca, Jerusalem, Medina, Najaf, Karbala, and Mashhad were all built upon Mazdean fire temples. The names of Islamic cities according to this report were Arabized forms of originally Persian names: Mecca was *Mah-gah* (Moon-place), Medina was *Mah-Dinah* (Moon of the Religion), Najaf a variation of *Na-akfat* (no-injury), Karbala an alteration of *Kar-i Bala* (sublime agency). It was further asserted that Buddhist holy places such as Gaya and Mathura were both alterations of Persian names *Gah-i Kayvan* (Abode of Saturn) and *Mihtara* (Resort of the eminent).[96] Retelling the views of the disciples of Azar Kayvan (*Abadiyan*) concerning the relation of Mazdean fire-places to Muslim, Christian, and Buddhist shrines, Kaykhusraw Isfandyar wrote: "When the Abadiyan come to such places, they visit them with the accustomed reverence, as, according to them, holy places are never liable to abomination or pollution, as they still remain places of worship and adoration: both friends and foes regarding them as a *Qibla*, and sinners, notwithstanding all their perverseness, pray in those sacred edifices."[97] This view gained currency among the Persianate literati. For instance Azar Bigdili (fl. 1134–95/1721–81) opened his famous biographical anthology of approximately 850 poets, *Atashkadah-'i Azar*, with the following verse, "I saw a child-prodigy circumventing the Shrine and uttering, 'Such a nice plac must have been a fire-place.'" The speculations concerning the hidden Persian meanings of non-Persian words also gave rise to an etymological mania that gained momentum in the nineteenth century, best exemplified by the effort of Mirza Aqa Khan Kirmani.[98]

Another text which contributed to the emergence of a new historiographical consciousness was *A'in-i Hushang*, compiled and edited by Darvish Fani Manekji Limji Hatara, an Indian–Persian who had traveled to Iran in the nineteenth century.[99] This collection was originally published in the 1830s and reprinted in 1879, and includes four books: *Khishtab*,[100] *Zar-i Dastafshar*,[101] *Zayandah Rud*,[102] and *Zawrah-'i Bastani*.[103] It was claimed that these books were written during the reign of Khusraw Parviz (590–628 CE) and translated into Persian by disciples of Azar Kayvan. These texts were used by the authors of *Dabistan* and *Sharistan*.

A historiographically significant aspect of this collection is Fani's introduction and postscript. Clearly influenced by the germinal texts of *Dasatir*, *Dabistan*, and *Sharistan*, Fani used a particular rhetoric which became the pervasive trope of historical discourse in the nineteenth century. He depicted the Muslim conquest of Iran as the "winter of Arab oppression and repression" (*zimistan-i zulm va sitam-i A'rab*) and the Qajar dynasty as the beginning of a new season of justice and fairness (*maratib-i 'adl va insaf va payah-'i ma'dilat va makrimat*). As an Indian Parsi, Fani argued that, like birds who leave their home with the arrival of winter, the winter of Arab oppression and tyranny in Iran resulted in the dispersion of Iranians from their homeland (*vatan*). With the beginning of a new season of Qajar rule, Iranian expatriates, like birds, begun to return to their ancestral home.[104] Like Fani, most nineteenth-century Iranian historians viewed the pre-Islamic era as a glorious ancient period that came to a tragic end with the Arab–Muslim conquest.

The nationalist "emplotment" of Iran's ancient history as a tragedy was based on the comprehension of the Muslim conquest as a force engendering "the reverse progress of Iran" (*taraqqi-i ma'kus-i Iran*).[105] Linking the end of the "enlightened" pre-Islamic times to origins identified with Iran through Mahabad or Kayumars, a new memory, identity, and political reality was fashioned. By inducing the desire and the will to recover "lost glories" of the past, the nationalist struggle for a new social order became intrinsically connected to the politics of cultural memory and its de-Arabizing projects of history and language. Juxtaposing Iran and Islam, these projects prompted the emergence of a schizochronic view of history and the formation of schizophrenic social subjects who were conscious of their belonging to two diverse and often antagonistic times and cultural heritages.[106] During Iran's Constitutional Revolution of 1905–9, these autonomous "Iranian" identities prefigured into the line-up of political forces to antagonistic "Constitutionalist" (*Mashru-tahkhwah*) and "Shari'atist" (*Mashru'ahkhwah*) camps. The shift in the 1970s from a regime glorifying Iran's ancient civilization to a revolution-ary regime extolling Islamic heritage is only the most recent example of the creative possibilities and insoluble dilemmas engendered by the contested memories of pre-Islamic Iran.

6
Crafting National Identity

Envisaging history

The formation of a modern Iranian national identity was linked intimately to the configuration of its national history and restyling of the Persian language. Informed by *dasatiri* texts and inspired by the *Shahnamah* of Firdawsi, modern historical writings harnessed the Iranian homeland (*vatan*) to an immemorial past beginning with Mahabad and Kayumars and pointing toward a future unison with Europe. Iran's pre-Islamic past was celebrated as a glorious and industrious age, and its integration into the Arab–Islamic world was shunned as a cause of its "reverse progress" (*tarraqi-i ma'kus*). To catch up with the "civilized world," the architects of Iranian nationalism sought to "reawaken" the nation to self-consciousness by reactivating and inventing memories of the country's pre-Islamic past. The simplification and purification of Persian were corollaries of this project of national reawakening. Like the glorification of the pre-Islamic past, these language-based movements helped to dissociate Iran from Islam and to craft a distinct national identity and sodality.

In an increasing number of eighteenth- and nineteenth-century Persian historical texts, "Iran" was constituted as the shifter and organizer of chains of narration and emplotment. For instance, *Rustam al-Tawarikh*, completed in 1800, referred to Karim Khan Zand (d. 1779) as "the architect of the ruined Iran" (*mi'mar-i Iran-i viran*) and "the kind father of all residents of Iran" (*pidar-i mihraban-i hamah-'i ahl-i Iran*). Among other compound constructions with Iran that were politically significant, Rustam al-Hukama, the author of this text, used *Iranmadar* (Iran-protector), *dawlat-i Iran* (government of Iran), *farmanrava'i-i Iran* (governing of Iran), *ahl-i Iran* (the people/residents of Iran), and territorial couplets such as *kishvar-i Iran*, *mamalik-i Iran*, *qalamraw-i Iran*, and *bilad-i Iran*.[1] Muhammad Hasan Khan I'timad al-Saltanah, like many other nineteenth-century historians, set himself the task of writing a geographical and historical "biography of Iran" (*sharh hal-i Iran*).[2] The narratological centrality of the entity "Iran" signified the emergence of a new conception of historical time that differed from the prevalent cyclical arrangement found in chronicles. While Iran had been previously conceived of as the center of the universe in the premodern Persian geographic imagination,[3] pre-nineteenth-century chronicles rarely temporized Iran. Rather, they were primarily concerned with chronicling the cycles of the rise and fall of dynasties. Making Iran the "ultimate referent" for the sequence of historical events allowed for the emergence of new modes of historical emplotment. Ancient history, which was for so long equated with the sacred history and the cycles of messengers and prophets from the time of Adam to the rise of Muhammad, was reenvisaged. The cyclical time of messengers and prophets gave way to an *Iran-time* connecting the "glorious pre-Islamic past" to a reawakened present and a rejuvenating future. These newer histories challenged the universality of biblical/Qur'anic stories. The new historians granted that Adam might have been the father of the Arabs, but he was not the father of humanity.

In the emerging Iran-time, the mythical tempos of *Dasatsir*, *Dabistan-i Mazahib*, *Sharistan*, and *Shahnamah* increasingly *displaced* the sacred time of Islam. Reading and (re)citing these Iran-glorifying texts in a period of societal dislocation, military defeats, and foreign infiltration during the nineteenth century allowed for the rearticulation of Iranian identity and the construction of alternative forms of historical narrations and periodizations. The authorization and popular (re)citation of these narratives resulted in a process of cultural *transference* that intensified the desire for a recovery of the "forgotten history" of ancient Iran. This awakening of interest in the country's pre-Islamic history provided a formative element in the discourse of constitutionalism. The Islamic master-narrative dividing history into civilized Islamic and uncivilized pre-Islamic periods was increasingly displaced with the meta-narratives and periodizations of *Dasatir* and *Shahnamah*. The eras of Adam, Noah, Moses, and Jesus were substituted with those of Kayumars, Hushang, Tahmuris, and Jamshid.

The dissemination of *dasatiri* texts heightened the interest in the *Shahnamah*, which was published in more than 20 editions in Iran and India in the nineteenth century.[4] The *Shahnamah* provided valuable semantic and symbolic resources for dissociating Iran from Islam and for fashioning an alternative basis of identity. Its accessibility contributed to its increased recitation in the coffeehouses, important sites for cultural and political production and dissemination. In fact, recitation of the *Shahnamah* in the coffeehouses increasingly displaced the narration of popular religious epics such as *Husayn-i Kurd-i Shabistari, Iskandar Namah, Rumuz-i Hamzah,* and *Khavar Namah*.[5] A number of nineteenth-century poets such as Sayyid Abu al-Hasan Harif Jandaqi (d. 1814), Hamdam Shirazi, and Mirza Ibrahim Manzur were, among others, well-known reciters of the *Shahnamah*.[6] The Qajar Aqa Muhammad Khan, Fath 'Ali Shah, Nasir al-Din Shah, and Muzaffar al-Din Shah were known to have had their own reciters or *Shahnamah'khwanan*.[7] Hearing that John Malcolm's *History of Persia* was read to Nasir-Din Shah at bedtime, Mirza Taqi Khan Amir Kabir (d. 1852) is reported to have suggested that the Shah should have the *Shahnamah* recited instead to him: "Why don't you read the *Shahnamah*. . . . You should know that for all Iranians, for the highest to the lowest, the *Shahnamah* is the best of all books."[8] The importance of the *Shahnamah*, and thus pre-Islamic Iran, in nineteenth-century Iran is also evident from the increased use of the names of its heroes and characters. For example, many Qajar princes were given names such as Kayumars, Jamshid, Farhad, Firaydun, Nushafarin, Isfand-yar, Ardashir, Bahman, Kaykavus, and Khusraw. This emerging popularity of ancient Iranian names signaled an important aesthetic shift in the constitution of both personal and national identities.

Mimicry of the *Shahnamah*, popular among eighteenth- and nineteenth-century poets, became an important means for literary and cultural creativity. Known as the Second Firdawsi (Firdawsi-i Sani), Muhammad 'Ali Tusi's *Shahanshah Namah-i Nadiri* began in 1721 with an account of the desolation of the provinces and the rise of revolts attributed to the "negligence of the King of Iran-land" (*ihmal-i sultan-i Iran zamin*). This, in his view, provided suitable conditions for the rise of Nadir Shah Afshar (r. 1736–47). The text ended by drawing a parallel between the fate of Jamshid and Zahhak in the *Shahnamah* and that of Nadir Shah who had become intoxicated with power. "Forgetting the truth like Jamshid" and "slaughtering the people like Zahhak," Nadir was beheaded by his own guards.[9] Likewise in "the Pahlavi author's style" (*bia'in-i guyandah-'i Pahlavi*), Fath 'Ali Khan Saba (d. 1822) described the Irano-Russian war of the 1810s in his *Shahanshahnamah*.[10] Among other poets imitating Firdawsi were Visal Shirazi (d. 1845) and his son, Muhammad Davari (d. 1866). Davari was an able calligrapher, transcribing one of the most beautiful copies of the *Shahnamah*.[11] In a versified introduction to his transcribed edition, Davari praised Firdawsi for glorifying the name of Iran and for revitalizing ancient history.[12] He wrote a versified history of Iran from the Mongol to the Safavid period, but owing to his early death it was never finished.[13] These imitations of Firdawsi reactivated and disseminated memories of pre-Islamic Iran and thus contributed to the recirculation of a large number of obsolete Persian oncepts and allusions.[14]

Veneration of Firdawsi was not limited to "traditionalist" poets. Nineteenth-century intellectuals such as Fath 'Ali Akhundzadah (1812–78), Mirza Aqa Khan Kirmani (1855–98), and Mirza Malkum Khan (d. 1908), who were critical of Iran's poetic tradition, respected Firdawsi's oeuvre. Mirza Aqa Khan Kirmani viewed the *Shahnamah* as a foundation for preserving the "people/nation of Iran" (*millat-i Iran*):

> If it were not for the *Shahnamah* of Firdawsi, the language and the race of the Iranian nation/people [*lughat va jinsiyat-i millat-i Iran*] would have been at once transformed into Arabic after the domination by the Arab tribes in Iran. Like the peoples of Syria, Egypt, Morocco, Tunisia, and Algeria, the Persian speakers would have changed their race and nationality [*milliyat va jinsiyat*].[15]

Imitating Firdawsi, Kirmani wrote a versified history entitled *Namah-'i Bastan* (The Book of Ancients).[16] In the introduction, he accused the classical poets of disseminating falsehoods, idleness, and moral corruption in the persons of kings and *vazirs*. Yet Kirmani praised Firdawsi for "inspiring in the hearts of Iranians patriotism, love of their race [*hubb-i milliyat va jinsiyat*], energy and courage; while here and there he also endeavored to reform their characters."[17] Akhundzadah, who was also critical of Persian poetic tradition, viewed Firdawsi as one of the best Muslim poets. Comparing Firdawsi to Homer and Shakespeare, he asserted, "It can be truthfully stated that amongst the Muslim people [*millat-i Islam*] only the work of Firdawsi can be considered poetry."[18] In his *Majma' al-Fusaha*, Riza Quli Khan Hidayat (1800–71) characterized *Shahnamah* as the "grand work" (*namah-'i 'azim*) of Persian poetry, comparable only to *Masnavi* of Mawlavi.[19] The nineteenth-century authorization and popular (re)citation of the epic *Shahnamah* resulted in a process of cultural transference that intensified the desire for the recovery of the "forgotten history" of ancient Iran. By transference, I have in mind the dialogic relation of cultural interlocutors and historical texts, that is, the *Shahnamah*-narrators and the *Shahnamah*, whereby the language and the themes of the *Shahnamah* reappear in the works of the interlocutor.[20] Identification with the ancient world of *Shahnamah* became a formative element of modern national identity.

Several historians contributed to the reactivation of Iran's ancient history and to the configuration of a glorious past. Mahmud Mirza Qajar's (b. 1799?) *Tazkirah at-Salatin* began with Kayumars and concluded with the reign of Fath'ali Shah.[21] *Khulasat al-Tawarikh*, another condensed general history of Iran from Kayumars to Fath'ali Shah, ended with the events of year 1798.[22] I'tizad al-Saltanah's *Iksir al-Tawarikh* of 1842 likewise began with Kayumars and ended with the reign of Muhammad Shah (1834–48), the ruler who had commissioned the work.[23] Muhammad Shah's interest in pre-Islamic history is evident from his support of Henry Rawlinson's research on Bistun, which was translated for him into Persian, with an introduction by Mirza Muhammad Taqi Lisan al-Mulk (1801–79).[24] Mirza Aqa Khan Kirmani's *Namah-'i Bastan*, clearly indebted to *Dasatir* and *Dabistan Mazahib*, also began with Kayumars and ended with his contemporary Nasir al-Din Shah. In his *Ayinah-'i Sikandari*, Kirmani synthesized Persian historical texts with Orientalist works on pre-Islamic Iran. *Ayinah-'i Sikandari* was hailed as "the geneology of this noble nation/people" (*shajarah namah-'i in millat-i najib*).[25]

Authors of these general histories viewed their efforts as attempts to overcome a debilitating historical amnesia. According to 'Itimad al-Saltanah, "for a civilized people and a great nation … no imaginable flaw is more severe than ignorance of the history of their country and a total forgetting of events of the former times."[26] In his tireless effort to recover the memory of Ashkanid history, I'timad al-Saltanah synthesized Orientalist works with classical Persian and Arabic mythistories.[27] His "discovery" that the Qajars were descendants of the Ashkanids was highly praised by Nasir al-Din Shah.[28] Jalal al-Din Mirza's *Namah-'i Khusravan*, a children's history book, was popular for its illustrations and for its use of "pure Persian" prose. Akhundzadah praised Jalal al-Din Mirza for his use of pure Persian language by saying, "Your excellency has freed our tongue from the domination of the Arabic language."[29] Jalal al-Din Mirza's illustrations invented a visual memory of the past and thus were further used for plaster-molding and interior decoration in Qajar houses and palaces.[30] Furughi, in his *Tarikh-i Salatin-i Sasani*, regretted that while "all over Europe, that is in London and Paris, people know the history of our land [*tarikh-i mamlikat-i ma*], but children of my own homeland are entirely ignorant of it." He celebrated the completion of his work by declaring, "I can now say that Iran has a Sasanid history."[31]

Historical research and the ensuing reconstruction of the pre-Islamic past helped to craft a distinctly nationalist memory and identity. With the rise of Iranian nationalism, pre-Islamic names lost their predominantly

Zoroastrian connotations and were adopted as proper names by Muslim Iranians. Likewise, Zoroastrian mythologies were cast as quintessentially Iranian. By anthropomorphizing the Iranian homeland (*vatan*), these mythologies were constitued as the nation's "spirit and character."

Emplotted in a tragic mode, these ancient histories of Iran signaled the will to recover lost national glories and to dissociate the Iranian Self from the "alien" Muslim-Arabs who had dominated Iran. Pre-Islamic myths and symbols were used by nationalists to fashion a new Iran and to reidentify the *millat*. The nationalist thinker Akhundzadah, for example, objected to using a picture of a mosque as the logo for the newspaper *Millat-i Saniyah-'i Iran*.[32] In a letter to the editor he argued that, "if by *millat-i Iran* you mean the specific connotation prevalent today, the mosque, which is a general symbol for all Muslims, is not an appropriate logo."[33] He suggested that the newspaper should use a combination of a pre-Islamic symbol, like an icon of Persepolis, and a picture of a Safavid building, in order to capture the spirit of the *millat-i Iran* (the people/nation of Iran).[34] Kavah the Blacksmith (Kavah-'i Ahangar), another character from the *Shahnamah* of Firdawsi, provided an inspiring icon. Furughi argued that Kavah's famous banner should be seen as the national flag of Iran.[35] Mirza Aqa Khan Kirmani portrayed Kavah as a revolutionary vanguard:

> Because of the courage and nationalist endeavors [*ghayrat va himmat-i milli*] of Kavah-'i Ahangar, who uprooted from Iran the rule of the Chaldean Dynasty, which had lasted for 900 years, Iranians can truthfully be proud that they taught the nations of the world how to remove oppression and repel the repression of despotic Kings.

Through a process of narrative recoding, Kavah, the restorer of monarchy to Faraydun, was refashioned as a revolutionary nationalist. Similarly, Faraydun, a pre-Islamic king, was depicted as a modernizing monarch who transformed the "indolent, fainéant, and world-resigning" Iranians into a people interested in "construction, cultivation, development, the pursuit of happiness and the reform of material life."[36] Anticipating the formation of a constitutional form of government in Iran, another pre-Islamic king, Anushirvan "Dadgar" (the Just), was depicted as a constitutional monarch.[37] In a critique of contemporary cultural practices, it was argued that veiling of women and polygamy were not aspects of the pre-Islamic past.[38] These "historical facts" were used rhetorically in a nationalist political discourse that projected Iran's "decadence" onto Arabs and Islam.

The protagonists of Iranian nationalism masterfully used history as a rhetorical resource. They inverted the Islamic system of historical narration, in which the rise of Muhammad constituted the beginning of a new civilization and which defined the pre-Islamic period as the age of infidelity and ignorance. Like Mirza Aqa Khan Kirmani, the forerunners of constitutionalism construed the pre-Islamic period as an "enlightened age" (*'asr-i munavvar*). They explained that the desperate conditions of their time were the result of the Muslim conquest of Iran.[39] Mirza Fath 'Ali Akhundzadah boldly asserted that "the Arabs were the cause of the Iranian people's misfortune."[40] In opposition to the "weak" and "despotic" state, which claimed to be the protector of Islam and the *Shari'a*, the protagonists of the "new age" (*'asr-i jadid*) looked back to the pre-Islamic era with great nostalgia. They borrowed pre-Islamic myths and images to articulate a new social imaginary and historical identity. In the emerging nationalist discourse Islam was defined as the religion of Arabs and as the cause of Iran's weakness and decadence.[41] Looking back to the idealized pre-Islamic Iran, Akhundzadah, addressing "Iran," stated:

> What a shame for you, Iran: Where is your grandeur? Where is that power, that prosperity that you once enjoyed? It has been 1,280 years now that the naked and starving Arabs have descended upon you and made your life miserable. Your land is in ruins, your people ignorant and innocent of civilization, deprived of prosperity and freedom, and your King is a despot.[42]

The same Arabophobic ideas, in remarkably similar language, were echoed in Kirmani's rhetorical masterpiece, *Sah Maktub*.[43] In such "novelized" and "dramatized" accounts of historical processes, the pre-Islamic era was viewed as a lost Utopia that possessed just rulers. By contrast, the Islamic period was projected as a time of misery, ruin, ignorance, and despotism. Mirza Aqa Khan Kirmani called the fall from this imaginary grace the "reverse progress of Iran" (*tarraqi-i ma'kus-i Iran*).[44] The rhetorical use of history, according to him, was "necessary for the uprooting of the malicious tree of oppression and for the revitalization of the power of *milliyat* [nationalism] in the character of the Iranian people."[45]

In a double process of projection and introjection Iranian nationalists attributed their undesirable customs and conditions to Arabs and Islam. Obversely, desirable European manners and cultures were appropriated and depicted as originally Iranian. In fact, contrary to the

"Westernization" thesis, identification with European culture provided an important component for the long process of historical dissociation from the Arab–Islamic culture that occured in the nineteenth century. In these endeavors fake etymology and assumed resemblance facilitated cultural appropriation of modern European institutions. Mirza Aqa Khan Kirmani, viewing history as the "firm foundation of the *millat*," speculated that the French term "histoire" was actually derived from the Persian word "*ustuvar*," meaning firm and sturdy.[46] After enumerating a number of Persian words with similar roots in French (i.e., pidar = père, dandan = dent, zanu = genou), he argued that the French and Iranians were "two nations born from the same father and mother." The French who moved to the West progressed and prospered, Iranians, by contrast, were raided by the Arabs in the East and as a result lost their reason, knowledge, and ethics and forgot their etiquette, norms of life, and means of progress, prosperity, happiness, and comfort.[47] Likewise Muhammad Shah (r. 1834–48), in a public proclamation calling for the adaptation for European-style military uniforms, had argued that these uniforms were really copies of ancient Iranian uniforms. He supported these claims by pointing to the similarities between the new uniforms and the uniforms of the soldiers engraved on the walls of Persepolis.[48] In a similar manner, I'tizad al-Saltanah attributed the "new order" (*nizam-i jadid*) of military reorganization to the pre-Islamic Iranians. Forgetting their military organization, he argued, Iranians were weakened and defeated by the Arabs whereas Europeans who imitated Iranians were empowered.[49] In another example, Mirza 'Abd al-Latif Shushtari (d. 1805) claimed the discovery of a Persian origin for the European custom of dining at a table. He argued that the term *mizban* (host) was etymologically connected to the word *miz* (table). Accordingly, the compound *miz-ban* [understood as table + keeper] constituted a trace of a forgotten Persian custom adopted by Europeans.[50] Similarly, Kirmani attributed the progress of Europe to the ideas of "liberty and equality" (*azadi va musavat*), which in his view had been introduced in Iran by the pre-Islamic reformer Mazdak.[51] In I'timad al-Saltanah's *Durrar al-Tijan*, modern political concepts such as *mashviratkhanah* and *majlis-i shura* (parliament), *jumhuri* (republic), and *mashrutah* (constitutional) were used to describe the pre-Islamic Ashkanid dynasty. I'timad al-Saltanah asserted that this dynasty "like the contemporary British monarchy was constitutional and not despotic."[52] Jamal al-Din Afghani, at the end of his brief outline of Iranian history from the time of Kayumars to Nasir al-Din Shah, similarly believed that most European industrial innovations, such as the telescope, camera, and telephone, had actually been invented by Iranians of earlier times.[53] Similar claims were promoted by Kirmani, who viewed Iranians as the inventors of devices as varied as the telegraph, postal service, and ships.[54] In this historical mode of self-refashioning, the architects of Iranian modernity crafted a past that mirrored, and even surpassed, that of nineteenth-century Europe.

Restyling Persian

The invention of a glorious past was contemporaneous with a through restylization of the Persian language. Restyling the Persian language, a process which continues today, was achieved in a dialogic relationship with Iran's Arab- and European-Other, but also with its often-ignored Indian-Other. The relationship with the Persian-speaking Indian-Other facilitated the renaissance and canonization of classical Persian literature. Fear of European colonization, experienced particularly in India where Persian served as an official language until the 1830s, led to a desire for neologism, lexicography, and the writing of grammar texts. The Arab-Other, on the other hand, provided Iranian nationalists with a scapegoat for the purging of the "sweet Persian language" (*zaban-i shirin-i Parsi*) from the influence of "the difficult language of the Arabs" (*zaban-i dushvar-i 'Arab*). Through these types of responses, the Persian language was instituted as essential to the formation of Iranian national identity. Kirmani's observation that "language is history," and that "the strength of each nation and people depends on the strength of their language," became accepted nationalist wisdom.[55] This development in Iran paralleled other nationalist movements worldwide.[56]

The rise of a Persian print culture in the late eighteenth century strengthened a literary style which resulted from a dispute among Persian poets of Iran and India. During the seventeenth and eighteenth centuries, India had been an important center for the development of Persian art, culture, and literature and was the site of the emergence of the "New Style" (*Tarz-i Naw*) poetry, known as the "Indian School" (*Sabk-i Hindi*).[57] The poets of the Indian School broke away from the conventional paradigms of the classical Persian poets in order to fashion a distinct style and language.[58] They created new conventions and systems of signification by altering poetic tropes and by coining new compound words. The liberty taken by Indian poets in constructing and shifting the meaning of terms and concepts came to be viewed by the Iranian literati as a sign of their basic unfamiliarity and incompetence in the Persian language.[59] This issue of linguistic competence served as the foundation for intense debates and disputes between

Iranian and Indian poets. Siraj ʿAli Khan Arzu (1689–1756), a leading Indian lexicographer and linguist, outlined in his famous essay *Dad-i Sukhan* one of these controversies that related to the problems of rhetoric, poetic creativity, and language identity. Reflecting on whether an Indian poet's resignification of idioms should be regarded as an error, Arzu took a pragmatic stance. He declared: "the Persian poets belonging to countries other than Iran, who are experts in language and rhetoric and have a long experience in poetic exercises, are qualified to amend or modify the meaning of words and idioms and use indigenous idioms in cases of poetic contingency." Such sentiments had been previously expressed by the poet Munir Lahuri (d. 1644) in his *Karnamah-i munir*. Munir criticized contemporary poets who claimed mastery of the Persian language because of their birth in Iran. Likewise the seventeenth-century poet Shayda Fatihpuri (d. 1632) criticized Iranians who dismissed him because of his Indian lineage.[60]

In an objection to *Tarz-i Naw* poets, Mir Sayyid ʿAli Mushtaq (1689–1757) and his disciples[61] – Lutf ʿAli Bayg Azar Baygdili (1721–80), Hatif Isfahani (d. 1784), Sabahi Bigdili (d. 1792) – negated the innovations of the Indian School, formulating a program explicitly aimed at returning to the images and language of classical poets.[62] Mushtaq believed that "poets must follow Saʿdi in *qazal*, Anvari in *qasidah*, Firdawsi and Nizami in *bazm*, Ibn Yamin in *qitʿah*, and Khayyam in *rubaʿi*; otherwise they drive on the path to falsity."[63] This authorization of classical poets, later labeled as *Bazgasht-i Adabi* (literary return), was an early expression of literary nationalism in Iran and has had a continuous influence on the modernist historiography of Persian literature. Even though in some instances it led to "mindless imitation" and to the rise of "Don Quixotes of Iran's poetic history"[64] or what Mahdi Akhavan Salis called "false Saʿdis, false Sanaʾis, [and] false Manuchihris," this literary return was a creative reauthorization of classical texts.[65] By authorizing classical poets and by recirculating their word choices, the literary return contributed to canon formation and a nineteenth-century literary renaissance.[66]

Notwithstanding the animosity of Iranian poets toward the Persianate poets of India, the development of Persian print culture in India did provide textual resources for a later poetic renaissance in Iran. As with the rise of Persian printing in India, a large number of classical texts became easily accessible for the first time. Printing made possible the formation of authoritative canons and facilitated the dissemination of seminal texts at an affordable price. Cultural and religious movements peripheral to the Shiʿi networks of knowledge and power gained new means of propagation and dissemination. Printed copies of *Dasatir*

(1818 and 1888), *Dabistan-i Mazahib* (1809, 1818, 1860), *Farhang-i Jahangiri*, and *Burhan-i Qati'* (1818, 1858),[67] for example, were widely disseminated in Iran and contributed to the vernacularization of the Persian language. These texts popularized a large number of supposedly obsolete Persian words reactivated by Azar Kayvan and his disciples. *Farhang-i Jahangiri* of Inju Shirzai (d. *c*.1626) included a chapter devoted to ancient Persian terms known as *zand va pazand or huzvarish*.[68] *Burhan Qati'* of Khalaf Tabriz embraced neologisms of Azar Kayvan and his disciples. These words quickly found their way into the works of Iranian poets such as Fath'ali Khan Saba (d. 1238/1822), Yaghma Jandagi (d. 1271/1859), Qa'ani (d. 1271/1854), Furughi Bistami (d. 1274/1857), Surush Isfahani (d. 1285/1868), Fursat Shirazi (1854–1920), and Fath Allah Shaybani (d. 1308/1890). Both Saba and Yaghma Jandaqi owned personal copies of *Burhan Qati'*.[69] Yaghma in many of his correspondences used unfamiliar and newly constructed Persian concepts instead of the popularly used Arabic equivalents.[70] He called this "recently appeared new style" (*tazah ravish-i naw didar*) pure Persian (*farsi-yi basit* or *parsinigari*)[71] and encouraged his disciples to practice *parsinigari*. In a letter Yaghma Jandaqi remarked that *parsinigari* was prevalent among many writers in Iran who were "highly determined in their endeavor and have written valuable materials."[72] The practitioners of *parsinigari* used terms such *amigh*, *akhshayj*, *farsandaj*, and *timsar*, which were recirculated by the followers of Azar Kayvan in *dasatiri* texts. Persian scholars and lexicographers Purdavud and 'Ali Akbar Dihkhuda have drawn attention to the inauthenticity of *dasatiri* terms. But the proliferation of these words, despite their "suspected" origin, signified a passion for semantic diversification and neologism in the nineteenth-century "invention of tradition."

An important context for the proliferation of neologism during the nineteenth century was the British policy of replacing Persian as the official language in India. Among the charges leveled against the Eastern languages, including Persian, was that they "greatly darken the mind and vitiate the heart" and are not an "adequate medium for communicating a knowledge of the higher departments of literature, science, and theology"[73] Such anti-Persian views justified the British government's abolition of Persian as the official language of India in 1834. At the same time this intensified the need for lexicography and neologism as anti-colonial defense mechanisms.[74] Abolition of Persian as the official language in India was noted in Iran. Persian dictionaries published in India provided the basic model and lexical resources for compilation of dictionaries such as *Farhang-i Anjuman Ara-yi Nasiri* (1871), *Farhang-i*

Nazim al-Atibba' (1900), and *Lughatnamah-'i Dihkhuda* (1958–66). Iranian neologists such as Isma'il Tuysirkani, Mirza Aqa Khan Kirmani, and Ahmad Kasravi used many of the terms and concepts objected to in the lexicographical controversies in India surrounding *Burhan Qati'*.[75]

With the nineteenth-century governmentalization of everyday life and the formation of the public sphere, Iranian bureaucrats recognized that a style of writing full of allusions and ambiguities was inappropriate for communication and popular politics. Bureaucrats and court historians, continuing a trend set by Indian Persophones, began to take pride in simple and comprehensible writing. Simple language meant de-Arabization and vernacularization of the Persian language. Among the leading practitioners of "simple prose" (*nasr-i sadah* or *sadah nivisi*) were 'Abd al-Razzaq Dunbuli (1753–1826), Qa'im Maqam Farahani (1779–1835 or 1836), Muhammad Ibrahim Madayihnigar (d. 1325/1907), Muhammad Khan Sinki Majd al-Mulk (1809–79), Hasan 'Ali Khan Amir Nizam Garusi (1820–99), Nadir Mirza Qajar (1826–85), and Amin al-Dawlah (1844–1904 or 5). With the expansion of the public sphere, these writers sought to close the gap between the written language of the elite and the spoken language of the masses by moving away from "sheer display of rhetorical cleverness and skill"[76] and adopting a style directed toward communication with the people (*mardum*).[77] This was the stated goal of official journals and news papers, *Kaqaz-i Akhbar*, *Vaqay'-i Ittifaqiyah*, *Iran*, *Ruznamah-'i Dawlat-i 'Illiyah-'i Iran*, and *Ruznamah-'i Millati*.

The need to communicate with the public was evident from two significant publicity pronouncements issued by Muhammad Shah in 1839. The first, as explained earlier, pertained to the adaptation of modern military uniforms. This announcement called for the standardization of uniforms with the intended function of promoting the "homogenization of all people" (*hamah mardum bih surat-i tawhid shavand*). The royal publicity explained that the new uniform, modeled after pre-Islamic attire, was lighter, easier to remove, and cheaper to produce. Signifying the formation of a national economy, it remarked that the fabric for these uniforms should no longer be imported from India but made of indigenous materials in Kirman and Shiraz. This printed publicity was disseminated in all the provinces and barracks (*buldan va amsar-i Iran*).[78] In the second public statement, the Shah explained why he had to retreat from his military campaign in Herat. Pressured by the British to withdraw from Herat, Muhammad Shah reassured "the people of Iran" (*mardum-i Iran*) that his retreat was not due to war fatigue or change of mind. He assured the soldiers, cavaliers, and tankers that he preferred an "honorable and virtuous/manly death" (*murdan-i ba ghayrat va mardanigi*) to a luxurious palace life. Here the Shah hailed the soldiers as his "brave religious brothers" (*hamana shuma baradaran-i dini va ghayur-i man hastid*).[79] The need to shape and to contain public opinion meant that these pronouncements had to be written in a simple and easily communicable language.

Along with the bureaucratic "simple prose" movement that addressed an enlarged critical reading public, there was a nascent nationalist attempt to purify the Persian language of Arabic words and concepts. The purist movement in language, contrary to the prevalent historical perception, predated the Riza Shah period (1925–41).[80] Amongst the nineteenth-century practitioners of "pure Persian" were: Mirza Razi Tabrizi, Farhad Mirza, Ahmad Divan Baygi Shirazi, Jalal al-Din Mirza, Isma'il Khan Tusirkani, Gawhar Yazdi, Riza Bagishlu Ghazvini, Manakji Limji Hataria, Aqa Khan Kirmani, Abu al-Fazl Gulpaygani,[81] Baha'u'llah,[82] and Kaykhusraw Shahrukh Kirmani.[83] In addition, the Qajar statesman Mirza 'Ali Amin al-Dawlah demonstrated an ability to write in "pure Persian" prose in the introduction to his memoirs, but refrained from doing so in the body of the text, arguing that "children of Iranian descent" (*kudakan-i Irani nizhad*) would understand him better in the contemporary language that is mixed with Arabic (*zaban-i imruzi-i Iran kah amikhtah bah navadir-i Tazi ast*).[84] Directly or indirectly these authors were informed by *Dasatir*'s examplary prose. While Persian purism found a nationalist expression in Iran, as a literary movement it was not limited to Iranian writers. Indeed the Indian poet Asadallah Ghalib (1797–1896) was an unquestionable nineteenth-century master of Persian purism.[85]

The movement for the simplification and purification of the Persian language coincided with the movement for the simplification of Ottoman Turkish. Both were intimately tied to the struggle for constitutionalism. The language reform was not an after-effect of the constitutional revolutions in Iran and the Ottoman Empire but a prelude to them. Purists viewed language as essential to national identity. As Mirza Aqa Khan Kirmani argued, "*Millat* means a people [*ummat*] speaking in one language. The Arab *millat* means Arabophones, Turkish *millat* means Turkophones, and Persian *millat* means Persophones."[86] The purist movement in Iran, by recirculating and resignifying archaic concept, provided the semantic field for the dissociation of Iran from Islam and formation of a nationalist system of signification and political imagination.

Consciousness of language did not stop with the attempt to purify the Persian language and substitute Arabic terms with their Persian equivalents. There were also attempts to study and to reform the structure of the Persian language. In 1286/1869 Riza Quli Khan Hidayat, lamenting the state of the language, wrote:

> In the 1286 years since the *hijra* of Muhammad, the Arabic language has continuously developed and evolved; but because of religious enmity and opposing natures, the Persian language has become obsolete, disordered, and obliterated, and nothing remains of the Ancient Persian texts.[87]

Such observations were important components of the rhetoric of language reform and purification. Compiling dictionaries and writing grammar texts were responses to a regressive comprehension of the history of the Persian language. During this period there were many important books written on Persian grammar: 'Abd al-Karim Iravani's *Qava'id-i Sarf va Nahv-i Farsi* (1262/1848), Hajj Muhammad Karim Khan Kirmani's *Sarf va Nahv-i Farsi* (1275/1858), Muhammad Husayn Ansari's *Tanbiyah al-Sibyan* (1296/1878), Mirza Habib Isfahani's *Dastur-i Sukhan* (1289/1872) and *Dabistan-i Parsi* (1308/1890), Mirza Hasan Taliqani's *Kitab-i Lisan al-'Ajam* (1305/1887), Ghulam Husayn Kashif's *Dastur-i Kashif* (1316/1898), and Mirza 'Ali Akbar Khan Nafisi's *Zaban Amuz-i Farsi* (1316/1898). These grammar texts, although modeled on studies of Arabic grammar, and while they often had Arabic titles, nevertheless provided the ground for developing and identifying the rules of the Persian language.

Protagonists of the constitutional order in Iran were conscious of the importance of language in the struggle for a new identity. The reconstruction of history would not have been possible without the transformation of the language, the locus of culture and memory. Mirza Aqa Khan Kirmani argued that language is in reality "a history which signifies the general and specific characteristics, behaviors, manners, and forms of belief of a people." He held the view that "the strength of the *millat* depends on the strength of the language."[88] Kirmani thought of writing as a creative act. He argued that the Persian word *nivishtan* (writing) was derived from *naw* (new) and "it means creating something original."[89] His *Ayinah-'i Sikandari*, a creative act of historical writing, subverted not only the dominant system of historical narration but also the system of signification, by creating an Iran-centered political discourse and identity.

Most nationalists viewed writing as a crucial but problematic element for the progress and development of Iran. Some, like Akhundzadah, Mirza Riza Khan Bigishlu, and Mirza Malkum Khan, argued that the proliferation of scientific thinking was not possible as long as the Arabic script was used. Akhundzadah argued that the reforms in Iran and the Ottoman Empire could not bring about the desired changes without the dissemination of modern sciences, which was only possible with a change in the alphabet. Such a change was necessary because scientific terms had to be borrowed from European languages: "How can we translate European books into Arabic, Persian, or Turkish when our three languages lack scientific terminologies? We have no choice but to adopt those terms into our language".[90] Akhundzadah devised a new alphabet based on Latin and Cyrillic, arguing, "The old alphabet should be used for the affairs of the hereafter, and the new alphabet for the affairs of this world."[91] Viewing the Arabic script as a cause of Iran's destruction, he revealed, "My outmost effort and hope today is to free my people [*millat-i khudam*] from this outdated and polluted script which was imposed on us by that nation [*an qawm*] and to guide my people [*millatam*] from the darkness of ignorance to the enlightenment of knowledge."[92] Likewise Malkum argued, "The ignorance of the people of Islam and their seperation from present-day progress are caused by the defectiveness of the alphabet."[93] As Bernard Lewis observed, "In the inadequecy of the Arabic alphabet, Malkom Khan saw the root cause of all the weakness, the poverty, insecurity, despotism, and inequity of the lands of Islam."[94] Despite Akhundzadah and Malkum's nationalist enthusiasm, their argument against the Arabic script was similar to that of the British promoters of Romanization, who considered Devi Nagari and Arabic scripts as "barbarous characters." For instance, C. E. Trevelyan, arguing for Romanization, stated that the words of "the English language are so generally indeclinable that their introduction into the Indian dialects may be accomplished with peculiar ease." Looking forward to a heavy borrowing from "the more scientific and cultivated language," he exclaimed: "How desirable would be to engraft upon the popular languages of the East such words as *virtue, honour, gratitude, patriotism, public spirit*, and some others for which it is at present difficult to find any synonym in them!"[95] The hidden logic of such arguments was clearer to those who were familiar with the British colonial projects. In a sophisticated rebutting of Malkum Khan's argument, Dardi Isfahani, who had lived in India for many years, argued that the Roman script, as used in English and French, was more irregular and more difficult to master than Arabic.[96]

Instead of importing European terms via the adaptation of the Roman script, I'timad al-Saltanah and Jalal al-Din Mirza called for the establishment of a language academy for the coining of new Persian scientific concepts.[97] This approach involved researching and rethinking history and language within the same scriptural culture. This was the stated goal of a Calcutta-based Persian journal, *Miftah al-Zafar*, which called for an active translation of European scientific texts. The journal's views on language were developed in a series of articles on "Falsafah-'i Qawmiyat va Lughat" (Philosophy of Nationalism and Language), arguing that "sciences could become popular only if they were made available in the national language." To support this claim it argued that if Iranian philosophers had written in Persian, instead of Arabic, "philosophical spirit would not have been lost amongst Iranians."[98] In an editorial, Mohammad Mahdi b. Musa Khan contended that the translation and publication of scientific texts was the secret of European progress. In order to advance, he suggested that Iranians must also translate European scientific texts and, when necessary, they should not hesitate to invent and to coin new concepts" (*alfaz-i naw barayi anha vaz' va ja'l kunad*).[99] In another article he noted that sending students to Europe did not promote the general interest of the nation: "The general benefit of the nation can only be promoted if all fields of knowledge are taught in public schools in the mother language [*zaban-i madari*]."[100]

To strengthen the Persian language, in a letter to the Prime Minister Mirza Ali Asghar Amin al-Sultan, *Miftah al-Zafar* called for the establishment of a scientific society in Calcutta for the sole purpose of translating European scientific texts into Persian. The response from Tehran was very positive. The editor of the journal, Mirza Sayyid Hasan al-Husayni Kashani, was granted the title "Mu'ayyad al-Islam" (Strengthener of Islam) and an annual salary of two thousand francs.[101] The journal followed its design with the establishment of *Anjuman-i Ma'arif*, which consisted of 73 scholars who were capable of translating from various languages.[102] A few years later a similar society, *Majlis-i Akadimi* (1903), was established by Nadim al-Sultan, the Minister of Publications.[103] These two societies were the forerunners of *Farhangistan-i Iran* (The Language Academy of Iran), which was established on the occasion of the Firdawsi Millennium (*Hizarah-'i Firdawsi*) in 1935 to advance Persian as the national language of Iran. Following the *Shahnamah* of Firdawsi, which was hailed as "the certification and documentation of the nobility of Iranian people" (*qabalah va sanad-i nijabat-i millat-i Iran*),[104] the members of Farhangistan sought to Persianize foreign terms and concepts. The purist movement, which was begun in the late sixteenth century by Azar Kayvan and his cohorts, was institutionalized in the form of Farhangistan in 1935.

The concern with language affected the development of the Constitutionalist discourse, a discourse best represented in the simple style of newspapers such as *Qanun, Sur-i Israfil, Musavat, Iran-i Naw,* and by writers such as Zayn al-'Abidin Maraghah'i, Mahdi Quli Hidayat, Hajj Muhammad 'Ali Sayyah Mahallati, Hasan Taqizadah, 'Ali Akbar Dihkhuda, and Mirza Jahangir Shirazi.[105] The nineteenth-century literary mimicry and canonization, restyling of language, and the reconfiguration of history provided the necessary components for the articulation of the constitutionalist discourse and institution of a new national popular imaginary. The constitutionalist discourse represented Iran as the motherland (*madar-i vatan*) and Persian as the mothertongue (*zaban-i madari*). By anthropomorphizing Iran, the protagonists of the constitutional order also instituted history and culture as expressions of its soul, a national soul that was inherited by all Iranians.

7
Patriotic and Matriotic Nationalism

Vatan-centered discourse

The emotive content of "homeland" (*vatan*) in Iranian nationalist discourse cannot be appreciated if it is uncritically assumed that the *vatan* was only a confused translation of "the French word *patrie*."[1] The nineteenth-century nationalist resignification of *vatan* as the familial home was made possible through the fusion of competing prenationalist notions of territorial and aterritorial "originary home" (*vatan-i asli*). The former embodied the nation and the latter endowed it with spirit and subjectivity. This metaphorical figuration of *vatan* involved two distinct, but overlapping, phases. In the official nationalist discourse, *vatan* was imagined as a "home headed by the crowned-father." This was contested by a counter-official matriotic discourse that imagined *vatan* as a dying 6,000-year-old mother. The engendering of the national body as a mother symbolically eliminated the father-Shah as the guardian of the nation and contributed to the emergence of the public sphere and popular sovereignty – the participation of "the nation's children" (both male and female) in determining the future of the "motherland" (*madar-i/mam-i vatan*). As for popular sovereignty, this changing gender of national-home was crucial to the resignification of *siyasat* from the infliction of physical pain on transgressive subjects to its modern definition as *politics*. The metaphorical familial relation of male and female citizens as national brothers and sisters also sanctioned the redrawing of the boundaries that separated the filiative home space (*andarun*) from the affiliative public male sphere (*birun*). The hybridiztion of male and female spaces – which was facilitated with the coming of Persian printing press, the conjoining of authorial voices of men and women, and the formation of a women-inclusive public sphere – made possible the formation of an imagined national sphere that sanctioned the mixing of "national sisters and brothers."

The nineteenth-century emergence of Iran as a "geobody" with bounded territory was linked to the global emergence of nation-states and the international demarcation of national boundaries.[2] Territorial enclosure was in part imposed on Iran via the treaties of Gulistan (1813), Turkmanchay (1828),[3] Erzurum (1823 and 1847),[4] and Paris (1857).[5] Studies of these treaties have been the focus of much research and lamentation in nationalist historiography.[6] But these boundary-formalizing treaties shaped the national body politic and prompted its full anthropomorphization.[7] Territorial enclosure shifted the characterization of Iran from a confederation of territories (*mamalik*) to a cohesive entity (*mamlikat-i Iran* or *kishvar-i Iran*). The displacement of *mamalik-i Iran* with *mamlikat-i Iran* marked the transition from an empire to a modern nation-state. The relative fixity of borders provided the *ground* upon which Iran could be conceived as a unified homeland (*vatan*) with a distinct character, identity, history, and culture.[8]

Like most political and philosophical concepts, *vatan* has a contested and multi-layered history. In prenationalist writings it connoted both territorial and aterritorial meanings. Territorially, *vatan* referred to either a person's "habitual-place" (*vatan-i ma'luf*)[9] or originary home (*vatan-i asli*).[10] These territorial definitions can be found in biographical dictionaries, travel accounts, and jurisprudential discussions of discount prayers (*namaz-i shikastah/qasr*) – that is, a reduction of the obligatory units of prayer for individuals traveling beyond the confines of their place of residence. For instance, in a discussion of prayers Hasan Lahiji (1635–1709) used the word *vatan* to mean an individual's intended settling-place, "even if s/he had been there no more than one day." Having constituted intentional residence as the primary criterion, he explained that if an individual, like a student or a merchant, does not "intend to settle" (*qasd/iradah-i tavvatun*) in a locality even after ten years of residence, "that place cannot be considered his/her *vatan*" (*anja bara-yi ishan vatan nashavad*). The special status of *vatan* was maintained as long as a traveler possessed property or a dwelling-place back "home." Failing to fulfill this basic requirement, the special status of a traveler's *vatan* was "annulled and became equivalent to all other localities."[11] In this operationalized definition, a person's birth-place was not necessarily the same as his/her *vatan* or place of residence.[12] A number of compound constructs such as "*tarh-i vatan rikhtan*" (planning to settle) and "*tavatun guzini*" (selecting a place of residence) implied the delectability of *vatan*, a choice seriously curtailed within the nationalist discourse and the modern system of nation-states.[13]

A second use of *vatan* as territory referred to a person's home. This was the implied meaning in Mulla Ahmad Naraqi's (1185–1245/1771–1829) "The Tale of the Mermaid and Her Travel on Earth." According to this tale, a mermaid who visited the earth reported back that the earthlings "are heart-attached to a place called *vatan* and sleep in it with corporal calm."[14] A later nineteenth-century abstraction of *vatan* as home made possible the metaphoric depiction of Iran as the national home and as a site for the cultivation of nationalist sentiments and "heart-attachments" (*dilbastigi*). In a unique way this usage of *vatan* was endowed with a subjectivity, identity, and agency. This was made possible by the intertextual linking of Iran with the "originary home" (*vatan-i asli*) of the human soul and subjectivity, an *aterritorial* "geosophical" conception prevalent among classical Islamic philosophers and mystics.[15]

As the originary home of the human soul, the aterritorial *vatan* was viewed as a *no-place* or *a-place* (*lamakan*) to which the soul (*nafs*) was destined to return after death. Explaining the soul's return to its originary home, Yahya Suhravardi (1153 or 1155–91) compared it to the outside leg of a drawing compass where "the point always returns to the locus of initiation."[16] Writing within the same paradigm, the nineteenth-century Iranian philosopher Mulla Ahmad Naraqi viewed the body as a "vehicle" (*markab*) for the soul. The soul had come to this world from its "originary home" (*mawtan-i asli*) in order "to trade and accumulate benefits, to adorn the self with many virtues and to acquire commendable qualities and laudable dispositions" before returning to its "original home" (*vatan-i asli*).[17] In a related conceptualization, the grave (*qabr*) was viewed as the originary home of human body: made of earth (*khak*), the body was ordained to return to its place of origin.[18]

Divergent understandings of *vatan* were authorized by a frequently cited aphorism attributed to Prophet Muhammad (570–632), "the love of *vatan* is of faith" (*Hubb al-watan min al-iman*).[19] In a poetic interpretation of this *hadith*, Baha' al-Din 'Amili (1547–1621) argued that the "adoration of vatan" endorsed by the Messenger of Islam was not that of territories like Egypt, Iraq, or Syria (*in vatan, Misr va Iraq va Sham nist*). The *vatan* that deserved love was an "aterritorial" (*la makan*) and "a nameless city" (*bi nam shahr*) considered as "the spiritual domain" (*iqlim-i ruh*).[20] Viewing the body as the prison house of the soul, Shaykh Baha'i evoked, "Turn away from the body and exult your soul; remember your originary home [*mawtin-i asli*]!" But for travelers, exiles, and immigrants – that is, those departed from their familial land (*jala'-i vatan kardah*) – the prophetic *hadith* was confirmation of their nostalgic longing for the home left behind.[21] The architects of Iranian nationalist discourse – many of whom lived in exile – imagined Iran as their originary *vatan* and employed this authorizing prophetic adage as a nationalist banner constituting the adoration of national-home as an obligatory religious duty. Didactic commentaries on this prophetic aphorism provided the cultural capital for the articulation of a persuasive and emotive *vatan*-centered discourse.

Nationalized subjectivity

The nationalist rearticulation of *vatan* was not simply a geographical expansion from a local domicile to a national homeland. What made this expansion inventive was the anthropomorphization of *vatan* through a dialogic and intertextual hybridization of territorial *vatan* and aterritorial "spiritual *vatan.*" By condensing the territorial and spiritual *vatan*s into one entity, the Iranian homeland (*vatan-i Iranian*) was endowed with subjectivity and agency. This spiritualization of territorial *vatan* provided the perspectival foundation for the articulation of a cohesive and unified "national" culture, literature, and history – all viewed as the manifestations of the homeland's soul, spirit, and biography. The historical process of spiritualizing *vatan* is beyond the scope of this study; I will, however, offer an outline of the nationalist discourse that conjoined the national *geobody* and the spiritual *geosophy* and endowed *vatan* with life and soul. Once fully incarnated, *vatan* became a site of matriotic love, possession, and protection.[22]

The fusion of the spirtual and physical *vatan*s was illustrated in a series of 1877 *Akhtar* articles – bearing initially as title the prophetic *hadith*, "Love of *vatan* is of faith." The series sought to explore the interrelationship of the concepts "love" (*hubb*), *vatan*, and "faith" (*iman*).[23] Writing from the Ottoman diaspora, the anonymous author asserted that, like a human body, the *vatan* possessed "nature, life, and reason" (*tabi'at, hayat, va 'aql*) and was endowed with its own "unique and apt spirit and life" (*ruh va jan-i makhsus va munasib*). Analogous to a human individual whose existence depended on both body and soul, he argued that the territorial and spirtual *vatan*s were fused: "the appearance and essence of *vatan* are inseparable. It is like spirit and body. Spirit cannot stand without the body and the body cannot live without the spirit."[24] By converging these two meanings of *vatan*, the author unified the territorial homeland with "the imaginary and spiritual worlds" (*avalim-i* *misaliyah va rawhaniyah*), the originary home of universal soul and reason. Possessing life and subjectivity, the fully anthropomorphized nationalist *vatan* was endowed with the exceptional power of shaping a person's life (*zindagani*), growth and thriving (*nashv va nama*), speech (*sukhanguyi*), logic (*mantiq*), ethics (*akhlaq*), knowledge ('*ilm*), manners, arts (*hunar*), profession (*makasib*), dignity (*sharaf*), honor ('*izzat*), religion (*diyanat*), and spirituality (*rawhaniyat*). The author summarized the overdetermining power of homeland by asserting that "the human self and all his/her possessions belong to *vatan* [*tamaman mal-i vatan ast*]." The constitutive function of *vatan* also comprised all that a person acquired beyond the boundaries of her/his national homeland. "By inference [a person's] existence and acquisitive power, which are products of a particular *vatan*, are like foundations and those which are acquired from abroad are like restorations [*tamirat*]. In reality s/he acquires that which is in the self." Having constituted the national homeland as the foundation of human abilities and potentialities, this anonymous architect of nationalist discourse concluded:

> Consequently, *vatan* is no other than the human self [*khud-i insan*]. *Vatan* is your existence [*vujud*]. *Vatan* is your disposition and behavior [*shu'un va atvar*]. *Vatan* is your foundation and origin [*asl va mabda'*]. *Vatan* is your materiality and physicality [*hayula va maddah*]. *Vatan* is your appearance and essence [*surat va ma'ni*]. *Vatan* is the locus of your dignity and glory [*sharaf va iftikhar*]. *Vatan* is the custodian of your existence and the inheritor of your life [*kafil-i hayat va varis-i zindigani*]. Conclusively, *vatan* is your initiation and consummation [*aqaz va anjam*].[25]

As defined here, the corporality and subjectivity of an individual were derivatives of *vatan*, and an individual's identity and attributes were viewed as identical to her/his national identity and attributes. In other words, the territorial *vatan* embodied a collective soul, personality, and individuality. These collective attributes found their profane expressions in the "national" literature (*adab*), culture (*farhang*), and history (*tarikh*), which were viewed as repositories of the national soul.

The territorializing of the soul's originary home allowed for the displacement of sovereignty over collective subjectivity from the Divine to national pedagogues. Unlike the serene celestial *vatan*, which was unchangeable by human design, the nationalized originary home – the residing place of collective mind and body – became the locus of nationalist pedagogy and developmental designs. To reawaken the collective soul of the nation, the educators of the nation, such as I'timad al-Saltanah and Mirza Aqa Khan Kirmani, sought to recover the history, literature, and language of the homeland. The recovered collective history and literature provided the pedagogical resources for the making of nationalist subjectivity and identity.

National–public sphere

With the coming of the printing press, Nasir al-Din Shah assumed the task of "disciplining/educating [*trabiyat*] the people of Iran and informing them of internal and external events." The official gazette, *Ruznamah-i Vaqayi'-i Ittifaqiyah*, which began publication in 1851, was to carry out the Shah's pedagogical task of fostering "the intelligence and perception of the residents of the Sublime State."[26] All governmental officials and "honest subjects" (*ra'aya-yi sadiq*) were encouraged to subscribe to the gazette, each issue of which included "the news of the capital," "the other Iranian territories," and "the affairs of foreign states." These included the publicizing of governmental appointments and policies, the institution of passports, punishment of transgressive soldiers, new industrial ventures, discussions of public health, reports of rape and theft, and the prices of commodities and books. With the publication of news and opinions, *Vaqayi'-i Ittifaqiah* and other official and non-official newspapers generated public knowledge and information vital to the formation of a critical national–public sphere.[27] The publicity of official decisions invited public criticism and this public criticism modified the state policies. As organs of enlightenment, official journals often published critical letters and essays by private individuals. To promote his image as an enlightened monarch, the Shah was advised to increase the number of journals and to allow the publication non-official newspapers.[28] The non-official (*ghayr-i rasmi*) newspapers, especially those published in the diaspora, assumed the role of the "people's tongue" (*zaban-i millat*) by evaluating and recommending policies. The dialogue between official and non-official papers was crucial to the familialization of *vatan* as a national home.

The inculcation of *vatan*-centered sentiments was an essential component of official and counter-official national pedagogical strategies. This involved the transferrence of familial loyalty, honor, and dignity from the family onto *vatan* – the national home. For instance *Mirikh* (Mars, the God of war), the official military journal, attempted to cultivate national honor and dignity amongst soldiers and officers. In a series of articles, Sani' al-Dawlah, the journal's editor who was a recipient of

Akhtar, associated individual dignity (*sharaf*) with the "love of home-land" (*hubb-i vatan*). Paraphrasing a passage from *Akhtar* cited above, Sani' al-Dawlah asserted, "Dignity and *vatan* are codependent [*malzum-i yikdigar*]. There can be no dignity without the love of *vatan* and the love of *vatan* is contingent upon dignity." To discern the value of "fervor" (*ghayrat*) and "nobility" (*sharafat*), he declared that the staffs of a victorious army must first learn the meaning of "the love of home-land." Essential to his official nationalist pedagogy, which emerged in a dialogic relation with the the non-official *Akhtar*, was the equation of "dignity" (*sharaf*) with a respectful relationship of "adherence and obedience" (*taqlid va mutabi'at*) among the lower and upper ranking officers. Dignified officers were to view as "obligatory the unquestioned compliance and pursuance" of their superiors' orders." "Until the last breath," all ranks of the military were obliged to avouch "their dignity [*sharafat*], love of land, fervor [*ghayrat*], and shah-adoration [*shah parasti*]."[29]

Shah-adoration and *vatan*-veneration were the nodal points of a *patri-otic* nationalist discourse which imagined the Shah as the father of *vatan*. An instance of this patriotic discourse was articulated by Sani' al-Dawlah in an article explicating the prophetic aphorism, "love of *vatan* is of faith." At the outset of this explication, he offered homage to the esoteric Sufi interpretations of *vatan* and invoked Shaykh Bahai's adage that "this *vatan* is not Egypt, Iraq, or Syria; this *vatan* is a nameless city." Shifting focus on the "exoteric" (*zahiri*) aspect, he then offered a nationalist definition of *vatan* as "a birth-place and the locus of growth and thriving and where one's kin, clan, and friends reside and speak in the main language [*zaban-i asli*] and the accustomed tongue [*lisan-i mu'tad*]." Elaborating the metaphorical equivalence of familial home and affilial homeland, he argued that in reality *vatan* "is the same as a person's family, clan, interior, and kinship [*khanivadah, tayifah, ihtisha', va 'ashirah*]." Condensing family and *vatan*, he concluded that, "A person who lacks the love of *vatan* lacks a kin and a clan."

Having equated homeland with family and clan, Sani' al-Dawlah extended the metaphor by asserting that the Shah's role "is analogous to the familial father [*bimanzilah-'i pidar-i khanivadah ast*]."[30] But this simile was not without its antecedent. In the late eighteenth century, the historian Rustam al-Hukama represented the Iranian ruler Karim Khan Zand (1750–79) as "the kind father of all residents of Iran [*pidar-i mihraban-i hamah-'i ahl-i Iran*]." Eight years before Sani' al-Dawlah, the Chief Minister Mirza Husayn Khan Sipahsalar declared that in reality "soldiers and subjects are the true royal children [*aulad-i vaqi'i-i saltanat qushun asl va ra'yat*]."[31]

As the chief publicist of Mirza Husayn Khan's reformist projects,[32] Sani' al-Dawlah was fully aware of the political implications of a metaphoric characterization of the Shah as "familial father" (*pidar-i khanivadah*). If the *vatan*, as affilial home, required mutual rights and responsibilities between its residents and its head (*ra'is-i vatan*), then its *familialized* political relations required that the residents of *vatan* remain loyal to the father-shah and that the Shah "guard and protect in a fatherly [fashion] the rights of *vatan*-adoring members of His community [*millat-i khud*]."[33] Having promoted the Shah to a new status as the father of the nation, Sani' al-Dawlah then *sanctified* the national–familial home by endowing it with "divine effulgence" (*farr-i izadi*):[34] "Fortunate is a community [*millat*] and divinely-effulgent is a *vatan* [*izzadi farr vatani*] that its chief [*ra'is*] behaves in a fatherly [manner] towards the descendant of *vatan* [*abna'-i vatan*]."[35] The ascription of "divine effulgence" to *vatan* constituted a radical break with the king-centered Perso-Islamic political discourse which conventionally sanctioned royal power by endowing it with divine effulgence. The displacement of effulgence invested *vatan* with a divinely sanctioned authority. Like the *relocation* of soul's originary home which endowed Iran with subjectivity and agency, the displacement of "divine effulgence" constituted *vatan* as the site of authorty. These double displacements provided the foundations for a *vatan*-centered political imagination.

In the king-centered classical political discourse the Shah's authority was viewed as a divinely granted "effulgence" (*farr*).[36] As a "distinct" (*khassah*) locus of power, the Shah/Sultan was invested with the right/ responsibility to protect and to discipline the residents of his "domain" (*mulk*). The residents were in turn obligated to obey their divinely appointed protector. Conventionally this hierarchic relation of power was imagined metaphorically in Jewish–Christian–Islamic traditions as a shepherd–flock relationship. Grounded on a widely acclaimed prophetic adage, the ruler was characterized as a shepherd (*ra'i*) herding his flock (*ra'i, ra'iyat*).[37] For instance, Najm Razi (d. 1256 or 7) stated, "the king is like a shepherd and his subjects are like a flock. It is incumbent on the shepherd to protect his flock from the wolf and strive to repel the wolf's evil."[38] This foundational metaphor constituted *sovereignty* as an individuated (*khassah*) authority belonging to a distinct person who differed from the "public" or "commoners" (*'ammah*).[39] Unlike modern political power, the Shah's authority was not publicly displayed through the pervasive royal *presence*. Royal authority, contrary to diverse narratives of "Asiatic despotism," lacked the institutional resources for a permanent *public* presence throughout the empire. The public display of royal authority was selective and swift. It was often publicized in the form of mutilated bodies bearing witness to royal wrath. Manifested upon bodies as a "political signature,"[40] this afflictive royal authority was conceptualized as *siyasat* – the right to punish and to shed the blood of transgressive subjects.[41] The characterization of the Shah as father of the homeland (*pidar-i vatan*) provided a new metaphorical foundation for the nationalist resignification of *siyasat* as politics and the displacement of royal with popular and national sovereignty.

The metonymic configuration of the Shah as familial father was a corollary to the nineteenth-century centralization of state and publicizing of royal authority. The private royal domain (*khassah*) was transposed into a new public sphere with Nasir al-Din Shah's well-orchestrated travels and and well-publicized travelogues, which were serialized in the official gazette.[42] Royal authority became more public with the utilization of new technologies of print, prisons, police, standing army, border-guards, passports, and public education, hygiene, and welfare. To curtail the rapid growth of prostitution, courtesans were arrested "gently" and sent to a correction house for rehabilitation.[43] The rise of homeless people in Tehran – attributed to "draught and inflation" – prompted the formation of the Poor Assistance Council (*Mjlis-i I'anat bah Fuqara*) in 1871.[44] With the help of the Qashqayi Brigade, the Assistance Council gathered 1,155 beggars in the newly built complexes (*mujtami'*) in Darwazah Dulab.[45] By mid-January 1865, four additional sites were established, housing a total 4,384 beggars. A Healthcare Council (*Majlis-i Hifz al-Sihah*) was also established to encounter the spread of contagious diseases.[46] To promote public health, the Council issued ordinances for cleaning public paths and waterways, discouraging the consumption of indigestible food, forbidding unnecessary gathering of crowds, and drafting guidelines for public health education.[47] To promote internal peace, the Public Order and Security Office (*Idarah-'i Nazmiyah va Amniyat-i 'Ammah*) was established and supplied with new ammunitions and uniforms.[48] Additionally, state-sponsored educational institutions, with curriculums noticeably different from seminary schools, enlarged the pedagogical task of the state while curtailing those of the *'ulama*. These new state institutions provided the material foundation for the symbolic characterization of the Shah as the father of *vatan*.

Ironically, the modern pedagogical state institutions, such as *Dar al-Funun* (established in 1851), played a crucial role in training individuals who constituted the core of an emerging critical public organized in secret societies and assemblies. Among such sodalities were *Faramushkhanah*, *Jami'ah-'i Adamiyat*, and *Atashkadah*. Founded in the 1850s,

Faramushkhanah (Amnesiac House) recruited many students and faculty of *Dar al-Funun*. After the dissolution of *Faramushkhanah* by a royal decree in 1861, a successor organization, *Jami'ah-'i Adamiyat* (the Society of Humanity), continued to provide a forum for the discussion of national political issues.[49] *Atashkadah*, another public sodality, met at least once a week and their monthly decisions and teachings were widely distributed.[50] Women of the court also established a secret organization, discussing the principles of humanity.[51] These sodalities, contrary to the conspiratorial studies,[52] constituted an expanding public sphere and provided the sites for the later articulation of a counter-official national imagination during the Constitutional Revolution of 1905–9.

Maternal homeland (*madar-i vatan*)

The state-initiated modernization was viewed as a sign of the increased tyranny of the Shah and was challenged by adversely affected social sectors. Awareness of social and political developments beyond Iran, promoted by journals and journeymen, made the state and the royal court targets of moral censure by citizens. The moral authority of the state was effectively challenged on two occasions that led to the repealing of the Reuter Concession of 1872 and the Tobacco Concession of 1890.[53] Consciousness of a more glorious past, engendered by a nineteenth-century historical comprehension, translated into an effective dis-crediting of authorities who were held responsible for the degradation of Iran and the selling of the country to Europeans. The critical public sphere – formed of private reading groups, secret societies, and publicly-aware citizens, each with its own communicative resources – became more vigorous and self-assured of its own judgments of the state officials as corrupt and as obstacles to *vatan*'s progress. Speaking in the name of *vatan* and *millat*, the public challenged the legitimacy and the moral authority of the state. The national–public sphere became a site of intensified struggle between the state and "the people" (*millat*), both of which understood themselves to be representing the interests of *vatan*.

With the polarization of public–political space into the spheres of the state (*dawlat*) and the people (*millat*), the familial trope provided the symbolic resources for the articulation of an effective counter-state discourse. In contradistinction to the characterization of the Shah as the father of the homeland, an increasing number of late nineteenth- and early twentieth-century non-official newspapers and journals char-acterized the homeland as a dying 6,000-year-old mother. Instead of the all-powerful father-Shah who had to be obeyed courteously, the image of a dying mother-*vatan* created an urgent situation obligating her "children" to rush to save her life. Whereas the earlier characterization of the authorities as shepherds constituted them as superior, they were now held accountable for the motherland's suffering and imminent death. To criticize the ruling elite, the end-of-the-century *milli* and *vatani* newspapers constituted Europe as a rhetorical referent for highlighting the severity of "motherland's illness." In a bi-temporal narrative, Iranian homeland was recounted as an exhausted body lagging behind in the forward march of the caravan of nations. The back-lagging of mother-Iran, formerly a caravan-guard of civilization, was blamed on the ruling elite who were censured for their corruption and negligence. It was this rhetorical utility, and not an inherent superiority, that accounts for the working of Europe as a "referent" in the nationalist political discourse that constituted Iran as a belated nation.

The private moral censuring of the state authority was publicized via the characterization of *vatan* as a mother infected by multiple diseases. Unlike the official *patriotic* discourse that constituted *vatan* as a healthy body symbolically headed by the Shah, the *matriotic* counter-state discourse represented *vatan* as an ailing mother in need of immediate care. Expressing anxiety over the motherland's future, Shayk al-Ra'is (1264–1336/1847–1917) lamented, "If the Angel of Death does not kill me, the trepidation of Iran will kill me . . . This *vatan* is extremely ill and says: if you do not cure me, the high fever will kill me."[54] *Iblaq*, "a free paper" (*jaridah-'i azad*), reported that the "delicate and endeared *vatan*" is confined in bed and the corrupt "Iranian physicians" (a metonym for statesmen), instead of curing her illness are prescribing mortal poison.[55] Her anxious children sought the assistance of a Russian physician who agreed to cure Iran under the condition of gaining total control over her life and belongings.[56] In another non-official paper, *Tarraqi*, the Minister of Internal Affairs was warned, "This bedridden sacred body that moves like a slaughtered animal is infected with chronic and immobilizing diseases." *Tarraqi* suggested that the dying body of *vatan* could be saved only by vaccinating her with "knowledge" (*'ilm*) against the disease of "ignorance" (*jahl*).[57] *Habl al-Matin*, a distinguished newspaper that initially began publication in Calcutta (1311/1893), inaugurated its Tehran edition with a series of articles inquiring, "Is Iran Ill?" and "What is Iran's Illness?"[58] Published between August 1906 and May 1908, *Rahnama*'s serialized "Identification of Illnesses of Vatan or Diagnosis of Iran" was an exemplary historical censure of royal authority and the pedagogy of popular self-care and self-governance. The synecdochic characterization of *vatan* as a dying mother provided a popularly accessible and incisive moral censure of political authority in Iran. The diagnosis of body politic implicitly and explicitly challenged the royal and state authority and authorized the people to take charge of the ailing motherland.

Rahnama's "Diagnosis of Iran" began with the recognition that the 6,000-year-old mother-*vatan* was infected by an incurable disease endangering her survival. The news of her impending death led to the gathering of her children who conferred about the possible course of action. Having reached the conclusion that they must consult an experienced physician, one suggested hiring a Russian doctor. Another recommended a British physician, arguing that the British are familiar with similar cases in India and Egypt. Another argued that an Ottoman physician would be more familiar with the peculiarities of her nature. Still another recommended a German physician. But others questioned the competence of foreigners in curing an adored Iranian mother. They argued that each homeland has her own unique climate and the body of her residents correspond to her habitat. Since foreign physicians cure patients in accordance with their own customs and habitat, they argued that the remedy prescribed by foreign physicians may hasten the motherland's death. "To diagnose and cure the illness of the dear mother-*vatan*," at last they concurred to form a "health-care commission" (*Majlis-i hafiz al-Sihhah*)[59] consisting of "skillful physicians and knowledgeable *hakims*."[60] They all agreed that the commission's decisions were incumbent on all of the motherland's descendants.

Distressed about the motherland's future, one of her sons consulted an independent physician who informed him of her suffering from melancholy, apoplexy, paralysis, dropsy, and rabies – all transmitted to her by foreign invaders. These perennial illnesses of the motherland were metonyms for the social crises of the social body and the body politic. The unpredictability of the conduct of Iranian rulers was attributed to the ancient Greek invasion and its infliction of Iran with melancholy:

> She is happy for no reason and turns sad with no cause. In dangerous situations she is brave and in protected sites she is fearful. She perceives nothingness as being, being as nothingness, the probable as improbable, and the impossible as possible. Due to her psychic instability, she turns into a wicked blood-shedder; and because of her mental infirmity she is unable to distinguish the good from the bad. She can not comprehend what she does and she does not know what she wants.

Vatan's enduring melancholy was also a metaphor for the cruelty of Iranian authorities. "As we witness, the shedding of the blood of the sons of *vatan* instead of being shameful and deplorable is the foundation of power and the source of our authorities' glory." This ailment passed to all of motherland's descendants who in extreme poverty are "presumptuous" (*mutakabirand*), in extreme weakness "view themselves capable and empowered over all things," and in extreme ignorance "view themselves as the most knowledgeable."[61]

Apoplexy (*siktah*) was diagnosed as the motherland's second illness transmitted with the "Arab invasion" (*hujum-i 'Arab*). After enumerating the symptoms of this political disease, ranging from lack of reaction to the loss of territories, excessive taxation, and the selling of privileges to foreigners, the examination concluded, "If a sensation and movement was left in this people [*millat*] after the apoplexy, they would not have engaged in extreme adulation and flattery and tolerated excessive calamity and ignobility."[62] The insensitivity reached its peak with the Umayyid rule and domination, "which tore the national nerves" (*a'sab-i milli*) and the people's "human sensibilities" (*'uruq-i insaniyat*). This illness infected the "Iranian existence" (*vujud-i Irani*) from the time of 'Abd al-Malik bin Marwan's (r. 685–705) conquest of Mazandaran, leading to her "loss of sensation and comprehension resembling a paralyzed person who could not feel the amputation of her joints."

> Consequently, foreigners amputated this country from all sides and chopped the endeared *vatan* to pieces. But the people [*millat*] did not feel and sense it; or they were aware but did not rise up to resist it; this means that she lost the abilities of contraction, expansion, attraction, and reaction.[63]

Like melancholy, the diagnosis revealed that "this ominous illness still prevails in Iran-land and pervades the Iranian character [*dar jins-i Irani sarist*]."[64]

The toleration of extreme cruelty and oppression by Iranians was diagnosed as a symptom of the motherland's political paralysis. The physician observed that "in other countries torturers [*mirghazabha*] are unknown and [their names] is kept secret. Our torturers are the most renowned Iranians." He identified the frequent reply by Iranians, "'what is it to me' and 'what is it to you' as the symptom of a national paralysis [*falaj-i milli*]. It pervades the Iranian character to the extent that if a hundred people are beheaded or plundered no one would care to ask 'why?'"[65]

Dropsy (*istisqa'*), a pathological accumulation of diluted lymph in body tissues and cavities, was diagnosed as a disease that developed in the motherland's body since the Abbasid rule (749–1258). Murad Khan, a leading character in the story, conjoining medical diagnosis with political censure, explained that one can ascertain from the tales of *One Thousand and One Nights* and the poetry of Abi Nawwas how the Abbasids' negligence of governmental affairs and their engagement in worldly pleasures led to the mistreatment of the people and the destruction of the country (*kharabi-i mamlikat*). Like dropsy, which hinders the orderly distribution of blood, in the Iranian body politic "the government instead of spending the treasury funds on the welfare of the people [*millat*] and country [*mamlikat*] it spends it entirely on personal desires and pleasure of the king." As a result of this national illness "indolence, unemployment, and bodily comfort prevail in Iranian territories [*mamalik-i Iran*]."[66] Here the diagnosis of the motherland was a metonym for the collective diagnosis of Iran's population.

Finally, rabies (*maraz-i har* or *maraz-i kalib*) was diagnosed as "a lethal illness transmitted to the people of Iran [*millat-i Iran*] by Mongolian [*Changiziyan*] conquest."[67] The physician ascertained that "the oppression, incivility [*bimuruvvati*], and blood-shedding that endures in Iranian character,"[68] is a symptom of this infection.

Collectively, these maladies were thought to persist in the Iranian national character. According to the diagnoses, this "repulsive mixture" brought Iran to a state of coma by the time of Nadir Shah's murder (1160/1747), when it was no longer possible "to tell whether she was dead or alive." The coma continued until the eve of the Constitutional Revolution of 1905. According to the prognoses, "the excitements of the past two years made the experienced physicians hopeful of the patient's recovery."[69]

On this diagnosis, the past served as a sign of Iran's future survival and recovery. The physician prognosticated that "one of the signs of the survival of this patient is that the character of the people of this land is more noble [*asil*] than those of other nations and its people were brought up to rule over the nations of the world." He explained that, according to the Greek and European historians, from the time of Faraydun to Anushirvan for 4,000 years the nation of Iran [*millat-i Iran*] prevailed and ruled over most parts of the world. This history was taken as a sign that "mastery and nobility is ingrained in Iranian blood." Continuing the Iranian body politic's history of noble resistance, the physician concluded: "Like Faraydun who after a thousand-year overthrew the reign of Zahhakians and renewed Iranian royalty, this nation has never [permanently] lived and will never live under foreign management and rule." As a hopeful sign the "Diagnosis of Iran" concluded by recounting the Sasanian overthrowing of the Greeks, Abu-Mulim's leadership in bringing down the Ummayids and the Buyid's repelling of the Abassid rule in Iran.[70] The urgent condition of the motherland provided an opportunity for engaging her descendants in her "curing" and "welfare."

Matriotic sentiments

The display of filial sentiments toward the motherland invoked the training of loyalties and sensibilities toward a relatively alien entity and the publicity of one's "private" views of authorities.[71] The revolutionary crises of 1905–9 transformed the public sphere into a pedagogical institute for the nationalization of familial honor, zealotry, bravery, purity, sacrifice, intimacy, and affections. Iranians learned to hail one another as *vatani*-brothers and *vatani*-sisters and to urge one another to display zealotry (*ghayrat*) and dignity (*sharaf*) toward the dying motherland. The call for the demonstration of zeal and integrity became especially important during the political division of Iran into contesting constitutionalist and anti-constitutionalist forces in 1908–9. In an article explaining the frequent usage of dignity (*sharaf*) by both the elite and the populace, *Musavat* addressed "the newly emerged claimants of dignity [*sharaf*]" and inquired: "Which trace of oppression have we obliterated and whom amongst the oppressors have we punished? Which foundation of justice have we instituted and which pillar [*bunyan*] of exploitation and oppression have we destroyed?" In these and other articles the emotive *sharaf* was linked to individual responsibility for societal welfare. All Iranians were held accountable for the care of "the innocent infant of dignity [*sharaf*] who recently entered the world of Iran."[72]

In another article, "Khayr al-Umur Awsatuha," *Musavat* reported that "the wretched Iranians are many stations away from true justice and have been denied and dispossessed [*binasib*] of human happiness." In order to "guarantee the existence of our ethnicity and nation" *Musavat* called upon the oppressors to limit their oppression and upon the oppressed to limit the tolerance of oppression: "Oh unmerciful oppressors! Extreme oppression for how long? Oh wretched oppressed! The extremity of insensitivity to what limit?" The article concluded that only in such a reciprocal manner "Iranians will become human and the desolated village of Iran will join the rank of the renowned states of the world."[73]

Ghayrat was another highly contested familial terminology nationalized during the Constitutional Revolution. Traditionally linked to manliness, *ghayrat* can be rendered as zealotry, propriety, and jealousy, or more accurately as a condensation of all three terms. The evocation of this emotive concept assumed an immediate threat to familial honor and integrity. Individuals were expected to demonstrate outer zeal for the protection of familial honor. Similarly, at a time when the honor of the motherland was compromised, her national children were expected to take necessary actions to restore her honor and integrity. Lack of such initiatives was viewed as a sign of unmanliness. In a letter to *Musavat* a reader prescribed *ghayrat* as a remedy for the illness of the motherland. Addressing the people of Iran (*ahl-i Iran*), the author remarked, "*ghayrat* is your dignity and salvation [*sharaf va fallah*]; your wealth, your independence, and your nationality [*milliyat*] depends on *ghayrat*; you have no remedy but *ghayrat*. If Plato, Avicenna, and all [other] sages and physicians of the world gather, they will all prescribe the same medicine."[74]

Since the enemies of the motherland were depicted as rapists, the demonstration of zealotry and integrity was viewed as essential to nationalized manhood. Reporting on border clashes with the Ottomans in northeastern Iran (Urumiyah and Savajbulagh), *Musavat* warned that "the purity of motherland is threatened by the desirous adulterers [*zinakaran*] and the authorities are interested [only] in position and promotion." Censuring the Majlis deputies for "*partibazi*" (party-playing), the ministers for "*turktazi*" (plundering), and the Shah for "*ishqbazi*" (love-playing), *Musavat* admonished his countrymen for their unawareness and "women-like" (*misl-i zanan*) idleness: "Oh you slumberers on the bed of unawareness! Oh you subsiders of the path of ignorance! Oh you stragglers of the caravan of civilization! And oh you laggards of the road of world progress!...You are biding idly at home like women expecting others to endeavor for your happiness." Here the illness of the motherland was linked directly to the lack of initiatives and the straggling of her children from the "caravan of civilization." The threat of the raping of the motherland was used metaphorically and rhetorically to agitate and to mobilize men for political action in defense of Iran. With the intensification of anti-constitutionalist efforts and the division of Iran into British and Russian zones of influence, the call for action became ever more urgent:

> You descendants of Iran who responded to the cry of the kind motherland in the recent revolution and liberated her from the paws of internal road-plunderers! Today, the cries of this same estranged mother are blaring from the oppressions of foreign plunderers. The descendant of Iran is one who would rise up like a man and perform

his duties of Iranianness on the life-sacrificing field and does not grant to the enemy this historical glory and this gift of freedom and this new life and permanent happiness which was obtained with deep affection [*khun-i jigar* (blood of the liver)].[75]

Having portrayed the foreign intervention as motherland's rape, men were asked to reflect on how dishonorable life would be after the loss of motherland's chastity: "Iranians! Is there a doubt and incertitude that after the removal of the nation's chastity and honor of nationality, for the respectable [people] life would be a taboo and the living time would be ugly and undignified?"[76]

To mobilize for political action, men were often compared to women and stories of women's bravery and self-sacrifice were used rhetorically to put men to shame.[77] A declaration of intent by the revolutionaries of Azarbayjan, for instance, invited all Iranians to join them in "the holy pursuit of the lost beloved" – the Constitutional Monarchy and the Consultative Assembly." To arouse national sentiments, it recounted the story of a Georgian woman who volunteered to sacrifice her life for the rescue and freedom of Iranians. Having constituted the Georgian woman as an exemplar, the declaration then compared her deeds to that of the "home-destroying" Shaykh Fazl al-Allah Nuri, the leading Mujtahid of Tehran who was organizing the anti-constitutional camp. Thus, a foreign woman who supported the constitutionalist cause was viewed as more dignified than an arch-mujtahid who led the anti-constitutionalist camp. Reprimanding the people of Shiraz, Yazd, Kirman, Isfahan, Khurasan, and Gilan for their failure to join Azarbayjanis in the struggle against tyranny, the endeavor of the Georgian woman was taken as a *lack* of manliness:

Oh wicked children, oh disobeyers of kind motherland, if this pure-essence woman calls for resistance [*mujahidah*] and defense – in Islam this has always been the special duty of men – then why the residents of these provinces are sitting silently and do not perform their manly duties [*takalif-i mardanah*]? Is it that in these territories men and balls/seeds/testicles of manhood [*mard va tukhm-i mardan-igi*] have been razed? Are men all dead and non-men [*namardan*] have taken their place?

The declaration denounced the people of Shiraz – who were proud of "the chivalry and bravery their forefathers" – as a "disgrace to the descendants of Kayan" and "the windblowers of the honor of Fars" (*bar baddahandigan-i namus-i Fars*). Viewed as resigned from "the realm of manhood" (*da'irah-'i mardanigi*), the Shirazis were commanded to "bury themselves alive" for their lack of "bravery" (*rishadat*), "young-manliness" (*javanmardi*), and "zeal" (*ghayrat*). Likewise the Khurasanis were reminded of the brave history of their forefathers and were asked: "Aren't you the children of the same renowned fathers? What happened to that courage? Where is that agility?" The admonished people of Iran who had failed to join the revolutionaries of Azarbayjan were asked to recall the exclamations of the angel of fame and happiness:

> Oh people of Iran, oh residents of the territories of Khurasan, Kirman, Isfahan and other provinces...why are you sitting silently like the dead? Why have you stuffed your ears with the cotton of negligence and do not respond to this divine call? Fie with your courage. Fie with you manners! How dear is this wretched life and this base existence, [an existence] many degrees lower and viler than that the affairs of the women of the earth, that you prefer it to the salvation and liberation of your *vatan*?[78]

Such rhetorical questions prompted men to demonstrate their manhood by going public and taking sides in the revolutionary contestation. In this and many other revolutionary night-letters (*shab-namah*) the lack of concern for the affairs of the motherland was equated with the lack of masculine attributes of honor, integrity, and bravery.

By familializing the affilial national–public space, men were called upon to demonstrate the same compassionate and possessive feelings toward their motherland that they showed toward their mothers, sisters, and daughters.[79] The "reawakening" of the nation was indeed a pedagogical project for the projection of familial feelings toward the affilial nation-state. "To reawaken the nationalist feelings of the zealots of Iran [*hiss-i vatani-i ghayratmandan-i Irani*]," *Musavat* published two congratulatory letters addressed to Satar Khan, the commander of the revolutionary forces in Tabriz, who was hailed as *Sardar-i Milli* (National Commander). One letter was sent by the students of a school in Moscow and another by the members of the Welfare Society of Iranian Women Residing in Istanbul. The newspaper explained that the letters were not intended for the flattery and the praise of the authorities but for the education of the people. "The demonstration of young students' zeal [*gharat*]" and "the expression of the manly fervor [*ta'assub*] of the Welfare Society of Iranian Women Residing in Istanbul" was intended to teach the people of Iran "the manners of *vatan*-adoration and the responsibilities of nationality-cultivation [*a'in-i vatanparasti va takalif-i milliyat parvari*]."[80] To provoke a sense of territorial loyalty and protectiveness, men's manhood was doubted and "manly fervor" (*ta'assub-i mardanah*) was attributed to women who showed revolutionary and nationalist fervor.

The attribution of manliness to women was a conventional trope of Iran's matriotic nationalism. Often men were incited to demonstrate the same feeling toward the homeland that they often demonstrated toward their extended families. The attribution of masculine qualities to the women of the nation was often followed by a pedagogical note of admonition and a call for reawakening.[81] Revealing its pedagogical intent, *Musavat* wrote,

> Oh people of the nation, oh reciters of the inauspicious words of 'I do not care, what is it to me' [*biman chah, biman chirah*], now that unfortunately you can not constitute as your national model [*sarmashq-i milli*] the men of history and follow the manly manners [*rasm-i futuvvat va mardanigi*] in accordance with the saying "acquire knowledge from the mouths of men" [*khadau al-'ilm min afwaha al-rijal*]," and can not follow the world-adoring actions of the courageous [men] of the early Islam [*rashidan-i sadr-i Islam*], the heroic [men] of the eighteenth century France, or the brave [men] of contemporary Japan, then at least be just and constitute as your life-guide [*pishnahad-i zindagi*], the saying "acquire knowledge from the mouths of women" [*khazaw al-'ilm min afwah al-nisa'*] and do learn from the women of this new age ['*asr-i jadid*] the path of propriety [*ghayrat*] and the creed of manliness [*shari'at-i ghayrat va kish-i futuwwat*].

The readers of *Musavat* were asked to reflect and to ponder on the content of these two letters and to ascertain why the young students of Moscow and the women "encampers of purity [*pardah nishinan-i 'iffat*]" from Istanbul expressed their thanks and their feelings about "our mother nation [*madar-i vatan-i ma*]." This rhetorical question had the clear pedagogical intent of prompting care for the motherland:

> For us, the children of Iran, who view ourselves as the worthy inheritors of this patient, it is becoming that jointly today we imitate the zeal [*ta'assub*] and propriety [*ghayrat*] of these school children and women of the Women Society and in cooperation with one another nurse this infirm mother and cure and remedy the perennial illnesses that have taken roots in the national body [*badan-i vatan*].

Mediated through a medicalized political discourse, the call for nursing and curing the motherland was a demand for "public security [*amniyat-i 'umumi*] and the protection of life, honor [*namus*], speech, and thought." The recovery of national-body was contingent upon "the implementation of the dictum of justice and equality – that is, a law treating the king and the beggar as equals." Without the absolute rule of law, Iranians were compelled "to bury [their] ethnicity [*qaumiyat*] and to say good-by to [their] independence [*istiqlal*]." The preservation of the dying mother-land was inextricably linked to the protection of her children's "personal happiness, honor, and life." The call for motherland-care was a synonym for civil self-care.[82]

Constituted as a maternal familial space, *vatan* became the site for redefining and nationalizing masculinity and its attributes. To mobilize *men* for political action and participatory politics, *Musavat*, like many other constitutionalist papers, constituted women as exemplars of bravery, courage, possessiveness, virtue, vigor, and honor. With women's public display of courage and devotion to mother-Iran, these masculine characteristics were increasingly identified in counter-examples with the women of the motherland. As national exemplars during the Consti-tutional Revolution of 1905–9, women demonstrated national *rishadat*, *sharaf*, and *ghayrt*, attributes identified historically with masculinity (*mardanigi*). The examples of women's devotion to the motherland were used rhetorically to prompt men to protect Iran's territorial integrity and its new constitutional and representative regime. The nationalizing of the filial traits of masculinity made possible the dissociation of zeal (*ta'assub*), propriety (*ghayrat*), and bravery (*rishadat*) from biological manliness. As exemplars of national honor, dignity, and zeal, women served as the teachers of matriotic nationalism and nationalized mascu-linity. The care for the territorial mother prompted women's entry into the public sphere.[83] Women initiated their organizational sodalities, political activities, and pedagogical praxis in the name of curing and strengthening the motherland.

The synecdochic characterization of *vatan* as a dying mother provided the imaginary foundation for the reconfiguration of disciplinary sys-tems, a corollary of the changing position of individual subjects within the modern nationalist political discourse. Significant to this change was the eventual displacement of the affliction of physical pain and visible marks of punishment with new "modes of subjection" inculcating a particular type of subjectivity.[84] Unlike the classical *ta'riz* and *siyasat*, the new regimes of power sought to reform the individual character and rationalize individual conduct. This change involved the resignification of *siyasat* from the affliction of physical pain to obligatory filial concern with the present and future of the motherland.

The mothering of territorial Iran provided the imaginative space for the scripting and enacting of an innovative vernacular nationalism and political modernity. As a metonym, motherland interiorized the exterior affilial space of Iran-land. It conjoined the affilial *birun* (outer space) with the filial *durum/andarun* (inner space). Interiorization of Iran-land via the familial metaphor familiarized the men and women of the nation as national (*vatani*) brothers and sisters. This gave the question of *mahramiyat* a new connotation. By familializing the national–public sphere, the filiative spatial metaphor provided the discursive terrain for the alteration of gender relations and enabled women to go public. Constituted as "national sisters," women were discursively authorized to shed the veil that segregated them from their national brothers.

The deployment of filial space in the matriotic discourse in Iran differed from its Indian counterpart. Just as the mother Iran was constituted as an interiorized filial space, fusing and condensing *andarun* and *birun*, so the colonized "mother India" was spatially bifurcated into the inner *ghar* (home) and the outer *bahir* (world). In India the public space was constituted as the "material" space of colonial domination and cultural mimesis. Given this colonial context, the inner sphere of *ghar* was established as the autonomous site of "spiritual" autonomy and cultural authenticity. The spatial bifurcation provided the "ideological principle of selection" for Indian nationalism. Whereas men were to "bear the brunt" of material activity in the outer world, women were assigned the "responsibility of protecting and nurturing" the home-based authentic social and spiritual life.[85] Located within "the inner domain of sovereignty," the women's question abated from the domain of *public* discourse with the intensification of anti-colonial national struggle at the end of the century.

Divergently, the matriotic domicilization of homeland in the formally independent Iran authorized the fusion of the women's question and the welfare of the motherland. As the actual and potential pedagogues of the children of the homeland, women assumed a strategically significant role in the developmentalist national discourse in Iran. "Since women are the foundational pillar of human societal formation [*hay'yat-i ijtima'iyah-'i bashariyah*]," explained the essayist Sayyid Husayn, "their education takes precedent and is more urgent than the education of men."[86] The centrality of women's education to national progress prompted the formation of schools for girls. Initially established in the residences of prominent women, these schools became sites for the formation of a women-inclusive public sphere.[87] The ingression of women into the public sphere was facilitated with the synecdochic characterization of *vatan* as a dying 6,000-year-old mother. Partially cured by the Constitutional Revolution, the strengthening of the mother-*vatan* was linked to the education of women, the first pedagogues of the people (*millat*).

The securing of women's position in the matriotic discourse was furthered with the invocation of the mother's body as the "originary *vatan*" (*vatan-i asli*). By constituting the woman's body as the "originary *vatan*," Tayirah Tihrani (1861 or 1865–1911), an outstanding essayist and educator,[88] *supplemented* the motherland with non-metaphoric corporeality. Addressing her national "brothers" she asked rhetorically, "Are we not the source of your life, being, and comfort? How have you forgotten this original *vatan* of yours?"[89] In this significant intervention, the woman's body was constituted as the "originary home" of all Iranians. The care for "future mothers" as the pedagogues of the nation was linked to the task of caring for the motherland.

8
Postscript

The dialogic interaction with India, Europe, and the Arab–Islamic culture in the eighteenth and nineteenth centuries contributed to the refashioning of Iran and rescripting of "the people" (*millat*) and "the nation" (*vatan*) in Iranian political and historical discourses. The newly imagined Iran, constructed of textual traces and archaeological ruins, fashioned a new syntax for reconfiguring the past and refiguring national time, territory, writ, culture, literature, and politics. Language, the medium of communication and the locus of tradition and cultural memory, was restyled. Arabic words were purged, "authentic" Persian terms forged, and neologism and lexicography were constituted as endeavors for "reawakening Iranians" (*bidari-i Iranian*). Iran-centered histories *displaced* dynastic and Islam-centered chronicles. To recover from a historical amnesia, pre-Islamic Iran was reinvented as a lost Utopia with Mahabad as the progenitor of humanity, Kayumars as the first universal king, Mazdak as a theoretician and practitioner of freedom and equality, Kavah-'i Ahangar as the originator of "national will" (*himmat-i milli*), and Anushirvan as a paradigmatic just-constitutional-monarch. This inventive remembrance of things pre-Islamic inspired a conscious effort to *dissociate* Iran from Islam and the Arabs.

The lamentation for bygone glories prompted a regenerative desire for a better future. These contemporaneous backward- and forward-gazings intensified the dissatisfaction with the *present* order of things, a dissatisfaction that informed the discourse of *mashrutah-talabi* (constitutionalism). The manifold aspects of the desired constitutional future were temporally registered in many key social and political concepts. The temporal reorientation of these concepts was induced by protracted theatrical and rhetorical acts involving maneuvers amongst alternative and often contradictory positions and identities. By shifting from one discursive frontier to another, the late nineteenth-century clerisy and literati created a discursive mélange that intertextualized pre-Islamic, Islamic, and contemporary European histories and ideals. The contested and uneven synchronization of these once autonomous universes expanded the horizon of expectation by providing alternative social and political scenarios for the future. In his famous essay *Yak Kalimah* (One Word), for example, Mirza Yusuf Khan Mustashar al-Dawlah (d. 1322/1888) grafted the 17 principles of the French *Declaration of the Rights of Man and Citizen* into Islamic legal culture.[1] Mirza Yusuf Khan's call for the cannonization of law (*qanun*) was not a passive immitation of the French Code but its creative relocation within a different textual and political universe. The popularity and effectiveness of this modern Iranian political manifesto was due to the author's rhetorical and theatrical competence in both Islamic and French revolutionary discourses. Like Mirza Yusuf Khan, the Iranian–Armenian Mirza Malkum Khan gained national prominence by his apt discursive maneuvers between Islamic and European political discourses and his multivalent articulation of contested concepts suh as *millat* and *qanun* (law). He established the demand for *qanun* as a populist slogan unifying a diverse ensemble of social and ideological forces. In the second issue of *Qanun*, a political periodical published in the 1890s, he wrote:

> If you have a religion, demand *qanun*! If you are detained by the state, demand *qanun*! If your home is destroyed, demand *qanun*! If your salaries have been plundered, demand *qanun*! If your positions and rights have been sold to the others, demand *qanun*! If you have a family, demand *qanun*! If you possess something, demand *qanun*! If your are poor, demand *qanun*! If you are human, demand *qanun*![2]

In his futurist endeavors Malkum Khan successfully wedded the notion of natural law to the Islamic *Shari'ah*.[3] He used the twofold connotations of *millat* as both a religious and a national community in order to gain the support of the clerisy and the political elite for an orderly and regulated future society. Other prominent figures like Malik al-Mutakalimin (1864–1908), Jamal al-Din Va'iz, and Yahya Dawlatabadi (1861–1939), who were educated in seminary schools, utilized their knowledge of Islam in order to articulate effectively a constitutionalist discourse and identity. The theatrical abilities of such rhetors and their mastery of Islamic discourse enabled them to win over to the cause of constitutionalism such leading Shi'i clerisy as Akhund Mulla Muhammad Kazim Khurasani (d. 1911), Sayyid Muhammad Tabataba'i (1841–1920), Sayyid

'Abdullah Bihbahani (d. 1910), and Mirza Muhammad Husayn Gharavi Na'ini (1860–1936). The double articulation of the interests of the *millat*, as both Iranian and Islamic, accounted for the changing grammar of Shi'i politics, a new grammar that rearranged classical Shi'i concepts into a modernist syntax. With the expanding horizon of expectation grounded in a firm belief in human progress, Islamic political concepts were deployed for the actualization of an orderly constitutional society.

These protracted maneuvers account for the foundational reenvisaging of the *millat* from the "Shi'i people" (*millat-i Shi'ah-'i isna 'ashari*) to the "people of Iran" (*millat-i Iran*). As collective formation associated with the community of believers, *millat* was dissociated from Islam and the creator, God, and was anchored to the life-giving mother-nation (*madar-i vatan*) and the mother-tongue (*zaban-i madari*). Recognized as the mother-tongue, the Persian language became a pivotal instrument for homogenizing "the people" and the "nation." *Vatan*, previously one's birth-place, became inclusive of territorial Iran. Collectively imagined as a 6,000-year-old mother, the rejuvenation of *vatan* became a central project of Iranian nationalism, a project that shaped the modern Iranian subjectivity. Individually hailed as a beloved, *vatan*-adoration (*vatan-parasti/vatan-dusti*) fostered *individualization* and individual devotion and obligation towards the Iranian homeland. The crafting of a de-differentiated *milli* and *vatani* identity linked to ancient history and the Persian language subverted "the twinship of state and religion," a basic mechanism of political consensus and coercion in premodern Persianate political discourse. As described in Chapter 7, the relocation of "divine effulgence" from the Shah onto the *vatan* contributed to a radical resignification of *siyasat*. Considered as the right of the sovereign to punish and even execute "his subjects" in classical political manuals, *siyasat* was recoded as the right of the *millat* – the responsible children of *vatan* – to promote the welfare of the motherland and to participate in its rejuvenation and progress. *Inqilab*, formerly considered as disorder created by unruly subjects, was redefined as the endeavor of the *millat* to reestablish the bygone glories of "Iran-land" (*Iran-shahr/kishvar-i Iran*) and to rebuild the *now* "desolate Iran" (*iran-i viran*), a degeneration "brought about" by the tyranny (*istibdad*) and injustice of the shahs. The regeneration of Iran was linked to the "acquisition of knowledge" (*kasb-i 'ilm*), which was considered as a remedy for the illness of the motherland. Previously delimited by the clerisy to Qur'an-centered knowledge, *'ilm* was resignified by the new intellectuals (*munavvar/munavvar al-fikran*) who sought to regenerate Iran by inheriting the scientific knowledge of the "cultured Europe" (*Farang-i ba farhang*).

Hailing Europe as the heterotopia of knowledge and progress, "catching-up with Europe" served as an affective rhetorical topos for inspiring collective action for the revitalization of the "desolate Iran." Thus Orientalism's device of temporal distancing, as explored in Chapter 1, was affectivity utilized by Iranian nationalists to foster urgent actions for closing the temporal gap between Europe and Iran, this once "caravan-guard of civilization."

The rejuvination of Iran was mediated through a sustained struggle against the Qajar "tyrannical state" (*dawlat-i mustabid*).[4] The fight against "tyranny" (*istibdad*) was a corollary of temporal concepts that anticipated a constitutional social and political order. The coalescing of the dissatisfaction with the *present* and the anticipation of the *future* contributed to a successful fracturing of the political space into two antagonist camps of the people (*millat*) and the state (*dawlat*). The *dawlat* was portrayed as tyranical and unjust (*zalim*), and the *millat* as oppressed (*mazlum*) and justice-seeking ('*adalatkhwah*).[5] Consequently, the 'ulama, who were viewed as *ru'asa-yi millat* (leaders of the nation/people), could not openly support the *dawlat*, the enemy of the *millat*. The clerisy's dual and precarious position at this conjuncture explains their contradictory roles during the events that led to the constitutional rupture in 1905–9. The arch-Mujtahids, who synchronized their position with the *millat*, were given the honorary title of *Ayat Allah* (Sign of God). This title was discursively important since it was parallel to the Shah's title of *Zill Allah* (Shadow of God). Members of the clerisy who did not support the *millat* were branded as religious impostors and seekers of worldly privilege.

The hybridization of the idea of the equality of all Muslims before God with the principles of the French *Declaration of Rights* empowered the *millat* as a new source of sovereignty. The sovereignty of "the people" not only challenged the symbolic power of the Shah, but also the function of the clerisy as the guardians of the legal basis of the society. The society that was conceived and institutionalized in the course of the Constitutional Revolution was based not on the divine *Shari'ah* supervised by the 'ulama but on the *Shari'ah*-informed *qanun* legislated by the representatives of the *millat*. The discursive rearticulation of the *millat* as a national sodality and the establishment of the National Consultative Assembly (*Majlis-i Shura-yi Milli*), the institutional expression of national will, provided the key components of popular politics and polity.

A decisive historical moment in the recognition of "the people" was the popular struggle that compelled Muzaffar al-Din Shah to consent to the convening of the National Consultative Assembly (*Majlis-i Shura-yi*

Milli) in August of 1906. In the course of negotiations that led to the drafting of the Shah's proclamation, the Prime Minister proposed the establishment of an Islamic Assembly (*Majlis-i Islami*).[6] But the protestors disagreed, insisting: "With the power of the *millat*, we will obtain a National Consultative Assembly [*Majlis-i Shura-yi Milli*]." In the proclamation (5 August 1906), which was addressed to the newly appointed Prime Minister, Nasr Allah Mushir al-Dawlah, Muzaffar al-Din Shah called for the convening of an assembly in which the representatives of "crown princes and Qajars, 'ulama and theology students, nobles and notables, landowners, merchants and craftsmen" were to participate.[7] While the proclamation included the constitutionalist demand for the founding of a *Majlis*, it failed to make mention of the *millat*. The exclusion of the *millat* from the "Constitutional Proclamation" (*Farman-i Mashrutah*) was unacceptable to the Constitutionalists who spoke in the name of the people.[8] The text of the Shah's widely distributed proclamation was torn off the walls. Protesters who had taken sanctuary in the British Embassy refused to leave until the word *millat* was added to the Constitutional Decree.[9] A few days later, Muzaffar al-Din Shah issued a supplementary *farman* noting, "I have explicitly ordered the establishment of a Majlis, an assembly of the representatives of the people [*majlis-i muntakhibin-i millat*]."[10]

Although the Shah was forced to recognize the *millat* as a unified political sodality, he made an important rhetorical move to subvert the Constitutionalist contingent that had united a wide spectrum of ideological and religious forces. In the supplementary letter the Shah changed the name of the assembly from *Majlis-i Shura-yi Milli* (National/Popular Consultative Assembly) to *Majlis-i Shura-yi Islami* (Islamic Consultative Assembly). At that enthusiastic moment, the importance of this strategic shift was disregarded by the Constitutionalists, who were busy organizing for the convening of the Majlis.[11] At the inauguration of the Majlis on the October 7, 1906, crowds, reportedly for the first time, chanted "Long live the people of Iran" (*zindah bad millat-i Iran/payandah bad millat-i Iran*).

Recognition of the *millat* in the Constitution provided the foundation for a new age of popular politics. In Iranian political discourse prior to this period the civil society was viewed as an ensemble of various classes, ranks, professions, and religious groups. This was evident from the Shah's *farman* dividing society into six classes.[12] But the constitutionalist discourse broke away from the hierarchical language of politics and introduced the *millat* as a unified and homogeneous force, the source of sovereignty, with the right to determine the policies of the government through its representatives to the Majlis.[13] In the constitutionalist discourse, *millat* signified everyone without regard to professional, social, and religious status. This view of *millat* radically differed from the hegemonic ranking of Muslims over the protected non-Muslim communities (*millal/millats*). This de-differentiation of the people provided the discursive terrain for the expansion of democratic rights. A 1910 *Iran-i Naw* editorial viewed the division of the people into separate religious *millats* as a tyrannical design. The editorial asserted that "Iranians are of one *millat*, a *millat* who speak in different dialects and worship God in various ways."[14]

The recognition of the *millat* as a people with diverse languages and religions equal before the law challenged the most basic hierarchy of the *millat* as a Shi'i-Muslim sodality. The ambiguous double articulation of the *millat* that had earlier united both the nationalist and Islamist forces reached an impasse with the constitutional debates over the questions of "equality and parity" (*barabari va musavat*) and "freedom and liberation" (*azadi va hurriyat*), two basic ideals of the French Revolution integrated into the Iranian revolutionary discourse. With the death of the ailing Muzaffar al-Din Shah after the convening of the Majlis and the ratification of the Fundamental Laws on December 30, 1906, his son Muhammad 'Ali, an antagonist of the constitutional movement, moved to Tehran as the new Shah.[15] Muhammad 'Ali Shah refused to invite the deputies of the Majlis, "the representatives of the *millat*," to his coronation. In his speech he spoke not of *mashrutah* (constitutionalism) but of *mashrutah-'i mashru'ah*, (Shari'atist Constitutionalism), a government based on the Shari'ah. By using *mashrutah-'i mashru'ah*, the new Shah used the Shari'ah as a mechanism to subvert the constitutionalist discourse and to divide the constitutionalist contingent. The drafting of Supplementary Fundamental Laws was divisive. It included controversial issues such as the curbing of royal authority and the equality of all citizens. With the assistance of Shaykh Fazl'allah Nuri, a leading mujtahid of Tehran, Muhammad 'Ali Shah managed to organize the *mashru'ahkhvah* camp, which thought of constitutionalism not as a government based on *qanun* (Majlis-legislated law) but the divine Shari'ah. Unlike the constitutionalists who were moving towards secular politics, the *mashrutahkhwah*'s emphasized the importance of the Shari'ah as the legal foundation of the society. In the Shari'atist discourse, because of the centrality of Islam, *millat* had a clearly religious definition and the equality of Muslims and non-Muslims was viewed as a heretical stand. Shaykh Fazl'allah Nuri, the intellectual leader of the *mashru'ah* contingent, argued against the constitutional idea of equality (*musavat*). Pointing to the *mashrutahkhwahs* (constitutionalists), he stated: "Oh you who lack integrity and honor, the founder of the *Shari'a* has granted you integrity and privileges because you belong to [the community of] Islam! But you disenfranchise yourself, and demand to be brother of and equal with Zoroastrians, Armenians, and Jews?"[16]

The same protestation against the equality of Muslims and non-Muslims was voiced in a gathering for the election of the Majlis deputies in the city of Yazd, a city with a large Zoroastrian population. One of the clerics present in the session pointed out that: "We should not allow Zoroastrians to become dominant. I hear that one of the articles of the laws of the Majlis is equality. Zoroastrians must be wretched and held in contempt."[17] The Shari'atists viewed the superiority of Muslims over non-Muslims as divine privilege. The equality of all citizens was thus perceived as detrimental to Islam and the privileges of the Muslim community.

Shaykh Fazl'allah, as the leader of the Shari'atist camp, also argued against the Constitutionalists' notion of "freedom" (*azadi*): "The strength of Islam is due to obedience and not to freedom. The basis of its legislation is the differentiation of groups and the summation of differences, and not equality."[18] Admonishing the Constitutionalists, whom he labeled "Paris worshipers" (*Paris parastha*), Shaykh Fazl'allah argued, "Oh, you God worshipers, this National Assembly [*Shura-yi Milli*], liberty and freedom [*hurriyat va azadi*], equality and parity [*musavat va barabari*], and the principles of the present constitutional law [*asas-i qanun-i mashrutah-'i haliyah*] is a dress sown for the body of Europe [*Farangistan*], and is predominantly of the naturalist school [*tabi'i mazhab*] and transgresses the Divine law and the holy book." Shaykh Fazl'allah asked the Constitutionalists why among "so many banners of long live, long live, long live equality, equality and fraternity, why don't you once write: long live the Shari'a, long live the Qur'an, long live Islam?"[19] He explained that "In Islam the verdict of equality is impossible (*mahal ast ba Islam hukm-i musavat*)."[20] Shaykh Fazl'allah clearly understood that the new conception of politics – the equality and freedom of all citizens regardless of their religious affiliation – would undermine the political primacy of Islam and the Shi'i clerisy.

With the discursive articulation of *mashrutah* as anti-Islamic, the campaign against it was depicted as an attempt to "protect the citadel of Islam against the deviations willed by the heretics and the apostates."[21] The Shari'atists demanded an *Islamic* Consultative Assembly and the Constitutionalists a *National* Consultative Assembly (*Majlis-i Shura-yi Milli*). This intensified the antagonism between an exclusionary conception of Islam and an inclusionary view of *millat-i Iran* as an undifferentiated collective sodality. To ground themselves in Iranian history and culture and to guard against the charges of inauthenticity and "Paris-worshiping," the Constitutionalists turned increasingly to pre-Islamic myths, symbols, and system of historical narration. In this way, the concept of the *millat* gained the meaning of "the people" of Iran, with an increasingly secular and non-Islamic connotation. While in the pre-Constitutional period the leading 'ulama were viewed as the leaders (*ru'asa*, sing. *ra'is*) of the *millat*, in the period immediatly after the Revolution this title (*ra'is-i millat*) was granted to the head of the Majlis.

The Constitutionalist movement that had started with dialogism and mutual influencing of nationalist and Islamic discourses ended with a civil war. The Constitutionalist and Shari'atist contingents, with Iran and Islam respectively as the primary loci of their identity, clashed during the 1908–9 Civil War. In the final battles of the Civil War in July 1909, the Constitutionalists captured Tehran, deposed the Shah, and executed some of the leading anti-Constitutionalists, among them Shaykh Fazl'allah Nuri. This seems to have been the first time in the history of Iran that an orthodox Shi'i cleric was hanged from the gallows in public. The execution of Shaykh Fazl'allah, the cultural equivalent of the execution of Louis XVI, marked a radical rejection of the previous political and symbolic order. The Revolution instituted "Iran" and "*millat-i Iran*" as the legitimating loci of political discourse. Authoritarian, Islamist, and populist political forces that emerged in the aftermath of the Revolution all unavoidably authorized their sociopolitical projects in the name of Iran and *millat-i Iran*. These forces could only temporarily dispense with the Majlis, the legitimating institution of modern Iranian politics.

With the hegemony of the nationalist discourse a "bordered" historical perspective became the fashionable style of historical writing and thinking. This bordered history was a product of cultural sedimentation and historical amnesia instituted by the struggle for constitutionalism. The rhetorical depiction of the pre-Constitutional period as the age of darkness, despotism, and fanaticism, which was ingeniously used to legitimate the struggle for constitutionalism, gained factual authority. Likewise the ideas of the decline and the degeneration of Iran from its pre-Islamic luster, originally formulated by the eighteenth-century Orientalists, became a conventional wisdom that informed both scholarly and lay historical arguments. This historiographic assumption also grounded the prevalent view of the pre-Constitutional period as the age of literary, artistic, scientific and philosophical decadence. Thus Iranian modernity (*tajaddud*) came to be viewed as a byproduct of the Iranian Constitutional Revolution or the establishment of the "enlightened" Pahlavi Dynasty (1926–79).

These nationalist historical perspectives were often informed by and corroborated Orientalist historical writings. Both nationalist and Orientalist historiography assumed a continuity between the contemporary and ancient Iran and Iranian "character," an assumption that simultaneously spatialized and detemporalized history. This assumption involved the taxonomic partition of the history and destiny of peoples residing in the bounded territories of Iran from those of the Arabs, Indians, and Turks. While this partition invigorated Iranian nationalism and the Iranian nation-state, it also created what in Chapter 1 was identified as "homeless texts," the marginalized traces of a forgotten prenationalist modernity.

By reactivating the homeless texts of Persianate modernity, this book has tried to chart a different account of the making of modern Iranian history, culture, and identity. This account establishes a close connection between the homeless Persianate texts and eighteenth-century Orientalist works, a connection that is rarely admitted in the burgeoning scholarship on Orientalism. It also acknowledges the significance of Indian Persianate works in fashioning a historical perspective that informed the nineteenth-century Iranian nationalist historiography. It explains how this historical vista sought to dissociate Iran from Islam and to contrive a counter-Arab Iranian identity. While forgetting the Arabs and purging Persian of Arabic terms, the architects of modern Iranian nationalism sought to invent cultural and linguistic affinities between Iran and Europe. Having constituted Europe as the heterotopia of modernity and progress, they blamed the Arabs for the "reverse progress" of Iran and its "non-contemporaneity" with Europe. The nationalist project for the rejuvenation of Iran and the recovery of its "ancient luster" was rhetorically grounded in the Orientalist assumption of the non-contemporaneity of the contemporaneous Iranian and European societies. This rhetorical time-distancing has gained scientific validity in the scholarship on Iranian modernity. The seven chapters of this book have explored new issues that require further inquiry and documentation. They have raised more questions than they were able to answer. It is hoped that the exploratory spirit of this project is pursued by other historians of Persianate modernity.

Notes

Preface and Acknowledgments

1. Dariush Shayegan, *Cultural Schizophrenia: Islamic Societies Confronting the West*, trans. John Howe (London: Saqi Books, 1992), 12.
2. Riza Davari Ardakani, *Shimmah'i az Tarikh-i Gharbzadigi-i Ma: Vaz'-i Kununi-i Tafakkur dar Iran* (Tehran: Surush, 1363 [1984]), 88.
3. Juan Cole, "Invisible Occidentalism: Eighteenth-Century Indo-Persian Constructions of the West," *Iranian Studies*, 25: 3–4 (1992), 3–16; Mehrzad Boroujerdi, *Iranian Intellectuals and the West: The Tormented Triumph of Nativism* (Syracuse, NY: Syracuse University Press, 1996), particularly 10–11. Boroujerdi's characterization of Persianate Europology as "Orientalism in reverse" is informed by Sadik Jalal al-Azm, "Orientalism and Orientalism in Reverse," *Khamsin*, 8 (1981), 5–26.
4. On the Hegelian notion of *secondary identification* see Slavoj Zizek, *The Ticklish Subject: The Absent Center of Political Ontology* (London: Verso, 1999), 90.

Chapter 1 Modernity, Heterotopia, and Homeless Texts

1. See Lorraine Daston, "Historical Epistemology," in *Questions of Evidence: Proof, Practice, and Persuasion across the Disciplines*, ed. James Chandler, Arnold Davidson, and Harry Harootunian (Chicago: University of Chicago Press, 1991), 282–9.
2. On the Husserlian concept of "sedimentation" see Ernesto Laclau, *New Reflections on the Revolution of Our Time* (London: Verso, 1990), 34.
3. For instance see Benedict Anderson, *Imagined Communities: Reflections on the Origins and Spread of Nationalism*, rev. edn (New York: Verso, 1991); Partha Chatterjee, *The Nation and Its Fragments: Colonial and Postcolonial Histories* (Princeton, NJ: Princeton University Press, 1993).
4. Reinhart Koselleck, *Futures Past: On the Semantics of Historical Time*, trans. Keith Tribe (Cambridge, Mass.: MIT Press, 1985), 276.
5. Friedrich Nietzsche, *Beyond Good and Evil*, trans. Marianne Cowan (1955; South Bend, Ind.: Gateway, 1967), 210–11, 146–50.
6. Karl Marx, "Speech at the Anniversary of the People's Paper," in *The Marx–Engels Reader*, 2nd edn, ed. Robert Tucker (New York: W. W. Norton & Company, 1978), 577–8.
7. Koselleck, *Futures Past*, 287.
8. For instance see Enrique Dussel, "Eurocentrism and Modernity," *Boundary*, 2: 20/3 (1993), 65–76; idem., *The Underside of Modernity: Apel, Ricoeur, Rorty, Taylor, and the Philosophy of Liberation*, trans. Eduardo Mendieta (New Jersey: Humanities Press, 1996); Dipesh Chakrabarty, "Postcoloniality and the Artifice of History: Who Speaks for 'Indian' Pasts?" *Representation*, 37 (Winter 1992), 1–26.

9. Max Weber, *The Protestant Ethic and the Spirit of Capitalism* (New York: Scribner, 1958), 25; Jürgen Habermas, *The Philosophical Discourse of Modernity: Twelve Lectures*, trans. Frederick G. Lawrence (Cambridge, Mass.: MIT Press, 1987), 1.

10. For instance see Bernard Lewis, "The Impact of the West," in *The Emergence of Modern Turkey* 2nd edn, London: Oxford University Press, 1961), 40–73; Leonard Binder, "The Natural History of Development Theory, with a Discordant Note on the Middle East," in *Islamic Liberalism: A Critique of Development Ideology* (Chicago: University of Chicago Press, 1988), 24–84; Habermas, *Philosophical Discourse of Modernity*, 2.

11. G. E. von Grunebaum, *Modern Islam: The Search for Cultural Identity* (Berkeley, Cal.: University of California Press, 1962), 248–88.

12. Stuart Hall, "The West and the Rest: Discourse and Power," in *Modernity: An Introduction to Modern Societies*, ed. Stuart Hall, David Held, Don Hubert, and Kenneth Thompson (Cambridge, Mass.: Blackwell, 1996), 184–227; J. M. Roberts, *The Triumph of the West* (London: BBC Publications, 1985), particularly 194–202.

13. Hall, "The West and the Rest," 187. The dichotomy, the West and the Rest, was originally formulated by Marshall Sahlins in his *Culture and Practical Reason* (Chicago: University of Chicago Press, 1976).

14. Hall, "The West and the Rest," 221.

15. Michel Foucault, "Of Other Spaces", *Diacritics*, 16: 1 (Spring 1986), 22–7; quotes on 24 and 27.

16. Stephen Toulmin, *Cosmopolis: The Hidden Agenda of Modernity*, 2nd edn (Chicago: University of Chicago Press, 1992), 28.

17. Toulmin, *Cosmopolis*, 28.

18. For instance see Judith Shklar, *Montesquieu* (Oxford: Oxford University Press, 1987), 30.

19. The first edition of *The Persian Letters* was published in 1721. In Letter 91, documenting this evocative context, Montesquieu noted: "There has appeared a personage got up as a Persian ambassador, who has insolently played a trick on the two greatest kings in the world." See *The Persian Letters*, trans. C. J. Betts (New York: Penguin, 1973), 172–3.

20. Maria Rosa Menocal, *The Arabic Role in Medieval Literary History: A Forgotten Heritage* (Philadelphia: University of Pennsylvania Press, 1987), 2.

21. Ann Stoler, *Race and the Education of Desire: Foucault's History of Sexuality and the Colonial Order of Things* (Durham, NC: Duke University Press, 1995), 15. On "laboratory of modernity" see Paul Rabinow, *French Modern: Norms and Forms of the Social Environment* (Cambridge, Mass.: Press, 1989), 289 and 317.

22. For example see Rabinow, *French Modern*; Sidney Mintz, *Sweetness and Power* (New York: Viking, 1985); Timothy Mitchell, *Colonizing Egypt* (Berkeley, Cal.: University of California Press, 1991); Uday Mehta, *Liberalism and Empire: a Study in Nineteenth-century British Liberal Thought* (Chicago: University of Chicago Press, 1999); Nicholas B. Dirks, "Introduction: Colonialism and Culture," in *Colonialism and Culture* (Ann Arbor: University of Michigan Press, 1992).

23. Stoler, *Race and the Education of Desire*, 16.

24. Rabinow, *French Modern*, 289.

25. Anderson, *Imagined Communities*, 47–65; quote on 50 (emphasis in original).

26. Stoler, *Race and the Education of Desire*, 195.

27. According to Toulmin, "In four fundamental ways . . . 17th-century philosophers set aside the long-standing preoccupation of Renaissance humanism. In particular, they disclaimed any serious interest in four different kinds of practical knowledge: the oral, the particular, the local, and the timely" (*Cosmopolis*, 30).

28. For an critique of modern Indian historiography see Chakrabarty, "Postcoloniality and the Artifice of History," 1–26.

29. Johannes Fabian defines the denial of coevalness as "*a persistent and systematic tendency to place the referent(s) of anthropology in a Time other than the present of the producer of anthropological discourse* [emphasis in original]." See his *Time and the Other: How Anthropology Makes Its Object* (New York: Columbia University Press, 1983), 31.

30. For instance see Ahmad Ashraf, "Historical Obstacles to the Development of a Bourgeoisie in Iran," in *Studies in the Economic History of the Middle East: From the Rise of Islam to the Present Day*, ed. M. A. Cook (London, New York: Oxford University Press, 1970), 308–32; idem, *Mavani'-i Tarikhi-i Rushd-i Sarmayahdari dar Iran: Dawrah-'i Qajariyah* (Tehran: Zaminah, 1359).

31. John Malcolm, *The History of Persia from the Most Early Period to the Present Time* (London: John Murray, 1815), 2: 621; For the Persian translation see *Tarikh-i Iran*, trans. Mirza Isma'il Hayrat (Bombay: Matba'-i Datparsat, 1876).

32. George W. F. Hegel, *The Philosophy of History*, trans. J. Sibree (Buffalo, NY: Prometheus Books, 1991), 188.

33. Malcolm, *History of Persia*, respectively 2: 622, 2: 623, and 2: 624.

34. Ervand Abrahamian, *Iran Between Two Revolutions* (Princeton, NJ: Princeton University Press, 1982), 35, 38, 39, 40, 47.

35. Homa Katouzian, *The Political Economy of Modern Iran: Despotism and Pseudo-Modernism, 1926–1979* (New York: New York University Press, 1981), 7–26, 298–300; idem, "Arbitrary Rule: a Comparative Theory of State, Politics and Society in Iran," *British Society for Middle Eastern Studies*, 24: 1 (1977), 49–73; Ervand Abrahamian, "Oriental Despotism: the Case of Qajar Iran," *International Journal of Middle Eastern Studies*, 5 (1984), 3–31, and also his "European Feudalism and Middle Eastern Despotisms," *Science and Society*, 39 (1975), 135; George Curzon, *Persia and the Persian Question* (London: Longman, 1892), 1: 433.

36. Guity Nashat, *The Origins of Modern Reform in Iran, 1870–80* (Urbana: University of Illinois Press, 1982).

37. Meagan Morris, "Metamorphoses at Sydney Tower," *New Formations*, 11 (Summer 1990), 10, cited in Chakrabarty, "Postcoloniality and the Artifice of History," 17.

38. Mangol Bayat, *Iran's First Revolution: Shi'ism and the Constitutional Revolution of 1905–1909* (Oxford: Oxford University Press, 1991), 36.

39. 'Ali Quli Mirza I'tizad al-Saltanah, *Falak al-Sa'adah* (Tehran: Dar al-Taba'ah-'i Aqa Mir Muhammad Tihrani, 1278/1861).

40. Bayat, *Iran's First Revolution*, 37.

41. Elie Kedourie, *Afghani and Abduh: An Essay on Religious Unbelief and Political Activism in Modern Islam* (London: Cass, 1966), 44–5; Nikki Keddie, *Sayyid Jamal al-Din "al-Afghani": A Political Biography* (Berkeley: University of California Press, 1972), 197–9; Jamshid Bihnam, *Iraniyan va Andishah-'i Tajaddud* (Tehran: Farzan Ruz, 1375/1996), 32–4; Alireza Manafzadeh,

"Nukhustin Matn-i Falsafah-'i Jadid-i Gharbi bah Zaban-i Farsi," *Iran Nameh*, 9: 1 (Winter 1991), 98–108.

42. Faraydun Adamiyat, *Andishah-'i Tarraqi va Hukumat-i Qanun: 'Asr-i Sipahsalar* (Tehran: Khwarazmi, 1351/1972), 17 and 18.

43. On Gobineau's anti-Semitism see Peter Pulzer, *The Rise of Political Anti-Semitism in Germany and Austria* (New York: Wiley, 1964).

44. Arthur, Comte de de Gobineau, Les *religions et philosophies dans l'Asie centrale* ([Paris: Gallimard, 1957]), 98, 110–4; idem, *Trois ans en Asie, de 1855 a 1858* (Paris: E. Leroux, 1905).

45. Kamran Arjomand, "The Emergence of Scientific Modernity in Iran: Controversies Surrounding Astrology and Modern Astronomy in Mid-Nineteenth Century," *Iranian Studies*, 30: 1–2 (Winter/Spring 1997), 15.

46. Ibid., 5–24.

47. Bayat, *Iran's First Revolution*, 37.

48. Arjomand, "Emergence of Scientific Modernity," 17.

49. Edward Said, *Orientalism* (New York: Pantheon Books, 1978), 2–3.

50. A. Bausani, "The Qajar Period: an Epoch of Decadence?" in *Qajar Iran: Political, Social, and Cultural Changes, 1800–1925*, ed. Edmond Bosworth and Carloe Hillenbrand (Costa Mesa, Cal.: Mazda, 1992), 255–60.

51. See Said, *Orientalism*, 322.

52. Michel Foucault, "What is Enlightenment," in *Ethics, Subjectivity, and Truth*, ed. Paul Rabinow, trans. Robert Hurley and others (New York: New Press, 1994), 303–19; quotes on 312, 309–10, and 309–10.

53. Mahdi Akhavn Salis, "Akhir-i Shahnamah'" in *Akhir-i Shahnamah*, 8th edn (Tehran: Intisharat-i Murvarid, 1363/1984), 79–86, quote on 85.

54. "Anjuman-i Ma'arif," *Miftah al-Zafar*, 2: 12 (22 March 1899), 182–3.

55. François Bernier, *Travels in the Mogul Empire*, AD 1656–1668, trans. Archibald Constable, rev. by Vincent Smith (London: Oxford University Press, 1914; New Delhi: Atlantic Publishers, 1989), 324–5. Danishmand Khan, also known as Muhammad Shafi', was born in Iran and went to Surat, India, in 1646. Shah Jahan appointed him as a Bakhshi (military paymaster) and granted him the title of Danishmand Khan. Alamgir appointed him as Governor of Shah Jahan Abad or New Delhi, where he died in 1670. William Harvey was a lecturer at the Royal College of Physicians and discovered the circulation of blood. Jean Pecquet discovered the conversion of chyle into blood.

56. Raymond Schwab, *The Oriental Renaissance: Europe's Discovery of India and the East, 1680–1880*, trans. Gene Patterson-Black and Victor Reinking (New York: Columbia University Press, 1984), 142–6.

57. Bernier, *Travels in the Mogul Empire*, quotes on 324–5 and 352–3.

58. Samsam al-Dawlah Shahnavaz Khan, *Ma'asir al-Umara*, ed. Maulavi 'Abd al-Rahim and Maulavi Mirza Ashraf 'Ali (Calcutta: Asiatic Society of Bengal, 1892) 2: 30–2; quotes on 32.

59. François Bernier to M. Caron (10 March 1663) in François Martin, *François Martin Mémoires: Travels to Africa, Persia & India*, trans. Aniruddha Ray (Calcutta: Subarnarekha, 1990), 546–66; quote on 548.

60. This Persian translation of the *Upanishads* was rendered into French and Latin by Anquetil-Duperron in 1801–2.

61. Martin, *François Martin Mémoires*, 441–2.

62. Pietro della Valle, *Viaggi di Pietro della Valle il pellegrino* (Roma: Appresso Vitale Mascardi, 1650; Brighton, 1843), 326–8; cited in Arjomand, "Emergence of Scientific Modernity," p. 7; John D. Gurney, "Pietro Della Valle: the Limits of Perception," *Bulletin of the School of Oriental and African Studies* (1986), 103–16, particularly 112.
63. On the *Zij-i Muhammad Shahi* see William Hunter, "Some Account of the astronomical labours of Jaha Sinha, Raja of Ambhere, or Jayanagar," *Asiatic Society*, 5 (1799), 177–210. This article includes the Persian preface of the Zij and its English translation.
64. Phillipe de La Hire (1640–1718), *Tabulae astronomicae...* (Paris: Apud S. Michallet, 1687; Paris: Apud Joannem Boudot, 1702).
65. Muhammad 'Ali Mubashshir Khan, *Manahij al-Istikhraj* (Unpublished manuscript: Kitabkhanah-'i Astan-i Quds-i Razavi, #12302). On the influence of de La Hire see Virendra Nath Sharma, "Zïj Muhammad Shahi and the Tables of de La Hire," *Indian Journal of History of Science*, 25: 1–4 (1990), 36–41.
66. Many copies of *Zij-i Muhammad Shahi* are available in Iranian libraries. One of the earliest editions is reported "to be extant" in the library of Madrasah-'i 'Ali-i Sipahsalar, which was renamed after the 1979 Revolution as Madrasah-'i 'Ali-i Shahid Mutahhari. See S. M. Razaullah Ansari, "Introduction of Modern Western Astronomy in India during 18–19 Centuries," in *History of Astronomy in India*, ed. S. N. Sen and K. S. Shukla (New Delhi: Indian National Science Academy, 1985), 363–402; quote on 364.
67. 'Abbas Mazda, "Nufuz-i Sabk-i Urupa'i dar Naqashi-i Iran", *Payam-i Nau*, 2: 10 (1325 [1946]), 59–72, particularly 61; Husayn Mahbubi Ardakani, *Tarikh-i Muassasat-i Tamadduni-i Jadid Dar Iran* (Tehran: Anjuman-i Danishjuyan-i Danishgah-i Tihran, 1354–1368 [1975–1989]), 1: 234. The claim of Muhammad Zaman's travel to Europe is refuted by the Russian Orientalists Igor Akimushkin. See Abolala Soudavar, "European and Indian Influences," in *Art of the Persian Courts: Selections from the Art and History Trust Collection* (New York: Rizzoli International Publications, 1992), 365–79, particularly f.n. #16, 379. For a critical evaluation of the controversy over Muhammad Zaman's career see A. A. Ivanov, "Nadirah-'i Dawran Muhammad Zaman," in *Davazdah Rukh: Yadnigari az Dawazdah Naqash-i Nadirahkar-i Iran*, trans. Ya'qub Azhand (Tehran: Intisharat-i Mawla, 1377/1998), 313–28.
68. Mir 'Abd al-Latif Shushtari, *Tuhfat al-'Alam va Zayl al-Tuhfah*, ed. Samad Muvahhid ([Bombay: s.n. , 1847]; Tehran: Tahuri, 1363/1984), 363–7. See also: amonymous, "An Account of the Life and Character of Tofuzel Hussein Khan, the Vakeel, or Ambassador, of the Nabob Vizier Assof-Ud-Dowlah, at Calcutta, During the Government of Marquis Cornwallis," *The Asiatic Annual Register*, (1803), Characters, 1–8, quote on 1.
69. "An Account of the Life and Character of Tofuzel Hussein Khan," 1.
70. Ruben Burrows was supposed to write "notes and explanations" to Tafazzul Husayn Khan's translation of Newton's *Principia*. According to the *Asiatic Annual Register*, "The translation was finished, but it has not been printed; and we believe Mr. Burrows never added the annotations he mentions." See "An Account of the Life and Character of Tofuzel Hussein Khan," Characters, 7. Mir 'Abd al-Latif Shushtari noted that Tafazzul Husayn Khan aquired his knowledge of European philosophy (*hikamiyat-i farang*) from Mr Burrows (*Tuhfat al-'Alam*, 371). On Ruben Burrows see *Asiatic Researches*, 2 (1790), 489.

71. Tafazzul Husayn Khan, who "wrote the Persian language with uncommon elegance," had been appointed by Hastings to accompany David Anderson to Mahajee Scindiah. According to David Anderson, Husayn Khan learned English from "my brother, Mr. Blaine" and European mathematics and astronomy "from his communication with the learned Mr. Broome." In 1792, upon a friend's request, Anderson had asked Tafazzul Husayn Khan to inquire about "the ancient astronomy of the Hindus." All quotes are from a letter by David Anderson published in "An Account of the Life and Character of Tofuzel Hussein Khan," 2–3.

72. "An Account of the Life and Character of Tofuzel Hussein Khan," 8. For Husayn Khan's acquaintance with William Jones and Richard Johnson, see p. 4.

73. Juan Cole, "Invisible Occidentalism," 3–16.

74. Shushtari, *Tuhfat al-'Alam*, respectively 252, 255, 36–40, 299–315, 36; 34–40, and 36–40, particularly 38.

75. Shushtari, *Tuhfat al-'Alam*, respectively 303 and 307. For an alternative interpretation of this passage see Cole, "Invisible Occidentalism," 11–12. As it relates to the state of astronomical knowledge, Shushtari mentioned meeting the 90-year-old Mir Masih Allah Shahjahanabadi, who resided in Murshidabad and had spent most of his life mastering astronomy. He reports studying *Zij-i Muhammad Shahi*, the observations of Chayt Singh, and other astronomical texts which were in the possession of Mir Masih. It would be important to locate the works these two scholars. See Shushtari, *Tuhfat al-'Alam*, 374.

76. Mirza Muhammad Sadiq Marvazi Vaqyi' Nigar, *Qava'id al-Muluk* (Tehran: Iranian National Libray, MS F/1757).

77. See I'tizad al-Saltanah's biographical note on Vaqayi' Nigar in his *Iksir al-Tavarikh*, ed. Jamshid Kayanfarr (Tehran: Visman, 1370/1997), 274–7; Yahya Aryanpur, *Az Saba ta Nima: Taridh-i 150 Sal Adabi Farsi* (Tehran: Kitabba -yi Jibi, 1351/1972), 1: 75–7.

78. Aqa Ahmad Bihbahani Kirmanshahi, *Mir'at al-Ahval-i Jahan Nama*, ed. 'Ali Davani (Tehran: Intisharat-i Markaz-i Asnad-i Inqilab-i Islami, 1375 [1996]), 392. For a different rendering see Cole, "Invisible Occidentalism," 11.

79. For instance Kamaran Arjomand claims that "in the second half of the nineteenth century there were serious efforts to defend traditional Islamic cosmology against modern European astronomy" ("Emergence of Scientific Modernity," 10).

80. Mawlavi Abu al-Khayr, *Majmu'ah-i Shamsi: mushtamil-i bar masa'il-i 'ilm-i hay'at mutabiq-i tahqiqat-i 'ulama-yi muta'akhirin-i Farang* (Calcutta: Hindoostani Press, 1222/1807). In the introduction Mawlavi Abu al-Khayr notes that *Majmu'ah-'i Shamsi* is based on English language sources, which he translated with the encouragement and assistance of Dr William Hunter (1718–83). *Majmu'ah -'i Shamsi* bears the following note in English: "A Concise View of the Copernican System of Astronomy, by Mouluwee Ubool Khuer, under the superintendence of W. Hunter, M. D. Calcutta. Printed by T. Hubbard at the Hindoostanee Press, 1807."

81. Mawlavi Abu al-Khayr, *Majmu'ah-i Shamsi*, 2.

82. William Hunter, "Account of the Astronomical Labours of Jaya Sinha, Rajah of Ambhere, or Jayanagar," *Asiatic Researches Or Transactions of the Society Instituted in Bengal*, 5 (1799), 177–211.

83. Other texts on modern sciences, particularly astronomy, include Muhammad Isma'il Landani's *Tashil al-adrak fi sharh al-aflak*, available at Dar al-'Ulum Nadwat al-'Ulama, radif 3, no. 4; Muhammad Ayyub's *Risalah dar 'Ilm-i Nujum* (1801/1216), available at the Khuda Bakhsh Oriental Public Library, (Acc. 334); Sayyid Ahmad 'Ali's *Muqaddamat-i 'Ilm-i Hay'at* (Calcutta: n.p., n.d.), and Rathan Singh Zakhmi Lakhnavi's *Hadayiq al-Nujum* (1838).

84. Muhammad Rafi' al-Din Khan, 'Umdat al-Mulk, *Rafi' al-Basar* (Calcutta: C. V. William Press, 1841).

85. For a discussion of Martyn see 'Abd al-Hadi Ha'iri, *Nukhustin Ruyaruyiha-yi Andishahgaran-i Iran ba Du Ruyah-'i Tamaddun-i Burzhuvazi-i Gharb* (Tehran: Amir Kabir, 1367), 507–45.

86. For Martyn's Persian translation of the New Testament see *Kitab al-Muqaddas va Huwa Kutub-i al-'Ahd-i al-Jadid-i Khudavand va Rahanandah-'i Ma 'Isa-'i Masih [The New Testament of Our Lord Saviour Jesus Christ]* (London: The British and Foreign Bible Society, 1876).

87. Afzal-ul-Ulama Muhammad Yousuf Kokan, *Arabic and Persian in Carnatic, 1710–1960* (Madras: Hafiza House, 1974), 340–4.

88. Ibid., 340–4 and 345–8.

89. Malcolm, *History of Persia*, 2: 5536–537).

90. James B. Fraser, *Narrative of a Journey into Khorasan . . .* (London: Longman, 1825), respectively 152–3, 282, and 484.

91. Muhammad Qazi b. Kashif al-Din Muhammad Ardakani, *Tuhfah-'i Muhammadiyah*, (Mashhad: Kitabkhanah-'i Astan-i Quds-i Razavi, no. 583). The manuscript was copied in 1220/1805.

92. Fraser, *Narrative of a Journey*, 484.

93. For instance see, Buzurg 'Alavi, "Critical Writings on the Renewal of Iran," in *Qajar Iran: Political, Social, and Cultural Changes, 1800–1925*, ed. Edmond Bosworth and Carloe Hillenbrand (Costa Mesa, Cal.: Mazda, 1992), 243–54, quote on 253.

94. Writing on eighteenth-century Bengal, Richard Eaton has also observed, "Two stereotypes – one by students of Indian history, the other held by students of Islam – have conspired greatly to obscure our understanding of Islam in Bengal, and especially of the growth of a Muslim peasant community there. The first of these is the notion of eighteenth-century Mughal India as a period hopelessly mired in decline, disorder, chaos, and collapse." See his "The Growth of Muslim Identity in Eighteenth-Century Bengal," in *Eighteenth-Century Renewal and Reform in Islam*, ed. Nehemiah Levtzion and John Voll (Syracuse, NY: Syracuse University Press, 1987), 161–85; quote on 161.

Chapter 2   Orientalism's Genesis Amnesia

1. On "genesis amnesia" see Pierre Bourdieu, *Outline of a Theory of Practice*, trans. Richard Nice (Cambridge: Cambridge University Press, 1977), 79.

2. Raymond Schwab, *The Oriental Renaissance: Europe's Discovery of India and the East, 1680–1880*, trans. Gene Pattersan-Black and Victor Reinking (New York: Columbia University Press, 1984), 8, 7, 5, and 33.

3. Bernard Lewis, *The Muslim Discovery of Europe* (New York: W. W. Norton, 1982), 142, 168, and 170. In Lewis's account, "[i]t is not until the 1820s that for the first time we find in Egypt translations of Western books . . . " (170).

4. Bernard Lewis, *Islam and the West* (New York; Oxford: Oxford University Press, 1993), 123–4.

5. G. E. Von Grunebaum, *Modern Islam: The Search for Cultural Identity* (Berkeley: University of California Press, 1962), 233–4 and 234–5.

6. Edward Said, *Orientalism* (London: Routledge & Kegan Paul, 1978), respectively 204, 160, 50, 204.

7. Lewis, *Islam and the West*, 125.

8. Said, *Orientalism*, 2.

9. Max Müller, "Preface to the Sacred Books of the East," in *The Upanishads*, trans. F. Max Müller (Oxford: Clarendon Press, 1879; Delhi: Motilal Banarsidass, 1965), xvii.

10. Schwab, *The Oriental Renaissance*, 158.

11. For an erudite account of Anquetil-Duperron's residence in India see Jivanji Jamshedji Modi, "Anquetil Du Perron of Paris–India as Seen by Him (1755–60)," in *Anquetil Du Perron and Dastur Darab* (Bombay: *Times of India*, 1916), 1–69.

12. In conventional accounts of this relationship Anquetil is often lionized while his educators are demeaned. For instance see Martin Haug, *The Parsis: Essays on Their Sacred Language, Writings and Religion*, rev. K. W. West (Boston, Mass.: Houghton, Osgood, 1878; New Delhi: Cosmo Publications, 1978), 17–18. For a critical analysis of Anquetil-Duperron's exaggerations and self-glorification see Jivanji Jamshedji Modi, "Anquetil Du Perron of Paris and Dastur Drab of Surat," in *Anquetil Du Perron and Dastur Darab*, 70–141.

13. Schwab, *The Oriental Renaissance*, 7.

14. According to Schwab, "An Oriental Renaissance – a second Renaissance, in contrast to the first: the expression and the theme are familiar to the Romantic writers, for whom the term is interchangeable with Indic Renaissance. What the expression refers to is the revival of an atmosphere in the nineteenth century brought about by the arrival of Sanskrit texts in Europe, which produced an effect equal to that produced in the fifteenth century by the arrival of Greek manuscripts and Byzantine commentators after the fall of Constantinople." See Schwab, *The Oriental Renaissance*, 11.

15. Abu al-Fazl Allami, *The A-in-i Akbari*, trans. H. Blochman; edited by D. C. Phillott (Calcutta : [Royal] Asiatic Society of Bengal, 1872–7; Delhi: Low Price Publications, 1989), 1: 110–12.

16. For Persian translation of Sanskrit works see Fathullah Mujtabai, "Persian Hindu Writings: Their Scope and Relevance," in *Aspects of Hindu Muslim Cultural Relations* (New Delhi: National Book Bureau, 1978); Shriram Sharm, *A Descriptive Bibliography of Sanskrit Works in Persian* (Hyderabad: Abul Kalam Azad Oriental Research Institute, 1982); N. S. Shukla, "Persian Translations of Sanskrit Works," *Indological Studies*, 3 (1974), 175–91.

17. Cited in Mujtabai, *Aspects of Hindu Muslim Cultural Relations*, 66.

18. Quoted from a statement by Emperor Akbar appearing in Mir Jamal al-Din Husayn Inju Shirazi, *Farhang-i Jahangiri*, ed. Rahim 'Afifi (Mashhad: Danishgah-i Mashhad, 1354/1975), 4. The full text of Akbar's statement appears in

J. J. Modi, "Notes on Anquetile Du Perron (1755–61) on King Akbar and Dastur Meherji Rana" in *Contributions on Akbar and the Parsees*, ed. B. P. Ambashthya (Patna: Janaki Prakashan, 1976), 1–16, particularly 6.

19. V. S. Ghate, "Persian Grammar in Sanskrit," *The Indian Antiquary* (January 1912), 4–7.
20. Mirza Khan ibn Fakhr al-Din Muhammad, *Tuhfat al-Hind*, ed. Nur al-Hasan Ansari (Tehran: Bunyad-i Farhang-i Iran, 1975).
21. Dastur Ardshir Nawshirvan was invited on the recommendation of the Zoroastrian Dastur Meherji Rana. On this point see J. J. Modi, "The Parsees at the Court of Akbar and Dastur Meherji Rana," in *Contributions on Akbar and the Parsees*, 1–177, particularly 17; Mary Boyce, *Zoroastrians: Their Religious Beliefs and Practices* (London: Routledge & Kegan Paul, 1979), 183. For a list of "Zand and Pazand" terminologies compiled in cooperation with Ardshir Nawshirvan see Inju Shirazi, *Farhang-i Jahangiri*, 3: 553–700.
22. On "Eighteenth-Century Parsi Religious Disputes" see Boyce, *Zoroastrians*, 188–95.
23. *Zend-Avesta*, trans. A. H. Anquetil-Duperron and intro. Robert D. Richardson (New York: Garland, 1984), I: 326; Boyce, *Zoroastrians*, 189; Haug, *The Parsis*, 57; Modi, *Anquetil Du Perron and Dastur Darab*, 37.
24. On the eve of Anquetil's departure for Europe, Dasturs Darab and Kavus sued him for the failure to pay the price for purchased manuscripts and tutorial charges. For details see Modi, *Anquetil Du Perron and Dastur Darab*, 55 and 95.
25. For the Persian translation see Muhammad Dara Shukuh bin Shahjahan, *Sirr-i Akbar* = Sirr al-Asrar, ed. Tara Chand and Muhammad Riza Jalali Na'ini (Tehran: Taban, 1961). For a description of this translation see Mahesh Prasad, "The Unpublished Translation of the Upanishads by Prince Dara Shikoh," in *Dr. Modi Memorial Volume: Papers on Indo-Iranian and other Subjects*, ed. Darab Peshotan Sanjana, Bamanji Nasarwanji et. al. (Bombay: Fort Printing Press, 1930), 622–38.
26. Halhed's translation remains unpublished. On his contribution see Rosane Rocher, *Orientalism, Poetry, and the Millenium: The Checkered Life of Nathaniel Brassey Halhed, 1751–1830* (Delhi: Motilal Banarsidass, 1983); Wilhelm Halbfass, *India and Europe: An Essay in Understanding* (New York: State University of New York Press, 1988), 64.
27. *Oupenek'hat: id est, Secretum tegendum*, trans. A. H. Anquetil-Duperron (Strasbourg, 1801).
28. Schwab, *The Oriental Renaissance*, 143 and 142.
29. François Bernier, *Travels in the Moghul Empire, AD 1656–1668*, trans. Archibard Constable, rev. Vincent Smith (London: Oxford University Press, 1914; New Delhi: Atlantic Publishers, 1989), 323–4.
30. From the publisher's "Note" appearing in the reprint edition of Jones's *A Grammar of the Persian Language* (London: W. and J. Richardson, 1771; Menston: Scholar Press, 1969), v.
31. *The Letters of Sir William Jones*, ed. Garland Cannon (Oxford: Claredon Press, 1970), 2: 798.
32. In a letter to William Steuart dated 13 September 1789, Jones wrote: "Give my best compliments to Major Palmer & tell him that his friend Tafazzul Husain Khan is doing wonders in English & Mathematicks. He is reading

Newton with Borrow, & means to translate the *Principia* into Arabick." See
"To William Steuart," in *Letters of Sir William Jones*, no. 520, 838–40. On
Tafazzul Husayn Khan see Shushtari, *Tuhfat al-'Alam*, 363–67; Rahman 'Ali,
Tazkarah-'i 'Ulama-yi Hind (Luknow: Matba'-i Munshi Niwal Kishur, 1894),
36–7.

33. See William Jones, "The Sixth Discourse: On the Persians, Delivered 19
    February 1789," in *The Works of Sir William Jones in Six Volumes*, ed. Anna
    Maria Shipley Jones (London: G. G. and J. Robinson, 1799), 73–94, name
    on 77–78; idem, "A Conversation with Abram, an Abyssinian concerning
    the City of Gwender and the Source of the Nile," in *Works*, I: 515–518,
    name on 517.
34. For Bahman's cooperation with Jones see Jones, "On the Persians," 80, 81,
    82, 84, 89. In a letter to Sir John Macpherson dated 6 May 1786, Jones
    wrote, "I read with pleasure, while at breakfast, Mr. Forster's lively little
    tract, and having finished my daily task of Persian reading with a learned
    Parsi of Yazd, who accompanied me hither" (*Letters of Sir William Jones*, let-
    ter no. 433, p. 697). Also see Jones's letter to John Shore, dated 16 August
    1787, in *Letters of Sir William Jones*, letter no. 465, p. 763). Bahman's father,
    Bahram, was "a confidential servant of Carim Khan [Zand]..." (Jones,
    "Remark by the President," *Works*, supplement I: 443–4).
35. For instance Shushtari noted that Jones had written a commentary on
    Muhammad 'Ali Hazin and asked him "to note the deficiencies and excess"
    (*Tuhfat al-'Alam*, 370).
36. See *Letters of Sir William Jones*, f.n. no. 1, 659. 'Ali Ibrahim Khan provided
    Jones with a copy of *Tuhfat al-Hind*, which he used in writing "On the
    Musical Modes of the Hindus," in *Works*, I: 413–43. See Nur al-Hasan
    Ansari, "Muqaddimah-'i musahhah," in *Tuhfat al-Hind*, 41.
37. In a letter to Charles Wilkins dated 17 September 1785, Jones wrote, "In the
    meantime, pray tell Mohhammed Ghauth, that... I wish him to set about
    the Inscription from Gaia, which you so wonderfully deciphered..." (*Let-
    ters of Sir William Jones*, 682).
38. He was the author of *Siyar al-muta'akhirin*, which was published as *A Trans-
    lation of the Sëir Mutaqharin; or View of Modern Times* (Calcutta, 1799,
    Calcutta: T. D. Chatterjee, 1902).
39. On the last five scholars see Jones's letter to "the first Marquis of Cornwal-
    lis, Governor-General of Bengal in Council," dated 13 April 1788, in *Letters
    of Sir William Jones*, letter no. 487, p. 802.
40. See *Letters of Sir William Jones*, letter no. 465, p. 762.
41. Jones to Charles Wilkins, 17 September 1785, in *Letters of Sir William Jones*,
    683.
42. Mirza Itesa Modeen, *Shigurf Namah I Velaët, or Excellent Intelligence Con-
    cerning Europe; Being the Travels of Mirza Itesa Modeen, in Great Britain
    and France*, trans. James Edward Alexander (London: Parbury, Allen, 1827),
    65–6.
43. See Mirza Itesa Modeen, *Shigurf Namah*, 64–5.
44. The editor of Jones's *Works* has identified the "foreign nobleman" as Baron
    Reviski. See Jones, *Works*, I: f.n. 129.
45. William Jones, *A Grammar of the Persian Language* (London: W. and J. Rich-
    ardson, 1771), xvi–xvii.

46. According to Arberry, "Early in 1768 Jones made the aquaintance of Count Reviczki, at that time resident in London, and was delighted to hail him a fellow-admirer of Persian poetry." See A. J. Arberry, "The Founder: William Jones," in *Oriental Essays: Portraits of Seven Scholars* (London: Geoge Allen & Unwin, 1960), 48–86, quote on 50. For Jones's correspondences with Reviczky, see *Letters of Sir William Jones*, letters no. 2 (1768), 4–5; no. 3 (April 1768), 6–12; no. 4 (1768), 12–13; no. 9 (Nov. 1768), 20; no. 28 (1770), 49–51; no. 30 (May 1770), 52–4; no. 32 (1770), 56–62; no. 46 (1771), 82–7; no. 58 (1771), 105–9; no. 101 (1775), 179–80. Also see Garland Cannon, *Oriental Jones: A Biography of Sir William Jones, 1746–1794* (New York: Asia Publishing House, 1964), 14–15.
47. Cannon, *Oriental Jones*, 10–13; S. N. Mukherjee, *Sir William Jones: A Study in Eighteenth-Century British Attitudes to India* (Cambridge: Cambridge University Press, 1968), 22–3. It is probable that the so called "Syrian teacher" of Jones was no other than Mirza I'tisam al-Din.
48. Jones, *A Grammar of the Persian Language*, xiv.
49. On the limitation of Jones's knowledge of Persian see Garland H. Cannon, "Sir William Jones's Persian Linguistics," *Oriental Society*, 78 (1958), 262–73. Also reprinted in Thomas A. Sebeok, *Portraits of Linguistics: A Biographical Source Book for the History of Western Linguistics, 1746–1963* (Westport, Conn.: Greenwood Press, 1966), 36–57.
50. Jones, *A Grammar of the Persian Language*, xv.
51. William Jones, *Lettre á Monsieur A*** du P***, dans laquelle est compris l'examen de sa traduction des livres attribués á Zoroastre* (London, 1771). For summaries of this controversy see Arthur D. Waley, "Anquetil Duperron and Sir William Jones," *History Today* 2 (January 1952), 23–33; Haug, *The Parsis*, 18–23; Max Müller, "Introduction" in *The Zend-Avesta*, xiv–xxv; Edward G. Brown, *A Literary History of Persia: From the Earliest Times until Firdawsi* (New York: Charles Scribner's Sons, 1902), 44–59; Cannon, *Oriental Jones*, 14–15.
52. Jones, "The History of the Persian Language," in *Works*, ii: 303–28, quote on 306.
53. Jones continued, "But let the *rosy-cheeked Frenchman*, to give him his own Epithet, rest happy in the *contemplation of his personal beauty, and the vast extent of his learning*: it is sufficient for us to have exposed his follies, detected his imposture, and retold his invectives, without insulting a fallen adversary, or attempting, like the Hero in *Dryden's* Ode, to *slay the slain*." See Jones, "The History of the Persian Language," in *Works*, ii: 307.
54. John Richardson, "A Dissertation on the Languages, Literature, and Manners of Eastern Nations," in his *A Dictionary: Persian, Arabic, and English*, rev. Charles Wilkins (London: J. L. Cox, 1829), i–lxxxii, quote on p. vb.
55. Richardson, "A Dissertation," ivb–vb.
56. In 1675 Pierre Besnier wrote, "Besides the Latin makes a friendly meeting between the Eastern, and Western languages; as to the first alone it owns birth and rise, so the others do to it . . . I consider the Latin under three different regards, as the daughter of the languages of the East, as the Mother of those in the West, and as the Sister of the more Northerne." See Pierre Besnier, *A Philosophical Essay for the Reunion of Languages*, trans. Henry Rose (Oxford: J. Good, 1675; Menston: The Scholar Press, 1971), 14.

57. Jones, "On the Persians," 83; cited in Max Müller, *The Sacred Languages of the East, translated by various Oriental Scholars*, ed. F. Max Müller (Delhi: Motilal Banarsidass, 1965), 4: xx.
58. Max Müller, *The Sacred Languages of the East*, 4: xx. Hans Aarsleff also views Jones as the founder of modern philology. See his *The Study of Language in England, 1780–1860* (Minneapolis: University of Minnesota Press, 1983), 124.
59. Müller, *The Sacred Languages of the East*, 4: xx–xxi.
60. The history of linguistics texts often opens with entries on William Jones. For instance see Sebeok, *Portraits of Linguistics*. The first three articles in this volume are devoted to Jones.
61. Siraj al-Din Khan Arzu, *Muthmir [Musmir]*, ed. Rehana Khatoon (Karachi: The Institute of Central and West Asian Studies, 1991). According to Rehana Khatoon, "Khan-i Arzu is also the first scholar in both the East and the West who introduced the theory of similarities of two languages [*tavafuq-i lisanayn*], meaning that Sanskrit and Persian are sister languages. His ideas in this regard are contained in his monumental work being discussed here, i.e. the *Muthmir*. The work has not yet been thoroughly studied and made a subject of serious assessment; [a]nd this has prompted me to undertake and prepare a critical edition of the *Muthmir*." See Rehana Khatoon, "Introduction," in *Muthmir*, 43.
62. Müller, "Introduction," in *The Sacred Languages of the East*, iv: xx.
63. The term *tavafuq* literally means concordance or concurrence.
64. Arzu, *Muthmir*, 221.
65. Arzu offered a detailed definition of *tavafuq al-lisanayn* under the concept of *ang*. See his *Chiragh-i Hidayat*, published with Ghiyas al-Din Rampuri's *Ghiyas al-Lughat*, ed. Mansur Sirvat (Tehran: Amir Kabir, 1984), pp. 1017–18. The editor of this edition, without any explanation, has eliminated Arzu's introduction to *Chiragh-i Hidayat*.
66. For example see Arzu, *Chiragh-i Hidayat*, 1050, 1061, 1068, 1091, 1119, 1020–21, and 1214.
67. Julia Kristeva, *Language the Unknown and Initiation into Linguistics*, trans. Anne M. Menke (New York: Columbia University Press, 1989), 196
68. According to Muhammad Javad Mashkur, "In Pahlavi writing there is a certain number of pure Semitic words. These words which are the most frequent occurrence, are pronouns, particles, numerals, and auxiliary verbs. They are mostly Aramaic, that is of Semitic origin.... This Semitic element is called Huzvaresh. The Semitic words were used in writing only as representatives of Persian words that were spoken; for example, when the writer of a text wrote the Semitic word 'lahma' (bread) it was read 'nan' which was its Iranian equivalent." See *Farhang-i Huzvarish ha-yi Pahlavi* (Tehran: Bunyad-i Farhang-i Iran, 1346/1967), 303.
69. Jones, "The Sixth Discourse," 81.
70. Arzu, *Muthmir*, 13.
71. Arzu, *Muthmir*, 20.
72. "*Iraniyan mara bah Hindi nizhad budan bah miqdari nanahand.*" Cited in Sayyad Muhammad Akram's "Pish guftar" in Siraj al-Din 'Ali Khan Arzu, *Dad-i Sukhan*, ed. Sayyid Muhammad Akram (Rawalpindi: Iran Pakistan Institute of Persian Studies, 1974), xxxiv.

73. Akram, "Pish guftar" in *Dad-i Sukhan*, xxxiv.
74. Abu al-Barakat Munir Lahuri, *Karnamah*, ed. Sayyid Muhammad Akram (Islamabad: Iran Pakistan Institute of Persian Studies, 1977), 26.
75. Munir, *Karnamah*, 27.
76. Students and disciples of Arzu included Tik Chand Bahar, Rai Rayan Anand Ram Mukhlis (d. 1751), Bindraban Das Khushgu, Mir Taqi Mir (c.1722–1810), Mirza Muhammad Rafi' Sauda (1713–80), Najm al-Din Shah Mubarak Abru (1692–1747), Sharaf al-Din Mazmun (c.1689–1745), and Mustafa Khan Yakrang.
77. Muhammad Husayn Azad, *Ab-i Hayat*, 121; cited in Muhammad Sadiq's *A History of Urdu Literature* (Delhi: Oxford University Press, 1984), 91. Earlier than Azad, Qudartullah Qadiri remarked, "Just as all theologians are the lineal descendants of Abu Hanifa, similarly it would be quite appropriate to consider all Hindi [Urdu] poets as his [Arzu's] descendants." Cited in Sadiq's *A History of Urdu Literature*, 91.
78. In a letter to John Shore dated 24 June 1787, Jones wrote, "the Dabistan also I have read through twice with great attention . . . On the whole, it is the most amusing and instructive book I ever read in Persian." See *Letters of Sir William Jones*, no. 461, 739.
79. See Chapter 5.
80. Jones, "The Sixth Discourse," 77–8.
81. Jones, "The Sixth Discourse," 78.
82. Müller, like Jones, was interested in "the first ancestors of the Indians, the Persians, the Greeks, the Romans, the Slaves, the Celts and the Germans [one] living together within the same enclosure, nay under the same roof." See Max Müller, *Lectures on the Science of Language Delivered at the Royal Institution of Great Britain in April, May, and June 1861* (London, 1862), 213.
83. Jones, "The Sixth Discourse," 88.
84. Jones, "The Sixth Discourse," 90. For a discussion of controversies over the universal deluge before Kayumars see Chapter 5.
85. Jones, "The Sixth Discourse," 92.
86. Jones, "The Sixth Discourse," 79. The significance of such an assertion had been brought to Jones's attention by Lord Monboddo (James Burnet) who in a letter dated 20 June 1789, wrote, "if you can discover the central country from which all those nations, which you have named, have derived their affinity in language, manners and arts, which you observe, it will be a most wonderful discovery in the history of man." See Jones, *Letters of Sir William Jones*, f.n. 2; p. 818. On Lord Monboddo's argument concerning the affinity of Sanskrit and Greek see James Burnet, *Of the Origin and Progress of Languages* (1773; Menston: Scholar Press, 1967), 1: 472.
87. Jones, "The Sixth Discourse," respectively 79 and 80.
88. According to Garland Cannon, Bahman "had fled the wrath of Ali Murad (d. 1785), the Persian king, who had killed his family. He became a reader of Jones's law digest and other projects in Nov. [1785?]." See *Letters of Sir William Jones*, no. 433, fn. 3, 697.
89. Müller, "Introduction," in *The Sacred Books of the East* (Oxford: Clarendon Press, 1879), iv: xx.
90. Jones, "The Sixth Discourse," all quotes on 81; also appears in Arzu, *Muthmir*, 176–7.

91. Arzu, *Muthmir*, 175–9.

92. Discussing the "phenomenon of reification," Georg Lukacs explained that "[i]ts basis is that a relation between people takes on the character of a thing and thus acquires a 'phantom objectivity', an autonomy that seems so strictly rational and all-embracing as *to conceal every trace of its fundamental nature*: the relation between people" (emphasis added). See his *History and Class Consciousness: Studies in Marxist Dialectics*, trans. Rodney Livingstone (Cambridge: MIT Press, 1971), 83.

93. This analysis is based on a comparison with Shiv Parshad's *Tarikh-i Fayz Bakhsh* (Oxford: Bodleian, Caps.Or.C. 2).

94. William Francklin, *The History of the Reign of Shah-Aulum, the Present Emperor of Hindostaun* (London, 1798). The claim is based on Ghulam 'Ali Khan's *Ayi'in 'Alamshahi* (Oxford: Bodleian Library, Elliot 3).

95. My analysis is based on an examination of a collection of documents belonging to Samuel Turner, which are held at the Bodleian Library (shelfmark 2822, Ms. Pers.a.4). A French translation of the *Account* (London: W. Bulmer, 1800) was published in the same year, *Ambassade au Thibet et au Boutan* (Paris: F. Bussion, 1800). In the following year it was also translated into German, *Gesandtschaftsreise an den hof des teshoo lama durch Bootan und einen theil von Tibet* (Hamburg: B. G. Hoffman, 1801).

96. William Moorcroft, *Travels in the Himalayan provinces of Hindustan and the Panjab; in Ladakh and Kashmir; in Peshawar, Kabul, Kunduz, and Bokhara . . . from 1819 to 1825* (London: John Murray, 1841).

97. See Mir 'Izzat Allah, *Ahval-i Safar-i Bukhara* (Oxford: Bodleian Library, Bodl. OR. 745).

98. Among other English language texts that are based on Persian works is Captain William Henry Sleeman, *Ramaseeana, or a Vacabulary of the Peculiar Language Used by the Thugs* (Calcutta, 1836), which is based on *Mustalahat-i Thugan* of 'Ali Akbar.

99. On Sir Gore Ouseley's travel to Iran see Denis Wright, *The English Amongst the Persians During the Qajar Period, 1787–1921* (London: Heinemann, 1977), 12–17.

100. For a fraction of Mirza Salih's report see Mirza Salih Shirazi, "Safar Namah-'i Istahan, Kashan, Qum, Tihran," in *Majmu'ah-'i Safar namah-hayi Mirza Salih Shirazi* (Tehran: Nashr-i Tarikh-i Iran, 1364), 5–36. The official *mihmandar* of this delagation was Mirza Zaki Mustawfi-i Divan-i A'la. See 'Abd al-Razzaq Maftun Dunbuli, *Ma'asir-i Sultaniyah* (reprint of 1825/1241 edition; Tehran: Ibn Sina, 1351/1972), 247.

101. William Price, *A Grammar of the Three Principal Oriental Languages, Hindoostani, Persian, and Arabic on a Plan Entirely New, and Perfectly Easy; to Which is Added, a Set of Persian Dialogues Composed for the Author, by Mirza Mohammed Saulih, of Shiraz; Accompanied with an English translation* (London: Kingsbury, Parbury, and Allen, 1823).

102. Price, *A Grammar of the Three Principal Oriental Languages*, vi. The text of Mirza Salih's "Persian Dialogues" appear on p. 142–88, followed by a French translation, "Dialogues Persans et Français," 190–238.

103. William Ouseley, *Travels in Various Countries of the East, more Particularly Persia* (London: Redwell and Martil,1819–23) I: xvii.

104. The extract in Ouseley's *Travels in Various Countries of the East*, I: xvii, is identical to the opening of Mirza Salih's text as appeared in Price's *A Grammar of the Three Principal Oriental Languages*, 142–3.
105. The colophon of the manuscript, *Su'al va Javab*, held at the Bodleian Library, which belongs to the Ouseley Collection, notes that it was written for Sir William Ousely (Oxford: Bodleian Library, Ouseley 390).
106. Price, *A Grammar of the Three Principal Oriental Languages*, vii. In a note Price remarked: "Since that period Mirza Saulih came to England with Col. Darsy, in order to learn the English Language, returned to Persia in 1819, and lately arrived on a special Mission from the King of Persia to his Majesty George the Fourth. On my presenting him with a copy of his own dialogues, he expressed himself much pleased, and promised to compose a new set" (vi).
107. William Price, *Journal of the British Embassy to Persia; Embellished with Numerious Views Taken in India and Persia; Also, A Dissertation Upon the Antiquities of Persepolis*, 2 vols (London: Thomas Thorpe, 1932).
108. Ouseley, *Travels in Various Countries of the East*, III: 363.
109. *Ibid.*, II: 16.
110. Denis Wright, *The Persians Amongst the English: Episodes in Anglo-Persian History* (London: I. B. Tauris, 1985), 73.
111. John Binder and David Wellbery (eds.), *The End of Rhetoric: History, Theory, and Practice* (Stanford, Cal.: Stanford University Press, 1990), 16.

Chapter 3   Persianate Europology

1. As Jalal Al-i Ahmad (1923–69) has pointed out, "'East' and 'West' are not geographical concepts." See his *Plagued by the West (Gharbzadegi)*, trans. Paul Sprachman (Delmar, NY: Caravan Books, 1982), 4. Similarly Stuart Hall explains that "Our ideas of 'East' and 'West' have never been free of myth and fantasy, and even today they are not primarily ideas about place and geography." See his "The West and the Rest: Discourse and Power," in *Modernity: An Introduction to Modern Societies*, ed. Stuart Hall, et al. (Cambridge, Mass: Blackwell Publishers, 1996), 184–227, quote on 185.
2. Munshi I'tisam al-Din, *Shigirf namah-'i vilayat* (unpublished manuscript: British Museum: O.C. 13663), 58a.
3. James Ballie Fraser, *Narrative of the Residence of the Persian Princes in London in 1835 and 1836 . . .* (London: Richard Bentley, 1838), 83.
4. Fraser, *Narrative of the Residence*, 83.
5. R. C. Money, *Journal of a Tour in Persia During the Years 1824 & 1825* (London: Teape and Son, 1928), 110–11.
6. *Farang/Farangistan* (Europe/Frank-land) as it emerged in eighteenth- and nineteenth-century Persian, Arabic, and Turkish writings is epistemologically different from its classical equivalent, *Rum* (Rome/Byzantine).
7. On "cultural looking" see Sara Suleri, *The Rhetoric of English India* (Chicago: University of Chicago Press, 1992), 18–19.
8. Najaf Khoolee Meerza, *Journal of a Residence in England . . .*, 2 vols, trans. Assad Y. Kayat (London: William Taylor, 1839), vol. 1, xiii–xiv.
9. On the ideological construction of otherness see Homi Bhabha, "The Other Question . . . ," *Screen*, 24: 6 (1983), 18–36.

10. My analysis of self-fashioning is partly informed by Stephen Greenblatt, *Renaissance Self-Refashioning: From More to Shakespeare* (Chicago: University of Chicago Press, 1980), particularly 9.

11. My definition of mimicry parallels that of Luce Irigaray, for whom mimicry is a strategy in which women intentionally perform the feminine posture assigned to them in a phallocentric discourse. See Luce Irigaray, *This Sex which is not One* (Ithaca, NY: Cornell University Press, 1985), 76.

12. On *mehmandar* during the Safavid period see John Chardin [1643–1713], *Voyages du Chevalier en Perse, et autres lieux de l'Orient,* ed. Langlés (Paris, 1811), v: 372; Engelbert Kaempfer [1651–1716], *Amonitatum exoticarum politico-physico-medicarum fasciculi V* (Lemgoviate: Typis & impensis Henrici Wilhelmi Meyeri, 1712), 82; Nichola Sanson [1600–1667], *Voyage ou Relation de l'etat présent du royaume de Peres: avec une dissertation curieuse sur les moeurs, religion & gouvernement de cet etat* (Paris: Chez la veuve M. Cramoisi, 1695), 38.

13. James Justinian Morier, *A Second Journey Through Persia, Armenia, and Asia Minor...* (London: Longman, Hurst, Rees, Orme, and Brown, 1818), 46. Morier's reference to Tissaphernes was based on Xenophon's *Anabasis.*

14. See J. P. Ferrier, *Caravan Journeys and Wanderings in Persia, Afghanistan, Turkistan, and Beloochistan,* 2nd edn, trans. William Jesse; ed. H. D. Seymour (London: John Murray, 1857), 47.

15. Sir Thomas Herbert, *Travels in Persia, 1627–1629,* abr. and ed. Sir William Foster (originally published in 1634; New York: R. M. McBride, 1929; New York: Books for Libraries Press, 1972), 62.

16. Sir John Malcolm, *Sketches of Persia from the Journal of a Traveller in the East* (Philadephia: Carey, Lea, & Carey, 1828), 52. Fath'ali Khan Nuri, Nayib-i Ishik Aqasi was the head *mehmandar* for Sir John Malcolm. See 'Abd al-Razzaq Maftun Dunbuli, *Ma'asir-i Sultaniyah* (Tabriz: s.n., 1825/1241; Tehran: Ibn Sina, 1351/1972), 64; Hasan Husayni Fasa'i, *Farsnamah-'i Nasiri,* ed. Mansur Rastigar Fasa'i (Tehran: Amir Kabir, 1988), 1: 678; Lisan al-Mulk Sipihr, *Nasikh al-Tavarikh: Salatin-i Qajariyah,* ed. M. B. Bihbudi (Tehran: Kitabfurushi Islami, 1353), 198.

17. Malcolm, *Sketches of Persia,* 53.

18. Cited in Malcolm, *Sketches of Persia,* 52.

19. For an example of the responsibilities of a *mehmandar* see "Dastur al-'amal-i 'Ali Jah Muqqarib al-Hazrat al-Khaqaniyah 'Askar Khan Sartip Mihmandar-i Jinab-i Khayr Allah Afandi Vazir-i Mukhtar-i Dawlat-i 'Illiyah-'i 'Usmani [4 Zilqa'dah 1296 H. Q.]," in *Guzidah-'i Asnad-i Siyasi-i Iran va 'Usmani: Dawrah-'i Qajariyah* (Tehran: Daftar-i Mutali'at-i Siyasi va Bayn al-Milali va bastah bah Vizarat-i Umur-i Kharijah-'i Jumhuri-i Islami-i Iran, 1370/1991), 144–56. On the office of *akhbarnawis* see Michael Fisher, "The Office of Akhbar Nawis: the Transition from Mughal to British Forms," *Modern Asian Studies,* 27: 1 (1993), 45–82. On intelligence gathering see C. A. Bayly, "Knowing the Country: Empire and Information in India," *Modern Asian Studies,* 27: 1 (1993), 3–43.

20. It is reported that in 1238, during the reign of Henry III, an envoy was sent to England by 'Ala' al-Din Muhammad "to seek English help against the Mongol hord..." (see Wright, *The Persians Amongst the English,* 1).

21. Uruj Bayk, *Don Juan of Persia: A Shi'ah Catholic, 1560–1604,* trans. Guy Le Strange (New York: Harper & Brothers, 1926). According to Uruj Bayg Bayat,

Husayn ʿAli Bayg and Antony Sherley were jointly accredited as the Persian ambassadors to the following: "the Roman Pontiff, the Emperor of Germany, the King of Spain, the King of France, the King of Poland, the Signiory of Venice, the Queen of England and the King of Scotland" (*Don Juan of Persia*, 233). For further information see Najafquli Hissam Muʿizzi, *Tarikh-i Ravabit-i Siyasi* (Tehran: Nashr-ʿIlm, 1366/1987), 181–7; Wright, *The Persians Amongst the English*, 2–3.

22. The delegation led by Robert Sherley, like the earlier one led by his brother, was accompanied by a Persian co-ambassador, Changiz Bayg Shamlu. Changiz Bayg Shamlu returned to Iran in 1613. See Le Strange, "Notes," in *Don Juan of Persia*, 310, fn 7.

23. E. P. Shirley, *The Sherley Brothers: An Historical Memoir of the Lives of Sir Thomas Sherley, Sir Anthony Sherley, and Sir Robert Sherley, Knights* (Chiswick: Press of Charles Whittingham, 1848). The author of this informative book is identified as "one of the same house."

24. Shirley, *The Sherley Brothers*, 78–9.

25. Herbert, *Travels in Persia*, xviii–xix, xxiv, 157, 195; Le Strange, "Introduction," in Uruj Bayg, *Don Juan of Persia*, 1–29; Wright, *The Persians Amongst the English*, 5–8. It is commonly believed that Naqd ʿAli Bayg committed suicide on his way back to Iran. The incident of his death was rather mysterious and needs further investigation.

26. Nicius Erythræus, *Pinacotheca Tertia*, new edition (S.l.: s.n., 1712), 797–807, cited in "Shirley or Sherley, Robert," in *The Dictionary of National Biography*, vol. xviii: 137.

27. Herbert, *Travels in Persia*, 206–8, 324, quote in 206. Teresia was buried in the Church of Santa Maria della Scala.

28. On Lady Teresia Sherley see Shirley, *The Sherley Brothers*, 59, 75, 76, 78–79, 85, 85 f.n. 13, 89, 95, 98–9. For the careers of Antony Sherley, the older brother of Robert Sherley, see Antony Sherley, *Relation of his Travels into Persia, the Dangers and Distresses which Befell him in his Passage, both by Sea and Land* (London: Nathaniell Butter, 1613).

29. See Chapter 1.

30. Husayn Mahbubi Ardakani, *Tarikh-i Muʾassasat-i Tamadduni-i Jadid dar Iran* (Tehran: Anjuman-i Danishjuyan-i Danishgah-i Tihran, 1354/1975), 1: 234–5.

31. For further information on diplomatic relations with Europe see R. W. Ferrier, "The European Diplomacy of Shah Abbas I and the first Persian Embassy to England," *Iran: Journal of the British Institute of Persian Studies*, 9 (1973); Roger Stevens, "Robert Sherley: the Unanswered Questions," *Iran: Journal of the British Institute of Persian Studies*, 17 (1979).

32. ʿAbd al-Husayn Navaʾi, *Ravabit-i Siyasi-i Iran va Urupa dar ʿAsr-i Safavi* (Tehran: Visman, 1372/1993), 275–86, particularly 282–3 on his marriage.

33. Navaʾi, *Ravabit-i Siyasi-i Iran va Urupa*, 286.

34. Joseph Émïn, *The Life and Adventures of Joseph Émïn, an Armenian* (London: n. p., 1792). For Sir William Jones's editorial comments see xix–xx.

35. For a comparison of *Hayrat Namah* and *Shigirf Namah*, see Mohamad Tavakoli-Targhi, "Nigaran-i Zan-i Farang," *Nimeye Digar*, 2: 3 (Winter 1997), 24–6.

36. Simon Digby, "An Eighteenth Century Narrative of a Journey from Bengal to England: Munshi Ismaʿil's *New History*," in *Urdu and Muslim South Asia:*

Studies in Honour of Ralph Russel, ed. Christopher Schackle (London: School of Oriental and African Studies, 1989), 49–65.

37. James B. Fraser, *Narrative of a Journey into Khorasan in the years 1821–1822* . . . (London, Longman, 1825; Delhi: Oxford University Press, 1984), 484. Morier's Moomed Ispahani appears to be the same person as Mir Muhammad Husayn Isfahani who, according to Shushtari, had traveled to Europe (*Tuhfat al-ʿAlam*, 367–8).

38. Fraser, *Narrative of a Journey*, 484.

39. Mirza Abu Talib, *Khulasat al-Afkar* (Oxford, Bodleian Library, Oriental Collection, Elliot 181), 340.

40. Charles Ambrose Storey, *Persian Literture: A Bio-Bibliographical Survey* (London: Luzac, 1927), vol. 1, no. 1596, p. 1144. Another known work by Mir Muhammad Husayn is *Qavaʾid-i Husayn-i Landani* (Lucknow: Matbaʿ-i Mustafaʾi, 1269/1852).

41. Mirza Abu Talib Isfahani, *Masir-i Talibi Ya Safarnamah-ʾi Mirza Abu Talib Khan*, ed. Husayn Khadivjam (Tehran: Sazman-i Intisharat va Amnzish-i Inqibb-i Islami, 1363), 58–9. On Din Muhammad see Michael Fisher, *The Travels of Dean Mahomet: An Eighteenth-Century Journey Through India* (Berkeley, Cal.: University of California Press, 1997).

42. Mirza Abu Talib, *Lubb al-Siyar va Jahan Numa* (Bodleian Library, Oriental Collection), 300–429.

43. See Mirza Abu Taleb Khan, *The Travels of Mirza Abu Taleb Khan in Asia, Africa, and Europe during the years 1799, 1800, 1801, and 1802*, 2 vol, trans. Charles Stewart (London: Longman, 1810); idem, *Reizen Van Mirza Abu Talib Khan in Asia, Africa en Europa* (Bijvoegsel, Leeuwarden, 1813); idem, *Voyages du prince persan mirza Aboul Taleb Khan, en Asie, en Afrique, en Europe; écrits par lui-même, et publiés, pour la première fois, en français, par Charles Malo* (Paris, Impr. de P.F. Dupont fils, 1819).

44. Richard Herber, "Travels of Mirza Abu Talib . . . ," *The Quarterly Review* (1810), 80–93; quotes on 82, 80, 82, and 92.

45. The letter was reproduced in many newspapers and magazines. A copy of it appeared in E. Bronson, *Select Reviews and Spirits of the Foreign Magazines* (Philadephia: The Lorenzo Press, 1810), 335–6.

46. "Memoir of His Excellency Mirza Al Aboo Hassan, Envoy Extraordinary from the King of Persia to the Court of Great Britein," *Select Reviews and Spirits of the Foreign Magazines*, 334.

47. "Ibid.," 334.

48. Lord Radstock's biography of Mirza Abu al-Hasan was completed on January 10, 1810 and was privately circulated. It was reprinted on the occasion of Mirza Abu al-Hasan Khan's second European tour as "A Slight Sketch of the Character, Person, &c. of Aboul Hassen, Envoy Extraordinary From the King of Persia to the Court of Great Britain, in the Year 1809 and 1810," *The Gentleman's Magazine* (February, 1820), 119–122.

49. [?]Johnson, "Dinner in Honour of the Persian Ambassador," *The Examiner*, 107 (January 14, 1810), 17–18.

50. Augustus Andrea de Nerciat, "Memoirs of the Persian Ambassador," *The London Literary Gazette, Journal of Belles Letters, Arts, Sciences, etc*, 120 (May 8, 1819), 299–300, quote in 299.

51. Ibid., 299.

52. Mirza Abu al-Hasan Ilchi, *Hayrat Namah: Safar Namah-'i Mirza Abu al-Hasan Khan Ilchi bah Landan*, ed. Hasan Mursalvand (Tehran: Mu'assisah-'i Khadamat-i Farhangi-i Rasa, 1364/1985). For a translation of his travelogue see *A Persian at the Court of King George, 1809–10: The Journal of Mirza Abul Hasan Khan*, trans. by Margaret Morris Cloake (London: Barrie & Jenkins, 1988).
53. Fraser, *Narrative of a Journey*, quotes on 151.
54. James Alexander, *Travels from India to England* . . . (London: Parbury, Allen, 1827), 203–4.
55. Fraser, *Narrative of a Journey*, 152.
56. Mujtaba Minuvi, "Avvalin Karvan-i Ma'rifat," in *Tarikh va Farhang* (Tehran: Khwarazmi, 1990), 385–9; Wright, *The Persians Amongst the English*, 70–4.
57. Minuvi, "Avvalin Karvan-i Ma'rifat," 386; Wright, *The Persians Amongst the English*, 82. Muhammad Kazim, the other student , died on March 25, 1813.
58. This group included Mirza Salih Shirazi, Mirza Riza Tabrizi, Mirza Ja'far Husayni "Mushir al-Dawlah," Mirza Ja'far Tabib, and Muhammad 'Ali Chakhmaqsaz. See: *Safar-i Mirza Salih Shirazi Kaziruni*, ed. Humayun Shahidi (Tehran: Rah-i Naw, 1362/1983), Mirza Salih, *Guzarish-i Safar*, 371; Wright, *The Persians Amongst the English*, 77.
59. For more detail see Chapter 2.
60. Louis Rabino, *Diplumatha va Kunsulha-yi Iran va Inglis va Nukhustvaziran va Vuzara-yi Umur-i Kharijah-'i Iran va Inglis va Sufara va Firistadigan-i Iran dar Sayir-i Kishvarha-yi Jahan az Aqaz ta sal-i 1945 Miladi*, ed. Ghulamhusayn Mirza Salih (Tehran: Nashr-i Tarikh-i Iran, 1984), 74.
61. Muhammad Riza Tabrizi, *Havadis Namah* (Kitabkhanah-'i Milli-i Iran, no. F1615; F/1714; F/1057).
62. Assuming that these students were unfamiliar with the Persian language, Wright writes that Hartford Jones suggested that "they should spend their holidays at East India College Haileybury, where they could receive instruction in reading and writing their own language" (*The Persians Amongst the English*, 73).
63. Among his scientific writings are: *Qanun va Qava'id-i Tupkhanah* (Mashhad: Astan-i Quds-i Razavi, no. 12154) and *Badayi' al-Hisab* (Tehran: Dar al-Tiba'ah-'i Dar al-Khalafah, 1263/1846).
64. Mirza Ja'far Husayni, *Tarz-i Hukumat-i Iran va Muqayisah-'i an ba Hukumatha-yi Urupa* (Tehran: Ministry of Foreign Affairs, no. 794). Among his other essays and reports are: *Kitabchah-'i Sifarat-i Mirza Ja'far Khan Mushir al-Dawlah* (dated 8 Muharram 1255; Tehran: Ministry of Foreign Affairs), *Risalah-'i Tahqiqat-i Sarhadiyah*, ed. Muhammad Mushiri (Tehran: Bunyad-i Farhang-i Iran, 1348 [1969]).
65. For the first issue of *Kaghaz Akhbar* see, "Persian Newspaper and Translation," *The Journal of the Royal Asiatic Society of Great Britain and Ireland*, 5 (1939), 355–71.
66. A portion of Mirza Salih Shirazi's travelogue appeared in English as "Travels of a Persian," *The Asiatic Journal and Monthly Register for British India and its Dependencies*, 18 (July–December 1824), 365–71. According to this report, Mirza Salih "published an account of his journey, and likewise of his residence in England. The portion of his travels we are about to present to our readers appeared in *Oriental Magazine*, a Calcutta publication, in October last, translated from the original Persian. We hope to receive shortly, through

the same channel, a continuation of it, for we are anxious to read the observations of so intelligent a Persian upon the arts, sciences, and manners of our countrymen" (365). From this note it appears that Mirza Salih's *Guzarish-i Safar* was originally published prior to October 1824, a fact unknown to Qajar historians.

67. For instance see *Sharh-i Hal-i Iskandar va Napil'un-i Avval* (Tehran: Iranian National Library, no. F/1680; no. F/1714); *Tarikh-i Napil'un-i Avval* (Tehran: Iranian National.Libray, no. F/1615; F/1714; F/1057).

68. Mirza Riza Muhandis Tabrizi, *Tarikh-i Tanazul va Kharabi-i Dawlat-i Rum* (Kitabkhanah-'i Milli, no. F/77).

69. Riza Quli Mirza, *Safar Namah-i Riza Quli Mirza nayib al-Iyalah Narah-'i Fath 'Ali Shah*, ed. Asghar Farmanfarma'i Qajar (Tehran: Asatir, 1982), respectively 524, 524–5, 530.

70. Mirza Abu Talib, *Masir*, respectively 263–84, 276, 265, 275 and 275.

71. Ibid., all quotes on 263.

72. Ibid., 263.

73. For a valuable study of *nafs* see Peter Heath, *Allegory and Philosophy in Avicenna (Ibn Sina) With a Translation of the Book of the Prophet Muhammad's Ascent to Heaven* (Philadelphia: University of Pennsylvania Press, 1992), 52–79.

74. Mirza Abu Talib, *Masir*, 263.

75. Ibid., respectively 263, 264, 264.

76. Ibid., 264.

77. Koselleck, *Futures Past*, 278 and 279.

78. Mirza Abu Talib, *Masir*, all on 265.

79. Ibid., quotes on 265.

80. Immanuel Kant, "The Contest of Faculties," in *Kant: Political Writings*, ed. Hans Reiss; trans. H. B. Nisbet (Cambridge: Cambridge University Press, 1970), 176–90; quote on 181.

81. For the "age of revolution," see E. J. Hobsbawm, *The Age of Revolution, 1789–1848* (New York: Mentor Books, 1962).

82. Mirza Abu Talib, *Masir*, 266.

83. Ibid., 366, 266–7, 267.

84. Ibid., 267–8 and 268.

85. Ibid., 268.

86. Ibid., 259 and 269.

87. Ibid., 270–1.

88. Ibid., 271.

89. Ibid., 272.

90. Ibid., 272–3.

91. Ibid., 273, 274, 275, and 276.

Chapter 4 Imagining European Women

1. Respectively in Mirza Abu al-Hasan Khan Ilchi, *Hayrat Namah: Safar Namah-'i Mirza Abu al-Hasan khan Ilchi bah Landan*, ed. Hasan Mursavard (Tehran: Mu'assisah-'i Khadamat-i Farhangi-i Rasa, 1364/1985); Mirza I'tisam al-Din, *Shigirf Namah* (British Library, London, OR5848), 83b; and Mirza Abu Talib, *Masir*, 166.

2. Respectively in Riza Quli Mirza, *Safar Namah-'i Riza Quli Mirza Naqib al-Iyalah Yavah-'i Fath 'Ali Shah*, ed. Asghar Farmanfarma'i Qajar (Tehran: Asatir, 1982), 418; Mirza Abu Talib, *Masir*, 169; Riza Quli Mirza, *Safar Namah*, 322.
3. Qur'an, "The Beneficent," lv: 72–4. Also see, Qur'an: Baqarah 25, Safat, 48–49, Dakhan, 54, Tur 20, Rahman 56–61, 70–6; Vaqi'ah 22–3, 35–8. For a valuable study of paradise in the Qur'an see: Fatna Sabbah, *Women in Muslim Unconscious*, trans. Mary Jo Lakeland (New York: Pergamon Press, 1984), 91–7.
4. Itesa Modeen [I'tisam al-Din], *Shigurf Namah-i Velaét, or Excellent Intelligence Concerning Europe*, trans. James Edward Alexander (London: Parbury, Allen, 1827), 45–6; when necessary, all translated materials have been modified. For my modifications I consulted the Persian manuscripts at National Archives of India's Oriental Collections, Bodleian Library, and the British Library, Oriental Collections, OR5848.
5. Sir Gore Ouseley was Mirza Abu al-Hasan Khan's *mehmandar* who accompanied him back to Iran.
6. Mirza Abu al-Hasan Khan, *A Persian at the Court of King George: the Journal of Mirza Abul Hasan Khan, 1809–10*, trans. Margaret Morris Cloake (London: Barrie & Jenkins, 1988), 78. In a recently published Persian text of Abu al-Hasan Khan's travelogue, the editor, Hasan Mursalvand, has edited out this verse and a few other sentences arguing, "A few phrases which offer an anti-moral description of *mahruyan-i Landani* [the moon-faceds of London] have been taken out." See Mirza Abu al-Hasan Khan Ilchi, *Hayrat Namah*, 144.
7. I'tisan al-Din, *Shigirf Namah*, 66A.
8. Riza Quli Mirza, *Safar Namah*, 393.
9. Mirza Abu Talib, *Masir*, respectively 244, 160, 160, 160.
10. Ibid., all quotes on 315.
11. Albinia, Dowager Countess of Buckinghamshire, d. 1816.
12. Mirza Abu al-Hasan, *A Persian*, 98–9.
13. According to Margaret Cloake, Miss Pole was a daughter of William Wellesley-Pole, the younger brother of the Marquis Wellesley (*A Persian*, 100).
14. Mirza Abu al-Hasan, *A Persian*, 136. Mirza Abul Hasan mentioned "Miss Pole" many times throughout his travelogue (*A Persian*, 104, 138, 148, 157, 262v 283, 288).
15. Ibid., 290–291; idem, *Hayrat Namah*, 354.
16. Mirza Abu al-Hasan, *Hayrat*, 354. This verse does not appear in *A Persian*.
17. Riza Quli Mirza, *Safar Namah*, 360–1.
18. Mirza Abu Talib, *Masir*, 74 and 163.
19. Mirza Abu al-Hasan, *A Persian*, 76.
20. William Waldegrave Radstock, "A Slight Sketch of the Character, Person, & c. of Aboul Hassen, Envoy Extraordinary from the King of Persia to the Court of Great Britain, in the year 1809 and 1810, 'To the Countess of——'," *The Gentleman's Magazine* (February 1820), 119–22, quotes on 120; quoted in part in *A Persian*, 76–7.
21. Mirza Abu al-Hasan, *A Persian*, respectively on 92, 165, 165, and 263; idem, *Hayrat Namah*, 159, 159, 228–9, and 333.
22. Mirza Fattah Garmrudi, *Safar Namah-'i Mirza Fattah Khan Garmrudi bi-Urupa, Mawsum Bah Chahar Fasl va du Risalah-i Digar Binam-i Shab Namah va Safar*

Namah-'i Mamasani dar Zaman-i Muhammad Shah Qajar, ed. Fath al-Din Fattahi (Tehran: Chapkhanah-i Bank-i Bazargani-'i Iran, 1347/1968), 970.

23. Mirza Abu Talib, *Masir*, quotes on 189.
24. Concerning the title of the "Persian Prince," Abu Talib wrote, "When I went to Court, or paid my respects to one of the Princes or ministers of the state, the circumstance was always reported by the newspapers of the following day. In all these advertisements, they did me the honour of naming me the Persian Prince. I declared I never assumed the title; but I was so much better known by it than by my own name, that I found it in vain to contend with godfathers" (*Travels*, 111; *Masir*, 195).
25. Mirza Abu Talib, *Masir*, 189.
26. Mirza Abul Hasan, *A Persian*, 274; idem, *Hayrat*, 339.
27. On the European perception of "harem" see: Leila Ahmad, "Western Ethnocentrism and Perceptions of the Harem," *Feminist Studies*, 8: 3 (1982), 521–34; Suzanne Rodin Pucci, "The Discrete Charms of the Exotic: Fiction of the Harem in Eighteenth-Century France," in *Exoticism in the Enlightenment*, ed. G. C. Rousseau and Roy Porter (Manchester: Manchester University Press, 1990), 145–74.
28. James Justinian Morier, *A Second Journey through Persia, Armenia, and Asia Minar, to Constantinople, Between the years 1810 and 1816 . . .* (London: Longman, Hurst, Rees, Orme, and Brown, 1818), 39–40.
29. Edward Said, *Orientalism* (London: Routledge & Kegan Paul, 1978), 190.
30. G. S. Rousseau and Roy Porter, "Introduction: Approaching Enlightenment Exoticism," in *Exoticism in the Enlightenment*, ed. G. S. Rousseau and Roy Porter (Manchester: Manchester University Press, 1990), 1–22, quote on 10.
31. I'tisam al-Din, *Shigurf Namah*, respectively 157–9, 159, 168.
32. Mirza Abu Talib, *Masir*, all on 226.
33. Mirza Salih, *Guzarish*, 333–4.
34. Mirza Abu al-Hasan, *A Persian*, 98; idem, *Hayrat*, 163.
35. "Letter from the Persian Envoy, Mirza Abul Hassan to the Lord, or Gentleman, without name, who lately write Letter to him and ask very much to give Answer," *Morning Post* (May 29, 1810); reprinted in *A Persian*, 246–7; Denis Wright, *The Persians amongst the English: Episodes in Anglo-Persian History* (London: I. B. Tauris, 1985), 226–7.
36. Mirza Abu al-Hasan, *A Persian*, 135.
37. Bibi Khanum Astarabadi, *Ma'ayib al-Rijal [Vices of Men]*, ed. Afsaneh Najmabadi (New York: Nigarish va Nigarish-i Zan, 1992), 57.
38. I'tisam al-Din, *Shigirf Namah*, respectively 149–50 E, 131 U; 137 E; INA, fl. 187.
39. Ibrahim Sahhafbashi Tihrani, *Safar Namah-'i Ibrahim Sahhafbashi Tihrani*, ed. Muhammad Mushiri (Tehran: Shirkat-i Mu'allifan va Mutarjiman-i Iran, 1357/1978), 81.
40. Garmrudi, *Shab Namah*, 983.
41. For a concise account of this mission see Wright, *The Persians amongst the English*, 104–9.
42. Ibid., 49.
43. Palmerston to Ajudanbashi, July 11, 1839 (Iranian Foreign Ministry Archive, document no. 500). Also see Wright, *The Persians Amongst the English*, 109.

44. Wright observed that Palmerston's "high handed treatment" of this Iranian delegate "rankled deep in Persian minds and remained a bitter memory for many years to come" (*The Persians Amongst the English*, 109).
45. Iqbal al-Dawlah was the author of a bilingual Persian–English book, *Iqbal-i Farang: Dar Shammah-'i Siyar-i Ahl-i Farang-i ba Farhang* (Calcutta: Matba'-i Tibbi, 1834). He had gone to England to protest the British policy in Awadh.
46. Garmrudi, *Shab Namah*, respectively on 951, 951, 955–6, and 956.
47. Garmrudi, *Shab Namah*, respectively on 256, 959, 961, and 962.
48. James B. Fraser (1783–1856) served as *mehmandar* for this delagation.
49. Garmrudi, *Shab Namah*, 964 and 982.
50. "Story of Shaykh San'an" is a story within the chain of narratives known as *Mantiq al-Tayr*. For English translations see Farid al-Din 'Attar, *The Conference of the Birds, Mantiq ut-Tair: A Philosophical Religious Poem in Prose*, trans. C. S. Nott (1st edn, 1954; New York: Samuel Weiser, 1974), 34–44; idem, *The Conference of the Birds*, trans. Afkham Darbandi and Dick Davis (New York: Penguin Books, 1984), 57–75. For the Persian original see *Shaykh-i San'an*, ed. by Sadiq Gawharin (Tehran: Amir Kabir, 1345); 'Attar, *Mantiq al-Tayr*, ed. Ahmad Khushnivis (Isfahan: Sana'i, 1978), 66–85. For further information on 'Attar and his mystical poetry see: Margaret Smith, *The Persian Mystics 'Attar* (London: John Murray, 1932).
51. 'Attar, *The Conference of the Birds*, respectively on 34, 34–5, 37, 39, and 39.
52. Sahhafbashi, *Safar Namah*, 62.
53. For a detailed study of Karim Khan's thought see: Mangol Bayat, *Mysticism and Dissent: Socioreligious Thought in Qajar Iran* (Syracuse: Syracus University Press, 1982), 63–86; Abbas Amanat, *Resurrection and Renewal: The Making of the Babi Movement in Iran, 1844–1850* (Ithaca, NY: Cornell University Press, 1989), 286–94.
54. Quoted in Bayat, *Mysticism and Dissent*, 85.
55. This individual appears to be either Riza Quli Mirza or his brothers Najaf Quli and Taymur Mirza who settled in Iraq where Hajj Muhammad Karim Khan Kirmani was attending seminars offered by his master Sayyid Kazim Rashti (d. 1844).
56. Muhammad Karim Khan Kirmani, *Risalah-i Nasiriyah Dar Tahqiq-i Mu'ad-i Jismani* (Kirmani Sa'adat, 1375/1955), 388–9. For an alternative rendering see Bayat's *Mysticism and Dissent*, 388–9.
57. Quoted in Bayat, *Mysticism and Dissent*, 85.
58. Kirmani, *Risalah Nasiriyah*, 389.
59. Kirman, *Risalah Nasiriyah*, 389 and 390. It is important to note that Europeanization of education led to a different anxiety among European clerics. For example see "The Rev. A. Duff['s] . . . Address to the General Assembly of the Church of Scotland," *The Asiatic Journal and Monthly Register*, 18 (1836), Asiatic Intelligence section: 86–8, quotes on 87–8).
60. Kirmani, *Risalah Nasiriyah*, respectively 391 and 389.
61. Mirza Abu Talib, *Masir*, 408–20.
62. Mirza Abu Talib, *The Travels al Mirza Abu Tahib Khan in Asia, Africa, and Europe During the years 1799, 1800, 1801, and 1802*, trans. Charles stewart (London: Longman, 1810), 312.
63. I'tisam al-Din, *Shigirf Namah*, 59a.

64. Mirza Abu Talib, *Masir*, 83; idem, *Travels*, 64.
65. "Sketches of Society," *The London Literary Gazette, and Journal of Belles Lettres, Arts, Sciences etc.* (May 8, 1819), 299: 3.
66. *The Morning Herald* (29 March 1810); Mirza Abu al-Hasan, *A Persian*, 188.
67. Charles de Secondat Montesquieu, *The Persian Letters*, trans. C. J. Betts (New York: Penguin Books, 1973), letter XXX, 83.
68. Mirza Salih Shirazi, *Guzarish*, 201.

Chapter 5   Contested Memories

1. My usage of narrative "emplotment" is informed by Hayden White, *Metahistory: The Historical Imagination in Nineteenth-Century Europe* (Baltimore: Johns Hopkins University Press, 1973), 7.
2. The terms *Furs, 'Ajam*, and *Majus* were used interchangeably in Arabic and Persian historical works to refer to the people residing in the Iranian plateau. For general definition of these terms see F. Gabrieli, "Adjam," in *The Encyclopaedia of Islam* (Leiden: Brill, 1960–), 1: 206; Ch. Pellat, "al-Furs," in *The Encyclopaedia of Islam*, 2: 950–1; M. Morony, "Madjus," in *The Encyclopaedia of Islam*, 5: 110–18.
3. Zoroastrianism and Mazdaism are used interchangeably in this article. Mazdean (Mazdayasnian) and Mazdaism are both derived from the name of the supreme god, Mazda (wise) or Ahura Mazda (wise lord). See Mary Boyce, *Zoroastrians: Their Religious Beliefs and Practices* (London: Routledge & Kegan Paul, 1979), 36–7. On the etymology of *Mazdayasna* see H. W. Bailey, *Zoroastrian Problems in the Ninth-Century Books: Ratanbai Katrak Lectures* (reprint 1943; Oxford: Clarendon Press, 1971), 177–8.
4. See Chapter 2.
5. See James R. Rusell, "On Mysticism and Esotericism among the Zoroastrians," *Iranian Studies*, 26: 1–2 (Winter/Spring 1993), 73–94.
6. There is an intertextual link between *dasatiri* and some Baha'i texts. Inquiry into the nature of this linkage is significant for a full understanding of the nineteenth-century Persianate cultural and intellectual history.
7. See Chapter 2.
8. For structural differences of "annals," "chronicle," and "history" see Hayden White, "The Value of Narrativity in the Representation of Reality," *The Content of the Form: Narrative Discourse and Historical Representation* (Baltimore: Johns Hopkins University, 1987), 1–25.
9. As Hayden White has explained, "In order to qualify as historical, an event must be susceptible to at least two narrations of its occurrence. Unless at least two versions of the same set of events can be imagined, there is no reason for the historian to take upon himself the authority of giving the true account of what really happened. The authority of the historical narrative is the authority of reality itself; the historical account endows this reality with form and thereby makes it desirable by the imposition upon its processes of the formal coherency that only stories possess." See White, "The Value of Narrativity in the Presentation of Reality," 20.
10. Concerning the practice of synchronizations see Franz Rosenthal, *A History of Muslim Historiography* (Leiden: E. J. Brill, 1968), 92–3.

11. For a Zoroastrian view of Kayumars see *Avista: Namah-'i Minuvi-i Ayin-i Zartusht*, ed. Jalil Dustkhwah (Tehran: Murvarid, 1343 [1964]), 259. On Kayumars, Mashi, and Mashyanah, see Farnbagh Dadagi, *Bundahish* [Creation], ed. by Mihrdad Bahar (Tehran: Tus, 1369 [1990]), 40–1, 52–3, 66, 69–70, 80–3, 139, 146, 155; "Bundahish or the Original Creation," in *Pahlavi Texts*, ed. E. W. West (Oxford: Clarendon Press, 1880), 18–19, 52–7.

12. For differing accounts of Kayumars in Islamicate historical sources see Mohamad Tavakoli-Targhi, "Tarikh pardazi va Iran arayi: bazsazi-i huviyat-i Irani dar guzarish-i tarikh," *Iran Nameh*, 12: 4 (Fall 1994), 583–628, especially 593–4, 620–3.

13. Tabari, *The History of al-Tabari* (Tar'ikh al-rusul wa'l-muluk), vol. 1: *General Introduction and From the Creation to the Flood*, trans. and annotated by Franz Rosenthal (New York: New York University Press, 1989), I: 318.

14. For such characterizations see Ahmad M. H. Shboul, *Al-Mas'udi & His World: A Muslim Humanist and his Interest in Non-Muslims* (London: Ithaca Press, 1979), 108–9; and Tarif Khalidi, *Arabic Historical Thought in the Classical Period* (Cambridge: Cambridge University Press, 1994), 78–80.

15. Ahmad b. Abi Ya'qub Ya'qubi, *Tarikh al-Ya'qubi* (Beirut: Dar al-Sadir, 1960), I: 158; English translation cited in Khalidi, *Arabic Historical Thought*, 115; for Persian translation see *Tarikh-i Ya'qubi*, trans. Muhammad Ibrahim Ayati, p. 193; cited also in Tavakoli-Targhi, "Tarikh Pardazi," 621.

16. Ya'qubi, *Tarikh*, I: 159; idem, *Tarikh-i Ya'qubi*, 194; English translation in Tarif Khalidi's *Arabic Historical Thought*, 116.

17. Tabari, *The History*, I: 326, I: 319; I: 319. For Tabari's earlier reference to Kayumars see *The History*, I: 185–6 and 318.

18. On "colligation" see W. H. Walsh, *An Introduction to Philosophy of History* (London: Hutchinson's University Library, 1951), 59–64; Louis O. Mink, "The Autonomy of Historical Understanding," *History and Theory*, 1 (1966), 24–47.

19. Tabari, *The History*, 1: 318–19.

20. "Bundahish or the Original Creation," in West (ed.), *Pahlavi Texts*, 53; Mihrdad Bahar (ed.), *Bundahish*, 155.

21. See Abu Rayhan Muhammad ibn Ahmad Biruni, *The Chronology of Ancient Nations: An English Version of the Arabic Text of the Athar-ul-Bakiya of Albiruni or Vestiges of the Past*, trans. C. Edward Sachau (London, 1879; Frankfurt: Minerva GMBH, 1969), 107.

22. Ibid., 108. For Arabic text see *al-Asar al-Baqiyah 'an-il-Qurun al-Khaliya*, ed. C. Edward Sachau (Leipzig: Otto Harrassowitz, 1923), 99–100.

23. Tabari, *The History*, I: 325–7.

24. Tabari, *The History*, I: 369. The same opinion was reported by Biruni, *The Chronology of Ancient Nations*, 27–8. For the Arabic original see *al-Asar al-Baqiyah*, 23–4.

25. Qur'an, 37: 75–7.

26. Tabari, *The History*, I: 369.

27. 'Izz al-Din Ibn Athir, *al-Kamil fi Tarikh* (Beirut: Dar Sader, 1965–7); idem, *Tarikh-i Kamil*, trans. Muhammad Husayn Rawhani (Tehran: Asatir, 1370), respectively 15, 78–9, and 51.

28. Tabari, *The History*, I: 186 and 318.

29. Biruni, *The Chronology of Ancient Nations*, 28; idem, *al-Asar al-Baqiyah*, 24.

30. Explaining al-Mas'udi's synchronization of Persian and biblical history, Shboul wrote: "Persian scholars in the eighth and ninth centuries attempted to link the Furs [Persians] with Isaac, son of Abraham, and thus find a way of attacking the Arabs, especially the Southerns (Qahtanis) who could not claim such ties with the Patriarch." See Shboul, *al-Mas'udi & His World*, 109.

31. For examples of Kayumars as a Syriac name see Mir Khwand, *Tarikh-i Rawzat al-Safa*, ed. 'Abbas Parviz (Tehran: Markazi, 1338/1959), 1: 493; Khwand Mir, *Habib al-Siyar fi Akhbar Afrad al-Bashar*, ed. Jalal al-Din Huma'i (Tehran: Khayyam, 1333/1954), 175.

32. For the political life in Islamdom in "the Earlier Middle period" see Marshall G. S. Hodgson, *The Venture of Islam: Conscience and History in a World Civilization* (Chicago: University of Chicago Press, 1974), 2: 12–61, quote on 12.

33. Abu Hamid Muhammad Ghazzali, *Ghazali's Book of Council for Kings (Nasihat al-Muluk)*, trans. F. R. C. Bagley (London: Oxford University Press, 1964), 45, 45, 48; idem, *Nasihat al-Muluk*, ed. Jalal al-Din Huma'i (Tehran: Babak, 1361), 81, 81, 89.

34. In pre-Islamic Persian statecraft, state and religion were viewed as twins. Tansar, an arch-cleric of the court of Ardishir, wrote: "Religion and state were born of one womb, joined together and never to be sundered. Virtue and corruption, health and sickness are of the same nature for both." See *The Letter of Tansar*, trans. M. Boyce (Rome: Instituto Italiano per il Medio ed Estremo Oriente, 1968), 33–4.

35. Ghazzali, *Council for Kings*, 53, 53, 46–7; idem, *Nasihat al-Muluk*, 96, 96, 82–83. In one of the manuscripts mentioned by Jalal al-Din Huma'i, the list of tyrannical kings also includes the last Sasanid king, "Yazdigird-i bizihkar" (Yazdigird the Sinner).

36. Ghazzali, *Council for Kings*, 56; idem, *Nasihat al-Muluk*, 100–1.

37. For an illustration of the "circle of justice" see Rashid al-Din Fazl Allah Tabib, *Savanih al-Afkar-i Rashidi*, ed. Muhmmad Taqi Danishpazhuh (Tehran: Intisharat-i Danishgah-i Tihran, 1358/1979), 113.

38. R. Stephen Humphreys, "Qur'anic Myth and Narrative Structure in Early Islamic Historiography," in *Tradition and Innovation in Late Antiquity*, ed. F. M. Clover and R. S. Humphreys (Madison: University of Wisconsin Press, 1989), 271–90, quote on 278.

39. 'Abd Allah Bayzavi, *Nizam al-Tawarikh*, ed. Bahman Mira Karimi (Tehran: 'Ilmi, 1313), 9.

40. Bayzavi, *Nizam al-Tawarikh*, 42.

41. Hamd Allah Mustawfi Qazvini, *Tarikh-i Guzidah*, ed. 'Abd al-Husayn Nava'i (Tehran: Amir Kabir, 1362).

42. Mir Khwand, *Rawzat al-Safa*, 806.

43. Mir Khwand, *History of the Early Kings of Persia from Kaiomars the First of the Peshdadian Dynasty, to the Conquest of Iran by Alexander the Great Translated from the Original Persian of Mirkhond Entitled the Rauzat-us-Safa*, trans. David Shea (London: John Murray and Parbury, Allen, 1882), 51.

44. Ibid., p. 51. Shea incorrectly translates "*ma'dilat*" as "equality and benevolence." In the above quotation I have altered "the carpet of equality and benevolence" into "the carpet of justice" (*basat-i ma'dilat*). For the Persian original see Mir Khwand, *Rawzat al-Safa*, 494.

45. For a valuable study of the concept of justice ('adl) see A. K. Lambton, "Justice in the Medieval Persian Theory of Kingship," *Studia Islamica*, 17 (1962), 91–119. See also Majid Khadduri, *The Islamic Conception of Justice* (Baltimore: Johns Hopkins University Press, 1984).

46. Qur'an, 3: 26.

47. In addition Ghazzali cited Qur'an, 59: 59: "Believers, obey God and obey the Apostle and those in authority amongst you." See Ghazzali, *Council for Kings*, 45–6; idem, *Nasihat al-Muluk*, 82.

48. Discussing administrative theories and mirrors for princes, Ann Lambton wrote, "Although the concept of the Sultan [ruler] in the mirrors owes much to the Sasanian theory, the purpose of the Sultan's government is still the formal establishment of the religion of Islam and conditions in which his subjects can fulfil their destiny." See A. K. S. Lambton, *Theory and Practice in Medieval Persian Government* (London: Variorum Reprints, 1980), 417.

49. On Azar Kayvan and his disciples see Jivanji Jamshedji Modi, "A Parsee High Priest (Dastur Azar Kaiwan, 1529–1614 AD) with his Zoroastrian Disciples in Patna, in the 16th and 17th Centuries AC," *The Journal of the K. R. Cama Oriental Institute*, 16 (1930), 1–85; Muhammad Mu'in, "Azar Kayvan va payravan-i au," *Majallah-'i Danishkadah-'i Adabiyat-i Tihran*, 4: 3 (Farvardin 1336 [March 1957]), 25–42.

50. See M. A. Alvi and A. Rahman, *Fathullah Shirazi: A Sixteenth-Century Indian Scientist* (New Delhi: National Insitute of Sciences of India, 1968), 2, 29–30.

51. Kaykhusraw Isfandyar, *Dabistan-i Mazahib*, ed. Rahim Rizazadah Malik (Tehran: Tahuri, 1983), 300–1.

52. *Dasatir* was claimed to be a "collection of the writings of the different Persian Prophets, who flourished from the time of Mahabad to the time of the fifth Sasan, being fifteen in number, of whom Zerdusht or Zoroaster was the thirteenth and the fifth Sasan the last" (*The Desatir or Sacred Writings of the Persian Prophets*, 2 vols [Bombay: Courier Press, 1818], iii). The publication of *Dasatir* generated intense academic controversies. For the controversy on *Dasatir* see H. Corbin, "Azar (Adar) Kayvan," in *Encyclopaedia Iranica*, ed. Ehisan Yarshater (London: New York: Routledge & Kegan Paul, 1983–), 183–7; Jivanji Jamshedji Modi, "A Parsee High Priest," 1–85; Sheriarji Dadabhai Bharucha, *The Dasatir, Being a Paper Prepared for the Tenth International Congress of Orientalists in Geneva in 1894 AC* (Bombay: s.n., 1907).

53. For a "scholarly edition" see Kaykhusraw Istandyar, *Dabistan-i Mazahib*, ed. Rahim Rizazadah Malik, vol. 2 (Tehran: Tahuri, 1983). For an English translation see *The Dabistan or School of Manners, Translated from the Original Persian with Notes and Illustrations*, trans. David Shea and Anthony Troye, vol. 3 (Paris: Oriental Translation Fund of Great Britain and Ireland, 1843); also reprinted as *Oriental Literature or the Dabistan* (Lahore: Khalil, 1973). On Dabistan see S. H. Askari, "Dabistan-i Mazahib and Diwan-i-Mubad," in *Indo-Iranian Studies: Presented for the Golden Jubilee of the Pahlavi Dynasty of Iran*, ed. Fathullah Mujtabai (New Delhi: Indo-Iran Society, 1977), 85–110; Fath Allah Mojtaba'i, "Dabistan-i Madaheb," in *Encyclopaedia Iranica*, vi, l: 532–534.

54. Bahram ibn Farhad, *Sharistan-i Chahar Chaman: Chaman-i Avval va Duvvum va Chaman-i Sivvum, Naqis al-akhir*, ed. Manikji Suhrabji and Siyavakhsh Hurmuzdyar Irani (Bombay, 1223/1854).

55. *A'in-i Hushang*, ed. Manikji Limji Hushang Hatarya Darvish Fani (Tehran: Mirza Bahram Nasrabadi, 1296/1878).

56. See S. H. Nasr, "The Spread of the Illuminationist School of Suhrawardi," *The Islamic Quarterly*, 14: 3, 111–21, quote on 116.

57. On the religious policies of Akbar see Makhanlal Roy Choudhury, *The Din-i-Ilahi or, The Religion of Akbar* (Patna, India: Patna University, 1952); Khaliq Ahmad Nizami, *Akbar and Religion* (Delhi: Idarah-i Adabiyat-i Delhi, 1989); B. P. Ambashthya, *Contributions on Akbar and the Parsees* (Patna, India: Janaki Prakashan, 1976); Azra Alavi, *Socio-Religious Outlook of Abul Fazl* (Delhi: Idarah-i Adabiyat-i Delhi, 1983).

58. According to Suhrawardi, "there were among the ancient Persians a community of men who were guides towards the Truth and were guided by Him in the Right Path, ancient sages unlike those who are called the Magi. It is their high and illuminated wisdom, to which the spiritual experience of Plato and his predecessors are also witness, and which we have brought to life in our book called Hikmat al-Ishraq." Cited in Seyyed Hossein Nasr, "Shihab al-Din Suhrawardi Maqtul," in *A History of Muslim Philosohpy*, ed. M. M. Sharif (Wiesbaden: Otto Harrassowitz, 1963), 372–98, quote on 375–8, note 11. For a systematic study of Suhrawardi's Illuminationist philosophy see Hossein Ziai, *Knowledge and Illumination: A Study of Suhrawardi's Hikmat al-Ishraq* (Atlanta: Scholars Press, 1990).

59. For a definition of "Zoroastrian Ishraqi" see Corbin, "Azar (Adar) Kayvan," 183. For a discussion of the *Ishraqi* (Illuminationist) aspect of this school see Muhammad Mu'in, "Hikmat-i Ishraq va Farhang-i Iran", in *Majmu'ah Magalat-i Duktur Muhammad Mu'in*, ed. Mahdukht Mu'in (Tehran: Mu'assisah-'i Intisharat-i Mu'in, 1371/1983), 444–6.

60. The author of *Dabistan* argued that the views of Ishraqis were the same as those of Azaris. See *Dabistan*, 314.

61. *Dasatir* includes the books of Mahabad, Ji-Afram, Shay-Kaliv, Yasan, Gal-Shah (Kayumars), Siyamak, Hushang, Tahmuris, Jamshid, Faraydun, Manuchihr, Kay-Khusraw, Zartusht (Zoroaster), Sikandar (Alexander), Sasan-i Nukhust (Sasan I), and Sasan-i Panjum (Sasan V).

62. On *dasatiri* terms see Mulla Firuz, "Farhang-i Lughat-i Kitab-i Mustatab-i Dasatir," in *The Dasatir*, II: 1–81; Nazir Ahmad, *Naqd-i Burhan-i Qati'* (New Delhi: Ghalib Institute, 1985), 211–44.

63. See Mir Khwand, *History of the Early Kings of Persia*, 47–8; idem, *Rawzat al-Safa*, 493.

64. There is no scholarly consensus over the authorship of *Dabistan-i Mazahib*. Three individuals have been named as the author of this book: Muhsin Fani Kashmiri (d. 1081/1670), Mir Zulfiqar 'Ali, known as Mulla Mawbad (*c*.1026–81/1617–70), and Kaykhusraw Isfandyar (*c*.b. 1028/1618). On this issue see Siraj al-Din Khan Arzu, *Muthmir*, 18; Jalal al-Din Mirza Qajar, *Namah-'i Bastan*, 3; S. H. Askari, "Dabistan-i Mazhib and Diwan-i Mubad," in *Indo-Iranian Studies: Presented for the Golden Jubilee of the Pahlavi Dynasty of Iran*, ed. Fatullah Mujtabai (New Delhi: Indo-Iran Society, 1977), 85–104; Fath Allah Mojtaba'i, "Dabestan-e Madaheb" in *Encyclopaedia Iranica*, 6: 532–4; Rahim Rizazadah Malik, *Dabistan-i Mazahib*, 2: 9–76.

65. *Dabistan*, 8 and 12. "The followers of the ancient faith call one revolution of the regent Saturn [Kayvan], a day; thirty such days, one month; twelve

such months, one year; a million of such years, one *fard*; a million *fard*, one *vard*; a million *vard*, one *mard*; one million *mard*, one *jad*; three thousand *jad*, one *vad*; and two thousand *vad*, one *zad*." See *Dabistan*, 8; *The Dabistan*, 19. One Saturn year is equal to 30 solar years. It was argued that the Abadiyan, the original kings and prophets of Iran, ruled for 100 *zad* years (*sad zad sal-i kayvani*). Jayan, the second dynasty, ruled for one *aspar kayvani* year (*yak aspar sal-i kayvani*). The third dynasty, Sha'iyan, ruled for one *shumar-i kayvani* year (*yak shumar sal-i kayvani*). Yasa'iyan, the fourth dynasty, ruled for nine *salam* years. According to this reckoning, *salam* = 100,000 years; 100 *salam* = 1 *shumar*; 100 *shumar* = 1 *aspar*; 100 *aspar* = 1 *zad*.

66. Charles Lyell, *Principles of Geology* (London: John Murray, 1830).
67. *Dabistan*, 13. For Tabari's reckoning of time from the creation of Adam to the *hijra* of Muhammad, see Tabari, *The History*, 1: 184–5.
68. Bahram ibn Farhad, *Sharistan*, 4.
69. Ibid., 2.
70. "Bihisab-i asl-i falsafi afrad-i insani ra bidayati zamani nist." See *Sharistan*, 6 and 10. The same is also argued in *Dabistan* (*Dabistan*, 9).
71. For Hegel's discussion of this significant concept see, *The Philosophy of History*, trans. J. Sibree (Buffalo: Prometheus Books, 1991), 178–9. Hegel had become familiar with this significant Mazdean concept of time via Anquetil-Duperron's *Zend-Avesta*.
72. Bahram ibn Farhad, *Sharistan*, 4–22.
73. Ibid., respectively on 22, 6, 11–12, 22.
74. Mahabad's "achievements," according to *Dabistan*, were numerous: "He ordered persons to descend into deep waters and bring forth the shells, pearls, corals, etc. People were commanded to shear the fleece of sheep and other animals: by him also were invented the arts of spinning, weaving, cutting up, sewing, and clothing. He next organized cities, villages, and streets; erected palaces and colonnades; introduced trade and commerce; and divided mankind into four classes." See *The Dabistan*, 21; for the Persian text see *Dabistan*, 9.
75. Bahram ibn Farhad, *Sharistan*, respectively on 13, 13–14, 14, 14.
76. Tabari, *The History*, 348, 350. Transliterations altered.
77. Bahram ibn Farhad, *Sharistan*, 15 and 89; *Qur'an*, 7: 59. The Qur'anic verse continues, "He said: 'Serve God, my people, for you have no god but Him. Beware the torment of a fateful day'."
78. Abu Hanifa ad-Dinawari, *Kitab al-Akbar at-Tiwal*, ed. Vladimir Guirgass (Leiden: E. J. Brill, 1888), 9; idem, *Tarjumah-'i Akhbar al-Tiwal*, trans. Sadiq Nash'at (Tehran: Intisharat-i Bunyad-i Farhang-i Iran, 1346 [1967]), 6; cited in Edward G. Browne, *A Literary History of Persia from the Earliest Times until Firdawsi* (New York: Charles Scribner's Sons, 1902), I: 113.
79. Mir Khwand, *History of the Early Kings of Persia*, 118 and 100; idem, *Rawzat al-Safa*, 526 and 517.
80. See *Qur'an*, 2: 101–2: "And now that an apostle has come to them from God confirming their own Scripture, some of those to whom the Scriptures were given cast off the Book of God behind their backs, as though they know nothing, and accept what the devils tell of Solomon's kingdom. Not that Solomon was an unbeliever: it is the devils who are unbelievers."

81. Mir Khwand, *History of the Early Kings of Persia*, 100; idem, *Rawzat al-Safa*, 517.

82. See *The Epic of Kings: Shah-Nama the National Epic of Persia by Ferdawsi*, trans. by Reuben Levy (Chicago: The University of Chicago Press, 1967), 9–11; for the Persian text see Firdawsi, *Shahnamah*, ed. Sa'id Hamidiyan (Tehran: Qatrah, 1374 [1995]), I: 42–50.

83. *Avesta*, ed. Jalil Dustkhwah (Tehran: Murvarid, 1343), "Zamyad yasht," 30–6, pp. 294–5. For Tabari's recounting see *The History*, 1: 350.

84. *Avesta*, 294–5; Firdawsi, *Shahnamah*, 1: 42–50

85. Bahram ibn Farhad, *Sharistan*, 72–9, quote on 77.

86. According to Bahram b. Farhad, "Siyamak had a son named Taz who is the forefather of all Arabs who are also called Tazi." See *Sharistan*, 77. In a similar fashion he also Persianized Alexander by depicting him as a son of Nahid and the First Darab ibn Bahman and constituted him as a Persian sage-king whose epistle appeared in the *Dasatir*. The *dasatiri* account of Alexander differs from the Zoroastrian view of him as destroyer of their religous texts. See *Sharistan*, 564 and 572.

87. Ghiyas al-Din Khwand Mir, *Tarikh-i Habib al-Siyar fi Akhbar-i Afrad-i Bashar*, ed. Jalal al-Din Huma'i (Tehran: Khayyam, 1333 [1954]), 44.

88. See Mir Khwand, *History of the Early Kings of Persia*, 151; idem, *Rawzat al-safa*, 542. For textual traces of *Rawzat al-safa* in *Sharistan*, see Bahram b. Farhad, *Sharistan*, 83.

89. Bahram b. Farhad, *Sharistan*, respectively on 27, 232; 29, 232, 59, 232, 73, 233, 88, 196, 200, and 130.

90. For a differentially constructed identification of Persian and Biblical genealogy see Tabari, *The History*, 1: 326.

91. Bahram ibn Farhad, *Sharistan*, 54. For the original reference see Mir Jamal al-Din Husayn Inju Shirazi, *Farhang-i Jahangiri*, ed. Rahim 'Afifi (Mashhad: Intisharat-i Danishgah-i Mashhad, 1359/1980), 1: 22.

92. Bahram ibn Farhad, *Sharistan*, 54, 60–1, 62, 62, and 59. The sexual othering of the Arabs is an important component of Iranian oral culture and is in need of serious study.

93. Ibid., respectively on 65, 63, 65–66; 66.

94. For instances see Ghazzali, *Nasihat al-Muluk*, 82.

95. Bahram ibn Farhad, *Sharistan*, 66–7, 68.

96. Kaykhusraw Isfandyar, *Dabistan*, 19–20, 20.

97. Ibid., 19–20, 20; 20, *The Dabistan*, 32 (translation altered).

98. See Chapter 6.

99. *A'in-i Hushang*, compiled by Darvish Fani, ed. Mirza Bahram Rustam Nasrabadi (Tehran: Mirza Bahram Nasrabadi, 1296/1879). According to Mirza Bahram, the first edition of *A'in* was edited by 'Abd al-'Ali Khan Shushtari and published in 1849 (p. 4).

100. *A'in-i Hushang*, 2–31. Authorship of *Khishtab* is attributed to Hakim Pishtab, who is identified as a student of the Fifth Sasan. It was "translated" into Persian by Mubad Hush, the tutor of Azar Kayvan's son Kaykhusraw Isfandyar.

101. *A'in-i Hushang*, 32–76. *Zar-i Dastafshar* was "translated" into Persian by Mubad Surush Dadpuyah ibn Hush. See *A'in-i Hushang*, 32; *Dabistan*, 27, 38.

102. *A'in-i Hushang*, 77–148. *Zayandah Rud* is attibuted to Zindah Azarm and was "translated" into Persian by Farzanah Khushi. On a closer examination it appears that at least a section of *Zayandah Rud* parallels Shahab al-Din Suhravardi's *Hikmat al-Ishaq*.
103. *A'in-i Hushang*, 149–77. *Zawrah-'i Bastani* is attributed to Ibrahim Zardusht (Abraham-Zoroaster), "a prophet of Iran." It was "translated" into Persian by Azar Pazhuh (149).
104. *A'in-i Hushang*, respectively on 192 and 191–2.
105. Mirza Aqa Khan Kirmani, *Sah Maktub: Maktub-i Shahzadah Kamal al-Dawlah bah Shahzadah Jalal al-Dawlah*, ed. Bahram Chubinah ([Paris]: Mardé Emrouz, 1370/1991), 166; idem, *Ayinah-'i Sikandari* ([Tehran]: n.p., 1324/1906), 523.
106. By "schizophrenic" I have in mind not the clinical definition but a person's simultaneous identification with cultural discourses that are independent of one another. By schizochronia I intend a fractured view of historical time, which is elaborated in my forthcoming article "Modernity and Schizochronia."

Chapter 6   Crafting National Identity

1. Muhammad Hashim Rustam al-Hukama, *Rustam al-Tawarikh*, ed. Muhammad Mushiri (Tehran: n.p., 1969), 423; 309, 378, 391, 418, 459; 309; 61; 383, 392, 395, 458; 69, 396; 81, 82; 130; 466.
2. Muhammad Hasan Khan I'timad al-Saltanah, *Mir'at al-Buldan*, ed. 'Abd al-Husayn Nava'i (Tehran: Intisharat-i Danishgah-i Tihran, 1367 [1988]), 3.
3. See Henry Corbin, *Spiritual Body and Celestial Earth: From Mazdean Iran to Shi'ite Iran*, trans. Nancy Pearson, Bollingen Series xci: 2 (Princeton, NJ: Princeton University Press, 1977), 17–24.
4. For lists of *Shahnamah*s printed in the nineteenth century see Iraj Afshar, *Kitabshinasi-I Shahnamah* (Tehran: Anjuman-i Asar-i Milli, 1347 [1968]), 191–9; Javad Safinizhad, "Shahnamah ha-yi Chap Sangi," *Mirs-i Farhangi*, 14 (Zimistan 1374 [Winter 1996]), 21–4.
5. For studies of recitation traditions see Muhammad Ja'far Mahjub, "Sukhanvari," *Sukhan*, 9: 6 (Shahrivar 1337/1958), 530–5; idem, "Sukhanvari," *Sukhan* 9: 7 (1337/1958), 631–7; idem, "Sukhanvari," *Sukhan*, 9: 8, (1337 [1958]), 779–86; idem, "Tahavvul-i naqqali va qissah khwani, tarbiyat-i qissah khwanan va tumarha-yi naqqali," *Iran Nameh*, 9: 2 (Spring 1991), 186–211; Bahram Bayza'i, "Namayish dar Iran: Naqqali," *Majallah-'i Musiqi*, 3: 66 (1341 [1962]), 15–33; Mary Ellen Page, "Professional Storytelling in Iran: Transmission and Practice," *Iranian Studies*, 12 (Summer 1979), 195–215; 'Ali Al-e Dawud, "Coffeehouse," in *Encyclopaedia Iranica*, vi: 1, 1–4; Husayn Lisan, "Shahnamah khwani," *Hunar va Mardum*, 14: 159/160 (Day/Bahman 1354 [1975]), 2–16.
6. Ahmad Divan Baygi, *Hadiqat al-Shu'ara* (Tehran: Intisharat-i Zarrin, 1364 [1985]), 425–7.
7. Muhammad Ibrahim Bastani Parizi, "Shahnamah akhirash khush ast," *Nay-i Haft Band* (Tehran: 'Ata'i, 1353 [1974]), 259–373.
8. Cited in Lisan, "Shahnamah khwani," 15; Fath al-Din Fattahi, *Safar Namah-i Mirza Fattah Khan Garmrudi bi-Urupa*, ed. Fath al-Din Fattahi (Tehran: Bank-i Bazargani-i Iran, 1347/1968), 919.

9. Muhammad Ali Tusi, *Shahanshah Namah-i Nadiri*, ed. Ahmad Suhayli Khwansari (Tehran: Anjuman-i Asar-i Milli, 1339/1970), 22 and 224.

10. Mirza Fath'ali Khan Saba, *Shahanshahnamah* (Bombay: Malik al-Kuttab, 1867), 41.

11. According to Iraj Afshar, Davari's copy was in the possession of Farah Pahlavi and was held in her personal library. See his "Shahnamah, az khatti ta chapi," *Hunar va Mardum*, 14: 162 (1354 [1975]), 24.

12. For Davari's introduction see Mahdi Hamidi, *Shi'r dar 'Asr-i Qajar* (Tehran: Ganj-i Kitab, 1364/1985), 210–15.

13. Hamidi, *Shi'r dar 'Asr-i Qajar*, 175.

14. On this point see Malik al-Shu'ara Bahar, *Sabk Shinasi: Tarikh-i Tatavvur-i Nasr-i Farsi* (Tehran: Khudkar, 1337 [1958]), 3: 348.

15. Mirza Aqa Khan Kirmani, *Ayinah-'i Sikandari* (Tehran: [n. p.], 1324 [1906]), 14.

16. *Namah-'i Bastan*, which was completed by Shaykh Ahmad Adib Kirmani after the execution of Mirza Aqa Khan, was also known as *Salar Namah* (Shiraz: Matba'-i Muhammadi, 1316/1898). The alternative title bore the name of 'Abd al-Husayn Mirza Farmanfarma Salar Lashkar, who sponsored the publication of *Namah-'i Bastan* in Shiraz. On this point see Nazim al-Islam Kirmani, *Tarikh-i Bidari-i Iraniyan: Muqaddamah*, ed. 'Ali Akbar Sa'idi Sirjani (Tehran: Intisharat-i Bunyad-i Farhang-i Iran, 1346 [1967]), 175–88.

17. Nazim al-Islam Kirmani, *Tarikh-i Bidari-i Iraniyan* (Tehran: Intisharat-i Agah, 1362/1983), 1: 222–3.

18. Mirza Fath 'Ali Akhundzadah, *Maktubat-i Mirza Fath 'Ali Akhundzadah*, ed. M[uhammad Ja'far Mahjub] Subhdam ([Paris]: Mardé Imruz, 1364 [1985]), 33–5.

19. Riza Quli Khan Hidayat, *Majma' al-Fusaha* (Tehran: Karkhanah-'i Aqa Mir Muhammad Baqir, 1295/1878).

20. For a theoretical formulation of transference in the field of historical research see Dominick LaCapra, "History and Psychoanalysis," *Soundings in Critical Theory* (Ithaca, NY: Cornell University Press, 1989), 30–66.

21. Mahmud Mirza Qajar, "Tazkirah at-Salatin," in *Majma' al-Mahmud* (Tehran: Iranian National Library, MS F/2349).

22. *Khulasat al-Tawarikh* (Tehran: Iranian National Library, MS F/266).

23. 'Aliquli Mirza I'tizad al-Saltanah, *Iksir al-Tawarikh*, ed. Jamshid Kayanfarr (Tehran: Visman, 1370/1991). This edition only includes the Qajar period.

24. Henry Rawlinson, *Tarjumah-'i Kuh-i Bistun*, intr. Lisan al-Mulk (Kitabkhanah-'i Milli-i Iran, manuscript MS F/291); Henry Rawlinson, *Persian Cuneiform Inscription at Behistun Deciphered and Translated* (London: J. W. Parker, 1847).

25. Kirmani, *Ayinah-'i Sikandari*, 637.

26. I'timad al-Saltanah, *Durrar al-Tijan*, 4.

27. In an appendix to *Durrar al-Tijan* (vol. 1, 202–5) I'timad al-Saltanah introduced 82 European historians and classicists whose works he had used. Among the authors authorizing his text were: Edward Gibbon, Sivester de Sacy, Comte de Gobineau, Étienne Flandin, Friedrich Max Müller, John Malcolm, Victor Delacroix, Henry Rawlinson, and George Rawlinson. I'timad al-Saltanah had collected the works of these authors during his visits to Europe with Nasir al-Din Shah.

28. Nasir al-Din Shah's letter to I'timad al-Saltanah, dated 1309/1891, was added to the first volume of *Durrar al-Tijan*. For I'timad al-Saltanah's speculation see *Durrar al-Tijan*, 3: 154–7.

29. Akhundzadah to Jalal al-Din Mirza, 15 June 1870, in *Alifba-yi Jadid va Maktubat* (Baku: Farhangistan-i 'Ulum-i Jumhuri-i Shuravi-i Susiyalisti-i Azarbayjan, 1963) 172; quoted in Hamid Algar, *Mirza Malkum Khan: A Study in the History of Iranian Modernism* (Berkeley, Cal.: University of California Press, 1973), 92.

30. Dust 'Ali Khan Mu'ayyir al-Mamalik, *Rijal-i 'Asr-i Nasiri* (Tehran: Nashr-i Tarikh-i Iran, 1361/1982), 54.

31. Furughi, *Tarikh-i Salatin-i Sasani*, 1: 194, 2: 196.

32. The inaugural issue of *Millat-i Saniyah-'i Iran* was published on 15th of Muharram, 1283/1866. The logo appeared on the first page of issues 1–34.

33. Mirza Fath 'Ali Akhundzadah, *Maqalat*, ed. Baqir Mu'mini (Tehran: Intisharat-i Ava, 1351 [1972]), 44–5.

34. Ibid., 45. On Kavah-'i Ahangar see Jalil Dustkhwah, "Kavah-'i Ahangar bih rivayat-i naqqalan," *Iran Nameh*, 10: 1 (Winter 1992), 122–44; Turaj Darya'i, "Sahm-i manabi'-i Hind va Urupayi dar shinakht-i Shahnamah: Huviyat-i Kavah-'i Ahangar," *Iran Shenasi*, 11: 2 (Summer 1997), 279–84.

35. Furughi, *Tarikh-i Salatin-i Sasani*, 2: 194.

36. Kirmani, *Ayinah-'i Sikandari*, respectively 75–6 and 76–7.

37. For a study of Anushirvan's epithet, the Just (*dadgar*), see Jalal Khaliqi-Mutlaq, "Chira Anushirvan ra Dadgar Namidahand?" *Faslnamah-'i Hasti* (Summer 1993), 109–16.

38. Furughi, *Tarikh-i Salatin-i Sasani*, 2: 195–6; Kirmani, *Sah Maktub: Maktub-i Shahzadah Kamal al-Dawlah bah Shahzadah Jalal al-Dawlah*, ed. Bahram Chubinah ([S.l.: Mardé Emruz, 1370/1991), 80–7.

39. Kirmani, *Ayinah-'i Sikandari*, 9.

40. Akhundzadah, *Maktubat*, 32–3.

41. It should be pointed out that Persian chauvinism became a component of the new secular political strategy. This anti-Arab tendency was to some degree similar to the *Shu'ubiyah* movement which had developed as a reaction to the Muslim conquest of Iran.

42. Akhundzadah, *Maktubat*, 20–1.

43. Kirmani, *Sah Maktub*, 68–9.

44. Kirmani, *Sah Maktub*, 166; idem, *Ayinah-'i Sikandari*, 523.

45. Letter to Mirza Malkum Khan dated 15 Jumada I, 1311; cited in Faraydun Adamiyat, *Andishah'ha-yi Mirza Aqa Khan Kirmani* (Tehran: Payam, 1357/1978), 55.

46. Kirmani, *Ayanah-'i Sikandari*, 17 and 14.

47. Kirmani, *Sah Maktub*, 270–1.

48. Mirza Muhammad Taqi Lisan al-Mulk, *Nasikh al-Tawarikh* (Tehran: Islamiyah, 1344/1965), 2: 2, 359–61; I'tizad al-Saltanah, *Iksir al-Tawarikh*, 499–501, particularly 500. It is important to note that the proclamation was followed by three Qur'anic verses, which had been identified by Hajji Mirza Aqasi in support of the new uniform.

49. I'tizad al-Saltanah, *Iksir al-Tavarikh*, 290.

50. Mir 'Abd al-Latif Shushtari, *Tuhfat al-'Alam va Zayl al-Tuhfah*, ed. Samad Muvahhid (Tehran: Tahuri, 1363/1984) 268.

51. Kirmani, *Ayinah-'i Sikandari*, 522–3.
52. I'timad al-Saltanah, *Durrar al-Tijan*, I: 106.
53. Jamal al-Din Afghani, "Tarikh-i Ijmali-i Iran," appearing in Fursat Shirazi, *Divan Fursat*, ed. 'Ali Zarrin Qalam (Tehran: Kitabfurushi-i Sirus, 1337/1958), 28–73.
54. Kirmani, *Ayinah-'i Sikandari*, 106–110.
55. Kirmani, *Sah Maktub*, 260 and 266.
56. See Benedict Anderson, *Imagined Communities: Reflections on the Origin and Spread of Nationalism*, rev. edn (London: Verso, 1991), particularly 37–46 and 67–82.
57. On the Indian School see Aziz Ahmad, "The Formation of *Sabk-i Hindi*," in *Iran and Islam: In Memory of the late Vladimir Minorsky*, ed. C. E. Bosworth (Edinburgh: Edinburgh University Press, 1971), 1–9.
58. Among the leading figures of the Indian School were poets such as Kalim Kashani (d. 1650), Sa'ib Tabrizi (d. 1670), Ghani Kashmiri (d. 1667), Shawkat Bukhari (d. 1695), Nasir 'Ali Sirhindi (d. 1696), Juya Tabrizi (d. 1706).
59. See Chapter 2.
60. Siraj al-Din 'Ali Khan Arzu, *Dad-i Sukhan*, ed. Muhammad Akram (Rawalpindi: Iran-Pakistan Institute of Persian Studies, 1974), respectively, x, xxx–xxxii, xxxiv, and xxxiv.
61. 'Abd al-Razzaq Maftun Dunbuli, *Tajribat al-Ahrar va Tasliyat al-Abrar*, ed. Hasan Qazi Tabataba'i (Tehran: Mu'assisah-'i Tarikh va Farhang-i Iran, 1349/1970), 213–6.
62. Nostalgia for classical literature was also an important component of both Arab and Turkish nationalism. In this regard see S. Moreh, "The Neoclassical Qasida: Modern Poets and Critics," in *Arabic Poetry: Theory and Development*, ed. G. E. von Gruenbaum (Wiesbaden: Otto Harrassowitz, 1973), 156.
63. Cited in Mawlavi Muhammad Muzzafar Husayn Saba, *Tazkirah-'i Ruz-i Rawshan*, ed. Muhammad Husayn Ruknzadah Adamiyat (Tehran: Kitabkhanah-'i Razi, 1343/1964), 737.
64. Shams Langarudi, *Maktab-i Bazgasht: Barrasi-i Shi'r-i Dawrah'ha-yi Afshariyah, Zandiyah, Qajariyah* (Tehran: Chap va Intisharat-i Vizarat-i Umur-i Kharijah, 1375/1996), 129.
65. Mahdi Akhavan Salis, *Bid'at va Badayi'-i Nima Yushij* (Tehran: Intisharart-i Tuka, 1357/1978), 22.
66. For an insightful reevaluation of the "Return Movement" see Ghulam 'Ali Ra'di Azarakhshi, "Darbarah-'i sabkha-yi shi'r-i Farsi va nahzat-i bazgasht," in *Namvarah-'i Duktur Mahmud Afshar*, ed. Iraj Afshar and Karim Isfahaniyan (Tehran: Majmu'ah-'i Intisharat-i Adabi va Tarikhi, 1364/1985), 73–112.
67. Muhammad Mu'in has shown that words such as *akhshij, anbaz, tavanish, kunish, manish, nava,* and *niru*, which were considered as *dasatiri* inventions, are indeed words that can be found in older Persian texts. See his "Lughat-i Ibn Sina va ta'sir-i anha dar adabiyat," in *Majmu'ah Maqalat-i Duktur Muhammad Mu'in*, 529–71.
68. See Chapter 2.
69. See Fath'ali Khan Saba, *Divan-i Ash'ar*, ed. Muhammad 'Ali Nijati (Tehran: Iqbal, 1962), 676.
70. For a collection of Yaghma's writings see Abu al-Hasan Yaghma Jandaqi, *Majmu'ah-'i Asar-i Yaghma Jandaqi: Makatib va Munsha'at*, 2 vols, ed. 'Ali Al-i Davud (Tehran: Intisharat-i Tus, 1362/1983).

71. Abu al-Hasan Yaghma Jandaqi, *Kulliyat-i Yaghma Jandaqi* (Tehran: Ibn Sina, 1339/1960), 49; Yahya Aryanpur, *Az Saba ta Nima: Tarikh-i 150 Sal Adab-i Farsi* (Tehran: Kitabha-yi Jibi, 1351/1972), 114.
72. Yaghma Jandaqi, *Majmu'ah-'i Asar*, 2: 85; idem, *Kulliyat* (Tehran: Ufsit, 1339/1960), 56.
73. "The Rev. A. Duff['s]...address to the General Assembly of the church of Scotland," *The Asiatic Journal and Monthly Register*, 18 (1836), "Asiatic Intelligence" section, 86–8.
74. Among dictionaries edited and published in numerous editions in India were *Bahr-i 'Ajam, Bahar-i 'Ajam, Bahr al-Javahir fi Lughat al-Tibb, Burhan-i Qati', Chiragh-i Hidayat, Dari Gusha, Durr al-Fakhir Litaj al-Masadir, Farhang-i Anandraj, Farhang-i Farrukhi, Farhang-i Jahangiri, Farhang-i Rashidi, Ghiyas al-Lughat, Haft Qulzum, Kashf al-Lughat va al-Istilahat, Khazinat al-Amsal, Khiyaban-i Gulshan, Lughat Dari va Pahlavi, Lughat-i Firuzi, Madar al-Afazil, Majma' al-Furs-i Sururi, Mu'ayyad al-Fuzala, Mustalahat al-Shu'ara, Nafayis al-Lughat, Navadir al-Masadir, Nasir al-Lughat, Shams al-Lughat, Siraj al-Lughat, Tahqiq al-Istilahat, Surah*, and *Zubdat al-Lughat Ma'ruf bih Lughat-i Sururi*.
75. *Burhan Qati'*, written in 1652, became the locus of one of the most interesting and under-studied lexicographic controversies in Persian. Asad Allah Ghalib (1797–1869), the celebrated Urdu poet, in 1860 wrote a critical review of *Burhan-i Qati'* entitled *Qati'-i Burhan* (1862), and five years later he added a new introduction to it and renamed the work *Dirafsh-i Kavyani*. Ghalib's harsh criticisms of the author of *Burhan Qati'* led to a great literary controversy and publication of many responses and counter-responses.
76. Hafiz Farmanfarmayan, "Introduction," in 'Ali Khan Amin al-Dawlah, *Khatirat-i Siyasi Mirza 'Ali Khan Amin al-Dawlah*, ed. Hafiz Farmanfarma'iyan (Tehran: Kitabha-yi Iran, 1341/1962), 5.
77. On the simplification of Persian prose see Bahar, *Sabk Shinasi*, 3: 361; Shakoor Ahsan, *Modern Trends in the Persian Language* (Islamabad: Iran–Pakistan Institute for Persian Studies, 1976), 34; 'Abbas Zaryab Khu'i, "Sukhani darbarah-'i munsha'at-i Qa'im Maqam," in *Namvarah-'i Duktur Mahmud-i Afshar*, ed. Iraj Afshar (Tehran: Intisharat-i Adabi va Tarikhi, 1366 [1987]), 3: 1433–55.
78. "Sharh-i Manshuri kah Shahanshah-i Ghazi Muhammad Shah bikhatt-i Khwish Nigasht," in Lisan al-Mulk, *Nasikh al-Tawarikh*, 2: 326–8.
79. Ibid.
80. For studies of language reform and purism see John R. Perry, "Language Reform in Turkey and Iran," *International Journal of Middle Eastern Studies*, 17 (1985), 295–330; M. A. Jazayery, "The Modernization of the Persian Vocabulary and Language Reform in Iran," in *Language Reform: History and Future*, ed. I. Fodor and C. Hagége (Hamburg: Buske, 1983), 2: 241–68; Ahmad Karimi-Hakkak, "Language reform movement and its language: the case of Persian," in *The Politics of Language Purism*, ed. Björn Jernudd and Michael Shapiro (Berlin: Mouton de Gruyter, 1989), 81–104.
81. Abu al-Fazl Gulpaygani, *Rasa'il va Raqa'im*, ed. Ruhallah Mihrabkhani (Tehran: Mu'assasah-'i Milli-i Matbu'at-i Amri, 134 [1974?]). In a letter Gulpaygani lists the following individuals as practitioners of *parsinigari*: Mirza Muhammad Husayn Khan Suraya, Mirza Hasan Khushnivis Isfahani, Mirza Shaykh 'Ali Yazdi, who is viewed as the real author of *Namah-'i Khuwravan*

that is attributed to Jalal al-Din Mirza, Mirza Lutf 'Ali Danish (pp. 480–2). I thank Sholeh Quinn for making this collection available to me.

82. Baha'u'llah, "Tablet to Manackji Sahib," *Star of the West*, 1: 1 (March 21, 1910), 5–9. I am grateful to Juan Cole for making a copy of the "Tablet" accessible to me.

83. Kaykhusraw Shahrukh Kirmani, *Furugh-i Mizdisni* (Tehran: n.p., 1909).

84. Amin al-Dawlah, *Khatirat-i Siyasi*, 5.

85. For instance see Asadallah Ghalib, *Dastanbu* (Agrah: Matba'-i Mufid-i Khalayiq, 1858).

86. Kirmani, *Sah Maktub*, 265.

87. Riza Quli Khan Hidayat, *Farhang-i Anjuman Ara-yi Nasiri* (Tehran: Kargah-i 'Ali'quli Khan, 1288/1871), [2].

88. Adamiyat, *Andishah'ha-yi Mirza Aqa Khan-i Kirmani*, 162 and 274.

89. Kirmani, *Ayinah-'i Sikandari*, 118.

90. Akhundzadah, *Maqalat*, 187 and 193.

91. Letter to Mirza Muhammad Rafi' Sadr al-'Ulama, dated 18 Muharram 1129, appearing in *Maqalat*, 205.

92. Letter to Haji Shaykh Muhsin Khan, dated 4 February 1869, in Akhundzadah, *Alifba-yi Jadid va Maktubat*, 1137–40; quote on 1140.

93. See Algar, *Mirza Malkum Khan*, 90.

94. Bernard Lewis, *The Emergence of Modern Turkey*, 2nd edn (London: Oxford University Press, 1968), 428.

95. "To the President, Vice Presidents, and Committee of the Calcutta School Book Society," in *The Application of the Roman Alphabet to All the Oriental Languages Contained in a Series of Papers, Written by Messrs. Tryvelyan, J. Prinsep, and Tytler, Rev. A. Duff, and Mr. H. T. Prinsep* (Calcutta: Serampore Press, 1834), 1–30; quote on 13.

96. Mirza Isma'il Dardi Isfahani, "Tahrif-i Alifba-yi Musalmanan," in *Tarikh-i Jahan* (Qum: Kitabkhanah-'i 'Umumi-i Hazrat-i Ayat Allah al-'Uzma Mar'ashi, no. 2439), 550–643.

97. I'timad al-Saltanah, *Tatbiq-i Lughat-i Jughrafiya'i* (Tehran: Dar al-Intiba'at, 1311/1893), 68; Faraydun Adamiyat, *Andishah'ha-yi Talibuf-i Tabrizi*, 2nd edn (Tehran: Damavand, 1363 [1984]), 85.

98. "Falsafah-'i Qawmiyat va Lughat," *Miftah al-Zafar*, 4 (1897), 56.

99. "Falsafah-'i Tabi'i," *Miftah al-Zafar*, 2: 2 (September 15, 1898), 1–2; quote on 2.

100. Mirza Mahdi Khan, "Geology 'Ilm al-Arz," *Miftah al-Zafar*, 2: 5 (1998), 5–6.

101. "'Arz-i Tashakkur," *Miftah al-Zafar*, 2: 8 (November 22, 1898), 125, 127, 128.

102. "Vahdat-i Lughat," *Miftah al-Zafar*, 2: 11 (March 8, 1899), 16–17. In a following issue it was announced that Anjuman-i Ma'arif was modeled after the Royal Society of London and over 100 individuals had been accepted to join the Society. See "Anjuman-i Ma'arif," *Miftah al-Zafar*, 2: 12 (March 22, 1899), 182–3; "Anjuman-i Ma'arif," *Miftah al-Zafar*, 2: 13 (April 8, 1899), 201–2.

103. "I'lam," *Iran: Ruznamah-'i Sultani*, 56: 1 (March 31, 1903), 3. Neither Anjuman Ma'arif nor Majlis-i Akadimi is mentioned in any contemporary accounts of language reforms in Iran. Such a selective amnesia recurs in much of the literary historty of modern Iran, in which the Qajar period is emplotted as *'asr-i bikhabari* (the age of unawareness).

104.   Furughi Zuka' al-Mulk, "Maqam-i Firdawsi va Ahammiyat-i U," in *Hizarah-'i Firdawsi: Shamil-i Sukhanraniha-yi Jam'i az Fuzala-yi Iran va Mustashriqin-i Dunya dar Kungirah-'i Hizarah-'i Firdawsi* (reprint; Tehran: Dunya-yi Kitab, 1362/1983), 27–41, quote on 28.
105.   For studies of the constitutionalist literature, see Aryanpur, *Az Saba ta Nima*; Ahmad Karimi-Hakkak, *Recasting Persian Poetry: Scenarios of Poetic Modernity in Iran* (Salt Lake City: University of Utah, 1995), 23–99.

Chapter 7   Patriotic and Matriotic Nationalism

1.   Bernard Lewis, "Patriotism and Nationalism," in *The Shaping of the Modern Middle East* (Oxford: Oxford University Press, 1994), 71–98, quote on 76; idem, *The Emergence of Modern Turkey*, 334–5.
2.   "Geo-body" is a concept coined by Thongchai Winichahul, *Siam Mapped: A History of the Geo-Body of a Nation* (Honolulu: University of Hawaii, 1994).
3.   "This treaty permanently severed the Caucasian provinces from Iran and settled the Russo-Persian northwestern boundary along the Aras River." See Abbas Amanat, *Pivot of the Universe: Nasir al-Din Shah Qajar and the Iranian Monarchy, 1831–1896* (Berkeley, Cal.: University of California Press, 1997), 16. See also Fatmah Qaziha, *Asnadi Az Ravand-i Mu'ahidah-'i Turkmanchay, 1245–1250* (Tehran: Sazman-i Asnad-i Milli-i Iran, 1374/ 1995; Jamil Quzanlu, *Tarikh-i Nizami-i Iran: Jild-i Duvvum* (Tehran: Chap-khanah Firdawsi, 1315/1936).
4.   See Richard Schofield, "Interpreting a Vague River Boundary Delimitation: The 1847 Erzerum Treaty and the Shatt al-Arab before 1913," in *The Boundaries of Modern Iran*, ed. Keith McLachlan (New York: St Martin's Press, 1994), 72–92.
5.   The Treaty of Paris provided "the ground for the emergence of Iran's eastern boundaries." See Pirouz Mojtahed-Zadeh, "The Eastern Boundaries of Iran," in Schefield, *The Boundaries of Modern Iran*, 128–39, quote on 131.
6.   Firuz Kazemzadeh, *Russia and Britain in Persia, 1864–1914: A Study in Imperialism* (New Haven, Conn.: Yale University Press, 1968); Abbas Amanat, "'Russian Intrusion into the Guarded Domain': Reflections of a Qajar Statesman on European Expansion," *Journal of the American Oriental Society*, 113.1 (1993), 35–6; idem, *Pivot of the Universe*, 13–18.
7.   Reflecting on these treaties, Vanessa Martin aptly writes, "the growth of the modern state in Iran owed much to the influence of the foreign powers, a point which has been overlooked in discussions of their role in the politics of the period. By such measures as delineation of the borders and the ensuring of a peaceful succession, they contributed to security and stability.... Therefore it may be said that, in the period under question, the growth of the Iranian state, slow though it was, owed much to the strategic and commercial interests of Britain and Russia." See her "An Evaluation of Reform and Development of the State in the Early Qajar Period," *Die Welt des Islam*, 36: 1 (1996), 1–24, quote on 24.
8.   For a discussion of land-based rhetoric of Iranian nationalism see Firoozeh Kashani-Sabet, "Fragile Frontiers: The Diminishing Domains of Qajar Iran," *International Journal of Middle Eastern Studies*, 29 (1997), 205–34.

9. For instance see Mahmud ibn Muhammad Isfahani [d. 1215], *Dastur al-Vizarah*, ed. Riza Inzabi Nizhad (Tehran: Amir Kabir, 1364), 91. In this instance Isfahani linked "vatan-i ma'luf" to "mansha' va mawlid" (origin and birthplace). See *Dastur al-Vizarah*, 92. *Vatan Ma'luf* was used frequently in biographical dictionaries. For instance see Samsam al-Dawlah Shahnavaz Khan [1700–1757], *Ma'asir al-Umara*, ed. Mawlavi 'Abd al-Rahim and Mawlavi Mirza Ashraf 'Ali (Calcutta: Asiatic Society of Bengal, 1891), 2: 659; 3: 663.

10. For instance see Shahnavaz Khan, *Ma'asir al-Umara*, 1: 363.

11. Hasan Lahiji, "Hadiyyat al-Musafir" in *Ras'il-i Farsi*, ed. 'Ali Sadra'i Khu'i (Tehran: Nashr-i Qiblah, 1357), 304–20, quotes on 311.

12. In his biographical dictionary Shaykh 'Ali Hazin (b. 1103/1691) clearly distinguished *mawlid* (birthplace) from the place of residence (*mawtin/vatan*). See his *Tazkirah-'i Hazin*, ed. Muhammad Baqir Ulfat (Isfahan: Kitabfurushi-i Ta'yid, 1334/1955), particularly 38, 42, 44, 46, 72, 87, 100, 101, 110, 119.

13. For instance see Shahnavar Khan, *Ma'asir al-Umara*, 1: 303 and 1: 672 respectively.

14. *Dil bah an bandand va khvanandash vatan vandaran khusband ba aram-i tan.* See Mullah Ahmad Naraqi, "Hikayat-i Adam-i Abi va siyahat u dar ru-yi zamin," in *Masnavi-i Taqdis*, ed. Hasan Naraqi (Tehran: Amir Kabir, 1362), 64–9; quote on 65.

15. Henry Corbin coined the term "geosophy" in an attempt to explain the imaginary geography that rendered sensible the Mazdean profession of faith, "My mother is Spendarmat, Archangel of the Earth, and my father is Ohrmazd, the Lord of Wisdom." For details see Henry Corbin, *Spiritual Body and Celestial Earth: From Mazdean Iran to Shi'ite Iran*, trans. Nancy Pearson, Bollingen Series xci: 2 (Princeton, NJ: Princeton University Press, 1977), 15–16 and 36–50.

16. Shahab al-Din Yahya Suhravardi, "'Aql-i Surkh," in *Majmu'ah-'i Asar-i- Farsi-i Shaykh-i Ishraq = Oevres Philosophiques Et Mystiques*, ed. Husayn Nasr (Tehran: Department D'Iranologie de l'Institute Français de Recherche, 1970), 3: 226–39, quote on 229. Suhrawardi identified the "return to originary *vatan*" as "linkage with the celestial world [*al-'alam al-'alawi*]." He explained this "return" and "linkage" as the meaning of the Prophetic saying, "Love of *vatan* is of faith." See his "Kalimat Zawqiyah," in *Majmu'ah-'i Asar-i- Farsi*, 3: 463.

17. Mulla Ahmad Naraqi, *Mi'raj al-Sa'adah* (Tehran: Intisharat-i Rashidi, 1983), 9.

18. Abu al-Qasim ibn Adb al-Husayn, "Maktub-i yiki az faqihzadigan," *Hadid* 2: 10 (6 Rajab 1324), 3–4. When Shaykh Abu al-Qasim reminded the readers of *Hadid* of this definition of *vatan*, he was mocked as a "knowledge-deprived" cleric. See Muhammad Riza, "Hubb al-vatan min al-iman," *Hadid* 2: 11 (13 Rajab 1324), 3–4; quote on 3.

19. Ruzbihan Baqli Shirazi, *Sharh-i Shathiyat*, ed. Henry Corbin (Tehran: Tahuri, 1981), 622.

20. Baha' al-Din 'Amili, *Kulliyat-i Ash'ar va Asar-i Shaykh Baha'i*, ed. 'Ali Katibi (Tehran: Nashr-i Chigamah, 1372 [1993]), 160–2; idem, *Kulliyat-i Ash'ar-i Farsi va Mush va Gurbah-'i Shaykh Baha'i*, ed. Mahdi Tawhidipur (Tehran: Mahmudi, 1336/1157), 23; cited in Afsaneh Najmabadi, "The Erotic Vatan

[Homeland] as Beloved and Mother: to Love, to Possess, and to Protect," *Comparative Studies in Society and History*, (July 1997), 442–67, quote on 448.

21. For instance see Husayn Va'iz Kashifi, *Anvar-i Suhayli ya Kalilah va Dimnah* (Tehran: Amir Kabir, 1362), 551. In this reference Va'iz Kashifi equated "vatan" with "mawlid" (birth-place). See also Mirza Muhammad Husayn Fazil Jam [1840–1901], *Munsha'at-i Fazil Jami*, ed. Haybat Allah Maliki (Tehran: Intisharat-i Kavir, 1371/1992), 19.

22. Afsaneh Najmabadi views the "erotic mapping" of Iran, "as a body to love and possess, to protect and defend, to fight and to die for," as essential for the understanding of Iranian nationalism ("The Erotic Vatan," 450).

23. "Hubb al-watan min al-iman," *Akhtar*, 3: 8 (14 Safar 1294/28 February 1877), 1–2 [25–6].

24. "Baz az vatan bayad guft," *Akhtar*, 3: 10 (21 Safar 1294/7 March 1877), 1–2 [41–2]; quotes on 1 and 2.

25. "Hub al-watan min al-iman," *Akhtar*, 3: 9 (17 Safar 1294/3 March 1877), 33–4 [1–2], quotes on 1 and 2.

26. "Ruznamchah-'i Akhbar-i Dar al-Khalafah-'i Tihran," *Ruznamah-'i Vaqayi'-i Ittifaqiyah*, 1 (5 Rabi' al-Sani 1267), 1.

27. On "public sphere" see Jürgen Habermas, "The Public Sphere," *New German Critique*, 3 (1974), 49; Reinhart Koselleck, *Critique and Crisis: Enlightenment and the Pathogenesis of Modern Society* (Cambridge, Mass.: MIT Press, 1988), particularly 70–5.

28. Mirza Husayn Khan Sipahsalar to Nasir al-Din Shah Qajar, Shavval 1292; document no. 12–128 in *Hukumat-i Sayah'ha: Asnad-i Mahramanah va Siyasi-i Mirza Husayn Khan Sipahsalar*, ed. Muhammad Riza 'Abbasi (Tehran: Sazman-i Asnad-i Milli-i Iran, 1372/1993), nos 153, 152–1147; reference on 146.

29. Sani' al-Dawlah, "Sharaf," *Mirikh*, 3 (18 Safar 1296/10 February 1879), 2–3; quotes on 2, 2, 2–3.

30. Sani' al-Dawlah, "Vatan," *Mirikh*, 5 (25 Rabi' I 1296/19 March 1879), 2–4; quotes on 2, 2, and 3. For additional references to the shah as "the head and father of vatan" (*ra'is va pidar-i ahl-i vatan*) see: Sani' al-Dawlah, "Sharaf: baqiyah," *Mirikh*, 6 (20 Rabi' II 1296/13 April 1879), 1–3; quote on 1.

31. "Savad-i Ta'liqiyah . . . ," *Iran*, 67 (10 Zilqa'dah 1288), 1–2 [265–66], quote on 1. This was not a novel idea. For instance Najm Razi (b. 1177), discussing kings and their conducts, argued, "As for generosity to kinsfolk, this consists of respecting the rights of all subjects, for subjects stand in a relation of kinship to the king; indeed, they take the place of his family and kinsfolk." See Najm Razi, *The Path of God's Bondsmen from Origin to Return*, trans. Hamid Algar (Delamr, NY: Persian Heritage Series, Caravan Books, 1982), 415; idem, *Mirsad al-'Ibad*, ed. Muhammad Amin Riyahi (Tehran: Bungah-i Tarjumah va Nashr-i Kitab, 1352/1973), 436.

32. For an alternative characterization of Sani' al-Dawlah see Juan Cole, "Marking Boundaries, Marking Time: The Iranian Past and the Construction of the Self by Qajar Thinkers," *Iranian Studies*, 29: 1–2 (Winter/Spring 1996), 35–56; quotes on 46–7.

33. Sani' al-Dawlah, "Vatan," 3.

34. On "divine effulgence" see Said Amir Arjomand, *The Shadow of God and the Hidden Imam: Religion, Political Order, and Societal Change in Shi'ite Iran from the Beginning to 1890* (Chicago: University of Chicago Press, 1984), 94–5.

35. Sani' al-Dawlah, "Vatan," 4.
36. For a twelfth-century definition of *farr-i izadi* (divine effulgence) see Ghazali, *Nasihat al-Muluk*, ed. Jalal al-Din Huma'i (Tehran: Intisharat-i Anjuman-i Asar-i Milli, 1972) 81, 89, 127–8; idem, *Ghazali's Book of Council for Kings* (*Nasihat al-Muluk*), trans. F. R. C. Bagley (London: Oxford University Press, 1964) 45, 48.
37. The prophetic adage as cited by Najm Razi reads, "Each of you is a shepherd, and each will be called to account for his flock. Thus the prince is a shepherd for his subjects, and will be called to account for them." See Razi, *The Path of God's Bondsmen*, 415; idem, *Mirsad al-'Ibad*, 429. Also see 'Ali ibn Ahmad Ibn al-Qaza'i, *Tark al-Atnab Fi Sharh al-Shihab*, ed. Muhammad Shirvani (Tehran: Danishgah-i Tihran, 1343/1964), 102–3; Lewis, *The Political Language of Islam* (Chicago: University of Chicago Press, 1988), 61–2.
38. Razi, *The Path of God's Bondsmen*, 415; idem, *Mirsad al-'Ibad*, 438.
39. This is not to argue that the *ra'i-ra'yat* relations remained unchanged in the premodern period. The changing definitions of *ra'i* and *ra'yat* signify a sustained changing of relations within the same overarching metaphor.
40. Darius Rejali, *Torture and Modernity: Self, Society, and State in Modern Iran* (Boulder, Co.: Westview Press, 1994), 136 and 146.
41. For modernist rearticulation of *siyasat* in Egyptian political discourse see Timothy Mitchell, *Colonizing Egypt* (Berkeley, Cal.: University of California Press, 1991), 100–4.
42. Writing about Nasir al-Din Shah's travels, A. R. Sheikholeslami observed, "By bringing the government to the people, the Shah legitimized his government and integrated his realm.... The Shah, during his trips, enhanced his authority not only by positive rewards, such as exemption from taxes or ordering a governor to repair a certain irrigation system, but also by exposing his subjects to his royal pomp and power." See his *The Structure of Central Authority in Qajar Iran, 1871–1896* (Atlanta, Ga.: Scholars Press, 1996), 83.
43. "Vizarat-i Dar al-Khalafah," *Iran*, 7 (3 Safar 1288), 1–2 [25–6).
44. "Tafsil-i vaz'-i majlis-i i'anah," *Iran*, 56 (25 Ramazan 1288), 2 [222].
45. For the bylaws, members, and the proceedings of the Poor Assistance Council see "Tafsil va vaz'-i majlis-i i'anah," 2–3 [222–3]; "Majlis-i chaharum va panjum-i i'anat," *Iran*, 62 (20 shavval 1288), 2–3 [246 7].
46. "Baqiyah-'i dastur al-'amal-i hafiz al-sihhah," *Iran*, 61 (15 Shavval 1288), 3 [243]; "Akhbar-i ghayr-i rasmi," *Iran*, 86 (7 Safar 1289), 2–4 [342–4]; "I'lan-i Digar," *Iran*, 7 Sha'ban 1288), 1 [189].
47. "Baqiyah-'i dastur al-'amal-i Hafiz al-Sihhah," *Iran*, 63 (25 Shavval 1288/7 January 1871), 2–3 [250–1]; "Baqiyah-'i dastur al-'amal-i Hafiz al-Sihhah," *Iran*, 63 (28 Shavval 1288/10 January 1871), 2–3 [254–5].
48. "Idarah-'i jalilah-'i nazmiyah...," *Iran*, 387 (15 Jamadi II 1296/2 June 1879), 4 [1552]; "Idarah-'i jalilah-'i nazmiyah...," *Iran*, 388 (21 Jamadi II 1296/22 June 1879), 4 [1556].
49. Hamid Algar, *Mirza Malkum Khan: A Study in Iranian Modernism* (Berkeley, Cal.: University of California Press, 1973), 36–55.
50. "Muzakirat-i Javami'-i Iran...," *Qanun*, 11: 1.
51. "Yak shahzadah-'i ba shu'ur...," *Qanun*, 10: 2
52. For instance see Isma'il Ra'in, *Anjumanha-yi Sirri dar Inqilab-i Mashrutiyat*, 2nd edn (Tehran: Javidan, 1976).

53. Ervand Abrahamian, *Iran between Two Revolutions* (Princeton, NJ: Princeton University Press, 1982), 73. See also Nikki Keddie, *Religion and Rebellion in Iran: The Iranian Tobacco Protest of 1891–1892* (London: Frank Cass, 1996); Faraydun Adamiyat, *Shurish bar Imtiyaz Namah-'i Rizhi* (Tehran: Payam, 1981).

54. Cited in "Tashkhis-i amraz-i vatan," *Rahnama*, 5 (3 September 1907), 8.

55. "Mariz-i Irani va tibabat-i dakhilah va kharijah," *Iblaq*, 2 ([Zulqa'dah]1324 [December 1906]), 1; "Baqiyah-'i Mariz-i Irani," *Iblaq*, 2 (23 Zulhajjah 1324 [January 1907]), 2–3.

56. "Baqiyah-'i mariz-i Irani," *Iblaq*, 3 (Muharam 1325 [February/March 1907]), 1–2.

57. "Qabil-i tavvajuh-i vizarat-i jalilah-'i dakhilah," *Tarraqi*, 11 (3 Rabi' al-Awwal 1325), 1–2.

58. See "Aya Iran mariz ast?" *Habl al-Matin*, 2 (30 April 1907), 1–3; "Nakhushi-i Iran Chist?" *Habl al-Matin*, 3 (1 May 1907), 1–2.

59. "Tashkhis-i amraz-i vatan ya diagnusis-i Iran," *Rahnama*, 1 (26 Jamadi II 1325/6 August 1906), 5–7.

60. "Tashkhis-i amraz-i vatan," *Rahnama*, 2 (August 13 1907), 7.

61. "Tashkhis-i amraz," *Rahnama*, 7 (7 Sha'ban 1325/17 September 1907), 5–7; quotes on 6 and 7.

62. "Tashkhis-i amraz," *Rahnama*, 8 (15 Sha'ban 1325/24 September 1907), 6 and 7.

63. "Tashkhis-i amraz," *Rahnama*, 10 (15 Ramazan 1325/23 October 1907), 10–11.

64. "Tashkhis-i amraz," *Rahnama*, 11 (9 Shavval 1325/16 November 1907), 5.

65. "Tashkhis-i amraz," *Rahnama*, 12 (16 Shavval 1325/23 November 1907), 3 and 4.

66. "Tashkhis-i amraz," *Rahnama*, 13 (26 Shavval 1325/3 December 1907), quotes on 4, 4, 5.

67. "Tashkhis-i amraz," *Rahnama*, 18 (8 Muharram 1326/11February 1908).

68. "Tashkhis-i amraz," *Rahnama*, 19 (22 February 1908), 6.

69. "Tashkhis-i amraz," *Rahnama*, 23 (23 April 1908), 4.

70. "Tashkhis-i amraz," *Rahnama*, 24 (12 May 1908), 5 and 6.

71. Najmabadi, "The Erotic Vatan," 456.

72. "Sharaf bah tazigi vird-i zaban-i [khass?] va 'ami shudah, chira?" *Musavat*, 15 (27 Muharam 1326 [1 March 1908]), 2.

73. "Khayr al-Umur Awsatuha," *Musavat*, 15 (1 March 1908/27 Muharram 1326), 3–4, quotes on 3.

74. "Maktub-i Shahri," *Musavat*, 6 (17 Shavval 1325 [24 November 1907]), 6.

75. "Musavat," *Musavat*, 12 (6 Muharram 1326 [9 February 1908]), 3–4; quotes on 3.

76. "Subh-i sa'adat-i vatan ra sham-i nuhusat rasid," *Musavat*, 25 (31 May 1908), 1–4, quote on 1.

77. Afsaneh Najmabadi, "Is Our Name Remembered?" *Iranian Studies*, 29: 1–2 (Winter/Spring 1996), 85–109, particularly 91; idem, "The Erotic Vatan," 455–6.

78. "Maqasid-i Azarbayjan: Nida-yi Azarbayjan bi'umum-i vilayat-i mahrusah-'i Iran," *Musavat*, 27 (7 Muharram 1327 [30 January 1909]), 2, 3–4, 5, and 6.

79. For a thoughtful study of this issue see Afsaneh Najmabadi, "Zanha-yi Millat: Women or Wives of the Nation," *Iranian Studies*, 26: 1–2 (Winter/ Spring 1993), 51–71; particularly 61–5.

80. Respectively see "Maktub-i Anjuman-i Khayriyah-'i Nisvan-i Iranian-i Muqim-i Islambul kah bah Jinab-i Sardar-i Milli Tabrik Numudahand," *Musavat*, 28 (7 February 1909/14 Muharram 1327), 7; "Tarjumah-'i Layihah-'i Muta'alimin-i Dar al-Funun-i Muscaw . . . ," *Musavat*, 28, 7–8.
81. According to Najmabadi, "The women's presence in the battlefield in a space presumably belonging to men or male lions, though initially admired, became immediately rescribed as a shame for men." See her "Zanha-yi Millat," 63.
82. "Musavat," *Musavat*, 28 (14 Muharram 1327 [7 February 1909]), 8–9.
83. Najmabadi, "The Erotic Vatan," 459–60.
84. For Darius Rejali there are four modes of subjection (statutory, disciplinary, tutelary, and carceral), see *Torture and Modernity*, 146–59.
85. Partha Chatterjee, *The Nation and Its Fragments: Colonial and Postcolonial Histories* (Princeton, NJ: Princeton University Press, 1993), 120–1, 121, 126.
86. "Dar farayiz-i murabiyan-i haqiqi-yi mardan ya'ni nisvan," *Hadid*, 13 (25 Rajab 1323), 4–6; quote on p. 4, col. 2.
87. Najmabadi, Afsaneh, "Crafting an Educated Housewife in Iran," in *Remaking Women: Feminism and Modernity in the Middle East*, ed. Lila Abu-Lughod (Princeton, NJ: Princeton University Press, 1998). 26.
88. On Tayirah Tihrani see Afsaneh Najmabadi, "Tayirah: Namah'ha, Nivishtah'ha, va Ash'ar Hamrah ba Barghayi az Zindigani-i U," *Nimah–'i Digar*, 2: 3 (Winter 1997), 146–95.
89. Tayirah Tihrani, "Maktub-i khanum-i danishmand," *Iran-i Naw*, 78 (16 Ziga'dah 1327/30 November 1909), 2–3; cited in Najmabadi, "The Erotic Vatan," 461.

Chapter 8 Postscript

1. Mohamad Tavakoli-Targhi, "Constitutionalist Imaginary in Iran and the Ideals of the French Revolution," *Iran Nameh*, 8: 3 (Summer 1990), 421–2.
2. *Qanun*, 2 ([Sha'ban 1308/22 March 1890]), 3.
3. See Mirza Malkum Khan, "Ishtihar Namah-'i Awliya-yi Adamiyat," in *Majmu'ah-'i Asar*, ed. Muhit Tabatab'i (Tehran: Intisharat-i 'Ilmi, n.d.), 182–7; idem, "Risalah 'i Ghaybiyah," in *Majmu'ah-'i Asar*, 219–37 [1–19].
4. *Istibdad* is usually translated as "despotism" and/or "tyranny." What was viewed as *istibdad* from the late nineteenth century onward was not "oppression" but increased governmentalization of everyday life. Additionally "despotism" has a highly charged connotation within the Orientalist discourse. Therefore, I find "authoritarianism" as a more appropriate translation of *istibdad*. For a historical study of this concept see 'Abd al-Hadi Ha'iri, "Sukhani Piramun-i Vazhah-'i *Istibdad* dar Adabiyat-i Inqilab-i Mashrutiyat-i Iran," *Iran va Jahan-i Islam: Pazhuhish'hayi Tarikhi Piramun-i Chihrah'ha, Andishah'ha, va Junbishha* (Mashhad: Intisharat-i Astan-i Quds-i Razavi, 1368), 223–31.
5. For a more elaborate study of the changing connotation of the "millat" and the polarization of the political space, see Mohamad Tavakoli-Targhi, *The Formation of Two Revolutionary Discourses in Modern Iran: The Constitutional Revolution of 1905–1909 and the Islamic Revolution of 1978–1979*, Ph.D dissertation, University of Chicago, 1988.

6. Nazim al-Islam Kirmani, *Tarikh-i Bidari-yi Iraniyan: Muqaddamah*, ed. 'Ali Akbar Sa'idi Sirjani (Tehran: Intisharat-i Bunyad-i Farhang-i Iran, 1346/1967), 1: 561.

7. On the class belonging of the elected deputies to the First Majlis, see Mansurah Ittihadiyah, *Paydayish va Tahavvul-i Ahzab-i Siyasi-i Mashrutiyat: Dawrah-'i Avval va Duvvum-i Majlis-i Shura-yi Milli* (Tehran: Nashr-i Gustarah, 1361 [1982]), 101–18.

8. On the concept of *mashrutah* see 'Abd al-Hadi Ha'iri, "Sukhani Piramun-i Vazhah-'i *Mashrutah*," in *Iran va Jahan-i Islam*, 212–22; Hasan Taqizadah, "Mashrutiyat," *Iran Nameh*, 1: 4 (Summer 1983), 511–12. For one of the earliest usage of the Persian usage of *shurut* in relation to a parliamentary form of government see Mirza Salih Shirazi, *Guzarish-i Safar*, 310.

9. Kasravi, *Tarikh-i Mashrutah-'i Iran*, 120; Malikzadah, *Tarikh-i Inqilab-i Mashrutiyat-i Iran* (Tehran: 'Ilmi, 1363), 2: 176; Bastani-Parizi, *Talash-i Azadi*, 89.

10. For this decree see Kasravi, *Tarikh-i Mashrutah-'i Iran*, 120.

11. The inauguration was initially planned for the 15th of Sha'ban, but since it coincided with the birthday of the "Twelfth Shi'i Imam," and since the constitutionalists wanted it to be an independent day, the Majlis was inaugurated on the 18th of Sha'ban of 1324. In a message by the Shah, the inauguration of the Majlis was regarded as "the strengthening of the unity between the representatives of *dawlat* and *millat*." See Kashani, *Vaqi'at-i ttifaqiyah dar Tarikh*, 1: 106; [Ibrahim Safa'i], *Nihzat-i Mashrutah bar Payah-'i Asnad-i Vizarat-i Umur-i Kharijah* (Tehran: Daftar-i Mutali'at-i Siyasi va Bayn al-Milali, 1370), 184.

12. See Ahmad Ashraf, "Maratib-i ijtima'i dar dawran-i Qajariyah," *Kitab-i Agah*, 1 (Zimistan 1360/Winter 1981): 72–3.

13. According to the 26th article of the Supplementary Constitutional Law, "All powers of the state are derived from the *millat*."

14. *Iran-i Naw*, 134 (16 February 1910).

15. Concerning the circumstances leading to the drafting of the Fundamental Laws, see 'Abd al-Husayn Nava'i, "Qanun-i Asasi va mutammam-i an chigunah tadvin shud?" *Yadgar*, 4: 5 (Bahman 1326 [Jan. 1947]), 34–47.

16. Shaykh Fazl'allah Nuri, *Majmu'ah-'i az Rasayil, I'lamiyah'ha, Maktubat, . . . va 'Ruznamah-'i Shaykh-i Shahid Fazl'allah Nuri*, ed. Muhammad Turkuman (Tehran: Khadamat-i Farhangi-i Rasa, 1962 [1983]), 1: 108. For an analysis of Nuri's political positions during this period see Firaydun Adamiyat, "Aqayid va ara-yi Shaykh Fazl'allah Nuri," *Kitab-i Jum'ah*, 31 (28 Farvardin 1359 [April 17, 1980]), 52–61.

17. "Surat majlis va nutqha-yi ahali-i Yazd barayi intikhab-i vakil, shab-i 6 Ramazan 1325," *Sur-i Israfil*, 17 (14 Shavval 1325), 4.

18. Nuri, *Majmu'ah*, 320.

19. Shaykh Fazl'allah Nuri, *Lavayih-i Aqa Shaykh Fazl'allah Nuri*, ed. Huma Rizvani (Tehran: Nashr-i Tarikh-i Iran, 1362), 29, 62, and 62.

20. Nuri, *Rasa'il*, 107.

21. Said Amir Arjomand, "The Ulama's Traditionalist Opposition to Parliamentarianism: 1907–1909," *Middle Eastern Studies*, 17 (1981), 179.

Select Bibliography

Manuscripts

Ardakani, Muhammad Qazi, *Tuhfah-'i Muhammadiyah*, Mashhad, Astan-i Quds Library, MS 583.

Dardi Isfahani, Mirza Isma'il, "Tahrif-i Alifba-yi Musalmanan," in *Tarikh-i Jahan*, Qum: Kitabkhanah-'i 'Umumi-i Hazrat-i Ayat Allah al-'Uzma Mar'ashi, MS 2439.

Ghulam 'Ali Khan, *Ayi'in 'Alamshahi*, Oxford, Bodleian Library, O. C. Elliot 3.

Mirza Abu Talib Isfahani, *Lubb al-Siyar va Jahan Numa*, Oxford, Bodleian Library, Oriental Collection.

Mir 'Izzat Allah, *Ahval-i Safar-i Bukhara*, Oxford, Bodleian Library, O.R. 745.

Mirza Abu Talib Isfahani, *Khulasat al-Afkar*, Oxford, Bodleian Library, MS Elliot 181.

Mirza I'tisam al-Din, *Shigirf Namah-'i Vilayat*, Oxford, Bodleian Library, Caps. OR.A.8; London, British Library, OR5848; London, British Museum, O.C. 13663.

Mirza Ja'far [Mushir al-Dawlah] Husayni, *Kitabchah-'i Sifarat-i Mirza Ja'far Khan Mushir al-Dawlah*, Tehran, Ministry of Foreign Affairs.

Mirza Ja'far [Mushir al-Dawlah] Husayni, *Qanun va Qava'id-i Tupkhanah*, Mashhad, Astan-i Quds-i Razavi, MS 12154).

Mirza Ja'far [Mushir al-Dawlah] Husayni, *Tarz-i Hukumat-i Iran va Muqayisah-'i an ba Hukumatha-yi Urupa*, Tehran, Ministry of Foreign Affairs, MS 794.

Mirza Salih Shirazi, *Su'al va Javab*, Bodleian Library, Ouseley 390.

Mubashshir Khan, Muhammad 'Ali. *Manahij al-Istikhraj*, Mashhad, Astan-i Quds Library, MS 12302.

Muhammad Ayyub, *Risalah dar 'Ilm-i Nujum*, Panta, Khuda Bakhsh Oriental Public Library, Acc. 334.

Muhammad Isma'il Landani, *Tashil al-Adrak fi Sharh al-Aflak*, Lucknow, Dar al-'Ulum Nadwat al-'Ulama, Radif 3: no. 4.

Muhammad Riza Tabrizi, *Havadis Namah*, Tehran, Iranian National Library, MS F1615, F/1714, F/1057.

Muhammad Riza Tabrizi, *Sharh-i Hal-i Iskandar va Napil'un-i Avval*, Tehran, Iranian National Library, MS F/1680, F/1714.

Muhammad Riza Tabrizi, *Tarikh-i Napil'un-i Avval*, Tehran, Iranian National Library, MS F/1615, F/1714, F/1057.

Qajar, Mahmud Mirza. *Majma' al-Mahmud*, Tehran, Iranian National Library, MS F/2349.

Rawlinson, Henry, *Tarjumah-'i Kuh-i Bistun*, trans. Lisan al-Mulk, Tehran, Iranian National Library, MS F/291.

Shiv Parshad, *Tarikh-i Fayz Bakhsh*, Oxford, Bodleian Library, Caps. OR.C.2.

Siraj al-Din Khan Arzu, *Majma' al-Nafa'is*, Oxford, Bodleian Library, MS Elliot 399.

Turner, Samuel, *Letters, Passports, and Documents*, Oxford, Bodleian Library, O.C. 2822, Ms. Pers.a.4.

Vaqyi' Nigar, Mirza Muhammad Sadig Marvazi, *Qava'id al-Muluk*, Tehran, Iranian National Library, MS F/1757.

Zakhmi Lakhnavi, Rathan Singh, *Hadayiq al-Nujum*, Patna, Khuda Bkhsh Oriental
Public Library.

Persian Newspapers

Habl al-Matin
Hadid
Iblaq
Iran
Iran: Ruznamah-'i Sultani
Iran-i Naw
Miftah al-Zafar
Mirikh
Musavat
Namah-'i Parsi
Qanun
Rahnama
Ruznamah-'i Millat-i Saniyah-'i Iran
Ruznamah-'i Vaqayi'-i Ittifaqiyah
Suraya
Tamadun
Tarraqi

Books and Articles

'Amili, Baha' al-Din, *Kulliyat-i Ash'ar-i Farsi va Mush va Gurbah-'i Shaykh Baha'i*, ed.
Mahdi Tawhidipur (Tehran: Mahmudi, 1958).

Aarsleff, Hans, *The Study of Language in England, 1780–1860* (Minneapolis: University of Minnesota Press, 1983).

Abrahamian, Ervand, "European Feudalism and Middle Eastern Despotisms,"
Science and Society, 39 (1975).

Abrahamian, Ervand, "Oriental Despotism: the Case of Qajar Iran," *International
Journal of Middle Eastern Studies*, 5 (1984), 3–31.

Abrahamian, Ervand, *Iran Between Two Revolutions* (Princeton: Princeton University Press, 1982).

Adamiyat, Firaydun, *Andishah'ha-yi Talibuf-i Tabrizi*, 2nd edn (Tehran: Damavand,
1363/1984]).

Adamiyat, Firaydun, *Andishah'ha-yi Mirza Aqa Khan Kirmani* (Tehran: Tahuri,
1346/1967; Tehran: Payam, 1357/1978).

Adamiyat, Firaydun, *Andishah'ha-yi Mirza Fath 'Ali Akhunzadah* (Tehran: Intisharat-i
Khwarazmi, 1349/1970).

Adamiyat, Firaydun, *Andishah-'i Tarraqi va Hukumat-i Qanun: 'Asr-i Sipahsalar*
(Tehran: Khwarazmi, 1351/1972).

Adamiyat, Firaydun, "'Aqayid va Ara-yi Shaykh Fazl'allah Nuri," *Kitab-i Jum'ah*,
31 (28 Farvardin 1359/April 17, 1980), 52–61.

Adamiyat, Firaydun, *Shurish Bar Imtiyaz Namah-'i Rizhi* (Tehran: Payam, 1981).

Afghani, Jamal al-Din, "Tarikh-i Ijmali-i Iran," in Fursat Shirazi, *Divan Fursat*, ed.
'Ali Zarrin Qalam (Tehran: Kitabfurushi-i Sirus, 1337) 28–73.

Afshar, Iraj, "Shahnamah, az khatti ta chapi," *Hunar va Mardum*, 14: 162 (1354/ 1975).

Afshar, Iraj, *Kitabshinasi-i Shahnamah* (Tehran: Anjuman-i Asar-i Milli, 1347/ 1968).

Ahmad, Aziz, "The Formation of *Sabk-i Hindi*," in *Iran and Islam: In Memory of the late Vladimir Minorsky*, ed. C. E. Bosworth, 1–19 (Edinburgh: Edinburgh University Press, 1971).

Ahmad, Leila, "Western Ethnocentrism and Perceptions of the Harem," *Feminist Studies*, 8: 3 (1982), 521–34.

Ahmad, Nazir, *Naqd-i Burhan-i Qati'* (New Delhi: Ghalib Institute, 1985).

Ahsan, Shakoor, *Modern Trends in the Persian Language* (Islamabad: Iran–Pakistan Institute for Persian Studies, 1976).

Akhavan Salis, Mahdi, *Bid'at va Badayi'-i Nima Yushij* (Tehran: Intisharart-i Tuka, 1357/1978).

Akhavan Salis, Mahdi, *Akhir-i Shahnamah*, 8th edn (Tehran: Intisharat-i Murvarid, 1363/1984).

Akhundzadah, Mirza Fath 'Ali, *Maktubat-i Mirza Fath 'Ali Akhundzadah*, ed. M. Subhdam [Muhammad Ja'far Mahjub] ([Paris]: Mardé Imruz, 1364/1985).

Akhundzadah, Mirza Fath 'Ali, *Maqalat*, ed. Baqir Mu'mini (Tehran: Intisharat-i Ava, 1351/1972).

Akhundzadah, Mirza Fath 'Ali, *Alifba-yi Jadid va Maktubat* (Baku: Farhangistan-i 'Ulum-i Jumhuri-i Shuravi-i Susiyalisti-i Azarbayjan, 1963).

Alavi, Azra, *Socio-Religious Outlook of Abul Fazl* (Delhi: Idarah-i Adabiyat-i Dihli, 1983).

Alavi, Buzurg, "Critical Writings on the Renewal of Iran," in *Qajar Iran: Political, Social, and Cultural Changes, 1800–1925*, ed. Edmond Bosworth and Carloe Hillenbrand (Costa Mesa, CA: Mazda Publishers, 1992).

Al-e Dawud, Ali, "Coffeehouse," in *Encyclopaedia Iranica*, ed. Ehsan Yarshater (Boston, Mass.: Routledge & Kegan Paul, 1983–), VI: 1, 1–4.

Alexander, James, *Travels from India to England: Comprehending a Visit to the Burman Empire, & c., in 1825–26* (London: Parbury, Allen, 1827).

Algar, Hamid, *Mirza Malkum Khan: A Study in the History of Iranian Modernism* (Berkeley: University of California Press, 1973).

Al-i Ahmad, Jalal, *Plagued by the West (Gharbzadegi)*, trans. Paul Sprachman (Delmar, NY: Caravan Books, 1982).

Allami, Abu al-Fazl ibn Mubarak, *The A-in-i Akbari*, trans. H. Blochman; ed. D. C. Phillott (Calcutta: Asiatic Society of Bengal, 1872–1877; Delhi: Low Price Publications, 1989).

Alvi, M. A. and Rahman, A., *Fathullah Shirazi: A Sixteenth Century Indian Scientist* (New Delhi: National Insitute of Sciences of India, 1968).

Amanat, Abbas, "'Russian Intrusion into the Guarded Domain': Reflections of a Qajar Statesman on European Expansion," *Journal of the American Oriental Society*, 113.1 (1993), 35–56.

Amanat, Abbas, *Pivot of the Universe: Nasir al-Din Shah Qajar and the Iranian Monarchy, 1831–1896* (Berkeley: University of California Press, 1997).

Amanat, Abbas, *Resurrection and Renewal: The Making of the Babi Movement in Iran, 1844–1850* (Ithaca: Cornell University Press, 1989).

Ambashthya, B. P., *Contributions on Akbar and the Parsees* (Patna, India: Janaki Prakashan, 1976).

Amin al-Dawlah, Mirza 'Ali Khan, *Khatirat-i Siyasi-i Mirza 'Ali Khan Amin al-Dawlah*, ed. Hafiz Farmanfarma'iyan (Tehran: Kitabha-yi Iran, 1341/1962).

Anderson, Benedict, *Imagined Communities: Reflections on the Origin and Spread of Nationalism*, rev. edn (London: Verso, 1991).

Anonymous, "Dastur al-'Amal-i 'Ali Jah Muqqarib al-Hazrat al-Khaqaniyah 'Askar Khan Sartip Mihmandar-i Jinab-i Khayr Allah Afandi Vazir-i Mukhtar-i Dawlat-i 'Illiyah-'i 'Usmani [4 Zilqa'dah 1296 H. Q.]," in *Guzidah-'i Asnad-i Siyasi-i Iran va 'Usmani: Dawrah-'i Qajariyah* (Tehran: Daftar-i Mutali'at-i Siyasi va Bayn al-Milali, 1370/1991).

Anonymous, "An Account of the Life and Character of Tofuzel Hussein Khan, the Vakeel, or Ambassador, of the Nabob Vizier Assof-Ud-Dowlah, at Calcutta, During the Government of Marquis Cornwallis," *The Asiatic Annual Register, or, A View of the History of Hindustan, and of the Politics, Commerce and Literature of Asia for the Year 1803* (London: Cadell and Davies, 1804), Characters: 1–8.

Anquetil-Duperron, Abraham Hyacinthe, "Oupnek'hat. . . . Argentorati: Typis et impensis fratrum Levrault, 1801–1802,".

Anquetil-Duperron, Abraham Hyacinthe, *Zend-Avesta* (Paris: N. M. Tilliard, 1771).

Anquetil-Duperron, A. H., *Zend-Avesta*, intro. Robert D. Richardson (New York: Garland, 1984).

Ansari, S. M. Razaullah, "Introduction of Modern Western Astronomy in India During 18–19th Centuries," in *History of Astronomy in India*, ed. S. N. Sen and K. S. Shukla (New Delhi: Indian National Science Academy, 1985).

Arberry, A. J., "The Founder: William Jones," in *Oriental Essays: Portraits of Seven Scholars* (London: George Allen & Unwin, 1960).

Arjomand, Kamran, "The Emergence of Scientific Modernity in Iran: Controversies Surrounding Astrology and Modern Astronomy in Mid-Nineteenth Century," *Iranian Studies*, 30: 1–2 (Winter/Spring 1997).

Arjomand, Said Amir, "The Ulama's Traditionalist Opposition to Parliamentarianism: 1907–1909," *Middle Eastern Studies*, 17 (1981).

Arjomand, Said Amir, *The Shadow of God and the Hidden Imam: Religion, Political Order, and Societal Change in Shi'ite Iran from the Beginning to 1890* (Chicago: University of Chicago Press, 1984).

Aryanpur, Yahya, *Az Saba ta Nima: Tarikh-i 150 Sal Adab-i Farsi* (Tehran: Kitabha-yi Jibi, 1351/1972).

Arzu, Saraj al-Din 'Ali Khan, *Muthmir [Musmir]*, ed. Rehana Khatoon (Karachi: The Institute of Central and West Asian Studies, 1991).

Arzu, Siraj al-Din 'Ali Khan, *Chiragh-i Hidayat*, ed. Mansur Sirvat (Tehran: Amir Kabir, 1984).

Arzu, Siraj al-Din 'Ali Khan, *Dad-i Sukhan*, ed. Muhammad Akram (Rawalpindi: Iran Pakistan Institute of Persian Studies, 1974).

Ashraf, Ahmad, "Historical Obstacles to the Development of a Bourgeoisie in Iran," in *Studies in the Economic History of the Middle East: from the Rise of Islam to the Present Day*, ed. M. A. Cook (London, New York: Oxford University Press, 1970).

Ashraf, Ahmad, *Mavani'-i Tarikhi-i Rushd-i Sarmayahdari dar Iran: Dawrah-'i Qajariyah* (Tehran: Zaminah, 1359).

Ashraf, Ahmad, "Maratib-i Ijtima'i dar Dawran-i Qajariyah," *Kitab-i Agah*, 1 (Zimistan 1360/Winter 1981), 72–3.

Asil, Hujjat-allah, *Zindagi va Andishah-yi Mirza Malkum Khan Nazim al-Dawlah* (Tehran: Nashr-i Nay, 1997).

Askari, S. H., "Dabistan-i Mazahib and Diwan-i-Mubad," in *Indo-Iranian Studies: Presented for the Golden Jubilee of the Pahlavi Dynasty of Iran*, ed. Fathullah Mujtabai (New Delhi: Indo-Iran Society, 1977).

Astarabadi, Bibi Khanum, *Ma'ayib al-Rijal [Vices of Men]*, ed. Afsaneh Najmabadi (New York: Nigarish va Nigarish-i Zan, 1992).

'Attar, Farid al-Din, *Shaykh-i San'an*, ed. Sadiq Gawharin (Tehran: Amir Kabir, 1345/1966).

'Attar, Farid ad-Din, *The Conference of the Birds, Mantiq ut-Tair: A Philosophical Religious Poem in Prose*, trans. by C. S. Nott (1st edn, 1954; New York: Samuel Weiser, 1974).

'Attar, Farid al-Din, *Mantiq al-Tayr*, ed. Ahmad Khushnivis (Isfahan: Sana'i, 1978).

'Attar, Farid al-Din, *The Conference of the Birds*, trans. Afkham Darbandi and Dick Davis (New York: Penguin Books, 1984).

Avista: Namah-'i Minuvi-i Ayin-i Zartusht, ed. Jalil Dustkhwah (Tehran: Murvarid, 1343/1964]).

Baha' al-Din 'Amili, *Kulliyat-i Ash'ar va Asar-i Shaykh Baha'i*, ed. 'Ali Katibi (Tehran: Nashr-i Chigamah, 1372/1993).

Baha' al-Din 'Amili, *Kulliyat-i Ash'ar-i Farsi va Mush va Gurbah-'i Shaykh Baha'i*, ed. Mahdi Tawhidipur (Tehran: Mahmudi, 1336/1957).

Baha'u'llah, Mirza Husayn Ali Nuri, "Tablet to Manackji Sahib," *Star of the West*, 1: 1 (March 21, 1910), 5–9.

Bahar, Malik al-Shu'ara, *Sabk Shinasi: Tarikh-i Tatavvur-i Nasr-i Farsi* (Tehran: Khudkar, 1337/1958).

Bahram ibn Farhad, *Sharistan-i Chahar Chaman: Chaman-i Avval va Duvvum va Chaman-i Sivvum, Naqis al-akhir*, ed. Manikji Suhrabji and Siyavakhsh Hurmuzdyar Irani (Bombay, 1223 Yazdigirdi).

Bailey, H. W., *Zoroastrian Problems in the Ninth-Century Books: Ratanbai Katrak Lectures* (Oxford: Clarendon Press, 1943).

Bastani Parizi, Muhammad Ibrahim, *Nay-i Haft Band* (Tehran: 'Ata'i, 1353/1974).

Bastani Parizi, Muhammad Ibrahim, *Talash-i Azadi: Muhit-i Siyasi va Zindagani-i Mushir al-Dawlah Pir niya* (Tehran: Intisharat-i Nuvin, 1354/1975).

Bausani, A., "The Qajar Period: An Epoch of Decadence?" In *Qajar Iran: Political, Social, and Cultural Changes, 1800–1925*, ed. Edmond Bosworth and Carloe Hillenbrand (Costa Mesa, CA: Mazda Publishers, 1992).

Bayat, Mangol, *Iran's First Revolution: Shi'ism and the Constitutional Revolution of 1905–1909* (Oxford: Oxford University Press, 1991).

Bayat, Mangol, *Mysticism and Dissent: Socioreligious Thought in Qajar Iran* (Syracuse: Syracuse University Press, 1982).

Bayly, C. A., "Knowing the Country: Empire and Information in India," *Modern Asian Studies*, 27: 1 (1993).

Bayza'i, Bahram, "Namayish dar Iran: Naqqali," *Majallah-'i Musiqi*, 3: 66 (1341/1962), 15–33.

Bayzavi, 'Abd Allah, *Nizam al-Tawarikh*, ed. Bahman Mira Karimi (Tehran: 'Ilmi, 1313/1935).

Bernier, François, *Travels in the Mogul Empire, AD 1656–1668*, trans. Archibald Constable; rev. Vincent Smith (London: Oxford University Press, 1914; New Delhi: Atlantic Publishers & Distributers, 1989).

Besnier, Pierre, *A Philosophical Essay for the Reunion of Languages*, trans. Henry Rose (reprint of 1st English edn, Oxford: J. Good, 1675; Menston: The Scholar Press, 1971).

Bhabha, Homi, "The Other Question . . . ," *Screen*, 24: 6 (November–December 1983), 18–36.

Bharuch, Sheriaji Dadabhai, *The Dasatir, Being a Paper Prepared for the Tenth International Congress of Orientalists in Geneva in 1894 A.D.* (Bombay: s.n., 1907).

Bihbahani Kirmanshahi, Aqa Ahmad, *Mir'at al-Ahval-i Jahan Nama*, ed. 'Ali Davani (Tehran: Intisharat-i Markaz-i Asnad-i Inqilab-i Islami, 1375/1996).

Bihnam, Jamshid, *Iraniyan va Andishah-'i Tajaddud* (Tehran: Farzan Ruz, 1375/1996).

Binder, John and Wellbery, David (eds), *The End of Rhetoric: History, Theory, and Practice* (Stanford, Cal.: Stanford University Press, 1990).

Binder, Leonard, *Islamic Liberalism: A Critique of Development Ideology* (Chicago: University of Chicago Press, 1988).

Biruni, Abu Rayhan Muhammad ibn Ahmad, *al-Asar al-Baqiyah 'an-il-Qurun al-Khaliya*, ed. C. Edward Sachau (Leipzig: Otto Harrassowitz, 1923).

Biruni, Abu Rayhan Muhammad ibn Ahmad, *The Chronology of Ancient Nations: An English Version of the Arabic Text of the Athâr-ul-Bâkiya of Albîrûnî, or "Vestiges of the Past,"* trans. C. Edward Sachau (London: Oriental Translation Fund of Great Britain & Ireland, 1879).

Boroujerdi, Mehrzad, "Westoxication and Orientalism in Reverse," *Iran Nameh*, 8: 3 (Summer 1990), 375–90.

Boroujerdi, Mehrzad, *Iranian Intellectuals and the West: The Tormented Triumph of Nativism* (Syracuse, NY: Syracuse University Press, 1996).

Bourdieu, Pierre, *Outline of a Theory of Practice*, trans. Richard Nice (Cambridge: Cambridge University Press, 1977).

Boyce, Mary (trans.), *The Letter of Tansar* (Rome: Instituto Italiano per il Medio ed Estremo Oriente, 1968).

Boyce, Mary *Zoroastrians: Their Religious Beliefs and Practices* (London: Routledge & Kegan Paul, 1979).

Breckenridge, Carol A. and Van der Veer, Peter, *Orientalism and the Postcolonial Predicament: Perspectives on South Asia* (Philadelphia: University of Pennsylvania Press, 1993).

Bronson, E., *Select Reviews and Spirits of the Foreign Magazines* (Philadephia, Penn.: The Lorenzo Press, 1810).

Browne, Edward G., *A Literary History of Persia: From the Earliest Times until Firdawsi* (New York: Charles Scribner's Sons, 1902).

Brown, Edward G., *The Press and Poetry of Modern Persia: Partly Based on the Manuscript Work of Mirza Muhammad Ali Khan "Tarbiyat" of Tabriz* (Cambridge: University Press, 1914).

Burnet, James (Lord Monboddo), *Of the Origin and Progress of Languages* (1773; Menston: Scholar Press, 1967).

Cannon, Garland H., "Sir William Jones's Persian Linguistics," *Oriental Society*, 78 (1958), 262–73.

Cannon, Garland H., *Oriental Jones: A Biography of Sir William Jones, 1746–1794* (New York: Asia Publishing House, 1964).

Chakrabarty, Dipesh, "Postcoloniality and the Artifice of History: Who Speaks for 'Indian' Pasts?" *Representations*, 37 (Winter 1992), 1–26.

Chardin, John, *Voyages du Chevalier en Perse, et autres lieux de l'Orient*, ed. Langlés (Paris, 1811).

Chatterjee, Partha, *Nationalist Thought and the Colonial World: A Derivative Discourse* (Minneapolis: University of Minnesota Press, 1986).

Chatterjee, Partha, *The Nation and Its Fragments: Colonial and Postcolonial Histories* (Princeton: Princeton University Press, 1993).

Choudhury, Makhanlal Roy, *The Din-i-Ilahi or, The Religion of Akbar* (Patna, India: Patna University, 1952).

Chubinah, Bahram, "Yiksadumin sal-i shahadat-i Mirza Aqa Kirmani va Shykh Ahmad Ruhi," *Iran Shenasi*, 7: 2 (Summer 1996), 339–53.

Cole, Juan, "Invisible Occidentalism: Eighteenth-Century Indo-Persian Construction of the West," *Iranian Studies*, 25: 3–4 (1992), 3–16.

Cole, Juan, "Marking Boundaries, Marking Time: The Iranian Past and the Construction of the Self by Qajar Thinkers," *Iranian Studies*, 29: 1–2 (Winter/Spring 1996), 35–56.

Corbin, Henry, "Azar (Adar) Kayvan," in *Encyclopaedia Iranica*, ed. Ehsan Yarohater (London, Boston: Routledge & Kegan Paul, 1983–), 183–7.

Corbin, Henry, *Spiritual Body and Celestial Earth: From Mazdean Iran to Shi'ite Iran*, trans. Nancy Pearson, Bollingen Series xci: 2. (Princeton, NJ: Princeton University Press, 1977).

Curzon, George, *Persia and the Persian Question* (London: Longmans, 1892).

Dara Shukuh bin Shahjahan, Muhammad, *Sirr-i Akbar = Sirr al-Asrar*, ed. Tara Chand and Muhammad Riza Jalali Na'ini (Tehran: Taban, 1961).

Darya'i, Turaj, "Sahm-i Manabi'-i Hind va Urupayi dar Shinakht-i Shahnamah: Huviyat-i Kavah-'i Ahangar," *Iran Shenasi*, 11. 2 (Summer 1997), 279–84.

Daston, Lorraine, "Historical epistemology," in *Questions of Evidence: Proof, Practice, and Persuasion across the Disciplines*, ed. James Chandler, Arnold Davidson, and Harry Harootunian (Chicago: University of Chicago Press, 1991), 282–9.

Davari Ardakani, Riza, *Shimmah'i az Tarikh-i Gharbzadigi-i Ma: Vaz'-i Kununi-i Tafakkur dar Iran* (Tehran: Surush, 1363 [1984]), 88.

De Nerciat, Augustus Andrea, "Memoirs of the Persian Ambassador," *The London Literary Gazette, Journal of Belles Letters, Arts, Sciences, etc.*, 120 (May 8, 1819), 299–300.

Digby, Simon, "An Eighteenth-Century Narrative of a Journey from Bengal to England: Munshi Isma'il's *New History*," in *Urdu and Muslim South Asia: Studies in Honour of Ralph Russel*, ed. Christopher Schackle (London: School of Oriental and African Studies, University of London, 1989), 49–65.

Dinawari, Abu Hanifa, *Kitab al-Akhbar at-Tiwal*, ed. Vladimir Guirgass (Leiden: E. J. Brill, 1888).

Dinawari, Abu Hanifa, *Tarjumah-'i Akhbar al-Tiwal*, trans. Sadiq Nash'at (Tehran: Intisharat-i Bunyad-i Farhang-i Iran, 1346/1967).

Dirks, Nicholas B., "Introduction: Colonialism and Culture," in *Colonialism and Culture* (Ann Arbor: University of Michigan Press, 1992).

Divan Baygi, Ahmad, *Hadiqat al-Shu'ara* (Tehran: Intisharat-i Zarrin, 1364/1985).

Duff, Rev. A., "The Rev. A. Duff['s] . . . Address to the General Assembly of the Church of Scotland," *The Asiatic Journal and Monthly Register*, 18 (1836), Asiatic Intelligence section, 86–8.

Dunn, Stephen P., *The Fall and Rise of the Asiatic Mode of Production* (London: Routledge and Kegan Paul, 1982).

Dussel, Enrique, "Eurocentrism and Modernity," *Boundary* 2, 20/3 (1993): 65–76.

Dussel, Enrique, *The Underside of Modernity: Apel, Ricoeur, Rorty, Taylor, and the Philosophy of Liberation*, trans. Eduardo Mendieta (New Jersey: Humanities Press, 1996).

Dustkhwah, Jalil, "Kavah-'i Ahangar bih rivayat-i naqqalan," *Iran Nameh*, 10: 1 (Winter 1992), 122–44.

Eaton, Richard, "The Growth of Muslim Identity in Eighteenth-Century Bengal," in *Eighteenth-Century Renewal and Reform in Islam*, ed. Nehemiah Levtzion and John Voll (Syracuse: Syracuse University Press, 1987), 161–85.

Ekhtiar, Maryam, *The Dar al-Funun: Educational Reform and Cultural Development in Qajar Iran* (Ann Arbor: UMI Dissertation Services, 1995).

Eley, Geoff, "Nations, Publics, and Political Cultures: Placing Habermas in the Nineteenth Century," in *Culture/Power/History: A Reader in Contemporary Social Theory*, ed. Nicholas B. Dirks, Geoff Eley, and Sherry Ortner (Princeton: Princeton University Press, 1994) pp. 297–335.

Émïn, Joseph, *The Life and Adventures of Joseph Émïn, an Armenian* (London: n. p., 1792).

Fabian, Johannes, *Time and the Other: How Anthropology Makes Its Object* (New York: Columbia University Press, 1983).

Fallah, Ghulam Faruq, *Mawj-i Ijtima'i-i Sabk-i Hindi* (Mashhad: Intisharat-i Taranah, 1360/1981).

Fani, Darvish Manikji Limji Hushang Hatarya (ed.), *A'in-i Hushang* (Tehran: Mirza Bahram Nasrabadi, 1296/1879).

Farmanfarma'iyan, Hafiz, "Introducton," in 'Ali Khan Amin al-Dawlah, *Khatirat-i Siyasi-i Mirza 'Ali Khan Amin al-Dawlah*, ed. Hafiz Farmanfarma'iyan (Tehran: Kitabhay-i Iran, 1341/1962).

Farmayan, Hafez F., *Kitabshinasi-i Tarikh-i Mashrutiyat-i Iran; Fihrist-i Tawzihi az Ma'akhiz va Kutub va Maqalat-i Chapi dar Barah-i Tarikh-i Mashrutiyat* (Tehran: Amir Kabir, 1345/1966).

Farmayan, Hafez F., *The Beginnings of Modernization in Iran: The Policies and Reforms of Shah Abbas I, 1587–1629* (Salt Lake City: Middle East Center, University of Utah, 1969).

Farmayan, Hafez F., *The Foreign Policy of Iran: A Historical Analysis, 559 B.C.–A.D. 1971* (Salt Lake City: Middle East Center, University of Utah, 1971).

Farnbagh Dadagi, *Bundahish*, ed. Mihrdad Bahar (Tehran: Tus, 1369/1990).

Fazil Jam, Mirza Muhammad Husayn, *Munsha'at-i Fazil Jami*, ed. Haybat Allah Maliki (Tehran: Intisharat-i Kavir, 1371/1992).

Ferrier, J. P., *Caravan Journeys and Wanderings in Persia, Afghanistan, Turkistan, and Beloochistan; with Historical Notices of the Countries Lying between Russia and India*, trans. William Jesse, ed. H. D. Seymour, 2nd edn (London: John Murray, 1857).

Ferrier, R. W., "The European Diplomacy of Shah Abbas I and the First Persian Embassy to England," *Iran: Journal of the British Institute of Persian Studies*, 9 (1973).

Firdawsi, Abu al-Qasim, *Shahnamah*, ed. Sa'id Hamidiyan (Tehran: Qatrah, 1374/1995).

Firdawsi, Abu al-Qasim, *The Epic of the Kings; Shah-Nama, the National Epic of Persia*, tran. Reuben Levy (Chicago: University of Chicago Press 1967).

Fisher, Michael, "The Office of Akhbar Nawis: The Transition from Mughal to British Forms," *Modern Asian Studies*, 27: 1 (1993), 45–82.

Fisher, Michael, *The First Indian Author in English: Dean Mahomed (1759–1851) in India, Ireland, and England* (Delhi: Oxford University Press, 1996).

Fisher, Michael, *The Travels of Dean Mahomet: An Eighteenth-Century Journey Through India* (Berkeley, Cal.: University of California Press, 1997).

Forbes, Eric, "The European Astronomical Tradition: Its Transmission into India, and its Reception by Sawai Jai Singh II," *Indian Journal of History of Science*, 17: 2 (1982), 234–43.

Foucault, Michel, "Of Other Spaces," *Diacritics*, 16: 1 (Spring 1986), 22–7.

Foucault, Michel, "What is Enlightenment," in *Ethics: Subjectivity and Truth*, ed. Paul Rabinow (New York: New Press, 1994), 303–19.

Francklin, William, *The History of the Reign of Shah-Aulum, the Present Emperor of Hindostaun* (London, 1798).

Fraser, James B., *Narrative of a Journey into Khorasan in the Years 1821 and 1822 Including Some Account of the Countries to the North-East of Persia; with Remarks upon the National Character, Government, and Resources of that Kingdom* (London: Longman, 1825).

Fraser, James Ballie, *Narrative of the Residence of the Persian Princes in London in 1835 and 1836 with an Account of Their Journey from Persia, and Subsequent Adventures* (London: Richard Bentley, 1838).

Fursat Shirazi, *Divan Fursat*, ed. 'Ali Zarrin Qalam (Tehran: Kitabfurushi-i Sirus, 1337/1958).

Furughi, Muhammad 'Ali, *Payam-i man bih Farhangistan* (Tehran: Intisharat-i Payam, 1354/1975).

Furughi, Muhammad 'Ali, "Maqam-i Firdawsi va Ahammiyat-i U," in *Hizarah-'i Firdawsi: Shamil-i Sukhanraniha-yi Jam'i az Fuzala-yi Iran va Mustashriqin-i Dunya dar Kungirah-'i Hizarah-'i Firdawsi* (Tehran: Dunya-yi Kitab, 1362/1983), 27–41.

Gabrieli, F., "'Adjam," in *The Encyclopaedia of Islam* (Leiden: Brill, 1960–), 1: 206.

Garmrudi, Mirza Fattah, *Safar Namah-'i Mirza Fattah Khan Garmrudi bi-Urupa, Mawsum Bah Chahar Fasl va du Risalah-i Digar Binam-i Shab Namah va Safar Namah-'i Mamasani dar Zaman-i Muhammad Shah Qajar*, ed. Fath al-Din Fattahi (Tehran: Chapkhanah-i Bank-i Bazargani-i Iran, 1347/1968).

Garusi, Hasan 'Ali Khan, *Munsh'at Jinab-i Fakhamat Nisab* (Tehran: Matba'ah-'i Mirza 'Ali Asghar, 1324/1906).

Ghalib, Asadallah, *Dastanbu* (Agrah: Matba'-i Mufid-i Khalayiq, 1858).

Ghate, V. S., "Persian Grammar in Sanskrit," *The Indian Antiquary* (January 1912): 4–7.

Ghawsi, Muhammad 'Ali, "Nadir Mirza va Tarikh-i Tabriz," *Yadgar*, 5 (1965): 15–26.

Ghazzali, Abu Hamid Muhammad, *Ghazali's Book of Council for Kings (Nasihat al-Muluk)*, trans. F. R. C. Bagley (London: Oxford University Press, 1964).

Ghazzali, Abu Hamid Muhammad, *Nasihat al-Muluk*, ed. Jalal al-Din Huma'i (Tehran: Babak, 1361).

Ghori, S. A. Khan, "Development of Zîj Literature in India," in *History of Astronomy in India*, ed. S. N. Sen and K. S. Shukla (New Delhi: Indian National Science Academy, 1985), 20–47.

Gibb, H. A. R., "The Social Significance of the Shu'ubiyya," in *Studia Orientalia Janni Pedersen dicata* (Copenhagen, 1953), 105–14.

Gobineau, Arthur Comte de, *Trois ans en Asie, de 1855 a 1858* (Paris: E. Leroux, 1905).

Gobineau, Arthur Comte de, *Les religions et philosophies dans l'Asie centrale* (Paris: Gallimard, 1957).

Greenblatt, Stephen, *Renaissance Self-Refashioning: From More to Shakespeare* (Chicago: University of Chicago Press, 1980).

Gulchin Ma'ani, Ahmad, *Karvan-i Hind: Dar Ahval va Asar-i Sha'iran-i 'Asr-i Safavi kah bah Hindustan Raftahand* (Mashhad: Intisharat-i Astan-i Quds-i Razavi, 1369/1990).

Gulpaygani, Abu al-Fazl, *Rasa'il va Raqa'im*, ed. Ruhallah Mihrabkhani [Tehran]: Mu'assasah-'i Milli-i Matbu'at-i Amri, 134/1974?].

Gurney, John D., "Pietro Della Valle: the Limits of Perception," *Bulletin of the School of Oriental and African Studies* (1986), 103–16.

Guzidah-'i Asnad-i Siyasi-i Iran va 'Usmani: Dawrah-'i Qajariyah (Tehran: Daftar-i Mutali'at-i Siyasi va Bayn al-Milali-i Vizarat-I Umur-i Kharijah, 1370/1991).

Ha'iri, 'Abd al-Hadi, *Nukhustin Ruyaruyiha-yi Andishahgaran-i Iran ba Du Ruyah-'i Tamaddun-i Burzhuvazi-i Gharb* (Tehran: Amir Kabir, 1367).

Ha'iri, 'Abd al-Hadi, *Iran va Jahan-i Islam: Pazhuhish'hayi Tarikhi Piramun-i Chihrah'ha, Andishah'ha, va Junbishha* (Mashhad: Intisharat-i Astan-i Quds-i Razavi, 1368), 223–31.

Habermas, Jürgen, "The Public Sphere," *New German Critique*, 3 (1974).

Habermas, Jürgen, *The Philosophical Discourse of Modernity: Twelve Lectures*, trans. Frederick G. Lawrence (Cambridge, Mass.: MIT Press, 1987).

Habermas, Jürgen, *The Structural Transformation of the Public Sphere: An Inquiry into a Category of Bourgeois Society*, trans. Thomas Burger (Cambridge, Mass.: MIT Press, 1991).

Halbfass, Wilhelm, *India and Europe: An Essay in Understanding* (New York: State University of New York Press, 1988), 64.

Hall, Stuart, "The West and the Rest: Discourse and Power," in *Modernity: An Introduction to Modern Societies*, ed. Stuart Hall, David Held, Don Hubert, and Kenneth Thompson (Cambridge, Mass.: Blackwell Publishers, 1996), 184–227.

Hamidi, Mahdi, *Shi'r dar 'Asr-i Qajar* (Tehran: Ganj-i Kitab, 1364/1985).

Haug, Martin, *The Parsis: Essays on Their Sacred Language, Writings and Religion*, rev. K. W. West. (Bombay: "Bombay Gazette" Press, 1862; New Delhi: Cosmo Publications, 1978).

Hazin, Shaykh 'Ali, *Tazkirah-'i Hazin*, ed. Muhammad Baqir Ulfat (Isfahan: Kitab-furushi-i Ta'yid, 1334/1955).

Heath, Peter, *Allegory and Philosophy in Avicenna (Ibn Sina) with a Translation of the Book of the Prophet Muhammad's Ascent to Heaven* (Philadelphia: University of Pennsylvania Press, 1992).

Hegel, George W. F., *The Philosophy of History*, trans. J. Sibree (Buffalo, NY: Prometheus Books, 1991).

Herber, Richard, "Travels of Mirza Abu Talib . . . ," *The Quarterly Review* (1810), 80–93.

Herbert, Morris, *Muhammad Riza Bayk: Safir-i Iran dar Darbar-i Lu'i-i Chahardahum*, trans. 'Abd al-Husayn Vujdani (Tehran: Guzarish-i Farhang va Tarikh-i Iran, 1362/1983).

Herbert, Thomas, *Travels in Persia, 1627–1629*, abr. and ed. Sir William Foster (New York: R. M. McBride, 1929; New York: Books for Libraries Press, 1972).

Hidayat, Riza Quli Khan, *Farhang-i Anjuman Ara-yi Nasiri* (Tehran: Kargah-i ʿAliʾquli Khan, 1288/181).

Hidayat, Riza Quli Khan, *Majmaʿ al-Fusaha* (Tehran: Karkhanah-ʾi Aqa Mir Muhammad Baqir, 1295/1878).

Hissam Muʿizzi, Najafquli, *Tarikh-i Ravabit-i Siyasi* (Tehran: Nashr-i ʿIlm, 1366/1987).

Hobsbawm, E. J., *The Age of Revolution, 1789–1848* (New York: Mentor Books, 1962).

Hodgson, Marshall G. S., *The Venture of Islam: Conscience and History in a World Civilization*, 3 vols (Chicago: University of Chicago Press, 1974).

Humphreys, R. Stephen, "Qurʾanic Myth and Narrative Structure in Early Islamic Historiography," in *Tradition and Innovation in Late Antiquity*, ed. F. M. Clover and R. S. Humphreys (Madison: University of Wisconsin Press, 1989), 271–90.

Hunter, William, "Some Account of the Astronomical Labours of Jaya Sinha, Rajah of Ambhere, or Jayanagar," *Asiatic Researches or Transactions of the Society Instituted in Bengal*, 5 (1799), 177–211.

Husayni Fasaʾi, Hasan, *Farsnamah-ʾi Nasiri*, ed. Mansur Rastigar Fasaʾi (Tehran: Amir Kabir, 1988).

Ibn al-Qazaʾi, ʿAli ibn Ahmad, *Tark al-Atnab fi Sharh al-Shihab*, ed. Muhammad Shirvani (Tehran: Danishgah-i Tihran, 1343/1964),

Ibn Athir, ʿIzz al-Din, *al-Kamil fi Tarikh* (Beirut: Dar Sader, 1965–7).

Ibn Athir, ʿIzz al-Din, *Tarikh-i Kamil*, trans. Muhammad Husayn Rawhani (Tehran: Asatir, 1370/1991).

Iʾtimad al-Saltanah, Muhammad Hasan Khan, *Mirʾat al-Buldan*, ed. ʿAbd al-Husayn Navaʾi (Tehran: Intisharat-i Danishgah-i Tihran, 1367/1988).

Iʾtimad al-Saltanah, Muhammad Hasan Khan, *Tatbiq-i Lughat-i Jughrafiyaʾi* (Tehran: Dar al-Intibaʾat, 1311/1893).

Iʾtizad al-Saltanah, ʿAliquli Mirza, *Falak al-Saʿadah* (Tehran: Dar al-Tabaʿah-ʾi Aqa Mir Muhammad Tihrani, 1278/1861).

Iʾtizad al-Saltanah, ʿAliquli Mirza, *Iksir al-Tawarikh*, ed. Jamshid Kayanfarr (Tehran: Visman, 1370/1991).

Iftikharzadah, Muhammad Riza, *Shuʿubiyah: Nasiunalism-i Irani* (Tehran: Nashr-i Maʿarif i Islami, 1376/1997).

Inju Shirazi, Mir Jamal al-Din Husayn, *Farhang-i Jahangiri*, ed. Rahim ʿAfifi (Mashhad: Intisharat-i Danishgah-i Mashhad, 1359/1980).

Iqbal al-Dawlah, *Iqbal-i Farang: Dar Shammah-ʾi Siyar-i Ahl-i Farang-i ba Farhang* (Calcutta: Matbaʿ-i Tibbi, 1834).

Irigaray, Luce, *This Sex Which Is Not One* (Ithaca: Cornell University Press, 1985).

Isfahani, Mahmud ibn Muhammad, *Dastur al-Vizarah*, ed. Riza Inzabi Nizhad (Tehran: Amir Kabir, 1364/1985).

Iʾtimad al-Saltanah, Muhammad Hasan Khan, *Mirʾat al-Buldan*, ed. ʿAbd al-Husayn Navaʾi (Tehran: Intisharat-i Danishgah-i Tihran, 1367/1988).

Ittihadiyah, Mansurah, *Paydayish va Tahavvul-i Ahzab-i Siyasi-i Mashrutiyat: Dawrah-ʾi Avval va Duvvum-i Majlis-i Shura-yi Milli* (Tehran: Nashr-i Gustarah, 1361/1982).

Ivanov, A. A., "Nadirah-ʾi Dawran Muhammad Zaman," in *Davazdah Rukh: Yadnigari az Dawazdah Naqash-i Nadirahkar-i Iran*, trans. Yaʿqub Azhand (Tehran: Intisharat-i Mawla, 1377/1998), 313–28.

Jalal al-Azm, Sadik, "Orientalism and Orientalism in Reverse," *Khamsin*, 8 (1981), 5–26.

Jamal al-Din Afghani, "Tarikh-i Ijmali-i Iran," in Fursat Shirazi, *Divan Fursat*, ed. 'Ali Zarrin Qalam (Tehran: Kitabfurushi-i Sirus, 1337/1958), 28–73.

James, Alexander, *Travels from India to England: Comprehending a Visit to the Burman Empire, and a Journey Through Persia, Asia Minor, European Turkey, &c. in the Years 1825–26* (London: Parbury, Allen, 1827).

Jazayery, M. A., "The Modernization of the Persian Vocabulary and Language Reform in Iran," in *Language Reform: History and Future*, ed. I. Fodor and C. Hagége (Hamburg: Buske, 1983), 5: 2, 241–68.

Johnson, [?], "Dinner in Honour of the Persian Ambassador," *The Examiner*, 107 (January 14, 1810), 17–18.

Jones, William, "The Sixth Discourse: On the Persians, Delivered 19 February 1789," in *The Works of Sir William Jones in Six Volumes*, ed. Anna Maria Shipley-Jones (London: G. G. and J. Robinson, 1799), 73–94.

Jones, William, *A Grammar of the Persian Language* (London: W. and J. Richardson, 1771; Menston: Scholar Press, 1969).

Jones, William Sir, *Lettre à monsieur A*** du P***, dans laquelle est compris l'examen de sa traduction des livres attribués à Zoroastre* (London, 1771).

Jones, William, *The Letters of Sir William Jones*, ed. Garland Cannon (Oxford: The Clarendon Press, 1970).

Kaempfer, Engelbert, *Amonitatum exoticarum politico-physico-medicarum fasciculi V* (Lemgoviate: Typis & impensis Henrici Wilhelmi Meyeri, 1712).

Kant, Immanuel, *Kant: Political Writings*, ed. Hans Reiss, trans. H. B. Nisbet (Cambridge: Cambridge University Press, 1970).

Karimi-Hakkak, Ahmad, *Recasting Persian Poetry: Scenarios of Poetic Modernity in Iran* (Salt Lake City: University of Utah, 1995).

Karimi-Hakkak, Ahmad, "Language Reform Movement and its Language: the Case of Persian," in *The Politics of Language Purism*, ed. Björn Jernudd and Michael Shapiro (Berlin: Mouton de Gruyter, 1989), 81–104.

Kashani-Sabet, Firoozeh, "Fragile Frontiers: The Diminishing Domains of Qajar Iran," *International Journal of Middle Eastern Studies*, 29 (1977), 205–34.

Kashifi, Husayn Va'iz, *Anvar-i Suhayli ya Kalilah va Dimnah* (Tehran: Amir Kabir, 1362).

Kasravi, Ahmad, *Tarikh-i Mashrutah-'i Iran* (Terhran, 1330/1951).

Katouzian, Homa, "Arbitrary Rule: A Comparative Theory of State, Politics and Society in Iran," *British Society for Middle Eastern Studies*, 24: 1 (1977), 49–73.

Katouzian, Homa, *The Political Economy of Modern Iran: Despotism and Pseudo-Modernism, 1926–1979* (New York: New York University Press, 1981).

Kaye, G. R., *The Astronomical Observatories of Jai Singh* (Calcutta: Archaeological Survey of India, 1918).

Kaykhusraw Isfandyar, *Dabistan-i Mazahib*, ed. Rahim Rizazadah Malik (Tehran: Tahuri, 1983).

Kazemzadeh, Firuz, *Russia and Britain in Persia, 1864–1914: A Study in Imperialism* (New Haven, Conn.: Yale University Press, 1968).

Keddie, Nikki, *Religion and Rebellion in Iran: The Iranian Tobacco Protest of 1891–1892* (London: Frank Cass, 1996).

Keddie, Nikki, *Sayyid Jamal al-Din "al-Afghani": A Political Biography* (Berkeley: University of California Press, 1972).

Kedourie, Elie, *Afghani and Abduh: An Essay on Religious Unbelief and Political Activism in Modern Islam* (London: Frank Cass, 1966).

Khadduri, Majid, *The Islamic Conception of Justice* (Baltimore, Md: Johns Hopkins University Press, 1984).

Khalidi, Tarif, *Arabic Historical Thought in the Classical Period* (Cambridge: Cambridge University Press, 1994).

Khaliqi-Mutlaq, Jalal, "Chira Anushirvan ra Dadgar Namidahand?" *Faslnamah-'i Hasti* (Summer 1993), 109–16.

Khwand Mir, Ghiyas al-Din ibn Humam al-Din, *Habib al-Siyar fi Akhbar Afrad al-Bashar*, ed. Jalal al-Din Huma'i (Tehran: Khayyam, 1333/1954).

Kirmani, Kaykhusraw Shahrukh, *Furugh-i Mizdisni* (Tehran: n.p., 1909).

Kirmani, Mirza Aqa Khan, *Ayinah-'i Sikandari* (Tehran: [n. p.], 1324/1906).

Kirmani, Mirza Aqa Khan, *Namah-'i Bastan = Salar Namah* (Shiraz: Matba'-i Muhammadi, 1316/1898).

Kirmani, Mirza Aqa Khan, *Sah Maktub: Maktub-i Shahzadah Kamal al-Dawlah bah Shahzadah Jalal al-Dawlah*, ed. Bahram Chubinah ([Paris]: Mardé Emrouz, 1370/1991).

Kirmani, Muhammad Karim Khan, *Risalah-i Nasiriyah Dar Tahqiq-i Mu'ad-i Jismani* (Kirman: Sa'adat, 1375/1955).

Kirmani, Nazim al-Islam, *Tarikh-i Bidari-i Iraniyan: Muqaddamah*, ed. 'Ali Akbar Sa'idi Sirjani (Tehran: Intisharat-i Agah, 1362/1983).

Kokan, Afzal-ul-Ulama Muhammad Yousuf, *Arabic and Persian in Carnatic, 1710–1960* (Madras: Hafiza House, 1974).

Koselleck, Reinhart, *Critique and Crisis: Enlightenment and the Pathogenesis of Modern Society* (Cambridge, Mass.: MIT Press, 1988).

Koselleck, Reinhart, *Futures Past: On the Semantics of Historical Time*, trans. Keith Tribe (Cambridge, Mass.: MIT Press, 1985).

Kristeva, Julia, *Language the Unknown and Initiation into Linguistics*, trans. Anne M. Menke (New York: Columbia University Press, 1989).

La Hire, Phillipe, *Tabulae astronomicae Ludovici Magni jussu et munificentia exaratae et in lucem editae . . .* (Paris: Apud Joannem Boudot, 1702).

LaCapra, Dominick, "History and Psychoanalysis," in *Soundings in Critical Theory* (Ithaca: Cornell University Press, 1989), 30–66.

Laclau, Ernesto, *New Reflections on the Revolution of Our Time* (London: Verso, 1990).

Lahiji, Hasan, "Hadiyyat al-Musafir," in *Ras'il-i Farsi*, ed. 'Ali Sadra'i Khu'i (Tehran: Nashr-i Qiblah, 1357).

Lambton, A. K. S., "Justice in the Medieval Persian Theory of Kingship," *Studia Islamica*, 17 (1962), 91–119.

Lambton, A. K. S., *Theory and Practice in Medieval Persian Government* (London: Variorum Reprints, 1980).

Langarudi, Shams, *Maktab-i Bazgasht: Barrasi-i Shi'r-i Dawrah'ha-yi Afshariyah, Zandiyah, Qajariyah* (Tehran: Chap va Intisharat-i Vizarat-i Umur-i Kharijah, 1375/1996).

Lewis, Bernard, "The Impact of the West," in *The Emergence of Modern Turkey*, 2nd edn (London: Oxford University Press, 1968).

Lewis, Bernard, "Patriotism and Nationalism" in *The Shaping of the Modern Middle East* (Oxford: Oxford University Press, 1994), 71–98.

Lewis, Bernard, "Siyasa," in *In Quest of an Islamic Humanism: Arabic and Islamic Studies in the Memory of Muhammad al-Nowaihi*, ed. A. H. Green (Cairo: American University of Cairo, 1984), 3–13.

Lewis, Bernard, *The Muslim Discovery of Europe* (New York: W. W. Norton, 1982).

Lewis, Bernard, *The Political Language of Islam* (Chicago: University of Chicago Press, 1988).

Lewis, Bernard, *Islam and the West* (Oxford: Oxford University Press, 1993).

Lisan al-Mulk Sipihr, Muhammad Taqi, *Nasikh al-Tavarikh: Salatin-i Qajariyah*, ed. Muhammad Baqir Bihbudi (Tehran: Kitabfurushi Islami, 1353).

Lisan al-Mulk Sipihr, Mirza Muhammad Taqi, *Nasikh al-Tawarikh* (Tehran: Islamiyah, 1344/1965).

Lisan, Husayn, "Shahnamah khwani," *Hunar va mardum*, 14: 159/160 (Day/Bahman 1354), 2–16.

Lukacs, Georg, *History and Class Consciousness: Studies in Marxist Dialectics*, trans. Rodney Livingstone (Cambridge, Mass.: MIT Press, 1971).

Lyell, Charles, *Principles of Geology* (London: J. Murray, 1830).

Madayihnigar, Ibrahim Khan, *Tazkirah-'i Anjuman-i Nasiri*, ed. Iraj Afshar (Tehran: Intisharat-i Babak, 1363).

Maftun Danbali, 'Abd al-Razzaq, *Ma'asir-i Sultaniyah* (Tabriz: Dar al-Intiba', 1241/1826; Tehran: Ibn Sina, 1351/1972).

Maftun Dunbuli, 'Abd al-Razzaq, *Tajribat al-Ahrar va Tasliyat al-Abrar*, ed. Hasan Qazi Tabataba'i (Tehran: Mu'assisah-'i Tarikh va Farhang-i Iran, 1349/1970).

Mahbubi Ardakani, Husayn, *Tarikh-i Mu'assasat-i Tamadduni-i Jadid Dar Iran* (Tehran: Anjuman-i Danishjuyan-i Danishgah-i Tihran, 1354–68).

Mahjub, Muhammad Ja'far, "Sukhanvari," *Sukhan*, 9: 6 (Shahrivar 1337/1958), 530–5.

Mahjub, Muhammad Ja'far, "Tahavvul-i naqqali va qissah khwani, tarbiyat-i qissah khwanan va tumarha-yi naqqali," *Iran Nameh*, 9: 2 (Spring 1991), 186–211.

Majd al-Mulk, Mirza Muhammad Khan Sinki, *Risalah-'i Majdiyah*, ed. 'Ali Amini (Tehran: Iqbal, 1358/1979).

Malcolm, John, *Sketches of Persia from the Journal of a Traveller in the East* (Philadephia: Carey, Lea, & Carey, 1828).

Malcolm, John, *The History of Persia from the most early period to the present time; containing an account of the religion, government, usages, and character of the inhabitants of that kingdom* (London: John Murray, 1815).

Malikzadah, Mahdi, *Tarikh-i Inqilab-i Mashrutiyat-i Iran*, 3 vols (Tehran: 'Ilmi, 1363/1984).

Manafzadeh, Alireza, "Nukhustin Matn-i Falsafah-'i Jadid-i Gharbi bah Zaban-i Farsi," *Iran Nameh*, 9: 1 (Winter 1991), 98–108.

Martin, François, *François Martin: Mémoires, Travels to Africa, Persia & India*, trans. Aniruddha Ray (Calcutta: Subarnarekha, 1990).

Martin, Vanessa, "An Evaluation of Reform and Development of the State in the Early Qajar Period," *Die Welt des Islam*, 36: 1 (1996), 1–24.

Marx, Karl, "Speech at the Anniversary of the People's Paper," in *The Marx–Engels Reader*, ed. Robert Tucker, 2nd edn (New York: W. W. Norton, 1978), 577–8.

Mashkur, Muhammad Javad, *Farhang-i Huzvarish ha-yi Pahlavi* (Tehran: Bunyad-i Farhang-i Iran, 1346/1967).

Mawlavi Abu al-Khayr, *Majmu'ah-i Shamsi: mushtamil-i bar masa'il-i 'ilm-i hay'at mutabiq-i tahqiqat-i 'ulama-yi muta'akhirin-i Farang* (Calcutta: Hindoostani Press, 1222/1807).

Mazda, 'Abbas, "Nufuz-i Sabk-i Urupa'i dar Naqashi-i Iran," *Payam-i Nau*, 2: 10 (1325/1946), 59–72.

Mehta, Uday, *Liberalism and Empire: A Study in Nineteenth-Century British Liberal Thought* (Chicago: University of Chicago Press, 1999).

Menocal, Maria Rosa, *The Arabic Role in Medieval Literary History: A Forgotten Heritage* (Philadelphia: University of Pennsylvania Press, 1987).

Mercier, Raymond, "The Astronomical Tables of Rajah Jai Singh Sawa'i," *Indian Journal of History of Science*, 19 (1984), 143–71.

Mink, Louis O., "The Autonomy of Historical Understanding," *History and Theory*, 1 (1966), 24–47.

Mintz, Sidney, *Sweetness and Power* (New York: Viking, 1985).

Minuvi, Mujtaba, *Tarikh va Farhang* (Tehran: Khwarazmi, 1990).

Mir Khwand, Muhammad ibn Khavandshah, *Tarikh-i Rawzat al-Safa*, ed. 'Abbas Parviz (Tehran: Markazi, 1338/1959).

Mir Khwand, Muhammad ibn Khavandshah, *History of the Early Kings of Persia from Kaiomars the First of the Peshdadian Dynasty, to the Conquest of Iran by Alexander the Great Translated from the Original Persian of Mirkhond Entitled the Rauzat-us-Safa.*, trans. David Shea (London: John Murray and Parbury, Allen, & Co., 1882).

Mir Muhammad Husayn Landani, *Qava'id-i Husayn-i Landani* (Lucknow: Matba'-i Mustafa'i, 1269/1852).

Mirza Abu al-Hasan Ilchi, "Memoir of His Excellency Mirza Al Aboo Hassan, Envoy Extraordinary from the King of Persia to the Court of Great Britain," *Select Reviews and Spirits of the Foreign Magazines*, 334.

Mirza Abu al-Hasan Ilchi, *A Persian at the Court of King George, 1809–10: The Journal of Mirza Abul Hasan Khan*, trans. Margaret Morris Cloake (London: Barrie & Jenkins, 1988).

Mirza Abu al-Hasan Ilchi, *Hayrat Namah: Safar Namah-'i Mirza Abu al-Hasan Khan Ilchi bah Landan*, ed. Hasan Mursalvand (Tehran: Mu'assisah-'i Khadamat-i Farhangi-i Rasa, 1364/1985).

Mirza Abu Talib Khan Istanhani, *The Travels of Mirza Abu Taleb Khan in Asia, Africa, and Europe during the years 1799, 1800, 1801, and 1802*, 2 vols, trans. by Charles Stewart (London: Longman, 1810).

Mirza I'tisam al-Din [Itesa Modeen], *Shigurf Namah i Velaët, or Excellent Intelligence Concerning Europe; Being the Travels of Mirza Itesa Modeen, in Great Britain and France*, trans. James Edward Alexander (London: Parbury, Allen, 1827).

Mirza Ja'far [Mushir al-Dawlah] Husayni, *Badayi' al-Hisab* (Tehran: Dar al-Tiba'ah-'i Dar al-Khalafah, 1263/1846).

Mirza Ja'far [Mushir al-Dawlah] Husayni, *Risalah-'i Tahqiqat-i Sarhadiyah*, ed. Muhammad Mushiri (Tehran: Bunyad-i Farhang-i Iran, 1348/1969).

Mirza Khan ibn Fakhr al-Din Muhammad, *Tuhfat al-Hind*, ed. Nur al-Hasan Ansari (Tehran: Bunyad-i Farhang-i Iran, 1975).

Mirza Malkum Khan, *Majmu'ah-'i Asar*, ed. Muhit Tabatab'i (Tehran: Intisharat-i 'Ilmi, n.d.).

Mirza Salih Shirazi, "Safar Namah-'i Isfahan, Kashan, Qum, Tihran," in *Majmu'ah-'i Safar Namah'ha-yi Mirza Salih Shirazi* (Tehran: Nashr-i Tarikh-i Iran, 1364), 5–36.

Mirza Salih Shirazi, *Guzarish-i Safar-i Mirza Salih Shirazi Kazaruni*, ed. Humayun Shahidi (Tehran: Rah-i Naw, 1362/1983).

Mirza Salih Shirazi, "Travels of a Persian," *The Asiatic Journal and Monthly Register for British India and its Dependencies*, 18 (July–December 1824), 365–71.

Mirza Abu Talib Khan Isfahani, *Masir-i Talibi, ya Safarnamah-i Mirza Abu Talib Khan*, ed. Husayn Khadivjam (Tehran: Sazman-i Intisharat va Amuzish-i Inqilab-i Islami, 1363/1984).

Mirza Abu Talib Khan Isfahani, *Reizen Van Mirza Abu Talib Khan in Asia, Africa en Europa* (Bijvoegsel, Leeuwarden, 1813).

Mirza Abu Talib Khan Isfahani, *Voyages du prince persan mirza Aboul Taleb Khan, en Asie, en Afrique, en Europe*, trans. Charles Malo (Paris, Impr. de P. F. Dupont fils, 1819).

Mitchell, Timothy, *Colonizing Egypt* (Berkeley, Cal.: University of California Press, 1991).

Modi, Jivanji Jamshedji, "A Parsee High Priest: Dastur Azar Kaiwan (1529–1614 A.D.) with his Zoroastrian Disciples in Patna, in the 16th and 17th Centuries A.D," *The Journal of the K. R. Cama Oriental Institute*, 16 (1930), 1–85.

Modi, Jivanji Jamshedji, "*Anquuetile Du Perron and Dastur Darab* (Bombay: *Times of India*, 1916).

Modi, Jivanji Jamshedji, "Notes on Anquetile Du Perron (1755–61), on King Akbar and Dastur Meherji Rana," in *Contributions on Akbar and the Parsees*, ed. B. P. Ambashthya (Patna: Janaki Prakashan, 1976), 1–16.

Modi, Jivanji Jamshedji, *The Parsees at the court of Akbar and Dastur Meherjee Rana. Two papers read by Jivanji Jamshedji Modi, B. A., before the Bombay branch Royal Asiatic Society on 19th December 1901 and 13th July 1903* (Bombay: Bombay Education Society's Press, Byculla, 1903).

Mojtaba'i, Fath Allah, "Dabistan-i Madaheb," in *Encyclopaedia Iranica*, vi, I: 532–4.

Mojtahed-Zadeh, Pirouz, "The Eastern Boundaries of Iran," in *The Boundaries of Modern Iran*, ed. Keith McLachlan (New York: St. Martin's Press, 1994), 128–139.

Money, R. C., *Journal of a Tour in Persia During the Years 1824 & 1825* (London: Teape and Son, 1928).

Montesquieu, Charles de Secondat, *The Persian Letters*, trans. C. J. Betts (New York: Penguin Books, 1973).

Moorcroft, William, *Travels in the Himalayan Provinces of Hindustan and Panjab . . . from 1819 to 1825* (London: J. Murray, 1841).

Moreh, S., "The Neoclassical Qasida: Modern Poets and Critics," in *Arabic Poetry: Theory and Development*, ed. G. E. von Gruenbaum (Wiesbaden: Otto Harrassowitz, 1973).

Morier, James Justinian, *A Second Journey Through Persia, Armenia, and Asia Minor, to Constantinople, Between the Years 1810 and 1816* (London: Longman, Hurst, Rees, Orme, and Brown, 1818).

Morris, Meaghan, "Metamorphoses at Sydney Tower," *New Formations*, 11 (Summer 1990).

Morony, M, "Madjus," in *The Encyclopaedia of Islam*, 5: 110–18.

Mottahedeh, Roy, "The Shu'ubiyah Controversy and the Social History of Early Islamic Iran," *International Journal of Middle East Studies*, 7: 2 (January 1976), 161–82.

Mu'ayyir al-Mamalik, Dust 'Ali Khan, *Rijal-i 'Asr-i Nasiri* (Tehran: Nashr-i Tarikh-i Iran, 1361/1982).

Mu'in, Muhammad, *Majmu'ah Maqalat-i Duktur Muhammad Mu'in*, ed. Mahdukht Mu'in (Tehran: Intisharat-i Mu'in, 1364–67/1985–8).

Mu'in, Muhammad, "Azar Kayvan va Payravan-i u," *Majallah-'i Danishkadah-'i Adabiyat-i Tihran*, 4: 3 (Farvardin 1336/March 1957), 25–42.

Muhammad Rafi' al-Din Khan, 'Umdat al-Mulk, *Rafi' al-Basar* (Calcutta: C. V. William Press, 1841).

Muhammad Sadiq, *A History of Urdu Literature* (Delhi: Oxford University Press, 1984).

Mujtabai, Fathullah, "Persian Hindu Writings: Their Scope and Relevance," in *Aspects of Hindu Muslim Cultural Relations* (New Delhi: National Book Bureau, 1978).

Mukherjee, S. N., *Sir William Jones: A Study in Eighteenth-Century British Attitudes to India* (Cambridge: Cambridge University Press, 1968).

Mulla Firuz bin Kaus, "Farhang-i Lughat-i Kitab-i Mustatab-i Dasatir," in *The Desatir; or, Sacred writings of the Ancient Persian Prophets, in the Original Tongue, Together with the Ancient Persian Version and Commentary of the Fifth Sasan,* 2 vols (Bombay: Courier Press, 1818).

Müller, Max, "Preface to the Sacred Books of the East," in *The Upanishads*, trans. F. Max Müller (Oxford: Clarendon Press, 1879; Delhi: Motilal Banarsidass, 1965).

Müller, Max, *Lectures on the Science of Language Delivered at the Royal Institution of Great Britain in April, May, and June 1861* (London, 1862).

Müller, Max, *The Sacred Languages of the East translated by various Oriental Scholars*, ed. F. Max Müller (Delhi: Motilal Banarsidass, 1965).

Mumtahin, Husayn 'Ali, *Nahzat-i Shu'ubiyah: Junbish-i Milli-i Iraniyan dar Barabar-i Khilafat-i Umavi va 'Abbasi* (Tehran: Amir Kabir, 1975).

Munir Lahuri, Abu al-Barakat, *Karnamah*, ed. Sayyid Muhammad Ikram (Islamabad: Iran Pakistan Institute of Persian Studies, 1977).

Mustawfi Qazvini, Hamd Allah, *Tarikh-i Guzidah*, ed. 'Abd al-Husayn Nava'i (Tehran: Amir Kabir, 1362/1983).

Najaf Khoolee Meerza, *Journal of a Residence in England, and of a Journey from and to Syria of their Highnesses Reeza Koolee Meerza, Najaf Koolee Meerza, and Taymoor Meerza, of Persia,* 2 vols, trans. Assad Y. Kayat (London: William Taylor Printer, 1839).

Najm Razi, *The Path of God's Bondsmen from Origin to Return*, trans. Hamid Algar (Delamr, NY: Persian Heritage Series, Caravan Books, 1982).

Najmabadi, Afsaneh, "Zanha-yi Millat: Women or Wives of the Nation," *Iranian Studies*, 26: 1–2 (Winter/Spring 1993), 51–71.

Najmabadi, Afsaneh "Is Our Name Remembered?" *Iranian Studies*, 29: 1–2 (Winter/Spring 1996), 85–109.

Najmabadi, Afsaneh, "Tayirah: Namah'ha, Nivishtah'ha, va Ash'ar Hamrah ba Barghayi az Zindigani-i U," *Nimah–'i Digar*, 2: 3 (Winter 1997), 146–95.

Najmabadi, Afsaneh, "The Erotic Vatan [Homeland] as Beloved and Mother: to Love, to Possess, and to Protect," *Comparative Studies in Society and History*, July 1997, 442–67.

Najmabadi, Afsaneh, "Crafting an Educated Housewife in Iran," in *Remaking Women: Feminism and Modernity in the Middle East*, ed. Lila Abu-Lughod (Princeton, NJ: Princeton University Press, 1998).

Najm Razi, 'Abd Allah ibn Muhammad, *Mirsad al-'Ibad*, ed. Muhammad Amin Riyahi (Tehran: Bungah-i Tarjumah va Nashr-i Kitab, 1352/1973).

Naraqi, Mulla Ahmad, *Mi'raj al-Sa'adah* (Tehran: Intisharat-i Rashidi, 1983).

Naraqi, Mullah Ahmad, *Masnavi-i Taqdis*, ed. Hasan Naraqi (Tehran: Amir Kabir, 1362).

Nashat, Guity, *The Origins of Modern Reform in Iran, 1870–80* (Urbana: University of Illinois Press, 1982).

Nasr, Seyyed Hossein, "Shihab al-Din Suhrawardi Maqtul," in *A History of Muslim Philosohpy*, ed. M. M. Sharif (Wiesbaden: Otto Harrassowitz, 1963), 372–98.

Nasr, Seyyed Hossein, "The Spread of the Illuminationist School of Suhrawardi," *The Islamic Quarterly*, 14: 3, 111–21.

Natiq, Huma, "Pishguftar," in *Namah'ha-i Tab'id*, ed. Huma Natiq and Muhammad Firuz (Bonn: Hafif-Verlag, 1365/1986), 13–43.

Nava'i, 'Abd al-Husayn, "Qanun-i Asasi va mutammam-i an chigunah tadvin shud?" *Yadgar*, 4: 5 (Bahman 1326 [Jan. 1947]), 34–47.

Nava'i, Abd al-Husayn, *Ravabit-i Siyasi-i Iran va Urupa dar 'Asr-i Safavi* (Tehran: Visman, 1372/1993).

Nietzsche, Friedrich, *Beyond Good and Evil*, trans. Marianne Cowan (1955; South Bend, Ind.: Gateway, 1967).

Nizami, Khaliq Ahmad, *Akbar and Religion* (Delhi: Idarah-i Adabiyat-i Delhi, 1989).

Nuri, Shaykh Fazl'allah, *Lavayih-i Aqa Shaykh Fazl'allah Nuri*, ed. Huma Rizvani (Tehran: Nashr-i Tarikh-i Iran, 1362/1983).

Nuri, Shaykh Fazl'allah, Majmu'ah-'i az Rasayil, I'lamiyah'ha, Maktubat, . . . va Ruznamah-'i Shaykh-i Shahid Fazl'allah Nuri, ed. Muhammad Turkuman (Tehran: Khadamat-i Farhangi-i Rasa, 1962/1983).

Ouseley, William, *Travels in Various Countries of the East, More Particularly Persia* (London: Rodwell and Martil, 1819–23).

Page, Mary Ellen, "Professional Storytelling in Iran: Transmission and Practice," *Iranian Studies*, 12 (Summer 1979), 195–215.

Parsinejad, Iraj, *Mirza Fath Ali Akhundzadeh and Literary Criticism* (Tokyo: Institute for the Study of Languages and Cultures of Asia and Africa, 1988).

Pellat, Ch, "al-Furs," in *The Encyclopaedia of Islam*, 2: 950–1.

Perry, John R., "Language Reform in Turkey and Iran," *International Journal of Middle Eastern Studies*, 17 (1985), 295–330.

Peshotan Sanjana, Darab and Nasarwanji, Bamanji (eds), *Dr. Modi Memorial Volume: Papers on Indo-Iranian and other Subjects* (Bombay: Fort Printing Press, 1930), 1–22.

Porter, Roy, "Introduction: Approaching Enlightenment Exoticism," in *Exoticism in the Enlightenment*, ed. G. S. Rousseau and Roy Porter (Manchester: Manchester University Press, 1990), 1–22.

Price, William, *A Grammar of the Three Principal Oriental Languages, Hindoostani, Persian, and Arabic on a Plan Entirely New, and Perfectly Easy; to Which is Added a Set of Persian Dialogues Composed for the Author, by Mirza Mohammed Saulih, of Shiraz; Accompanied with an English translation* (London: Kingsbury, Parbury, and Allen, 1823).

Price, William, *Journal of the British Embassy to Persia; Embellished with Numerous Views Taken in India and Persia; Also, a Dissertation upon the Antiquities of Persepolis* (London: Thomas Thorpe, 1932).

Pucci, Suzanne Rodin, "The Discrete Charms of the Exotic: Fiction of the Harem in Eighteenth-Century France," in *Exoticism in the Enlightenment*, ed. G. C. Rousseau and Roy Porter (Manchester: Manchester University Press, 1990), 145–74.

Pulzer, Peter, *The Rise of Political Anti-Semitism in Germany and Austria* (New York: Wiley, 1964).

Purdavud, Ibrahim, *Farhang-i Iran-i Bastan* (Tehran: Anjuman-i Iranshinasi, 1326/1947; Tehran: Danishgah-i Tihran, 1355).

Purdavud, Ibrahim, *Hurmazd Namah* (Tehran: Société d']Iranologie, 1953).

Qajar, Farhad Mirza, *Zanbil* (Tehran: Kalalah-'i Khawar, 1345/1966).

Qaziha, Fatmah, *Asnadi Az Ravand-i Mu'ahidah-'i Turkmanchay, 1245–1250 Hÿri* (Tehran: Sazman-i Asnad-i Milli-i Iran, 1374/1995).

Quzanlu, Jamil, *Tarikh-i Nizami-i Iran* (Tehran: Chapkhanah Firdawsi, 1315/1936).

Ra'di Azarakhshi, Ghulam 'Ali, "Darbarah-'i sabkha-yi shi'r-i Farsi va nahzat-i bazgasht," in *Namvarah-'i Duktur Mahmud Afshar*, ed. Iraj Afshar and Karim Isfahaniyan (Tehran: Majmu'ah-'i Intisharat-i Adabi va Tarikhi, 1364/1985), 73–112.

Ra'in, Isma'il, *Anjumanha-yi Sirri dar Inqilab-i Mashrutiyat*, 2nd edn (Tehran: Javidan, 2535/1976).

Rabino, Louis, *Diplumatha va Kunsulha-yi Iran va Inglis va Nukhustvaziran va Vuzara-yi Umur-i Kharijah-'i Iran va Inglis va Sufara va Firistadigan-i Iran dar Sayir-i Kishvarha-yi Jahan az Aqaz ta sal-i 1945 Miladi*, ed. Ghulamhusayn Mirza Salih (Tehran: Nashr-i Tarikh-i Iran, 1984).

Rabinow, Paul, *French Modern: Norms and Forms of the Social Environment* (Cambridge, Mass.: MIT Press, 1989).

Radstock, William Waldegrave, "A Slight Sketch of the Character, Person, & c. of Aboul Hassen, Envoy Extraordinary from the King of Persia to the Court of Great Britain, in the year 1809 and 1810, 'To the Countess of——'", *The Gentleman's Magazine* (February 1820), 119–22.

Rahman, 'Ali, *Tazkarah-'i 'Ulama-yi Hind* (Luknow: Matba'-i Munshi Niwal Kishur, 1894).

Rashid al-Din Fazl Allah Tabib, *Savanih al-Afkar-i Rashidi*, ed. Muhmmad Taqi Danishpazhuh (Tehran: Intisharat-i Danishgah-i Tihran, 1358/1979).

Rejali, Darius M., *Torture and Modernity: Self, Society, and State in Modern Iran* (Boulder, Col.: Westview, 1994).

Richardson, John, "A Dissertation on the Languages, Literature, and Manners of Eastern Nations," *A Dictionary, Persian, Arabic, and English*, rev. Charles Wilkins (London. J. L. Cox, 1829), 1–82.

Richter-Bernburg, Lutz, "Linguistic Shu'ubiya and Early Neo-Persian Prose," *Journal of the American Oriental Society*, 94 (1974) 55–64.

Riza Quli Mirza Qajar, *Safar Namah-'i Riza Quli Mirza Nayib al-Iyalah Navah-'i Fath 'Ali Shah*, ed. Asghar Farmanfarma'i Qajar (Tehran: Asatir, 1982).

Rizazadah Malik, Rahim (ed.), *Dabistan-i Mazahib* (Tehran: Tahuri, 1983).

Roberts, J. M., *The Triumph of the West* (London: British Broadcasting Corporation, 1985).

Rocher, Rosane, *Orientalism, Poetry, and the Millennium: The Checkered Life of Nathaniel Brassey Halhed, 1751–1830* (Delhi: Motilal Banarsidass, 1983).

Rosenthal, Franz, *A History of Muslim Historiography* (Leiden: E. J. Brill, 1968).

Rousseau, G. C. and Porter, Roy, "Introduction: Approaching Enlightenment Exoticism," in *Exoticism in the Enlightenment* (Manchester: Manchester University Press, 1990), 1–22.

Rusell, James R., "On Mysticism and Esotericism among the Zoroastrians," *Iranian Studies*, 26: 1–2 (Winter/Spring 1993), 73–94.

Rustam al-Hukama, Muhammad Hashim, *Rustam al-Tawarikh*, ed. Muhammad Mushiri (Tehran: n.p., 1969).

Ruzbihan Baqli Shirazi, *Sharh-i Shathiyat*, ed. Henry Corbin (Tehran: Tahuri, 1981).

Saba, Fath'ali Khan, *Divan-i Ash'ar*, ed. Muhammad 'Ali Nijati (Tehran: Iqbal, 1962).

Saba, Mirza Fath'ali Khan, *Shahanshahnamah* (Bombay: Malik al-Kuttab, 1867).

Saba, Muhammad Muzzafar Husayn, *Tazkirah-'i Ruz-i Rawshan*, ed. Muhammad Husayn Ruknzadah Adamiyat (Tehran: Kitabkhanah-'i Razi, 1343/1964).

Sabbah, Fatna, *Women in Muslim Unconscious*, trans. Mary Jo Lakeland (New York: Pergamon Press, 1984).

Sadiq, Muhammad, *A History of Urdu Literature* (Delhi: Oxford University Press, 1984).

Sadiqi, 'Ali Ashraf, "Zaban-i Farsi va Farhangistan," *Rahnama-yi Kitab*, 16 (January 1974), 8–31.

Safa'i, Ibrahim, *Nihzat-i Mashrutah bar Payah-'i Asnad-i Vizarat-i Umur-i Kharijah* (Tehran: Daftar-i Mutali'at-i Siyasi va Bayn al-Milali, 1370/1991).

Safinizhad, Javad, "Shahnamah ha-yi Chap Sangi," *Mirs-i Farhangi*, 14 (Zimistan 1374/Winter 1996), 21–4.

Sahhafbashi Tihrani, Ibrahim, *Safar Namah-'i Ibrahim Sahhafbashi Tihrani*, ed. Muhammad Mushiri (Tehran: Shirkat-i Mu'allifan va Mutarjiman-i Iran, 1357/1978).

Sahlins, Marshall, *Culture and Practical Reason* (Chicago: University of Chicago Press, 1976).

Said, Edward, *Orientalism* (New York: Pantheon Books, 1978).

Sanjabi, Maryam, "Rereading the Enlightenment: Akhundzada and His Voltaire," *Iranian Studies*, 28: 1–2 (Winter/Spring 1995), 39–60.

Sanson, Nichola, *Voyage ou Relation de l'etat présent du royaume de Peres: avec une dissertation curieuse sur les moeurs, religion & gouvernement de cet etat* (Paris: Chez la veuve M. Cramoisi, 1695).

Sayyid Ahmad 'Ali, *Muqaddamat-i 'Ilm-i Hay'at* (Calcutta: n.p., n.d.).

Schofield, Richard, "Interpreting a Vague River Boundary Delimitation: The 1847 Erzerum Treaty and the Shatt al-Arab before 1913," in *The Boundaries of Modern Iran*, ed. Keith McLachlan (New York: St. Martin's Press, 1994), 72–92.

Schwab, Raymond, *The Oriental Renaissance: Europe's Discovery of India and the East, 1680–1880*, trans. by Gene Patterson-Black and Victor Reinking (New York: Columbia University Press, 1984).

Schwartz, M., "The Old Eastern Iranian World View According to Avesta," in *The Cambridge History of Iran: Volume 2, The Median and Achaemenian Periods*, ed. Ily Gershevitch (Cambridge: Cambridge University Press, 1985), 640–63.

Sebeok, Thomas A., *Portraits of Linguistics: A Bibliographical Source Book for the History of Western Linguistics, 1746–1969* (Bloomington: Indiana University Press, 1966; Westport, CT: Greenwood Press, 1966).

Shafi'i Kadkani, Muhammad Riza, "Persian Literature (Belles-Letters) from the Time of Jami to the Present," in *History of Persian Literature: From the Beginning of the Islamic Period to the Present Day*, ed. George Morrison (Leiden: E. J. Brill, 1981), 145–65.

Shahnavaz Khan, Samsam al-Dawlah, *Ma'asir al-Umara'*, ed. Maulavi 'Abd al-Rahim and Maulavi Mirza Ashraf 'Ali (Calcutta: Asiatic Society of Bengal, 1892).

Sharif Kashani, Muhammad Mahdi, *Vaqi'at-i Ittifaqiyah dar Ruzgar*, ed. Mansurah Ittihadiyah (Nizam Mafi), Sirus Sa'dvandiyan, 3 vols (Tehran: Nashr-i Tarikh-i Iran, 1362/1983).

Sharm, Shriram, *A Descriptive Bibliography of Sanskrit Works in Persian* (Hyderabad: Abul Kalam Azad Oriental Research Institute, 1982).

Sharma, Virendra Nath, "Jai Singh, His European Astronomers and its Copernican Revolution," *Indian Journal of History of Science*, 18: 1 (1982), 333–44.

Sharma, Virendra Nath, "Zïj Muhammad Shahi and the Tables of De La Hire," *Indian Journal of History of Science*, 25: 1–4 (1990), 36–41.

Shayegan, Dariush, *Cultural Schizophrenia: Islamic Societies Confronting the West*, trans. John Howe (London: Saqi Books, 1992).

Shboul, Ahmad M. H., *Al-Mas'udi & His World: A Muslim Humanist and his Interest in non-Muslims* (London: Ithaca Press, 1979).

Shea, David and Troye, Anthony (trans.), *The Dabistan or School of Manners: Translated from the Original Persian with Notes and Illustrations* (Paris: Oriental Translation Fund of Great Britain and Ireland, 1843).

Sheikholeslami, A. R., *The Structure of Central Authority in Qajar Iran, 1871–1896* (Atlanta: Scholars Press, 1996).

Sherley, Antony, *Relation of his Travels into Persia, the Dangers and Distresses which Befell him in his Passage, both by Sea and Land* (London: Nathaniell Butter, 1613).

Shirley, Evelyn Philip, *The Sherley Brothers: An Historical Memoir of the Lives of Sir Thomas Sherley, Sir Anthony Sherley, and Sir Robert Sherley, Knights* (Chiswick: Press of Charles Whittingham, 1848).

Shklar, Judith, *Montesquieu* (Oxford: Oxford University Press, 1987).

Shukla, N. S., "Persian Translations of Sanskrit Works," *Indological Studies*, 3 (1974), 175–91.

Shushtari, Mir 'Abd al-Latif, *Tuhfat al-'Alam va Zayl al-Tuhfah*, ed. Samad Muvahhid (Tehran: Tahuri, 1363/1984).

Sleeman, William Henry, *Ramaseeana, or a Vocabulary of the Peculiar Language Used by the Thugs, with an Introduction and Appendix, Descriptive of the System Pursued by that Fraternity and of the Measures which have been Adopted by the Supreme Government of India for its Suppression* (Calcutta, 1836).

Smith, Margaret, *The Persian Mystics 'Attar* (London: John Murray, 1932).

Soudavar, Abolala, "European and Indian Influences," in *Art of the Persian Courts: Selections from the Art and History Trust Collection* (New York: Rizzoli International Publications, 1992).

Stevens, Roger, "Robert Sherley: the Unanswered Questions," *Iran: Journal of the British Institute of Persian Studies*, 17 (1979).

Stoler, Ann, *Race and the Education of Desire: Foucault's History of Sexuality and the Colonial Order of Things* (Durham: Duke University Press, 1995).

Suhravardi Shahab al-Din Yahya, *Majmu'ah-'i Asar-i- Farsi-i Shaykh-i Ishraq = Oeuvres Philosophiques et Mystiques*, ed. Husayn Nasr (Tehran: Department D'Iranologie de l'Institute Français de Recherche, 1970).

Suleri, Sara, *The Rhetoric of English India* (Chicago: University of Chicago Press, 1992).

Tabari, *The History of al-Tabari* (Tar'ikh al-rusul wa'l-muluk), vol. 1: *General Introduction and From the Creation to the Flood*, trans. Franz Rosenthal (New York: New York University Press, 1989).

Tabataba'i, Gholam-Hoseyn Khan, *A Translation of the Sëir Mutaqherin; or, View of Modern Times* (Calcutta, 1799; Calcutta: T. D. Chatterjee [1902]).

Taqizadah, Hasan, "Luzum-i hifz-i Farsi-i fasih," *Yadgar*, 5: 6 (Isfand 1326/February 1948).

Tavakoli-Targhi, Mohamad, "The Formation of Two Revolutionary Discourse in Modern Iran: The Constitutional Revolution of 1905–1909 and the Islamic Revolution of 1978–1979" (Ph.D. Dissertation, University of Chicago, 1988).

Tavakoli-Targhi, Mohamad, "The Constitutionalist Imaginary in Iran and the Ideals of the French Revolutions" [Asar-i Agahi-i az Inqilab-i Faransah dar Shikl'giri-i Angarah-'i Mashrutiyat dar Iran], *Iran Nameh*, 8.3 (Summer 1990), xxx–xxxii, 411–39.

Tavakoli-Targhi, Mohamad, "Refashioning Iran: Language and Culture during the Constitutional Revolution," *Iranian Studies*, 23: 1–4 (1992), 77–101.

Tavakoli-Targhi, Mohamad, "Imagining Western Women: Occidentalism and Euro-eroticism," *Radical America*, 24: 3 (1993), 73–87.

Tavakoli-Targhi, Mohamad, "Tarikh'pardazi va Iran'arayi: Baz'sazi-yi Huvviyat-i Irani dar Guzarish-i Tarikh," *Iran Nameh*, 12: 4 (1994), xxix–xxx, 583–628.

Tavakoli-Targhi, Mohamad, "Women of the West Imagined: the Farangi Other and the Emergence of the Women Question in Iran," in *Identity Politics and Women: Cultural Reassertions and Feminisms in International Perspective*, ed. Valentine Moghadam (Boulder, Col.: Westview Press, 1994), 98–120.

Tavakoli-Targhi, Mohamad, "Contested Memories: Narrative Structures and Allegorical Meanings of Iran's Pre-Islamic History," *Iranian Studies*, 29: 1–2 (1996), 149–75.

Tavakoli-Targhi, Mohamad, "Orientalism's Genesis Amnesia," *Comparative Studies of South Asia, Africa and the Middle East*, 16: 1 (Spring 1996), 1–14.

Tavakoli-Targhi, Mohamad, "Women of the West Imagined: Persian Occidentalism, Euro-eroticism, and Modernity," *CIRA Bulletin*, 13: 1 (March 1997), 19–22.

Tavakoli-Targhi, Mohamad, "Nigaran-i Zan-i Farang," *Nimeye Digar*, 2: 3 (Winter 1997), 24–6.

Tavakoli-Targhi, Mohamad, "Modernity, Heterotopia, and Homeless Texts," *Comparative Studies of South Asia, Africa and the Middle East*, 18: 2 (1998), 2–13.

Tavakoli-Targhi, Mohamad, "Contested Memories of Pre-Islamic Iran," *Medieval History Journal*, 2: 2 (1999), 245–75.

Tavakoli-Targhi, Mohamad, "Going Public: Patriotic and Matriotic Homeland in Iranian Nationalist Discourses," *Strategires*, 13: 2 (2000), 175–200.

Tavakoli-Targhi, Mohamad, "Eroticizing Europe," in *Society and Culture in Qajar Iran: Studies in Honor of Hafez Farmayan*, ed. Elton L. Daniel (Costa Mesa, Cal.: Mazda Publishers, 2001).

Tavakoli-Targhi, Mohamad, "The Homeless Texts of Persianate Modernity," *Cultural Dynamics* (2001).

The Desatir; or, Sacred Writings of the Ancient Persian Prophets, in the Original Tongue, Together with the Ancient Persian Version and Commentary of the Fifth Sasan, ed. Mulla Firuz bin Kaus (Bombay: Courier Press, 1818).

Toulmin, Stephen, *Cosmopolis: The Hidden Agenda of Modernity*, 2nd edn (Chicago: University of Chicago Press, 1992).

Trevelyan, C. E., J. Prinsep, Rev. A. Duff, and H. T. Prinsep, *The Application of the Roman Alphabet to All the Oriental Languages . . .* (Calcutta: Serampore Press, 1834).

Turner, Samuel, *Account of an Embassy to the Court of the Teshoo Lama, in Tibet; Containing a Narrative of a Journey Through Bootan, and Part of Tibet* (London: W. Bulmer and Co., 1800).

Tusi, Muhammad Ali, *Shahanshah Namah Nadiri*, ed. Ahmad Suhayli Khwansari (Tehran: Anjuman-i Asar-i Milli, 1339/1970).

Uruj Bayk [Don Juan], *Don Juan of Persia: A Shi'ah Catholic, 1560–1604*, trans. Guy Le Strange (New York: Harper & Brothers, 1926).

Von Grunebaum, Gustave E., *Modern Islam: The Search for Cultural Identity* (Berkeley, Cal.: University of California Press, 1962).

Waley, Arthur D., "Anquetil Duperron and Sir William Jones," *History Today*, 2 (January 1952), 23–33.

Walsh, W. H., *An Introduction to Philosophy of History* (London: Hutchinson's University Library, 1951).

Weber, Max, *The Protestant Ethic and the Spirit of Capitalism* (New York: Charles Scribner's, 1958).

West, E. W., *Pahlavi Texts* (Oxford: Clarendon Press, 1880).

White, Hayden, "The Value of Narrativity in the Representation of Reality," *The Content of the Form: Narrative Discourse and Historical Representation* (Baltimore: Johns Hopkins University, 1987), 1–25.

White, Hayden, *Metahistory: The Historical Imagination in Nineteenth-Century Europe* (Baltimore: Johns Hopkins University Press, 1973).

Winichahul, Thongchai, *Siam Mapped: A History of the Geo-Body of a Nation* (Honolulu: University of Hawaii, 1994).

Wright, Denis, *The English Amongst the Persians During the Qajar Period, 1787–1921* (London: Heinemann, 1977).

Wright, Denis, *The Persians Amongst the English: Episodes in Anglo-Persian History* (London: I. B. Tauris, 1985).

Yaghma Jandaqi, Abu al-Hasan, *Kulliyat-i Yaghma Jandaqi* (Tehran: Ibn Sina, 1339/1960).

Yaghma Jandaqi, Abu al-Hasan, *Majmu'ah-'i asar-i Yaghma Jandaqi: Makatib va Munsha'at*, ed. 'Ali Al-i Davud (Tehran: Intisharat-i Tus, 1362/1983]).

Yarshater, Ehsan, "Iranian National History," in *The Cambridge History of Iran*, vol. 3: *The Seleucid, Parthian and Sasanian Periods*, ed. Ehsan Yarshater (Cambridge: Cambridge University Press, 1983), 359–477.

Yaqubi, Ahmad ibn Abi Yaqub, *Tarikh al-Yaqubi* (Beirut: Dar Sadir, 1960).

Yaqubi, Ahmad ibn Abi Yaqub, *Tarikh-i Yaqubi*, trans. Muhammad Ibrahim Ayati (Tehran: Markaz-i Intisharat-i Ilmi va-Farhangi, 1362/1983).

Zaryab Khu'i, 'Abbas, "Sukhani Darbarah-'i Munsha'at-i Qa'im Maqam," in *Namvarah-'i Duktur Mahmud-i Afshar*, ed. Iraj Atshar (Tehran: Intisharat-i Adabi va Tarikhi, 1366/1987), 3: 1433–55.

Ziai, Hossein, *Knowledge and Illumination: A Study of Suhrawardi's Hikmat al-Ishraq* (Atlanta: Scholars Press, 1990).

Zizek, Slavoj, *The Ticklish Subject: The Absent Center of Political Ontology* (London: Verso, 1999).

Index